IMPLEMENTING ARTICLE 3 UNITED NATIONS CONVENTIC RIGHTS OF THE CHILD

Best Interests, Welfare and Well-being

The UN Convention on the Rights of the Child is acknowledged as a landmark in the development of children's rights. Article 3 makes the child's best interests a primary consideration in all actions concerning children and requires States Parties to ensure their care and protection. This volume, written by experts in children's rights from a range of jurisdictions, explores the implementation of Article 3 around the world. It opens with a contextual analysis of Article 3, before offering a critique of its implementation in various settings, including parenting, religion, domestic violence and baby switching. Amongst the themes that emerge are the challenges posed by the content of 'best interests', 'welfare' and 'well-being'; the priority to be accorded them; and the legal, socio-economic and other obstacles to legislating for children's rights. This book is essential for all readers who interact with one of the Convention's most fundamental principles.

ELAINE E. SUTHERLAND is Professor of Child and Family Law at the Law School, University of Stirling, Scotland, and Distinguished Professor of Law at Lewis & Clark Law School, Portland, Oregon.

DR LESLEY-ANNE BARNES MACFARLANE is Lecturer in Child and Family Law at Edinburgh Napier University and has practised as a solicitor in Scotland, specialising in Child and Family Law.

IMPLEMENTING ARTICLE 3 OF THE UNITED NATIONS CONVENTION ON THE RIGHTS OF THE CHILD

Best Interests, Welfare and Well-being

Edited by

ELAINE E. SUTHERLAND
University of Stirling and Lewis & Clark Law School

LESLEY-ANNE BARNES MACFARLANE
Edinburgh Napier University

CAMBRIDGE
UNIVERSITY PRESS

University Printing House, Cambridge CB2 8BS, United Kingdom

One Liberty Plaza, 20th Floor, New York, NY 10006, USA

477 Williamstown Road, Port Melbourne, VIC 3207, Australia

314-321, 3rd Floor, Plot 3, Splendor Forum, Jasola District Centre, New Delhi - 110025, India

79 Anson Road, #06-04/06, Singapore 079906

Cambridge University Press is part of the University of Cambridge.

It furthers the University's mission by disseminating knowledge in the pursuit of education, learning and research at the highest international levels of excellence.

www.cambridge.org
Information on this title: www.cambridge.org/9781316610879

© Cambridge University Press 2016

This publication is in copyright. Subject to statutory exception and to the provisions of relevant collective licensing agreements, no reproduction of any part may take place without the written permission of Cambridge University Press.

First published 2016
First paperback edition 2018

A catalogue record for this publication is available from the British Library

Library of Congress Cataloging in Publication data
Names: Sutherland, Elaine E., editor. | Macfarlane, Lesley-Anne Barnes, editor.
Title: Implementing Article 3 of the United Nations Convelntion on the Rights of the Child : best interests, welfare and well-being / Edited by Elaine E. Sutherland, University of Stirling and Lewis & Clark Law School and Lesley-Anne Barnes Macfarlane, Edinburgh Napier University.
Description: New York : Cambridge University Press, 2016. | Includes bibliographical references and index.
Identifiers: LCCN 2016019203| ISBN 9781107158252 (Hardback : alk. paper) | ISBN 9781316610879 (pbk. : alk. paper)
Subjects: LCSH: Convention on the Rights of the Child (1989 November 20) | Children (International law) | Children's rights.
Classification: LCC K639.A41989 I47 2016 | DDC 344.03/17–dc23 LC record available at https://lccn.loc.gov/2016019203

ISBN 978-1-107-15825-2 Hardback
ISBN 978-1-316-61087-9 Paperback

Cambridge University Press has no responsibility for the persistence or accuracy of URLs for external or third-party internet websites referred to in this publication, and does not guarantee that any content on such websites is, or will remain, accurate or appropriate.

CONTENTS

Notes on Contributors viii
Preface xxi

Introduction   1
ELAINE E. SUTHERLAND AND LESLEY-ANNE BARNES MACFARLANE

PART I   Best Interests, Welfare and Well-being: A Contextual Overview   19

1   Article 3 of the United Nations Convention on the Rights of the Child: The Challenges of Vagueness and Priorities   21
ELAINE E. SUTHERLAND

2   The Best Interests of the Child: A Gateway to Children's Rights?   51
URSULA KILKELLY

3   Conflict between Human Rights and Best Interests of Children: Myth or Reality?   67
JANYS M. SCOTT

4   Final Appeal Courts and Article 3 of the United Nations Convention on the Rights of the Child: What Do the Best Interests of the Particular Child Have to Do with It?   81
MARK HENAGHAN

PART II   Confronting the Challenges of Article 3   97

5   Two Dimensions of the Best Interests Principle: Decisions About Children and Decisions Affecting Children   99
JOHN EEKELAAR

CONTENTS

6   A Developmental Equality Model for the Best Interests of Children   112
    NANCY E. DOWD

7   A Long Lesson in Humility? The Inability of Child Care Law to Promote the Well-Being of Children   131
    ALISON CLELAND

    PART III   Best Interests and Bestowing Parentage   147

8   Serving Best Interests in 'Known Biological Father Disputes' in the United Kingdom   149
    LESLEY-ANNE BARNES MACFARLANE

9   Surrogacy in the United Kingdom: An Inappropriate Application of the Welfare Principle   165
    KENNETH MCK. NORRIE

10 Baby Switching: What Is Best for the Baby?   180
    TRYNIE BOEZAART

11 Primacy, Paramountcy and Adoption in England and Scotland   197
    BRIAN SLOAN

12 Article 3 and Adoption in and from India and Nepal   213
    RICHARD W. WHITECROSS

    PART IV   Parenting Disputes and the Best Interests of the Child   231

13 Canada's Controversy over Best Interests and Post-Separation Parenting   233
    NICHOLAS BALA

14 In Harm's Way: The Evolving Role of Domestic Violence in the Best Interests Analysis   249
    D. KELLY WEISBERG

15 The Best Interests of the Child When There Is Conflict About Contact   265
    LINDA D. ELROD

16 Relocation Disputes Following Parental Separation: Determining the Best Interests of the Child   280
    NICOLA TAYLOR

    PART V   Best Interests and State Intervention   293

17 Making Best Interests Significant for Children Who Offend: A Scottish Perspective   295
    CLAIRE MCDIARMID

18 The Child's Best Interests and Religion: A Case Study of the Holy See's Best Interests Obligations and Clerical Child Sexual Abuse   310
    IOANA CISMAS

19 'Best Interests' in Care Proceedings: Law, Policy and Practice   326
    JUDY CASHMORE

20 Judicial Discretion and the Child's Best Interests: The European Court of Human Rights on Adoptions in Child Protection Cases   341
    MARIT SKIVENES AND KARL HARALD SØVIG

    Appendix I   Convention on the Rights of the Child (1989) 1577 U.N.T.S. 3   358
    Appendix II United Nations Committee on the Rights of the Child: General Comment No. 14 (2013) on the Right of the Child to Have His or Her Best Interests Taken as a Primary Consideration (art. 3, para. 1), CRC/C/GC/14   381
    Index   410

NOTES ON CONTRIBUTORS

NICHOLAS BALA Nicholas Bala is a leading Canadian expert on legal issues related to children, youth and families in the justice system, and also teaches and writes about contract law. He has law degrees from Queen's University (JD, 1977) in Canada and Harvard (LLM, 1980). He has been a professor at the Faculty of Law at Queen's since 1980, and has also been a visiting professor at McGill, Duke and the University of Calgary. Professor Bala's research focuses on issues related to children and families in the justice system, including: judicial interviews with children and legal representation of children; the role of experts in the family justice process; child welfare law; youth justice and young offenders; parental rights and responsibilities after divorce, including parental alienation; spousal abuse and its effects on children; child witnesses in the criminal courts; and child abuse; the Charter of Rights and the family; the Hague Convention on Child Abduction; and access to family justice. Much of his research work is interdisciplinary; he has undertaken many collaborative projects with psychologists, social workers, criminologists and health professionals. His work is cited by all levels of court in Canada, including the Supreme Court of Canada as well as trial and appellate courts across the country, and has also been cited by courts in the United States, England and Australia. Professor Bala has presented at many conferences and professional education programs for judges, lawyers, probation officers, youth workers, teachers, doctors, psychologists, child welfare workers and social workers in Canada, the United States, the United Kingdom, Australia, Italy, Trinidad, Jamaica and Hong Kong. His contributions to family law research and professional education were recognized in awards from Ontario's Law Society and the Ontario Bar Association in 2009. In 2013, Professor Bala was elected a Fellow of the Royal Society of Canada.

TRYNIE BOEZAART Trynie Boezaart (previously Davel) is Professor of Private Law at the University of Pretoria. She was the founder of the Centre for Child Law at that university in 1998 and Director thereof until 2008. Under her supervision, the Centre for Child Law launched a litigation section in August 2003. To date, the Centre's litigation project is the only project in South Africa with the sole focus on litigation with regard to children's rights. In 2008 she acted as a Judge in the North Gauteng High Court. She still serves on the Board of the Centre for Child Law and is the deputy chairperson of the Board of the Centre for Education Law and Policy (CELP). Trynie Boezaart specialises in child law, the law of persons and the law of delict. Her publications include textbooks such as *Law of Persons* (6th ed., 2016), various chapters in books, the most recent on the position of minor and dependent children of divorcing and divorced spouses or civil union partners in J. Heaton (ed), *The Law of Divorce Dissolution of Life Partnerships in South Africa* (edited by J. Heaton, 2014) and articles in peer-reviewed journals. She is the editor of, and contributed a chapter to, *Child Law in South Africa* (2009) and the co-editor of and contributor to *Commentary on the Children's Act* (2007), a regularly updated looseleaf publication (the most recent update being Revision Service 7 in 2015) dealing comprehensively with the intricacies of the Children's Act 38 of 2005. Her doctoral students include the Executive Dean of the School of Law at the University of South Africa (Unisa), Professor R. Songca, and the Directorof the Centre for Child Law, Professor A. Skelton. She has acted as external examiner for the doctoral theses of child law experts such as Professors J. Sloth-Nielsen (University of the Western Cape), N. Zaal (University of Kwazulu-Natal), S. Ferreira (University of South Africa) and B. Kruger (University of the Free State).

JUDY CASHMORE Professor Judy Cashmore, AO has a PhD in developmental psychology, and a Master's degree in education. She is Professor of Socio-Legal Research and Policy at the University of Sydney Law School. Her research concerns children's involvement in civil and criminal proceedings and other processes in which decisions are made about children's lives. The special focus of this research has been on children's experience and perceptions of the process and the implications for social policy. She has worked as a consultant to various federal and state government agencies and been involved in numerous state and federal government committees concerning children and families. She has been integrally involved with the presentation of the alternative report for Australian NGOs to the UN Committee on the Rights of the Child on several occasions, and invited to participate in expert roundtables on child protection and children's rights in the United States, Thailand and Vietnam, and Turkey. She and her colleague and co-researcher, Professor Patrick Parkinson, AM, were jointly awarded the 2013 Stanley Cohen Distinguished Research Award by the Association of Family and Conciliation Courts (AFCC) for outstanding research and/or research achievements in the field of family and divorce.

IOANA CISMAS Dr Ioana Cismas is Lecturer in Law at the Stirling Law School. Prior to moving to Scotland, Ioana was a scholar-in-residence at the Center for Human Rights and Global Justice at NYU School of Law. In 2013, she served as Consultant to the UN Special Rapporteur on transitional justice while working at the Office of the High Commissioner for Human Rights in Geneva, and was the coordinator and instructor of the Law Clinic at the Geneva Academy of International Humanitarian Law and Human Rights. Previously, she was a researcher, then research fellow at the Geneva Academy and provided legal and policy advice to a number of stakeholders, including the Swiss Federal Department of Foreign Affairs. From 2009 to 2012, she acted as legal advisor to a member of the UN Human Rights Council Advisory Committee. In the past, her work for international NGOs and research institutions centered on humanitarian engagement and accountability of non-state actors, including corporate complicity in international crimes. Ioana holds a PhD in International Law (summa cum laude) from the Graduate Institute of International and Development Studies in Geneva. Her book *Religious Actors and International Law* (2014) explores the rights and obligations of the Holy See, the Organization of Islamic Cooperation, churches and other religious non-state actors under international law, including obligations arising from child rights instruments.

ALISON CLELAND Alison Cleland qualified as a solicitor in Scotland in 1990. She was the Scottish Child Law Centre's first advice worker. She represented children and young people in family law, child protection and youth justice proceedings in private practice in Edinburgh. She was advisor to the Scottish Parliament's Education, Culture and Sport committee during its work on establishing a Commissioner for Children and Young People. Alison joined academia in Scotland in 1999. Her research there focused on child protection law and children's rights. She is author of *Child Abuse, Child Protection and the Law* (2008) and co-editor (with Elaine E. Sutherland) of *Children's Rights in Scotland* (3rd ed., 2009). Alison and her husband Jim emigrated to Aotearoa New Zealand in 2007. She is now a senior lecturer in the Faculty of Law at the University of Auckland. Her research there has focused on youth justice. She is author of *Youth Advocates in Aotearoa/New Zealand's Youth Justice System* (2012) and (with Khylee Quince) *Youth Justice in Aotearoa New Zealand: Law Policy and Critique* (2014). Alison and Jim's daughter Rachael was born in 2010. She has deepened considerably her parents' understanding of children's rights in practice. Experiential learning has never been so tiring, or so much fun.

NANCY E. DOWD Nancy E. Dowd is the David Levin Chair in Family Law at the University of Florida Levin College of Law. She is the immediate past Director of the Center on Children and Families at UF. She is widely published in areas of non-traditional families, fathers and fatherhood, juvenile justice, and race and gender analysis. Most recently she has edited two collections on juvenile justice and completed a volume on masculinities theory, as well as a series of articles on African American boys.

JOHN EEKELAAR John Eekelaar, LLB (London, 1963), BCL (Oxon, 1965), MA (Oxon, 1967) held a Rhodes Scholarship from 1963 to 1965, and was awarded the Vinerian Scholarship in 1965. He was called to the bar in 1968 at the Inner Temple. He was a tutorial fellow at Pembroke College from 1965 to 2005; held a CUF lecturership from 1966 to 1991, and was Reader in Law until 2005. He was a founder member of the International Society of Family Law and its President from 1985 to 1988, and founding co-editor of the *International Journal of Law, Policy and the Family*. In collaboration with social scientists, he has carried out empirical research into child protection, financial consequences of divorce, post-separation parenting and the delivery of family justice, and he has written on a wide range of topics, including children's rights. He was elected to a Fellowship of the British Academy in July 2001 and to a Distinguished Visiting Fellowship by the New Zealand Law Foundation in 2005. He retired from teaching in 2005. From 2005 to 2009 he was Academic Director at Pembroke College. His books include *Family Security and Family Breakdown* (1971), *Family Law and Social Policy* (1978, 1984), *Regulating Divorce* (1991), *Family Law and Personal Life* (2006, 2007) and (with Mavis Maclean) *Family Justice* (2013).

LINDA D. ELROD Linda D. Elrod is the Richard S. Righter Distinguished Professor at Washburn University School of Law and Director of the Children and Family Law Center. She was a Fulbright Senior Specialist for the Dublin Institute of Technology and received the Roy A. Myers Excellence in Research faculty award. She serves on the Council for the American Bar Association Family Law Section and on the US Secretary of State Legal Adviser's Advisory Committee on Private International Law. She has been Editor-in-Chief of the ABA *Family Law Quarterly* since 1992; is past chair of the ABA Family Law Section; was co-chair of the ABA Child Custody Pro Bono Advisory Board; and served on the Steering Committee on the Unmet Legal Needs of Children. She chaired the drafting committee for the ABA Standards for Lawyers Who Represent Children in Abuse and Neglect Cases. In 2000, she coordinated an international, interdisciplinary think tank on 'High Conflict Custody Cases – Reforming the System for Children'. She was an official observer to the Hague Conference, which drafted the Hague Convention on the International Enforcement of Child Support and Other Forms of Family Maintenance (2007). For the Uniform Law Commission, she is the Reporter for drafting a Family Law Arbitration Act; Reporter for the Joint Editorial Board on Family Law; and was previously the Reporter for the Uniform Child Abduction Prevention Act. She founded and chaired the Family Law Section of the Kansas Bar Association and has served on the Kansas Supreme Court Child Support Advisory Committee since its inception in 1987. She has authored a national child custody treatise, a two-volume Kansas family law treatise and co-authored a family law textbook. She has written dozens of articles and has spoken at international, national and regional programs.

MARK HENAGHAN Mark Henaghan, BA, LLB (Hons) (Otago) is Professor and Dean of the Faculty of Law at Otago University in New Zealand and is a barrister and solicitor of the High Court of New Zealand. Mark specialises in family law and is particularly interested in children's rights. Mark has written extensively on family law matters and he is co-author of *Family Law Policy in New Zealand* (4th ed., 2013) and joint author of *Family Law in New Zealand* (16th ed., 2014). Mark is also the joint author of *Relationship Property on Death* (2004), which won the 2004 JF Northey prize for the best published law book by legal academics in New Zealand. He is the sole author of *Health Professionals and Trust: The Cure for Healthcare Law and Policy* (2012) and *Care of Children* (2005). He has written more than 150 articles and book chapters on family law published in family law journals and books around the world. Mark also provides legal advice on family law matters to lawyers and barristers from New Zealand and overseas on a regular basis.

URSULA KILKELLY Ursula Kilkelly is Professor of Law at the School of Law, University College Cork (UCC). She has published many books and peer-reviewed articles on children's rights, focusing on challenges of implementation in different settings like youth justice and healthcare. She has undertaken multiple empirical studies into children's rights, examining national implementation against the standards of the UN Convention on the Rights of the Child working with national and international human rights institutions like the (Irish) Ombudsman for Children and the Council of Europe with whom she has worked closely for many years. She has been undertaking a major study on child rights advocacy in Ireland, with the support of the Atlantic Philanthropies, seeking to understand how civil society works with children's rights. She directs the Child Law Clinic at UCC supporting her students to work with lawyers to advance children's rights through litigation and law reform. Together with her research team, she is undertaking research on issues like child participation, children and the environment and child-friendly social services. Her research is funded by the Department of Children and Youth Affairs, the Irish Penal Reform Trust, the Heritage Council, the International Juvenile Justice Observatory and the Irish Research Council. She is currently partner with London's Coram Children's Legal Centre, the International Juvenile Justice Observatory and the Aire Centre on three EU-funded projects to advance children's rights training for professionals. Her profile can be found on ResearchGate, Academia.edu and LinkedIn, and she is on Twitter @ukilkelly.

CLAIRE MCDIARMID Dr Claire McDiarmid is Reader in Law at the University of Strathclyde in Glasgow where she has worked since 1999. Her teaching is in the area of criminal law in which she has published widely, and she has a particular research interest in children who commit serious crimes and, more generally, in the way in which the law impacts on and deals with children. She has recently introduced a master's-level class, which she coordinates and teaches, in childhood and crime. She has written on the Scottish children's hearings system and she was a member of the children's panel for the city of Glasgow from 1996 to 2006. Her work is underpinned by an interest in rights as they apply to and are used by children. She is the author of *Childhood and Crime* (2007) and, more recently, she has been undertaking work on a defence for children who offend. She was a member of the programme team for the Scottish Universities Insight Institute's 2015 series of events on 'Children and Young People's Experiences and Views of Poverty and Inequality: Policy and Practice Implications' and co-authored its policy briefing paper on *Poverty and Children's Rights, Civic and Political Engagement*. She has just completed a term as the Head of the Humanities and Social Sciences Graduate School at Strathclyde and the Associate Dean (Postgraduate Research).

LESLEY-ANNE BARNES MACFARLANE Dr Lesley-Anne Barnes Macfarlane is Lecturer in Child and Family Law at Edinburgh Napier University. Her research interests lie mainly in the fields of child law, private law and children's rights. She practiced as a solicitor for six years before taking up her present position. While in practice, she specialised in child and family law, becoming an accredited lawyer-mediator and an associate with MHD Solicitors, Edinburgh. She received child client referrals from lawyers throughout the UK and was routinely appointed as Court Welfare Reporter and Curator ad Litem in complex proceedings involving children. Lesley-Anne has been a trustee on the board of the *Scottish Child Law Centre,* edited the child law sections of *Butterworths Scottish Family Law Service* and was Division Head for Children and Childcare in *Greens Annotated Social Work Statutes*. Recent publications with a focus on children and their best interests include: 'The Children and Young People (Scotland) Bill' (2013)'*F* v *F*: MMR Vaccine – welfare need or welfare norm?' (2014); 'Taking care of the small: Article 6 of the Convention on the Rights of the Child and childhood accidental injury claims in Scotland' (2015).

KENNETH MCK. NORRIE Kenneth McKenzie Norrie has taught family law for over thirty years. Though originally a medical lawyer, he developed, via his early work on children's consent to medical intervention, an interest in the parent-child relationship. His main interests today include child protection processes and families revolving around same-sex couples. He has published extensively in Scottish child law, including the major works *The Law Relating to Parent and Child in Scotland*, now in its third edition, and *Children's Hearings in Scotland*. As well, he writes on private international law aspects of family law, especially same-sex families, comparative law and legal history. Professor Norrie served as Head of Strathclyde Law School between 2001 and 2007, and acted as a member of the Children's Panel (the quasi-judicial tribunal dealing with vulnerable, neglected and abused children, and children who have committed offences) for ten years. He has been a visiting scholar at a number of institutions around the world, including the Universities of Regensburg (Germany), Vienna (Austria), Sydney (Australia) and Cape Town (South Africa), and the Victoria University of Wellington in New Zealand. He acted as Parliamentary Adviser to the Scottish Parliament as it considered the Family Law (Scotland) Act 2006, the Adoption and Children (Scotland) Act 2007 and the Children's Hearings (Scotland) Act 2011.

JANYS M. SCOTT Janys M. Scott is a graduate of Cambridge University where she studied history and law at Newnham College. She qualified as a solicitor in England and then in Scotland and was called to the Bar in Scotland in 1992. She was appointed part-time sheriff in 2005 and took silk in 2007. She is a noted authority on family law at the Scottish Bar. She regularly appears in the Inner House and Outer House of the Court of Session, and has made successful appeals to the UK Supreme Court. She has particular expertise in matters relating to child care and financial cases arising from family disputes. She has been instructed counsel in numerous reported cases, including *Principal Reporter* v *K* [2010] UKSC 56, which involved an unmarried father's right to be heard, challenging legislation on human rights grounds. She featured as The Times Newspaper's "Lawyer of the Week" on 2 August 2012, following victory in the Supreme Court for Jessamine Gow, who was claiming financial provision after the breakdown of a cohabiting relationship. Her publications include *Education Law in Scotland* 2nd ed. (2016); *The Laws of Scotland, Stair Memorial Encyclopaedia* (education section) (2010) and *Scottish Human Rights Service* (family and education sections). She co-edits *Family Law Reports*, and is the Chairman of the Advocates' Family Law Association.

MARIT SKIVENES Professor Marit Skivenes has a PhD in political science and is a faculty member at the Department of Administration and Organization Theory, University of Bergen, Norway. She is the principal investigator on several international research projects on child protection system in Norway, Finland, England and the United States. Skivenes has written numerous scientific works on child protection decision making, migrant children, and child welfare system and broader welfare issues, as well as the impact of communication and publicity in theory and practice. Her work has been published in the *Journal of Children's Rights*; *Child and Family Social Work*; *Human Relations*; *International Social Work*; *Acta Sociologica*, to mention some. She has published two books on whistle blowing, and co-edited three books for Oxford University Press with a comparative focus: *Child Protection Systems* (2011), *Child Welfare Systems and Migrant Children* (2015) and *Taking Children into State Care: A Cross-Country Analysis of Child Welfare Decision-Making Systems* (2016).

BRIAN SLOAN Brian Sloan read for his BA in Law (scholar) and LLM (Wright Rogers scholar) at Robinson College, Cambridge. He then took up a W. M. Tapp doctoral studentship at Gonville and Caius College, and his PhD was supervised by Professor Kevin Gray and Dr Jens Scherpe. After three years as Bob Alexander Fellow at King's College, Brian returned to Robinson as a College Lecturer in October 2012, where he teaches equity, family law and land law. Brian's research interests lie mainly in the fields of family law (including succession law), property law and comparative law. His previous work on adoption law and the UN Convention on the Rights of the Child has been cited by the UK Supreme Court.

KARL HARALD SØVIG Dr. juris Karl Harald Søvig is Professor of Law at the Faculty of Law, University of Bergen, where he is leader of the PhD program and chairing the research group on administrative law. He has previously worked as a temporary judge at the district and high court and as ad hoc chairman of the county board. He wrote his dissertation on detention of alcoholics and drug addicts ('Incarceration of alcohol or drug addicts – The Norwegian Social Services Act sections 6-2 till 6-3', Fagbokforlaget 2007, with a summary in English), where he inter alia analyzed the special provision in the Norwegian legislation warranting detention of pregnant women abusing alcohol or other substances. His research has focused on different forms of coercive measures *within the* welfare state, as well as rights of the children. He has authored a report for the government on the implementation of the UN Convention on the Rights of the Child into the Norwegian legal system and chaired an expert committee drafting a new act on adoption (NOU 2014:9). His most recent project was PROVIR (provision of welfare to irregular migrants) funded by the Norwegian research council. He is currently working on a project funded by the Norwegian Directorate for Children, Youth and Family Affairs exploring legal challenges for adolescents in institutions in need of both child protection services and health care. Sovig is a member of the regional committee of medical ethics and vice-chair of the European Association of Health Law (EAHL). He has acted as opponent for PhD theses in all Scandinavian countries and is also supervising PhD students writing dissertations in child law. He is a member of the editorial board of a Norwegian journal on family, heritage and child care law, where he writes comments on new recent decisions by the European Court of Human Rights.

ELAINE E. SUTHERLAND Elaine E. Sutherland is Professor of Child and Family Law at the Law School, University of Stirling, Scotland, and Distinguished Professor of Law at Lewis & Clark Law School, Portland, Oregon, spending six months of the year researching, writing and teaching at each. She has lectured on child and family law around the world and, in addition to her work in the Scottish and US domestic contexts, has long pursued her interest in the comparative dimensions of child and family law. One aspect of that was establishing the United Nations Convention on the Rights of the Child Implementation Project (CRC-IP), which brings together an invited group of respected child law scholars from around the world on a regular basis to offer critical analysis of the implementation of the Convention, one article at a time. The author of some 100 articles and book chapters, she contributes the chapter on Scotland to the *International Survey of Family Law*. Her books reflect the spectrum of her child and family law interests, as well as concern for wider legal developments in her native Scotland, and include *Child and Family Law*, 2nd ed. (2008); *Children's Rights in Scotland*, 3rd ed. (2009) (with Alison Cleland); *Scots Law Tales* (2010) (with John P. Grant); *Law Making and the Scottish Parliament: The Early Years* (2011) (with Kay E. Goodall, Gavin F. M. Little and Fraser P. Davidson); *The Future of Child and Family Law: International Predictions* (2012); *Pronounced for Doom: Early Scots Law Tales* (2013) (with John P. Grant) and *Family Law Basics*, 3rd ed. (2014).

NICOLA TAYLOR Associate Professor Nicola Taylor is the Director of the Children's Issues Centre at the University of Otago in New Zealand. She also holds the Alexander McMillan Leading Thinker Chair in Childhood Studies. Nicola has a Bachelor's of Social Work (Hons) degree, a Bachelor's of Laws (Hons) degree, a PhD, and has been admitted as a barrister and solicitor of the High Court of New Zealand. She is also an accredited family mediator. Nicola has a particular interest in socio-legal research with children, parents and professionals. Her research interests include guardianship and parental responsibility, day-to-day care and contact issues; relocation following parental separation; international child abduction; children's views and participation in family law proceedings; family dispute resolution and child-inclusive practice; judicial meetings with children; evaluation of family justice initiatives and reforms; international law and human rights issues affecting children; and the ethics of research with children and young people.

D. KELLY WEISBERG D. Kelly Weisberg is Professor of Law at Hastings College of the Law, University of California, San Francisco. She joined UC Hastings College of the Law after obtaining a JD at UC Berkeley School of Law and a PhD in Sociology at Brandeis University. She is a sociologist as well as a lawyer. She has participated in federal studies of juvenile justice, intimate partner violence and child abuse. She testified before the Senate Subcommittee of Juvenile Justice and Delinquency Prevention on the relationship between runaway behaviour and juvenile prostitution. She also worked as a legal intern at the International Commission of Jurists in Geneva, conducting legal research on the rights of children during the International Year of the Child. At UC Hastings, she has served as Director of the Family Law Concentration. She has authored law review articles and books on the subjects of family law, domestic violence and children and the law. Her recent books include *Domestic Violence: Legal and Social Reality* (2012); *Modern Family Law: Cases and Materials* (with Susan F. Appleton) (6th ed., 2016), and *Child, Family, State: Cases and Materials on Children and the Law* (with Robert H. Mnookin) (7th ed., 2013). She is also the editor of *Domestic Violence Report*, a national newsletter on domestic violence.

RICHARD W. WHITECROSS Richard is Lecturer in Law at Edinburgh Napier University. Richard has a broad range of academic and research interests. He holds degrees in history, law and anthropology. Before undertaking his LLM and subsequent degrees, Richard was a practising lawyer with a major Edinburgh law firm. He was awarded the Royal Anthropological Society Sutasoma Award for outstanding research merit in 2001 for his legal ethnography based on field work conducted in

Bhutan, Nepal and West Bengal. His principal research interests are on legal anthropology, legal consciousness and human rights policy. Richard was ESRC Postdoctoral Fellowship at the University of Edinburgh in 2003 and then a lecturer in anthropology. In 2005, he was appointed ESRC Research Fellow in socio-legal studies. Prior to joining Edinburgh Napier in 2012, Richard was a senior analyst in Justice Analytical Services where he led research to inform civil law development, notably in the area of child and family law. Based on his fieldwork in South Asia, Richard was an expert witness for asylum appeal cases in the UK. Richard is an honorary fellow of the School of Social and Political Science, University of Edinburgh. Richard is a fellow of the Royal Anthropological Institute and the Royal Asiatic Society. In addition, he is an associate member of the Centre National de le Recherche Scientifique, Paris and an alumnus of the Rockefeller Foundation.

PREFACE

There is no shortage of literature on the United Nations Convention on the Rights of the Child or aspects thereof. That is hardly surprising, given its critical importance in recognising children as rights-holders and its rapid and almost universal ratification by countries around the world. While ratification is vital, the real test of the impact of a treaty lies in the extent to which its provisions are being implemented at regional and local level. This volume addresses that issue in respect of one of the fundamental principles of this Convention, Article 3, which makes the child's best interest a primary consideration in all actions concerning children and requires States Parties to ensure their care and protection.

The origins of this volume lie in the *Convention on the Rights of the Child: Implementation Project* (CRC-IP) and its third, annual colloquium, which took place in Edinburgh, Scotland in June 2015. The CRC-IP was established by Elaine E. Sutherland in 2012 in the belief that, while large, multi-stream conferences have much to offer, there is a distinct value in bringing a smaller group of experts from around the world together to discuss the progress that had been made in implementing the Convention and to focus on one article at a time.

That validity of that belief was confirmed by the hugely successful colloquia that have taken place to date. The first, examining Article 12 (the child's right to be heard), was organised by Alison Cleland in 2013 at the University of Auckland, New Zealand, and the second, addressing article 6 (the child's right to life, survival and development), was arranged by Lize Mills at the University of Stellenbosch, South Africa in 2014. Articles expanding on papers from these colloquia can be found in the *New Zealand Law Review*[1] and the *Stellenbosch Law Review*,[2] respectively.

---

[1] [2013] *New Zealand Law Review* 333–504.
[2] (2015) 26 *Stellenbosch Law Review* 254–442.

The participants in the third colloquium gathered at the Mackenzie Building, Old Assembly Close, just off the High Street in Edinburgh, and we are immensely grateful to the Faculty of Advocates for donating the use of its superb conference facility and for providing refreshments throughout each day. The Clark Foundation for Legal Education kindly funded a reception each evening and met administrative and other essential expenses.

Following a welcome from James Wolffe, QC, Dean of the Faculty of Advocates, the Right Honourable Lord Gill, recently retired Lord President of the Court of Session, opened the colloquium. After two days of papers followed by lively discussion, both during the colloquium and in even more relaxed settings later in the day, the participants were charged to reflect on their papers and to write the chapters that follow.

Further hospitality, in the form of a closing dinner, was generously provided by the Law Society of Scotland and its President, Christine McLintock, gave a gracious farewell address to the participants. The enthusiasm with which all parts of the legal profession in Scotland embraced the colloquium is a tribute to the support for children's rights in the country.

We were most gratified when Cambridge University Press accepted our proposal for publication and we appreciate the work done by Finola O'Sullivan and her team.

A special word of thanks goes to our spouses, John P. Grant and Ross Macfarlane, for their unflagging support before, during and after the colloquium and throughout the preparation of this manuscript.

Finally, our deepest gratitude goes to the contributors to this volume. Not only were they a source of tremendous intellectual stimulation, but their enthusiasm, commitment and consummate professionalism made the task of editing the book a pleasure.

Elaine E. Sutherland
Lesley-Anne Barnes Macfarlane
June 2016
Edinburgh, Scotland

Introduction

ELAINE E. SUTHERLAND AND LESLEY-ANNE BARNES MACFARLANE

When the United Nations General Assembly adopted the Convention on the Rights of the Child[1] on 20 November 1989, it signalled a seismic shift in the legal status of children and young people. Rather than being the objects of adult munificence and protection, they became fully-fledged rights-holders, a point reinforced by the United Nations Committee on the Rights of the Child, established to monitor compliance with the Convention:

> States must see their role as fulfilling clear legal obligations to each and every child. Implementation of the human rights of children must not be seen as a charitable process, bestowing favours on children.[2]

The acid test, of course, lies in the extent to which the rights guaranteed to the world's children and young people by the Convention are being given effect in policy, law and practice in countries throughout the world. The focus of this volume is the implementation of Article 3, making the best interests of the child a primary consideration in all actions concerning children and requiring States Parties to ensure their care and protection. This Introduction provides an overview of the Convention before highlighting the salient themes surrounding implementation of Article 3 and discussed in the book.

Scope and Content of the Convention

While there had been previous domestic and international efforts directed at gaining recognition of children's rights,[3] none equalled the

---

[1] United Nations Convention on the Rights of the Child, 1577 UNTS 3, 20 November 1989, entered into force 2 September 1990.
[2] Committee on the Rights of the Child, *General Comment No. 5: General Measures of implementation of the Convention on the Rights of the Child* (2003), CRC/GC/2003/5, para. 11.
[3] Principal amongst them are the Geneva Declaration of the Rights of the Child of 1924 and the United Nations Declaration of the Rights of the Child of 1959, U.N. Doc. A/4354.

status and scope of this Convention.[4] It is global, holistic and specific. In global terms, it is designed to apply to all children and young people, regardless of where they are located, in peacetime and in time of conflict.

It is holistic in that it addresses the whole child by recognising his or her social, economic and cultural rights, as well as the child's civil and political rights. Historically, civil and political rights were accorded a degree of priority, placing them ahead of economic, social and cultural rights. That approach gave credence to the view of human rights as an essentially Western or European construct, unsuited to countries in Africa and Asia that were seeking to rid themselves of the residue of colonialism.[5] The Vienna Human Rights Declaration of 1993 has described all human rights as 'universal, indivisible, interdependent, and interrelated',[6] a stance endorsed by the Committee on the Rights of the Child in the context of that Convention with the words, 'Enjoyment of economic, social and cultural rights is inextricably intertwined with enjoyment of civil and political rights.'[7]

Alongside its global and holistic application is the Convention's emphasis on the unique nature of each child through its requirement for individualised decision-making focusing on the needs and circumstances of each specific child. The value placed by the Convention on the individual child is evident from the opening paragraphs of the Preamble and has been reiterated in successive General Comments issued by the UN Committee on the Rights of the Child.[8]

---

[4] On the history of children's rights, see, Philip Veerman, *The Rights of the Child and the Changing Images of Childhood* (Dordrecht: Martinus Nijhoff, 1992) and Philip Alston and John Tobin, *Laying the Foundation for Children's Rights* (Florence: UNICEF Innocenti Centre, 2005), pp. 3–9.

[5] José A. Lindgren Alves, 'The Declaration of Human Rights in Postmodernity' 22 *Human Rights Quarterly* 478 (2000) and Makau Mutua, 'Savages, Victims and Saviors: The Metaphor of Human Rights' 42 *Harvard International Law Journal* 201 (2001).

[6] Vienna Declaration and Programme of Action, UN Doc A/CONF.157/23, 25 June 1993, para. 5.

[7] United Nations Committee on the Rights of the Child, *General Comment No. 5: General measures of implementation of the Convention on the Rights of the Child* (2003), CRC/GC/2003/5, para. 6.

[8] The Preamble to the Convention refers to the requirement that the child be 'fully prepared to live an individual in society ... in the spirit of peace, dignity, tolerance, freedom, equality and solidarity'. See also, e.g., *General Comment No. 14 on the right of the child to have his or her best interests taken as a primary consideration (art. 3, para. 1)* (2013), CRC/GC/2013/14, para. 3, in which the UN Committee directs that 'the concept of the child's best interests ... should be adjusted and defined on an individual basis' and 'must be assessed and determined in light of the specific circumstances of the particular child'.

Opponents of children's rights often claim that, by accepting children as rights-holders, there is the danger of granting them autonomy and, thereby, depriving them of the protection adults should be providing for them.[9] Some see recognition of children's rights as posing a danger to the family and to society. In this, they misunderstand – one suspects, sometimes wilfully – the whole nature of the UN Convention on the Rights of the Child. Unlike the 'child liberationists' of the 1970s,[10] the drafters of the Convention did not seek to leave children to their own devices. Rather, their awareness of the rich and varied nature of childhood and of child development led them to recognise both the evolving capacities of children and young people and the central role of parents and, where appropriate, the wider family group, in the child's life.[11]

Many attempts have been made to classify Convention rights[12] and one of the best known – and appealing for its sheer simplicity – is that of

---

[9] See, for example, Michael King, 'Against Children's Rights' 1996 *Acta Juridica* 28; Bruce C. Hafen and Jonathan O. Hafen, 'Abandoning Children to their Autonomy: The United Nations Convention on the Rights of the Child' 37(2) *Harvard International Law Journal* 449 (1996); Martin Guggenheim, *What's Wrong with Children's Rights?* (Cambridge, MA: Harvard University Press, 2005); and Clark Butler (ed.), *Child Rights: The Movement, International Law and Opposition* (West Lafayette, ID: Purdue University Press, 2012).

[10] Richard Farson, for example, saw children's rights as including not only the more traditional rights to education and justice, but also the more controversial rights to sexual freedom and choice of living arrangements: Richard E. Farson, *Birthrights* (New York: Macmillan, 1974). John Holt's list was similar and included the right to experiment with drugs: John C. Holt, *Escape from Childhood* (New York: E.P. Dutton, 1974), pp. 249–265.

[11] Article 5 bring all of these elements together, referring to the 'evolving capacities of the child' as well as 'the responsibilities, rights and duties of parents or, where applicable, the members of the extended family or community as provided for by local custom, legal guardians and other persons legally responsible for the child'. By adopting this particular phraseology, the Convention recognises that the Western notion of the nuclear family is not the only model. Thus, the wider family groups, recognised in other cultures, like the African, First Nation Canadian and Native American tribe, the Hawaiian *'ohana*, the Maori *whānau* and so forth, are given their place in the Convention's scheme.

[12] Vitit Muntarbhorn classifies Convention rights as follows: general rights; rights requiring protective measures; rights concerning the civil status of children; rights concerning government and welfare; rights concerning children in special circumstances or in 'especially difficult circumstances'; and procedural considerations: Vitit Muntarbhorn, 'The Convention on the Rights of the Child: Reaching the Unreached?' (1992) 91 *Bulletin of Human Rights* 66, pp. 66–67. Lawrence J. LeBlanc adopts and adapts the classification of Jack Donnelly and Rhoda Howard, addressing human rights more generally, and classifies Convention rights under four heads: survival, membership, protection, and empowerment rights: Lawrence J. LeBlanc, *The Convention on the Rights of the Child: United Nations Lawmaking on Human Rights* (Lincoln, NE: University of Nebraska Press, 1995), pp. xviii–xix.

Thomas Hammarberg who grouped Convention rights according to 'the three Ps': provision or 'the right to get one's basic needs fulfilled'; protection or 'the right to be shielded from harmful acts or practices'; and participation or 'the right to be heard on decisions affecting one's own life'.[13]

Four general principles, themselves Convention rights, underpin the UN Convention: the child's right to freedom from discrimination (Article 2); the child's best interests as a primary consideration in all actions concerning children (Article 3); the child's right to life, survival and development (Article 6); and the child's right to participate in decision-making (Article 12).[14] It is through the application of these general principles that the Convention marries together the empowerment of children and seeks to ensure their protection.

Article 3

Due to their youth, inexperience and lack of political power, children and young people are not well placed to protect their own interests or to take care of themselves. Thus, Article 3 places the obligation to do so firmly on States Parties to the Convention and provides:

1. In all actions concerning children, whether undertaken by public or private social welfare institutions, courts of law, administrative authorities or legislative bodies, the best interests of the child shall be a primary consideration.
2. States Parties undertake to ensure the child such protection and care as is necessary for his or her well-being, taking into account the rights and duties of his or her parents, legal guardians, or other individuals legally responsible for him or her, and, to this end, shall take all appropriate legislative and administrative measures.
3. States Parties shall ensure that the institutions, services and facilities responsible for the care or protection of children shall conform with the standards established by competent authorities, particularly in the

---

[13] Thomas Hammarberg, 'The UN Convention on the Rights of the Child – And How to Make It Work' (1990) 12 *Human Rights Quarterly* 97, pp. 99–100.

[14] United Nations Committee on the Rights of the Child, *General Comment No. 3: HIV/AIDS and the rights of the child* (2003), CRC/GC/2003/3, p. 3, para. 5, referring to the 'rights embodied in the general principles of the Convention' and referring to these four articles. See also, *General Comment No. 5*, CRC/GC/2003/5, para. 12, again referring to the same 'general principles'.

areas of safety, health, in the number and suitability of their staff, as well as competent supervision.

In *General Comment 14*, the UN Committee on the Rights of the Child signalled the pervasive nature of 'best interests', describing it as 'a threefold concept', being a substantive right, a fundamental interpretive legal principle and a rule of procedure.[15] By according best interests the status of a substantive right, it had the following in mind:

> The right of the child to have his or her best interests assessed and taken as a primary consideration when different interests are being considered in order to reach a decision on the issue at stake, and the guarantee that this right will be implemented whenever a decision is to be made concerning a child, a group of identified or unidentified children or children in general.[16]

The effect of best interests being a fundamental interpretive legal principle is that, 'If a legal provision is open to more than one interpretation, the interpretation which most effectively serves the child's best interests should be chosen.'[17] In terms of best interests being a rule of procedure, the Committee meant that, where a decision will affect a child or children, the decision-making process must include evaluation of the impact of the decision on them, with the decision-maker demonstrating expressly how the child's or children's best interests have been taken into account.[18]

Article 3(2) and 3(3) lay the crucial foundations for the state's obligations in respect of the care and protection of children and its standard-setting and oversight role in respect of institutions, services and facilities designed to meet that end, obligations that are expanded upon later in the Convention.

The Dynamism, Evolution and Impact of the Convention

The speed with which the requisite twenty states ratified the Convention meant that it entered into force less than a year after its adoption by the UN, more quickly than any other human rights instrument.[19] By 2015,

---

[15] *General Comment No. 14 on the rights of the child to have his or her best interests taken as a primary consideration* (2013), CRC/C/GC/14, para. 6.
[16] Ibid., para. 6(a). [17] Ibid., para. 6(b). [18] Ibid., para. 6(c).
[19] Upon ratification, States may make reservations, excluding or modifying the legal effect of certain Convention provisions, albeit, no reservation 'incompatible with the object and

there were 196 parties to the Convention[20] and it is ironic, given its very significant contribution to the drafting process,[21] that the United States is the only UN Member State not to have ratified the Convention.

The Convention's entry into force was, of course, only the beginning of a dynamic and evolutive process. One part of that dynamism is provided for in the instrument itself through the mechanism whereby States Parties self-report, two years after ratification and periodically, every five years thereafter, on their progress in complying with the Convention.[22] These country reports are then scrutinised by the UN Committee on the Rights of the Child, which, in turn, publishes its Concluding Observations on the State Party's progress in fulfilling its obligations under the Convention. The premise is that, through this iterative process of reporting, evaluation and feedback, individual state compliance with all of the Convention's provisions will improve over time.

The Committee makes further contributions to the Convention's evolution through its *Days of General Discussion* when it explores specific aspects of, and challenges to, its implementation.[23] In the wake of the economic crisis that rocked the world in the early years of this century, for example, it devoted its 2007 *Day of General Discussion*, to the issue of limited state resources and the implications for children's rights, later publishing its recommendations.[24]

Rather more directive are the UN Committee's *General Comments*, where it provides guidance to States Parties and others on what it

---

purpose' of it is permissible: Vienna Convention on the Law of Treaties 1969, 1155 UNTS 331, Article 19(c).

[20] The total of 196 comprises 192 of the 193 UN Member States plus the Cook Islands, the Holy See, Niue and the State of Palestine. Up-to-date information on ratification can be found on the UN Treaty Collection website: https://treaties.un.org/ and the Office of the High Commissioner of Human Rights website: http://indicators.ohchr.org/ There was a frisson of excitement when, on 20 January 2015, UNICEF announced on its website that Somalia had ratified: www.unicef.org/media/media_78732.html In the event, it was not until 1 October 2015 that Somalia's instrument of ratification was lodged, bringing the Convention into force there, in accordance with Article 49(2), on 31 October 2015.

[21] Cynthia Price Cohen, 'The Role of the United States in the Drafting of the Convention on the Rights of the Child' (2006) 20 *Emory International Law Review* 185.

[22] Article 44.

[23] For details of the Days of General Discussion, see, www.ohchr.org/EN/HRBodies/CRC/Pages/DiscussionDays.aspx.

[24] Office for the High Commissioner for Human Rights, *Resources for the Rights of the Child – Responsibility of States* (2007): www.ohchr.org/EN/HRBodies/CRC/Pages/DiscussionDays.aspx.

understands the various Convention obligations to mean.[25] Strictly speaking, these interpretations are not binding on States Parties, since the UN Convention, like other human rights treaties, does not give the relevant treaty body express power to adopt binding interpretations of the treaty.[26] However, it is widely accepted that the views expressed in General Comments are 'non-binding norms that interpret and add detail to the rights and obligations'[27] contained in the treaty or as a distillation of the particular committee's views[28] and they are of immense help to those charged with implementing the obligations.

Nor has the Convention itself remained static and there are now three Optional Protocols to it. The first two, addressing the involvement of children in armed conflict[29] and the sale of children, child prostitution and child pornography,[30] each adopted in 2000, have garnered significant support.[31] The third, providing for a right of individual complaint to the UN Committee through what is described in UN parlance as a 'communications procedure', dates from 2011 and has not, as yet, proved particularly popular with states.[32]

The UN Convention has been in force for over a quarter of a century and there is no doubt that it has had significant impact on international, regional and domestic policy-makers, legislators, courts and those

---

[25] The Committee's General Comments can be found at: www2.ohchr.org/english/bodies/crc/comments.htm.
[26] International Law Association: Committee on International Human Rights Law and Practice, *Final Report on the Impact of Finding of the United Nations Human Rights Treaty Bodies* (London, 2004), paras. 16 and 18.
[27] Helen Keller and Leena Grover, 'General Comments of the Human Rights Committee and their Legitimacy' in Helen Keller, Geir Ulfstein and Leena Grover (eds.), *UN Human Rights Treaty Bodies: Law and Legitimacy* (Cambridge: Cambridge University Press, 2012), p. 131.
[28] Philip Alston, 'The Historical Origins of the Concept of "General Comments" in Human Rights Law' in de Laurence Boisson de Chazournes and Vera Gowlland-Debbas, *The International Legal System in Quest of Equity and Universality: Liber Amicorum Georges Abi-Saab* (The Hague: Matinus Nijhoff, 2001), p. 775.
[29] Optional Protocol to the Convention on the Rights of the Child on the involvement of children in armed conflict, 2172 UNTS 222, adopted 25 May 2000.
[30] Optional Protocol to the Convention on the Rights of the Child on the sale of children, child prostitution and child pornography, 2171 UNTS 227, adopted 25 May 2000.
[31] See, UN Treaty Collection website: https://treaties.un.org/ and the Office of the High Commissioner of Human Rights website: http://indicators.ohchr.org for details of the states that are parties and their current status.
[32] Optional Protocol to the Convention on the Rights of the Child on a Communications Procedure, A/RES/66/138, adopted 19 December 2011.

working with children and has been the catalyst for reform of policy, law and practice.[33]

That the Convention should hold considerable sway with international organisations is, perhaps, unsurprising. As Adam Lopatka, the Chair-Rapporteur of the Working Group that drafted the Convention, observed:

> The Convention has become the framework for all of UNICEF's programmes and activities. Moreover, provisions of the Convention are referred to by such international organizations as UNESCO, WHO and ILO. Improvement of the welfare of the child has been given priority in the activities of the United Nations and other international organizations.[34]

At a regional level, the Convention's impact on the content of regional children's rights instruments, including the African Charter on the Rights and Welfare of the Child[35] and the European Convention on the Exercise of Children's Rights,[36] is tangible. Regional human rights courts, like the Inter-American Court of Human Rights, use the provisions of the UN Convention when interpreting more general regional human rights instruments.[37] Indeed, the Grand Chamber of the European Court of Human Rights gave it the following unambiguous endorsement:

> The human rights of children and the standards to which all governments must aspire in realising these rights for all children are set out in the Convention on the Rights of the Child.[38]

The goal of the UN Convention, of course, is that it will have impact at the domestic level and Article 4 requires States Parties to 'undertake all appropriate legislative, administrative, and other measures for the implementation of the rights' contained in it. Implementation is defined

---

[33] For an analysis of the impact of the Convention in terms of a number of different steps or phases, see, for example, Philip Alston and John Tobin, *Laying the Foundation for Children's Rights* (Florence: UNICEF Innocenti Centre, 2005): www.unicef-irc.org/publications/pdf/ii_layingthefoundations.pdf.

[34] *Legislative History*, vol. 1, p. xlii.

[35] OAU Doc. CAB/LEG/24.9/49, 1990, entered into force 29 November 1999.

[36] CETS No. 160, 25 January 1996, entered into force 1 July 2000.

[37] See, Monica Feria-Tinta, 'The CRC as a Litigation Tool Before the Inter-American System of Protection of Human Rights' in Ton Liefgaard and Jaap Doek (eds.), *Litigating the Rights of the Child: The UN Convention on the Rights of the Child in Domestic and International Jurisprudence* (Dordrecht: Springer, 2015), pp. 231–248.

[38] *Sommerfeld v Germany* (2004) 38 EHRR 35, para. 37. For a recent and somewhat unusual use of the best interests principle by the European Court of Human Rights, see, *SL and JL v Croatia*, Application No 13712/11, judgment of 7 May 2015.

by the UN Committee on the Rights of the Child as, 'the process whereby states parties take action to ensure the realization of all rights in the Convention for all children in their jurisdiction'.[39]

When considering the impact of the Convention on the domestic law of a given jurisdiction, it is important to remember that the domestic status of international obligations varies from one country to another. In a 2007 study of the implementation of the Convention in fifty-two countries, chosen for geographic distribution, the UNICEF Innocenti Research Centre found that, in twenty-two of them, treaty obligations are not only incorporated into national law automatically, they take precedence over it.[40] In a further ten countries in the study, treaty obligations form part of domestic law, ranking equally with locally generated provisions. In either case, formal incorporation is unnecessary. In addition, some countries, like South Africa, have incorporated parts of the Convention into the domestic constitution.

In the absence of automatic or proactive incorporation, the status of Convention rights in a given jurisdiction will be dependent on domestic law. As many of the chapters in this volume demonstrate, countries around the world have passed legislation and adopted procedures designed to implement the Convention's provisions, and domestic courts make extensive use of them.[41] It is a tribute to the Convention that in the United States, which, it will be remembered, has not ratified it, the Convention featured in the landmark Supreme Court decision striking down the juvenile death penalty.[42]

Emerging Themes

While each of the following chapters offers its own exploration of the implementation of aspects of Article 3 and, thus, warrants reading in full,

---

[39] See the Introduction to United Nations Committee on the Rights of the Child, *General Comment No. 5: General measures of implementation of the Convention on the Rights of the Child* (2003), CRC/GC/2003/5.

[40] *Law Reform and Implementation of the Convention on the Rights of the Child* (Florence: UNICEF Innocenti Research Centre, 2007), pp. 5–7. More recent research examined twelve countries and found that the UN Convention had been formally incorporated into the law in three of them: Belgium, Norway and Spain. See, Laura Lundy, Ursula Kilkelly, Bronagh Byrne and Jason Kang, *The UN Convention on the Rights of the Child: A Study of Implementation in 12 Countries* (London: UNICEF UK, 2012), para. 1.3.

[41] Further illustrations of the use made of the convention in domestic courts in a range of countries can be found in Liefgaard and Doek, *Litigating the Rights of the Child*.

[42] *Roper v Simmons* 543 US 541, 577; 125 S Ct 1183, 1199 (2005).

some significant themes surrounding Article 3 and explored in this volume are highlighted in the sections that follow.

Article 3(1)

Article 3(1) has no shortage of supporters and critics in the courts, the academic literature and beyond and the contributors to this volume offer their own, sometimes challenging, observations on it and its place in the Convention. Ursula Kilkelly critiques its place in human rights discourse, noting that Article 3(1) is one of very few substantive provisions of the Convention that does not contain the word 'right' and she questions whether it contains an obligation.[43] She concludes, nonetheless, that the best interests principle can act as a unifying force between professionals and as 'a gateway to children's rights'.[44]

The potential for conflict between the best interests principle, as articulated in the UN Convention, and the protection against state interference afforded by the European Convention on Human Rights, is the subject of Janys M. Scott's analysis. She explores the application of each over a range of contexts and concludes that any such conflict is 'a myth'.[45] Marit Skivenes and Karl Harald Søvig reach a similarly encouraging conclusion, noting that the European Court of Human Rights sometimes references the UN Convention in the context of child protection and non-consensual adoption and is developing its own list of factors relevant to such decisions that bear 'a resemblance' to the elements found in *General Comment 14*.[46] Trynie Boezaart highlights subtle, but important, differences between the best interests test, as framed in in the UN Convention, with that in the African Charter on the Rights and Welfare of the Child.[47]

Elaine E. Sutherland notes that the twin concerns that so troubled the drafters of Article 3(1), the vagueness of the best interests test and the

---

[43] Ursula Kilkelly, 'The Best Interests of the Child: A Gateway to Children's Rights?', Chapter 2 in this volume, p. 58.
[44] Ibid., p. 66.
[45] Janys M. Scott, 'Conflict between Human Rights and Best Interests of Children: Myth or Reality?', Chapter 3 in this volume, p. 80.
[46] Marit Skivenes and Karl Harald Søvig, 'Judicial Discretion and the Child's Best Interests: The European Court of Human Rights on Adoptions in Child Protection Cases', Chapter 20 in this volume, p. 355.
[47] Trynie Boezaart, 'Baby Switching: What Is Best for the Baby?', Chapter 10 in this volume, pp. 186–187.

priority to be accorded to these interests, continue to be a source of debate in its application. Noting 'the Janus-like quality' of the best interests test,[48] whereby the flexibility that makes it applicable across the board is also the source of it being condemned as indeterminate, she concludes that 'if the price for ensuring tailor-made solutions, suited to the circumstances of the individual child, is a degree of unpredictability, then it is a price worth paying'.[49]

The Best Interests Principle: Vagueness and Content

The theme of the vagueness of the best interests (or welfare) test is taken up by numerous contributors,[50] including Kenneth McK. Norrie, who refers to 'the anchorless nature of the welfare principle' and the 'dangerous subjectivity of "welfare"'.[51] Judy Cashmore notes the 'value-laden indeterminacy' of the best interests principle, while recognising 'its capacity to reflect shifting social values and circumstances',[52] while Nicholas Bala highlights the danger of judges reaching decisions that are 'unpredictable or reflect their personal biases and experiences'.[53]

For some contributors, the problem lies not in vagueness, but in the way the best interest test is framed and applied. While Nancy E. Dowd welcomes the use of interdisciplinary research incorporating a developmental perspective in the assessment of best interests, she observes that such research too often uses a neutral or generic child as the focus of enquiry and, thus, fails to take account of developmental inequality

---

[48] Elaine E. Sutherland, 'Article 3 of the United Nations Convention on the Rights of the Child: The Challenges of Vagueness and Priorities', Chapter 1 in this volume, p. 36.
[49] Ibid., p. 49.
[50] See, John Eekelaar, 'Two Dimensions of the Best Interests Principle: Decisions About Children and Decisions Affecting Children', Chapter 5 in this volume; Mark Henaghan, 'Final Appeal Courts and Article 3 of the United Nations Convention on the Rights of the Child: What Do the Best Interests of the Particular Child Have to Do with It?', Chapter 4 in this volume; Sutherland, 'Article 3 of the United Nations Convention on the Rights of the Child'; and Nicola Taylor, 'Relocation Disputes Following Parental Separation: Determining the Best Interests of the Child', Chapter 16 in this volume.
[51] Kenneth McK. Norrie, 'Surrogacy in the United Kingdom: An Inappropriate Application of the Welfare Principle', Chapter 9 in this volume, pp. 173 and 177, respectively.
[52] Judy Cashmore, '"Best interests" in Care Proceedings: Law, Policy and Practice', Chapter 19 in this volume, p. 339.
[53] Nicholas Bala, 'Canada's Controversy over Best Interests and Post-Separation Parenting', Chapter 13 in this volume, p. 244.

stemming from poverty, gender or race.[54] Richard W. Whitecross argues that meaningful assessment of the best interests requires addressing the underlying cultural and social values of the state and its representatives.[55] The challenge of overcoming institutional bias in securing meaningful compliance with the Convention is discussed by Ioana Cismas in her chapter on the Holy See's handling of clerical child sexual abuse allegations.[56]

The vagueness – or flexibility – of the best interests test may lie at the heart of its appeal for the courts. Lesley-Anne Barnes Macfarlane identifies 'complex, fragmented and, at times, ambiguous' legislation governing the taxonomy of the parent-child relationship as the source of the problem in resolving disputes over parentage in the context of assisted reproduction in 'known donor' cases in the United Kingdom.[57] As a result, the courts have relied 'on the language of welfare' in resolving many of these disputes.[58] It is what he sees as judicial misuse of the best interests test that troubles Norrie. He examines a number of surrogacy cases in the United Kingdom and concludes that, 'the focus on the child's best interests has blinded the courts to the requirement to follow statutory language, which risks disrupting the balance of interests struck by Parliament', something he sees as a threat to the rule of law itself.[59]

Prioritisation

The priority to be accorded to best interests is another constant theme in this volume.[60] As Boezaart points out, in her discussion of resolving disputes over babies swapped accidentally shortly after birth, the African

---

[54] Nancy E. Dowd, 'A Developmental Equality Model for the Best Interests of Children', Chapter 6 in this volume, p. 118.

[55] Richard Whitecross, 'Article 3 and Adoption in and from India and Nepal', Chapter 12 in this volume, p. 229.

[56] Ioana Cismas, 'The Child's Best Interests and Religion: A Case Study of the Holy See's Best Interests Obligations and Clerical Child Sexual Abuse', Chapter 18 in this volume.

[57] Lesley-Anne Barnes Macfarlane, 'Serving Best Interests in "Known Biological Father Disputes" in the United Kingdom', Chapter 8 in this volume, p. 151.

[58] Ibid., p. 158.   [59] Norrie, 'Surrogacy in the United Kingdom', p. 166.

[60] See, Cashmore, '"Best Interests" in Care Proceedings'; Henaghan, 'Final Appeal Courts and Article 3 of the United Nations Convention on the Rights of the Child'; Kilkelly, 'The Best Interests of the Child'; Norrie, 'Surrogacy in the United Kingdom'; Sutherland, 'Article 3 of the United Nations Convention on the Rights of the Child'; and Taylor, 'Relocation Disputes Following Parental Separation'.

Charter on the Rights and Welfare of the Child accords greater priority to the best interests of the child than does the UN Convention since, under the Charter, the best interests of the child is not merely *a* primary consideration, but *the* primary consideration.[61]

Certainly, the UN Committee is uncompromising in criticising states that place the interests of others ahead of those of children[62] and Cismas highlights the Committee's condemnation of the Holy See for consistently placing 'the preservation of the reputation of the Church and the protection of the perpetrators above the child's best interests'.[63] Examining decision-making in respect of children who commit crime, Claire McDiarmid notes the danger of children's rights being trumped by public safety concerns with the result that the promise of Article 3(1) can remain unfulfilled for many young offenders.[64]

John Eekelaar argues that a difficulty in applying the best interests test is the failure of legal systems to develop a structured approach to prioritising the various interests at play in cases involving children.[65] He makes a persuasive case for drawing a distinction between 'decisions that are directly about children and decisions that affect children indirectly'.[66] Where a decision affects children indirectly, he advocates for finding the 'best' solution to the issue to be decided, not what is 'best' for the children. In contrast, if a decision is characterised as being about a child directly, that decision should focus on the outcome for the child from a wide range of perspectives.

It might be thought that, had those who favoured according 'paramount' status to the best interests of the child prevailed, this problem of prioritisation would have been avoided. That is not the verdict of Brian Sloan who explores the adoption of children in the England and Scotland, where legislation declares the child's best interests to be 'paramount'. He concludes that this does not guarantee Convention-compatible court decisions.[67]

---

[61] Boezaart, 'Baby Switching', p. 186.
[62] Sutherland, 'Article 3 of the United Nations Convention on the Rights of the Child', p. 47.
[63] Cismas, 'The Child's Best Interests and Religion', p. 315.
[64] Claire McDiarmid, 'Making Best Interests Significant for Children Who Offend: A Scottish Perspective', Chapter 17 in this volume.
[65] Eekelaar, 'Two Dimensions of the Best Interests Principle'. [66] Ibid., p. 99.
[67] Brian Sloan, 'Primacy, Paramountcy and Adoption in England and Scotland', Chapter 11 in this volume, p. 212.

Listening to Children's Views

The challenge of taking account of the child's views, as required by Article 12 of the Convention, alongside prioritising their best interests, is another theme explored by a number of contributors.[68] For Mark Henaghan, the views of the child form an inherent part of any best interests analysis and he offers a damning verdict on decision-making in a range of appellate courts around the world: 'Children are not heard nor seen in such decisions that are about them or "affect" them, even though the decisions are supposed to be made in their best interests.'[69]

Scott concludes that while the UN Convention has been effective in promoting international consensus on the need to listen to children, the European Convention on Human Rights has been more successful in encouraging legal representation of children.[70] Skivenes and Søvig note that reference is sometimes made to children's views in the judgments of the European Court of Human Rights[71] and offer the tantalising prospect that the Court may be moving towards greater inclusion of children's views.[72]

The legislation in many of the legal systems discussed in this volume make express reference to listening to the child's views in the decision-making process.[73] Even where legislation is silent, the judiciary, perhaps influenced by the UN Convention, sometimes consider their views nonetheless. Thus, in Canada, for example, Bala observes that the absence of statutory reference to listening to children has not prevented judges from taking the child's views into account in divorce proceedings.[74] Cashmore notes that children's views sometimes play a part in the decision-making process in Australia and she attributes any reluctance to place reliance on

---

[68] Alison Cleland, 'A Long Lesson in Humility? The Inability of Child Care Law to Promote the Well-Being of Children', Chapter 7 in this volume; Linda D. Elrod, 'The Best Interests of the Child When There Is Conflict About Contact', Chapter 15 in this volume; Sutherland, 'Article 3 of the United Nations Convention on the Rights of the Child'; and D. Kelly Weisberg, 'In Harm's Way: The Evolving Role of Domestic Violence in the Best Interests Analysis', Chapter 14 in this volume.

[69] Henaghan, 'Final Appeal Courts and Article 3 of the United Nations Convention on the Rights of the Child', p. 83.

[70] Scott, 'Conflict between Human Rights and Best Interests of Children', p. 79.

[71] Skivenes and Søvig, 'Judicial Discretion and the Child's Best Interests'.

[72] Ibid., p. 355.

[73] Macfarlane, 'Serving Best Interests in "Known Biological Father Disputes"'; Boezaart, 'Baby Switching'; Norrie, 'Surrogacy in the United Kingdom'; Sloan, 'Primacy, Paramountcy and Adoption in England and Scotland'; and Weisberg, 'In Harm's Way'.

[74] Bala, 'Canada's Controversy Over Best Interests and Post-Separation Parenting', p. 246.

their views to the courts' desire to protect children from the responsibility for decision-making and from adult pressure and manipulation.[75]

Certainly, research suggests that children themselves do not always feel that their views are listened to. McDiarmid refers to the findings of research in Scotland where child offenders speak of feeling 'judged, ignored' and 'not understanding' the decision-making processes affecting them.[76] Nicola Taylor stresses that research highlights the need for better understanding of children's daily, lived experiences.[77] Reminding us that giving effect to the child's participation rights requires having appropriate mechanisms in place, Boezaart highlights the value of using a *curator ad litem* as a means of providing the child with a safe space to air his or her views.[78]

Legislation and the Courts

Effective implementation of Article 3 requires its integration when policy is being developed, in the formulation of appropriate laws and in practice. What, then, are the challenges facing legal systems?

In her forthright analysis of the child protection systems in a range of common law countries and Scotland, Alison Cleland condemns their comprehensive failure to serve either the child's best interest or well-being.[79] At the heart of the problem is legislation that uses 'significant harm' or an equivalent as the threshold criterion for intervention in a child's life and Cleland recommends replacing it with a test that takes an 'ecological approach', substituting 'a central concept of the child's well-being' for the current threshold test.[80]

Framing and applying legislation requires being clear about what it is designed to achieve and how it will reach these goals. In the context of relocation disputes, Taylor observes that there is no consistent international approach to what will serve the child's best interests, in part, due to the lack of relevant large-scale longitudinal research on child outcomes. She proposes refocusing on the child-centeredness of the best interests principle.'[81] Discussing the use of social science research and the reports of social science experts in court decisions in Australia, Cashmore

---

[75] Cashmore, '"Best Interests" in Care Proceedings', p. 334.
[76] McDiarmid, 'Making Best Interests Significant for Children Who Offend', p. 308.
[77] Taylor, 'Relocation Disputes Following Parental Separation', p. 289.
[78] Boezaart, 'Baby Switching', p. 192.   [79] Cleland, 'A Long Lesson in Humility?'
[80] Ibid., p. 132.   [81] Taylor, 'Relocation Disputes Following Parental Separation', p. 292.

notes that, while the legislation and court procedures are broadly consistent with the UN Committee's recommendations in *General Comment 14*, there is a need for clear communication by researchers and for lawyers and judges to become 'intelligent consumers of research'.[82]

In many jurisdictions, the legislation dealing with disputes between parents provides a fairly refined best interests test, often reflecting at least some of the elements proposed by the UN Committee in *General Comment 14*.[83] Particular problems arise, however, with the 'difficult cases' – those involving parental relocation, allegations of domestic abuse and/or 'parental alienation' and a high degree of parental conflict. The danger is that adult interests and voices can overwhelm those of the children involved.

In his analysis of the various efforts in Canada to reform the law governing post-separation parenting, Bala highlights the difficulties caused by the failure of the relevant legislation to articulate the principles underpinning the best interests test.[84] While he offers guidance on how that legislation might be framed, he notes that previous efforts to do this have been impeded by the 'gender wars' of polemical rhetoric generated when the difficult issues come into play.[85]

Even where the elements of the best interests test are articulated, as is the case in many US states, the 'difficult cases' continue to present challenges. Discussing the situation where a child refuses contact with a non-resident parent,[86] Linda D. Elrod explores the intersection of allegations of parental alienation, abuse, shared parenting, the child's preference and 'friendly parent' laws, arguing that high-conflict parents benefit from early identification and quick interventions by the judiciary and other professionals.[87]

'Difficult cases' are a product, not of law, but of human interaction and it is the task of the legal system to address them. As Skivenes and Søvig remind us, while they are complex and challenging, decisions about what will serve the child's best interests are made by the courts all the time.[88]

---

[82] Cashmore, '"Best Interests" in Care Proceedings', p. 340.
[83] Kilkelly, 'The Best Interests of the Child'; Scott, 'Conflict between Human Rights and Best Interests of Children'; and Skivenes and Søvig, 'Judicial Discretion and the Child's Best Interests'.
[84] Bala, 'Canada's Controversy over Best Interests and Post-Separation Parenting'.
[85] Ibid., p. 239.
[86] Elrod, 'The Best Interests of the Child When There Is Conflict About Contact'.
[87] Ibid., p. 273.
[88] Skivenes and Søvig, 'Judicial Discretion and the Child's Best Interests', p. 356.

It is fitting, then, that the final words of this Introduction should be devoted to an encouraging example of the law evolving in order to apply the best interests principle in a particularly difficult setting. In her discussion of custody determinations in the context of domestic violence, Kelly Weisberg demonstrates how the best interests principle has influenced the 'safety-first' approach recently adopted by the state of Colorado and by Australia, prioritising the child's physical, mental and emotional safety above all other considerations.[89]

---

[89] Weisberg, 'In Harm's Way'.

PART I

Best Interests, Welfare and Well-being:
A Contextual Overview

1

Article 3 of the United Nations Convention on the Rights of the Child: The Challenges of Vagueness and Priorities

ELAINE E. SUTHERLAND

A   Introduction

We live in an era of rights when everyone is endowed, at least in theory, with a panoply of entitlements: rights in respect of each other, rights in respect of government and rights in the international arena. The United Nations Convention on the Rights of the Child[1] is justifiably regarded as a milestone in the acceptance of children as rights-holders. Yet there is no escaping the reality that because of their youth, inexperience and lack of political power, children are not well placed to protect their own interests or to take care of themselves. For that reason, Article 3 of the Convention places States Parties under an obligation to prioritise the child's best interests and requires states to ensure their care and protection. Along with the other general principles of the Convention,[2] Article 3 underpins the Convention as a whole.

The concept of the child's 'best interests' has a respectable pedigree, being found in earlier international instruments[3] and in

---

[1] United Nations Convention on the Rights of the Child, 20 November 1989, in force 2 September 1990, 1577 UNTS 3.
[2] The others are the child's right to non-discrimination (Art. 2); to life, survival and development (Art. 6) and to express his or her views freely and to have them taken into account (Art. 12). See, United Nations Committee on the Rights of the Child, *General Comment No. 3: HIV/AIDS and the rights of the child* (2003), CRC/GC/2003/3, p. 3, para. 5, referring to the 'rights embodied in the general principles of the Convention' and listing these four articles. See also, *General Comment No. 5*, CRC/GC/2003/5, para. 12, and *General Comment No. 14 on the right of the child to have his or her best interests taken as a primary consideration (art. 3, para. 1)*, CRC/C/GC/14 (2013), para. 1, again referring to the same 'general principles'.
[3] While not found in the Geneva Declaration on the Rights of the Child of 1924, it features in the United Nations Declaration of the Rights of the Child of 1959, G.A. Res. 1386 (XIV), U.N. Doc. A/RES/1386/XIV, Arts. 2 and 7, and the United Nations Convention on

domestic law.[4] Yet long before the Convention was a twinkle in the eye of the Polish government, the best interests test – or 'welfare' test as it is sometimes known in domestic law – had been dogged by the criticism that it was vague and indeterminate.[5] That concern was raised during the drafting of what became Article 3(1), but no alternative formulation was provided.[6] It was division over the priority to be accorded to the child's best interests – whether they should be accorded primary or paramount status – that dominated discussions on Article 3(1). In the event, those favouring primacy prevailed.

One might ask why the drafters of the Convention adopted a provision they knew to be plagued by such controversy. Many years before, Robert Mnookin, the arch-critic of the best interests test explained the test's enduring attraction: 'While the indeterminate best-interests standard may not be good, there is no available alternative that is plainly less detrimental'.[7] That, it is submitted, is unsurprising since the variety and complexity of the circumstances in which children live requires a standard for decision-making that is flexible and the price of flexibility is a degree of uncertainty. Describing best interests as 'a threefold concept...a substantive right...a fundamental interpretive principle and...a rule of procedure',[8] the UN Committee on the Rights of the Child has attempted to reduce the ambiguity surrounding the best interests test, most notably in *General Comment 14*.[9]

---

the Elimination of All Forms of Discrimination against Women, 18 December 1979, in force 3 September 1981, 1249 UNTS 13, Arts. 5 and 16.

[4] Domestic statutes use the terms 'best interests' and 'welfare'. See, for example, Family Law Act 1975, s. 64 (Australia) ('best interests'); Children Act 1989, s. 1 (England and Wales) ('welfare'); Care of Children Act 2004, s. 4 (New Zealand) (using 'welfare' and 'best interests'); Children (Scotland) Act 1995 (welfare), s. 11; Children's Act of 2005, s. 7 (South Africa) ('best interests'). In the United States, where family law is a state, rather than a federal, matter, the term has been used in legislation for decades.

[5] Robert H. Mnookin, 'Child Custody Adjudication: Judicial Functions in the Face of Indeterminacy' (1976) 39 *Law and Contemporary Problems* 226, 229.

[6] See footnotes 34–38 and accompanying text.

[7] Mnookin, 'Child Custody Adjudication', 282.

[8] *General Comment No. 14 on the rights of the child to have his or her best interests taken as a primary consideration* (2013), CRC/C/GC/14, para. 6.

[9] See footnotes 85–96 and accompanying text.

Such is the pervasive nature of Article 3(1) that Articles 3(2) and 3(3) are sometimes overshadowed by their omnipresent sibling in the academic literature on Article 3. Yet the second and third paragraphs of Article 3 lay the crucial foundations for the state's obligations in respect of the care and protection of children and its standard-setting and oversight role in respect of institutions, services and facilities designed to meet that end, obligations that are expanded upon later in the Convention.

Article 3(2) introduced another ambiguous term, 'well-being', but the uncertainty surrounding it did not seem to trouble the drafters of the Convention. While it lacks the cachet of 'best interests', not being mentioned in the 1959 Declaration of the Rights of the Child, 'well-being' has long been used by international organisations[10] and is found, sometimes in unhyphenated form, in modern domestic constitutions[11] and legislation.[12] The use in the Convention of a different term in such close proximity to 'best interests' suggests that 'well-being' must mean something different. As we shall see, rather than being a criterion for decision-making, well-being denotes an outcome to be achieved, and a measurable outcome at that.[13] Again, the UN Committee has sought to clarify its content.

This chapter sets the scene for those that follow by exploring what the drafters were seeking to achieve in Article 3 and drilling down into its content. Using the UN Committee's *General Comments* and *Concluding Observations* on State Parties' reports, in particular, it will assess the extent to which the UN Committee has been successful in clarifying precisely what Article 3 requires of States Parties.

---

[10] See, for example, the Preamble to the Constitution of the World Health Organisation, as adopted by the International Health Conference, New York, 19–22 June 1946, defining health as 'a state of complete physical, mental and social well-being and not merely the absence of disease or infirmity'.

[11] It is used in the constitutions of Burundi (2005), Ecuador (2008), Ethiopia (1994), Finland (1999), Iceland (1944), Kosovo (2008), Mozambique (2004), Peru (1993), Sierra Leone (1991), South Africa (1996), South Sudan (2011) and Zimbabwe (2013). See the *Constitute* website for the text of domestic constitutions: www.constituteproject.org/.

[12] See, for example, the Children and Families Act 2014, s. 25 (England and Wales), the Children and Young People (Scotland) Act 2014, s. 96, and the Vulnerable Children Act 2014, ss. 6 and 7 (New Zealand).

[13] See footnotes 101–108 and accompanying text.

B Drafting

The seeds of what was to become Article 3 of the Convention were present from the beginning of the drafting process[14] and Article II of the first Polish draft offered the following text:

> The child shall enjoy special protection and shall be given opportunities and facilities, by law and by other means, to enable him to develop physically, mentally, morally, spiritually and socially in a healthy and normal manner and in conditions of freedom and dignity. In the enactment of laws for this purpose, the best interests of the child shall be the paramount consideration.[15]

That formulation was modelled on a similar provision in the 1959 Declaration of the Rights of the Child[16] on which that draft was based and attracted a number of comments suggesting slight modifications.[17] The early comments flagged up two issues that were to dominate subsequent negotiations and to which we shall return presently: concern over the vagueness of the term 'best interests of the child' and disagreement over according 'paramount' status to these interests.

What is remarkable to the modern reader is the proposal from the French and German delegations that the provision 'should not be included in the convention itself but set out in the preamble or in an annexed recommendation of a pedagogical nature'.[18] What difference would that have made? While the preamble and annexes to an international instrument form part of its context for the purpose of interpretation,[19] the location of a provision is important when it comes

---

[14] This is in contrast to two of the other general principles, (most of) Article 6 and Article 12, neither of which was present in the first Polish draft. Only the elements of what became Articles 2 and 3 found expression there.

[15] Save the Children Sweden and the Office of the United Nations High Commissioner for Human Rights, *Legislative History of the Convention on the Rights of the Child* (New York and Geneva: UNHCHR, 2007), vol. 1, p. 335. Volumes 1 and 2 if this work can be located, respectively, at: www.ohchr.org/Documents/Publications/LegislativeHistorycrc1en.pdf *and* www.ohchr.org/Documents/Publications/LegislativeHistorycrc2en.pdf.

[16] General Assembly Resolution 1386(XIV), 20 November 1959.

[17] *Legislative History*, vol. 1, pp. 335–337. The delegation from the Dominican Republic, for example, sought inclusion of express reference to the children of working mothers, while the UN Food and Agriculture Organisation noted the absence of any reference to emotional development and UNESCO advocated for express reference to 'cultural development with due regard for national and regional realities'.

[18] *Legislative History*, vol. 1, p. 337.

[19] Vienna Convention on the Law of Treaties, Vienna, 23 May 1969, in force 27 January 1980, 1155 UNTS 331, Art. 31(2).

to reporting on compliance. Where the instrument is monitored by means of a reporting process, as is the case with this convention, there is no specific obligation on states to report on compliance with matters contained in the preamble or annexes and reports focus on the substantive articles of the instrument.[20] In short, had the Franco-German proposal been accepted, the effect would have been to downgrade what is a fundamental principle of the UN Convention to something of much lesser status. Happily, the proposal sank without trace at the First Reading Stage.

The Polish draft was revised in 1979 and what was now known as Article 3 acquired its more familiar three-part structure:

1. In all actions concerning children, whether undertaken by their parents, guardians, social or State institutions, and in particular by courts of law and administrative authorities, the best interest of the child shall be the paramount consideration.
2. The States Parties to the present Convention undertake to ensure the child such protection and care as his status requires, taking due account of the various stages of his development in family environment and in social relations, and, to this end, shall take necessary legislative measures.
3. The States Parties to the present Convention shall create special organs called upon to supervise persons and institutions directly responsible for the care of children.

Meanwhile, in 1980, alternative texts were proposed by Australia and the United States. Lack of time prevented their immediate consideration, but each was reintroduced in the Working Group in 1981. The Australian proposal did not address the first, crucial paragraph and we shall return to it in the context of paragraphs 2 and 3. The US text was more all-encompassing and provided:

1. In all official actions concerning children, whether undertaken by public or private social welfare institutions, courts of law, or administrative authorities, the best interests of the child shall be a primary consideration.

---

[20] The Committee's most recent reporting guidelines, *Treaty-specific guidelines regarding the form and content of periodic reports to be submitted by States parties under article 44, paragraph 1 (b), of the Convention on the Rights of the Child*, CRC/C/58/Rev.2 (2010), are discussed more fully at footnotes 120–122 and accompanying text.

2. In all judicial or administrative proceedings affecting a child that has reached the age of reason, an opportunity for the views of the child to be heard as an independent party to the proceedings shall be provided, and those views shall be taken into consideration by the competent authorities.
3. Each State party to this Convention shall support special organs which shall observe and make appropriate recommendations to persons and institutions directly responsible for the care of children.
4. The States parties to this Convention undertake, through passage of appropriate legislation, to ensure such protection and care for the child as his status requires.[21]

Common to the revised Polish and US texts was the absence of reference to the specific aspects of child development – physical, mental, moral, spiritual and social – that had been enumerated in the first Polish draft, nor is there any mention of health, freedom and dignity. Instead, the settings in which best interests fell to be considered were spelt out more fully and each version makes express mention of the obligation on states to oversee persons and institutions responsible for the care of children.

There are, however, significant differences between the two. Paragraph 1 of the Polish text includes the actions of parents and guardians within its ambit, while the US text confines itself to the public sphere. Given the keen US sensitivity to the need to respect family privacy, that was no accident, and while some delegates questioned the use of an international instrument to regulate parental conduct, others thought their inclusion offered greater protection to children.[22] While there is no reference to 'parents or guardians' in the final text of paragraph 1, their rights and duties received mention, in the context of their protective role, in paragraph 2, and Article 18 of the Convention, addressing the common responsibilities of parents for the upbringing and development of the child, contains the stark sentence: 'The best interests of the child will be their basic concern'. Whether that is a direction or an observation is, however, unclear.[23]

---

[21] *Legislative History*, vol. 1, p. 338.   [22] *Legislative History*, vol. 1, p. 339.
[23] Reference to parents and best interests in Article 18 was first suggested, in the context of education, by France: *Legislative History*, vol. 2, p. 501. In the revised Polish draft, the reference was more general and directive: that the parents 'should be guided' by the child's best interest: *Legislative History*, vol. 2, p. 504. The Brazilian representative offered the final, less directive formulation that was adopted by the Working Group of 1981 and made its way into the final text: *Legislative History*, vol. 2, p. 505. To the end, the US

Only the US text is gender neutral throughout and the use of the male pronoun was not laid to rest until UNICEF raised the matter, comparatively late on, during the 1988 Technical Review.[24] Another innovation was found in paragraph 2 of the US proposal: the child's right to participate in judicial and administrative proceedings. It was discussed extensively by the Working Group in its 1981 session and adopted at the First Reading stage, only to be deleted during the Second Reading so that it could be considered, where it truly belonged, under what was to become another of the fundamental values of the Convention, Article 12.[25] Since our focus is Article 3, paragraph 2 of the US text need not detain us further and our exploration will proceed by referring to the texts in terms of what ultimately became paragraphs 1 to 3.

Paragraph 1

From the outset of negotiations, there was division over whether the child's best interests should be regarded as 'the paramount consideration' or 'a primary consideration' and the delegates debated the matter throughout the First and Second Readings, with contributions being added during the Technical Review stages. At the heart of the debate, of course, is the level of priority to be extended to the child's best interests when other, pressing (or even, legitimate) interests come into play: essentially, should the child's best interests always trump all others? Those favouring paramountcy had international precedent on their side.[26] While some delegates noted that the Polish text of paragraph 1 offered greater protection to the child, early in the negotiations and 'in search for compromise', it was agreed that the US text should be used as the basis for discussion.[27]

---

delegation expressed disquiet over an international covenant imposing obligations on individuals when ratification was by governments: *Legislative History*, vol. 2, p. 511, para. 311.

[24] *Legislative History*, vol. 1, p. 344.   [25] *Legislative History*, vol. 1, pp. 346–347.

[26] The 1959 Declaration accorded best interests paramount status, as did Declaration on Social and Legal Principles relating to the Protection and Welfare of Children, with Special Reference to Foster Placement and Adoption Nationally and Internationally, A/RES/41/85, 20 November 1989, Preamble and Art. 5. The Convention on the Elimination of Discrimination against Women of 1979 uses the term 'primordial consideration' which is arguably more akin to 'paramount' than it is to 'primary'.

[27] *Legislative History*, vol. 1, p. 339.

Nor was the debate confined to 'paramountcy v primacy' and the use of the words 'a' and 'the' was also discussed, with UNICEF drawing the issues together elegantly in the following terms:

> The word 'primary' implies that other considerations, although not deemed primary, may nevertheless be taken into account. The article 'a' indicates that there may be several considerations, each of which is primary. The issue which arises by virtue of standards incorporated in other widely accepted human rights instruments is whether a single qualification is not sufficient.'[28]

That was enough to get the word 'the' back into the text, but the debate continued,[29] with the Canadian delegate noting that other international instruments adopting that formulation were directed at narrower circumstances and the Finnish representative suggesting confining 'the' to issues relating to the child's welfare. This latter proposal was opposed by the delegations from Australia, Canada, Portugal and Senegal. The United Kingdom representative sought to side-step the 'a versus the' problem, proposing that the child's best interests be stated to be simply 'of primary consideration', a position supported by Norway.[30] As we know, those supporting 'a primary consideration' prevailed in the end of the day. That the division of opinion continues is reflected in the fact that, while some later regional instruments have adopted primacy, others avoid committing one way or the other,[31] domestic constitutional documents reflect a split[32] and much domestic legislation treats the child's best interests as paramount.[33]

---

[28] *Legislative History*, vol. 1, p. 344. [29] *Legislative History*, vol. 1, pp. 345–346.

[30] *Legislative History*, vol. 1, p. 344.

[31] Both the African Charter and the Charter of Fundamental Rights of the European Union employ the notion of 'primacy', while the European Convention on the Exercise of Children's Rights sidesteps the issue neatly by providing that 'the rights and best interests of children should be promoted'. The Washington Declaration on International Family Location of 2010, point 3, produced by 50 judges and others from 14 countries, demonstrates the ultimate 'hedging of bets', when it provides, 'In all applications concerning international relocation the best interests of the child should be the paramount (primary) consideration'. See, www.icmec.org/missingkids/servlet/NewsEventServlet?LanguageCountry=en_X1&PageId= 4240. For a full account of the proceedings, see, *The Judges' Newsletter on International Child Protection – Special Edition No 1, 2010*: www.hcch.net/index_en.php?act=text.display&tid=1.

[32] The constitutions of Ethiopia (1994) and Fiji (2013) accord primacy to the best interests of the child, while the constitutions of Kenya (2010), Somalia (1996) and Zimbabwe (2013) accord paramount status and the constitution of Bolivia (2009) refers to 'the priority of best interests'. See the *Constitute* website for the text of domestic constitutions: www.constituteproject.org/.

[33] See for example, the Family Law Act 1975, s. 65AA (Australia), Children Act 1989, s. 1 (England and Wales); the Children (Scotland) Act 1995, s. 11, the Care of Children Act 2004, s. 4 (New Zealand) and the Children's Act of 2005, s. 9 (South Africa).

Prioritisation aside, discussion focussed on disquiet, familiar to domestic legal systems, over the vagueness of the term 'best interest'.[34] The New Zealand comments on the first Polish draft noted that the phrases 'will be open...to varied interpretations and will be defined nationally in terms of the laws and child-rearing practices which are adopted and acceptable within that nation'[35] and the World Health Organisation expressed its concern over the lack of clarity.[36] Much later in the negotiating process, the matter was raised again by the representative of Venezuela who objected that, with the removal of express reference to the physical, mental, spiritual, moral and social dimensions of best interests, interpretation would be left 'to the judgment of the persons, institutions or organisations applying the rule'.[37] Yet there was no real discussion of what 'best interests' might actually mean and it was many years before the Committee on the Rights of the Child sought to clarify its content.[38]

Paragraph 2

While both the revised Polish and US texts contained provisions addressing the state obligation to protect children, the Working Group used the following text, proposed by the Australian delegation in 1980, as the basis for its deliberations on what became paragraph 2 of Article 3:

> The States parties to the present Convention undertake to ensure the child such protection and care as is necessary for his well-being, taking into account the rights and responsibilities of his parents and the stage of the child's development towards full responsibility and, to this end, shall take all necessary legislative and administrative measures.[39]

The Australian representative pointed out that the provision took account of the basic aim of the 1979 Warsaw Conference on Legal Protection of the Rights of the Child: namely 'to secure the rights of the child through support for the family in need'.[40] There was little discussion of this provision and, perhaps surprisingly, no exploration of the ambiguity surrounding the term 'well-being'. Apart from minor

---

[34] The International Federation of Human Rights and others counselled that, in respect of children of dual origin, states might be tempted to give the concept 'a purely nationalist content and interpretation': *Legislative History*, vol. 1, p. 341.
[35] *Legislative History*, vol. 1, p. 336. [36] *Legislative History*, vol. 1, p. 336.
[37] *Legislative History*, vol. 1, p. 345. [38] See notes 85–96 and the accompanying text.
[39] *Legislative History*, vol. 1, p. 339. [40] *Legislative History*, vol. 1, p. 340.

textual amendments, it was adopted by the Working Group.[41] The importance of the provision should not be underestimated, however, since it articulates the crucial role of the state as the safety net for children. In this, it acknowledges the obligation on parents and legal guardians, but it leaves no doubt about where the ultimate responsibility lies.

Paragraph 3

The seeds of paragraph 3 were present in the revised Polish draft as well as those offered by the Australian and US delegation.[42] In the event, it was the following Australian text that was used as the basis for discussion:

> The States parties to the present Convention shall ensure competent supervision of persons and institutions directly responsible for the care of children.[43]

A textual amendment was proposed by the Canadian and New Zealand delegations to reflect the move away from institutional care in many countries,[44] while the Venezuelan representative made (and later withdrew) a proposal that there be technical supervision of children in institutions.[45]

Considerable debate was generated by the proposal from the International Labour Organisation (ILO) that express reference be made to the training and qualifications of those involved in the care of children.[46] This triggered discussion of whether such an addition was covered by what was to become Article 18(2)[47] and led, in turn, to a proposal from Australia, Canada and Norway that, since the whole of Article 3(3) was so covered, it should be deleted from Article 3.[48] The Indian representative opposed this move, pointing out that Article 18(2) applied only to children who had parents or guardians and that children who did not would be left out by the removal of Article 3(3). The observer from the

---

[41] It was rendered gender neutrality, the term 'legal guardians' was added and 'appropriate' was substituted for 'necessary'.
[42] *Legislative History*, vol. 1, p. 340.
[43] *Legislative History*, vol. 1, p. 339.
[44] *Legislative History*, vol. 1, p. 347.
[45] *Legislative History*, vol. 1, p. 347.
[46] *Legislative History*, vol. 1, p. 343.
[47] Article 18(2) provides, 'For the purpose of guaranteeing and promoting the rights set forth in the present Convention, States Parties shall render appropriate assistance to parents and legal guardians in the performance of their child-rearing responsibilities and shall ensure the development of institutions, facilities and services for the care of children'.
[48] *Legislative History*, vol. 1, p. 347.

ILO indicated that the Organisation saw the two articles as being different in scope but withdrew the proposal. The matter of overlap was referred to a drafting group and the alternative text proposed by the Finnish observer emerged from it, was adopted by the Working Group and, ultimately, became Article 3(3) of the Convention.[49]

Article 3 provides:

1. In all actions concerning children, whether undertaken by public or private social welfare institutions, courts of law, administrative authorities or legislative bodies, the best interests of the child shall be a primary consideration.
2. States Parties undertake to ensure the child such protection and care as is necessary for his or her well-being, taking into account the rights and duties of his or her parents, legal guardians, or other individuals legally responsible for him or her, and, to this end, shall take all appropriate legislative and administrative measures.
3. States Parties shall ensure that the institutions, services and facilities responsible for the care or protection of children shall conform with the standards established by competent authorities, particularly in the areas of safety, health, in the number and suitability of their staff, as well as competent supervision.

C The Content of the Obligations

Meaningful assessment of the impact of any of the Convention's provisions – in this case, Article 3 – requires exploring and clarifying the actual content of the obligations it places on states: essentially, deconstructing the article and examining its component parts in order to gain a better understanding of the whole. There is an abundant body of impressive academic literature to assist in that process and it is in the nature of scholarly discourse that it highlights problems and contradictions.

Through its *Days of Discussion* and its *General Comments*, the UN Committee on the Rights of the Child seeks to offer guidance by clarifying and amplifying Convention obligations so that states can implement them more effectively. Thereafter, it provides feedback to states in its *Concluding Observations* on their periodic reports and we shall return to the *Concluding Observations* presently, when we turn our attentions to the progress made in implementing Article 3. First, it will be helpful

---

[49] *Legislative History*, vol. 1, p. 348.

to explore the content of Article 3, the scholarly critiques thereof and the extent to which the UN Committee has been able to rise to the challenges they present.

Article 3(1)

The twin concerns that so consumed the drafters' energy – the vagueness of 'best interests' and the level of priority to be accorded to them – have continued to dominate discussions of Article 3(1) in operation. The UN Committee on the Rights of the Child was keenly aware of them, offering guidance in a number of *General Comments*.[50] However, it was in *General Comment No. 14*, adopted in 2013, that it provided a more comprehensive analysis of the content of Article 3(1) and its implications for states in terms of implementation.[51] In that document, the Committee celebrated the dynamic and evolutive nature of the best interests principle[52] and indicated the true magnitude of its application with the words,

> the best interests of the child is a threefold concept...a substantive right...a fundamental interpretive principle and...a rule of procedure.[53]

Like all rights embodied in the UN Convention, Article 3(1) applies to 'children', being persons under the age of 18, without discrimination of any kind.[54] Sometimes the matter at issue will relate to a single child while, in other cases, like the decision to close a particular school, a group of children may be affected. Indeed, as the UN Committee has observed, 'all actions taken by the State affect children one way or another'.[55] By the use of the words 'in all actions concerning children', it is made clear that

---

[50] See, for example, *General Comment No. 5: General measures of implementation of the Convention on the Rights of the Child* (2003), CRC/GC/2003/5, para. 12 (highlighting the pervasive and holistic nature of Article 3); *General Comment No. 7: Implementing child rights in early childhood* (2005), CRC/C/GC/7/Rev.1, para. 13(b) ('All law and policy development, administrative and judicial decision-making and service provision that affect children must take account of the best interests principle'.); and *General Comment No. 13: The right of the child to freedom from all forms of violence* (2011), CRC/GC/2011/13, para. 61 ('An adult's judgment of a child's best interests cannot override the obligation to respect all the child's rights under the Convention'.).

[51] *General Comment No. 14 on the right of the child to have his or her best interests taken as a primary consideration (art. 3, para. 1)*, CRC/C/GC/14 (2013), para. 12.

[52] *General Comment No. 14*, para. 11: 'The best interests of the child is a dynamic concept that encompasses various issues which are continuously evolving'.

[53] *General Comment No. 14*, para. 6.   [54] Articles 1 and 2.

[55] *General Comment 14*, para. 20.

Article 3 applies to decisions taken in all of these situations, albeit a formal process of prioritising the child's best interests will not necessarily be required in every instance, with the level of scrutiny depending on the impact on the child or children.[56] Lest there be any doubt about the pervasive application of Article 3(1), the provision itself spells out that it applies to decisions taken 'by public or private social welfare institutions, courts of law, administrative authorities or legislative bodies'.

Primacy

After considerable debate, the drafters of the Convention eventually settled the 'primacy v paramountcy' debate by opting for the formulation that the child's best interests are 'a primary consideration' in all actions concerning children. But what does being a primary consideration require?

Clearly, this becomes an issue when the child's best interests are in conflict with other rights and interests, either those of other persons or those of the child in question. Turning first to the interests of others, it is widely acknowledged that parental divorce can have an adverse impact on a child. If we were truly to prioritise the rights of the child, then we would not permit parents to divorce until their children grow up (or possibly not at all). Of course, the argument can be made that such a course would not be in the child's best interests, but the point is that legal systems do not prohibit divorce simply because the spouses have children. More conceptually problematic, perhaps, is the situation where one child's rights are in conflict with those of another child or a group of children. Suppose, for example, that separating two siblings after parental divorce would serve the best interests of one child, but would be detrimental to the interests of the other. How is the conflict to be resolved?

The UN Committee acknowledged that the wide range of circumstances in which the best interests principle must operate necessitates 'a degree of flexibility in its application'.[57] In cases of conflicting interests, it recommended balancing the interests of all concerned and seeking to find a compromise. With respect, were that possible, there would not be a problem. Assuming the various interests cannot be harmonised, then treating the child's interests as the primary consideration requires that they be accorded 'high priority', not simply being treated as 'one of several considerations', with 'larger weight' being attached to them.[58]

---

[56] Id. [57] *General Comment 14*, para. 39. [58] Id.

What of conflict between the best interests principle and other rights of the child in question? One of the fundamental criticisms of the application of the best interests test is that, by prioritising adult perceptions of the child's welfare, it undermines the place of the child's agency.[59] Legal systems are rightly cautious about forcing adults to do 'what is good for them' since proceeding down that path, if taken far enough, can result in the removal of personal autonomy. Yet, societies have always felt freer to impose adult perceptions of best interests on children, in part, as a direct result of acknowledging the need to protect them. Were the child's best interests to be the sole criterion in decision-making, it could lead to the complete disempowerment of children and young people. That, of course, is the point. While the best interests principle is important, it should not be the sole determinant in the decision-making process, something acknowledged and addressed, perhaps most directly and constructively, by John Eekelaar first, through his concept of 'dynamic self-determinism',[60] and later in this volume when he draws a distinction between decisions about children and decisions that affect them.[61]

The UN Convention, itself, acknowledges the danger of over-reliance on best interests in another of its general principles, Article 12, where it guarantees the child's right to have his or her views taken into account when decisions are being made that affect that child. It is widely recognised in the academic literature that this can lead to tension between welfare and rights, where the adult perception of what will serve the child's best interests is in direct conflict with the child's clearly articulated preference.[62] Initially, the UN Committee may have been in denial[63] when it expressed the view, in *General Comment 12*, that

> There is no tension between articles 3 and 12, only a complementary role of the two general principles: one establishes the objective of achieving the

---

[59] For an excellent overview, see, Jane Fortin, *Children's Rights and the Developing Law*, 3rd edn (Cambridge: Cambridge University Press, 2009), pp. 19–22. See also, Adrian James, 'Squaring the Circle – The Social, Legal and Welfare Organisation of Contact' in Andrew Bainham, Bridget Lindley, Martin Richards and Liz Trinder (eds.), *Children and their Families: Contact, Rights and Welfare* (Oxford: Hart Publishing, 2003), p. 145.

[60] John Eekelaar, 'The Interests of the Child and the Child's Wishes: The Role of Dynamic Self-Determinism' (1994) 8 *International Journal of Law and the Family* 42.

[61] See, Chapter 5, John Eekelaar, 'Two Dimensions of the Best Interests Principle: Decisions About Children and Decisions Affecting Children'.

[62] For an excellent overview, see, Fortin, *Children's Rights and the Developing Law*, pp. 22–30.

[63] Elaine E. Sutherland, 'Listening to the Voice of the Child: The Evolution of Participation Rights' (2013) *New Zealand Law Review* 335, 347.

best interests of the child and the other provides the methodology for reaching the goal of hearing either the child or the children.[64]

More recently, the Committee did a rather better job of addressing the tension in *General Comment 14*, first, by clarifying that 'an adult's judgment of a child's best interests cannot override the obligation to respect all the child's rights under the Convention'.[65] Second, it has indicated the priority to be accorded to best interests with the words, 'The child's best interests shall be applied to all matters concerning the child or children, and taken into account to resolve any possible conflicts among the rights enshrined in the Convention or other human rights treaties'.[66]

Best Interests

A starting point in understanding the best interests of the child is to appreciate what it is not. It is the antithesis of the approach, taken in centuries past, when children were often viewed as 'instruments for the promotion of the interests of others'[67] or as 'mere personal possessions to be sent hither and yon without regard to their feelings or well-being'.[68] Similarly, it replaces (and displaces) earlier tests that turned on the child's gender or the gender or wealth of the parent.[69]

Prioritising the best interests of the child stems from recognition of the obvious fact that due to their youth, inexperience and lack of political power, children are not well placed to protect their own interests.[70] That being the case, it falls to the wider community to ensure that their

---

[64] It continued, 'In fact, there can be no correct application of article 3 if the components of article 12 are not respected. Likewise, article 3 reinforces the functionality of article 12, facilitating the essential role of children in all decisions affecting their lives'. See, *General Comment No. 12: The right of the child to be heard* (2009), CRC/C/CG/12, para. 74.

[65] *General Comment 14*, para. 4, repeating what it said in *General Comment 13* (2011), para. 61.

[66] *General Comment 14*, para. 33.

[67] John Eekelaar, 'Beyond the Welfare Principle' (2002) 14 *Child and Family Law Quarterly* 237, 240.

[68] Barbara Bennett Woodhouse, 'Child Custody in the Age of Children's Rights' (1999) 33 *Family Law Quarterly* 815, 817.

[69] These were particularly evident in custody disputes: Mnookin, 'Child Custody Adjudication', 233–235. See also, Woodhouse, 'Child Custody in the Age of Children's Rights', 817–818.

[70] This point is recognised by countless scholars. See, for example, Mitchell Woolf, 'Coming of Age? – The Principle of "the Best Interests of the Child"' (2003) 2 *European Human Rights Law Review* 205, 208–209.

interests are respected and the law, whether international or domestic, is a valuable (but not the only) tool in securing that end.[71]

Perhaps the greatest strength of the best interests test is its flexibility since it can be applied in the vast array of circumstances in which children find themselves. Given the varied and complex nature of families this is important for decisions within families,[72] but it also means that the test can be used in decision making in other settings, like health care provision and education. Flexibility also allows for the accommodation of social and cultural factors that are relevant to the particular situation[73] and creates a degree of adaptability to changing social mores. The beneficiaries of this adaptability have often been the children of parents who do not live in what were seen as 'traditional' (which was often equated with 'acceptable') relationships or whose parents strayed from the path of conventional norms.[74]

Yet the best interests test has a Janus-like quality and its very strength – its flexibility – is often presented as one of its fundamental weaknesses, with it being condemned as vague and imprecise. Long before the UN Convention, Robert Mnookin articulated the problem thus: 'the determination of what is "best" or "least detrimental" for a particular child is usually indeterminate and speculative'.[75] Indeed, many of the other shortcomings attributed to the test by its critics flow from this basic flaw.

Much of the literature on the operation of the best interests test focusses on disputes between never-together or divorcing parents over their child's future living arrangements and care. Concern has been expressed over the vagueness of best interests opening the door to

---

[71] *X, Y and Z* v *United Kingdom*, (1997) 24 EHRR 143, para. 47 ('the community as a whole has an interest in maintaining a coherent system of family law which places the best interests of the child at the forefront').

[72] Elizabeth S. Scott and Robert E. Emery, *Gender Politics and Child Custody: The Puzzling Persistence of the Best-Interests Standard* (2014) 77 Law and Contemporary Problems 69, 73.

[73] Philip Alston, 'The Best Interests Principle: Towards a Reconciliation of Culture and Human Rights' in Philip Alston (ed.), *The Best Interests of the Child* (Alderley: Clarendon Press, 1994) 1, p. 19.

[74] In the past, the fact that a parent was cohabiting with a partner outside marriage or was living in a same-sex relationship often presented an insurmountable barrier to securing custody or residence of a child: *Early* v *Early* 1990 SLT 221 (Scotland); *Linda R* v *Richard E*, 561 N.Y.2d 29 (2d Dep't 1990). While many courts have moved on from that position, the shift is not universal: contrast *T.C.H.* v *K.M.H.*, 784 S.W.2d 281 (Mo. App. 1989) with *Tucker* v *Tucker*, 910 P.2d 1209 (Utah, 1996).

[75] Mnookin, 'Child Custody Adjudication', 229.

'capricious decision-making',[76] allowing the decision-maker to impose his or her preferred values, sometimes disguised as being based on 'neutral or scientific data'.[77] This can result in the values of the dominant political, cultural or religious group being imposed on those who do not fit the standard pattern, leading to discrimination against those who do not conform.[78] Similarly, judicial discretion 'allows gender biases and subjective value judgments to replace objective considerations'.[79] Individual authors variously claim that this results in systematic bias against either mothers[80] or fathers.[81]

As Mnookin pointed out, indeterminacy leads to unpredictability, which in turn reduces the incentive for the parties to negotiate a settlement and results in increased resort to litigation,[82] a theme taken up by numerous other commentators.[83] This has obvious implications for acrimony, delay, cost to litigants and court time, but it can also lead to increased reliance on expert evidence with the cost usually being borne by the parties, placing the economically weaker party (often the mother in a custody dispute) at a disadvantage.[84]

The UN Committee clearly had the issue of 'indeterminacy' in mind when it sought, in *General Comment 14*, to clarify what was involved in a

---

[76] Stephen Parker, 'The Best Interests of the Child – Principles and Problems' in *The Best Interests of the Child*, p. 3. See also, Helen Reece, 'The Paramountcy Principle: Consensus or Construct?' (1996) 49 *Current Legal Problems* 267, 273.

[77] Katherine Bartlett, 'Re-Expressing Parenthood' in M.D. Freeman (ed.), *Family, State and Law* (Farnham: Ashgate Publishing, 1999), p. 173.

[78] Kohm, for example, argues that bias against religion can be found in the application of the best interest standard: Lynne Marie Kohm, 'Tracing the Foundations of the Best Interests of the Child Standard in American Jurisprudence' (2008) 10 *Journal of Law & Family Studies* 337, 374. Atwood warns of similar prejudice in respect of Native American children: Barbara Ann Atwood, *Children, Tribes, and States: Adoption and Custody Conflicts over American Children'* (Durham, NC: Carolina Academic Press, 2010), p. 8. Reece makes much the same point in the context of gay and lesbian parents: Reece, 'The Paramountcy Principle', 291.

[79] Robert A Warshak, 'The Approximation Rule, Child Development Research, and Children's Best Interests After Divorce' (2007) 1(2) *Child Development Perspectives* 119, 120.

[80] Martha Albertson Fineman, *The Illusion of Equality: The Rhetoric and Reality of Divorce Reform* (Chicago: University of Chicago Press, 1991), p.149.

[81] Scott and Emery, 'Gender Politics and Child Custody', 81–82; Julie E. Artis, 'Judging the Best Interests of the Child: Judges' Accounts of the Tender Years Doctrine' (2004) 38 *Law & Society Review* 769, 785.

[82] Mnookin, 'Child Custody Adjudication', 262.

[83] Reece, 'The Paramountcy Principle', 273; Linda Jellum, 'Parents Know Best: Revising Our Approach to Parental Custody Agreements' (2004) 60 *Ohio State Journal* 615, 630.

[84] Jellum, 'Parents Know Best', 631.

'best interests assessment and determination'.[85] It advocated for the use of 'a non-exhaustive and non-hierarchical list of elements' that would provide decision-makers with 'concrete guidance, yet flexibility' in making a best interests assessment.[86] The elements are discussed under seven general headings and each is amplified in some detail: the child's views; the child's identity; preservation of family environment and maintaining relations; care, protection and safety; situations of vulnerability; right to health; right to education.[87]

Yet there is nothing new about 'welfare checklists', as they are often known in domestic law, and their use has been proposed by numerous academics as the antidote to indeterminacy,[88] with Warshaw going as far as positing that they can 'minimize the drawbacks of the best-interests standard while retaining its virtues'.[89] To date, the various attempts to devise and use checklists have not met with unmitigated success in living up to that promise. One objection to checklists is that they risk being incomplete and, in the attempt to avoid that danger, many legislative provisions sensibly permit the decision-maker to take account of 'all other relevant circumstances' or the like. There is also the very real prospect of different factors on the checklist pointing to opposite conclusions. Nor do checklists normally indicate the relative weight to be accorded to the different factors and, arguably, any attempt to do so would render them unduly rigid. What all of this means, of course, is that the doors are again opened to judicial discretion. As John Eekelaar observed many years ago, 'a judge can consider almost any factor which could possibly have a bearing on a child's welfare and assign to it whatever weight he or she chooses.'[90]

Since the UN Committee's list of elements is stated to be 'non-exhaustive', other elements can be considered and there is express mention of those that are 'in accordance with [the state's] own legal tradition'.[91] Only elements that 'are contrary to the rights enshrined in the convention' are ruled out.[92] The Committee acknowledges that not all of the elements will be present in every case and that, on occasion, the elements may conflict one with another. In a rather weak attempt to suggest a way

---

[85] *General Comment 14*, para. 46.   [86] *General Comment 14*, para. 50.
[87] *General Comment 14*, paras. 52–79.
[88] Mnookin, 'Child Custody Adjudications', 262; Woodhouse, 'Child Custody in the Age of Children's Rights', 829; Woolf, 'Coming of Age?', 208.
[89] Warshak, 'The Approximation Rule', 120.
[90] John Eekelaar, *Regulating Divorce* (Alderley: Clarendon Press, 1991), p. 125.
[91] *General Comment 14*, para. 51.   [92] Id.

to resolve conflicts, *General Comment 14* reminds us that the goal of determining best interests is 'to ensure the full and effective enjoyment' of the rights under the Convention and 'the holistic development of the child'.[93]

A great strength of *General Comment 14* lies in the fact that it does not confine itself to providing a list of the elements relevant to a best interests decision since it also offers guidance on how the assessment and determination should be carried out, requiring evaluation to be by means of a 'transparent and objective formal process'[94] that incorporates 'child-friendly procedural safeguards'.[95] The Committee did not anticipate this formal step applying strictly when day-to-day decisions are being taken by parents, guardians and the like, albeit it was clear that such decisions, like all others, 'must respect and reflect the child's best interests'.[96]

For all other decisions, the Committee again elaborated on what it meant by the requisite procedural safeguards. The first of these seeks to ensure respect for the child's participation rights, something the Committee had already stressed was important when it explored its interaction with best interests. The remaining safeguards require that facts be established by well-trained professionals; processes reflect a child's, rather than an adult's, perception of time; formal assessment be carried out by suitably qualified professionals and preferably involve a multidisciplinary team; the child be provided with a legal representative as well as a guardian or representative of views where a legal or administrative determination is being made; the reasoning behind any decision affecting a child be explained fully; all decisions should be subject to review or appeal; and a child-rights impact assessment should be provided in respect of all proposed policy, legislation, regulation, budget or other administrative decision.

Article 3(2)

The pervasive nature of Article 3(1), combined with the wide-ranging debate surrounding it, may explain why it can sometimes overshadow the obligations under Articles 3(2) and 3(3). Yet the final two subsections of Article 3 lay the crucial foundations for the state's obligations in respect of the care and protection of children, obligations that are expanded upon later in the Convention. Following the *Day of General Discussion*,

---

[93] *General Comment 14*, para. 82.
[94] *General Comment 14*, para. 87.
[95] *General Comment 14*, para 85.
[96] *General Comment 14*, para. 86.

in 2005, where the UN Committee on the Rights of the Child recommended the development of international standards for the protection and alternative care of children without parental care,[97] the UN General Assembly adopted *Guidelines for the Alternative Care of Children*,[98] in 2010, setting out 'desirable orientations for policy and practice'.[99]

Article 3(2) signals the proactive nature of the duty placed on the state by requiring it to 'ensure the child such protection and care as is necessary for his or her well-being'. As Alston has explained:

> The verb used to describe the obligation ('to ensure') is very strong and encompasses both passive and active (including pro-active) obligations. The terms 'protection and care' must also be read expansively, since their objective is not stated in limited or negative terms (such as 'to protect the child from harm') but rather in relation to the comprehensive ideal of ensuring the child's 'well-being'.[100]

Given the drafters' concern over the ambiguity surrounding the concept of 'best interests', it is curious that they expressed no similar disquiet over what is meant by 'well-being', a term that also appears elsewhere in the Convention.[101] There is no accepted legal definition of 'well-being', with the Oxford English Dictionary defining it as, 'the state of being healthy, happy, or prosperous; physical, psychological, or moral welfare'. In the UN Committee's *General Comments*, the term is frequently preceded by adjectives like 'physical', 'emotional' or 'social'[102] and often occurs alongside references to 'heath', 'survival' or 'safety'.[103] The abundance of legal scholarship analysing and critiquing 'best interests' is in stark contrast to

---

[97] Day of General Discussion, 'Children Without Parental Care', 16 September 2005, CRC/C/153, para. 688. This had been preceded by a Day of General Discussion, 'The Private Sector as Service Provider and its Role in Implementing Children's Rights', 20 September 2002, CRC/C/121, paras. 630–653. For the various Days of General Discussion, see, www.ohchr.org/EN/HRBodies/CRC/Pages/DiscussionDays.aspx.

[98] GA Res A/Res/64/142. [99] GA Res A/Res/64/142, para. 2.

[100] Philip Alston, 'The Legal Framework of the Convention on the Rights of the Child' (1992) 91(2) *Bulletin of Human Rights* 1, 9.

[101] The Preamble and Articles 9 and 17.

[102] See, for example, *General Comment No. 17 on the right of the child to rest, leisure, play, recreational activities, cultural life and the arts (art. 31)* (2013), CRC/C/GC/17, para. 43 ('Narrowly focusing all of a child's leisure time into programmed or competitive activities can be damaging to his or her physical, emotional, cognitive and social well-being'.).

[103] See, for example, *General Comment No. 7: Implementing child rights in early childhood* (2005) CRC/C/GC/7/Rev.1, para. 13 ('The principle of best interests applies to all actions concerning children and requires active measures to protect their rights and promote their survival, growth, and well-being'.).

the paucity of legal literature addressing the actual content of 'well-being'.[104] The same cannot be said, however, of the social science literature, where there is a constant lament over the lack of any agreed definition and debate over the indicators used to measure it.[105] Following the UN Millennium Declaration,[106] UNICEF articulated outcomes it seeks to achieve and a wide range of very specific performance indicators, some directed at child protection[107] and, through its Office of Research (the Innocenti Centre), has undertaken work to measure progress on well-being.[108]

Collections of indicators, however, are not the same thing as a definition. In short, internationally, everyone uses the term 'well-being', but no one defines it. Far from the lofty status of being 'a right, a principle and a rule of procedure', it becomes clear that well-being is simply an outcome, a view supported by the call from the UN Committee, in *General Comment 13*, for States Parties 'to establish national standards for child well-being, health and development as securing these conditions is the ultimate goal of child caregiving and protection'.[109] That process is

---

[104] Again, where it is addressed, it is usually in terms of indicators. See, for example, Eekelaar, who summarises what it means as 'being indicated by the degree of success achieved in realising the person's significant goals in life' and goes on to explore indicators: Eekelaar, 'Beyond the Welfare Principle', 243.

[105] See, for example, Gaelle Amerijckx and Perrine Claire Humblet, 'Child Wellbeing: What Does It Mean?' (2014) 28 *Children and Society* 404, at 405 ('to date, there is no consensus on a definition') and Virginia Morrow and Berry Mayall, 'Measuring Children's Well-Being: Some Problems and Possibilities' in Anthony Morgan, Maggie Davies and Erio Ziglio (eds.) *Health Assets in a Global Context* (Heidelberg: Springer, 2010), p. 151 (referring to well-being as a 'conceptually muddy' term).

[106] General Assembly Resolution 2/55. A/RES/55/2, 18 September 2000. The Declaration established Millennium Development Goals and all the constituent parts of the UN system, including UNICEF, were charged to elaborate the nature and extent of their role in achieving these goals.

[107] *UNICEF Strategic Plan, 2014–2017*, E/ICEF/2013/21 and the *Final Results Framework for the UNICEF Strategic Plan, 2014–2017*, E/ICEF/2014/8.

[108] Laura H. Lippman, Kristin Anderson Moore and Hugh McIntosh, *Positive Indicators of Child Well-being: A Conceptual Framework, Measures and Methodological Issues* (Florence: Innocenti Research Centre, 2009) (offering 'a new comprehensive framework which identifies constructs for positive well-being') and *Innocenti Report Card 11: Child Wellbeing in Rich Countries: A comparative overview* (Florence: UNICEF Office of Research, 2013) (essentially, measuring well-being by the use of a number of indicators).

[109] *General Comment No. 13: The right of the child to freedom from all forms of violence* (2011), CRC/C/GC/13, para. 18.

already underway and there are recent examples of domestic legislation that seek to formulate the goals to be achieved in terms of well-being.[110]

Throughout the Convention, emphasis is placed on the importance of the child's parents and guardians.[111] Article 3(2) acknowledges their role and the state's function in supporting them in fulfilling their obligations and in providing the necessary care and protection when they are not doing so. The United Nations *Guidelines for the Alternative Care of Children* repeat support for 'efforts to keep children in, or return them to, the care of their family or, failing this, to find another appropriate or permanent solution'.[112] Nonetheless, where a child has no parents or guardians or they are absent, incapacitated or offering inadequate care (for whatever reason), the responsibility for the child's care and protection falls upon the state and, as we shall see, the UN Committee on the Rights of the Child has not been slow to criticise states that have failed in one or other respect.[113]

Yet the state's obligation is broader than simply being a safety net since there are functions necessary to child well-being, like ensuring the highest attainable standard of health (Art. 24), social security (Art. 26), standard of living (Art. 27), education (Art. 28 and 29) and environmental protection (Art. 24(2)), that it is uniquely situated to discharge.

Article 3(3)

Article 3(3) amplifies the state's obligations by requiring 'competent authorities' to establish standards to which institutions, services and facilities responsible for child care must conform. While the areas of safety and health, as well as the number and suitability of staff and competent supervision, are emphasised (by the use of the word

---

[110] The Vulnerable Children Act 2014, s. 6 (New Zealand) is directed at improving the well-being of vulnerable children, which is defined as 'promoting the best interests of vulnerable children (having regard to the whole of their lives)' and it goes on to list a number of specific goals it seeks to achieve. The Children and Families Act 2014, s. 25 (England and Wales), dealing with the integration of educational provision and training provision with health care provision and social care provision, and includes a similar list of the kind of well-being it is aimed at. The Children and Young People Act 2014 (Scotland) is rather more vague. Where it requires assessment of the well-being of a child, that is to be done, by virtue of s. 96, 'by reference to the extent to which' the child is or would be 'safe healthy, achieving, nurtured, active, respected, responsible and included'.

[111] See also, Articles 5, 18 and 20.   [112] GA Res A/Res/64/142, para. 2(a).

[113] See footnotes 147–152 and accompanying text.

'particularly'), that language makes clear that the enumerated matters are not an exhaustive list and regulation should reach more broadly. Rather more detail is provided in the United Nations *Guidelines for the Alternative Care of Children*. It will be recalled that during the drafting of Article 3, there was a skirmish over the proposal from the ILO, subsequently withdrawn, that express reference should be made to the training and qualification of those providing alternative case. That idea re-emerged in the *Guidelines*, with the requirement that 'special attention should be paid to the quality of alternative care provision...in particular with regard to the professional skills, selection, training and supervision of carers'.[114]

Nor is the state's standard-setting and supervisory role confined to the services it provides directly. The UN Committee recognised that such services may be provided by the non-governmental sector and, in the context of early childhood development, reminded states that 'the role of civil society should be complimentary to – not a substitute for – the role of the State', emphasising that the obligation to ensure compliance with the Convention remains a state responsibility.[115] The same principles apply where the state outsources services to private providers.

D Progress

The real test of the impact of the Convention is how it affects the lives of children in their own countries, neighbourhoods, schools and families. Invaluable insights into how well Convention rights are being implemented can be gleaned from the *Concluding Observations* of the UN Committee on the Rights of the Child on the initial and periodic reports that States Parties are required to submit within two years of ratifying the Convention and every five years thereafter.[116] In the course of commenting on the progress and shortcoming in individual countries, the Committee clarifies further precisely what is expected of states.

The process of self-reporting is subject to a number of limitations and, when contrasted with a judicial process, is regarded as one of the weaker methods of enforcing treaty obligations, with it being described more

---

[114] GA Res A/Res/64/142, para. 71.
[115] *General Comment No. 7: Implementing child rights in early childhood* (2005), CRC/C/GC/7/Rev.1, para. 32.
[116] Article 44.

accurately as monitoring compliance.[117] Some states report late or do not report at all and it may be tempting for a state to be highly selective in terms of the content of reports, emphasising the positive and downplaying or ignoring the negative. In addition, the very part-time status of the Committee resulted in a substantial backlog of country reports awaiting its attention. The UN General Assembly sough to alleviate the backlog by authorising the Committee to receive combined periodic reports, covering more than one five-year period, from states, something that helped to address the problem of late reporting as well.[118] The backlog continued and the General Assembly permitted the Committee to meet in parallel chambers 'as an exceptional and temporary measure'.[119]

The UN Committee does not rely solely on the state's own periodic reports and receives information from other sources, including UN Special Rapporteurs and non-governmental organisations. That contributes to offsetting any 'selective reporting' by states, as do the Committee's own guidelines on what it expects in terms of the structure and content of reports. Revised most recently in 2010, the guidelines on periodic reports anticipate each report will be comprised of two parts: the common core and the treaty-specific report.[120] The common core is designed to save the state from duplicating its efforts since it will form the basis of reports by it to other human rights bodies, like the Human Rights Committee and the Committee on Economic, Social and Cultural Rights, as well as the Committee on the Rights of the Child, and provides general information about the state and its overall framework for the protection and promotion of human rights.[121] The treaty-specific report is when we get to the heart of the state's progress on children's rights since it should

---

[117] See John P. Grant, 'Monitoring and Enforcing Children's International Human Rights' in Alison Cleland and Elaine E. Sutherland (eds.), *Children's Rights in Scotland*, 3rd edn (Edinburgh: W Green, 2009).

[118] *Report of the Committee on the Rights of the Child, General Assembly Official Records, Sixty-seventh session, Supplement No 41 (A/67/41)*, Annex II. In 2008, for example, the United Kingdom submitted a combined third and fourth report and, in 2013, South Africa submitted a periodic report covering 1998–2013.

[119] A/RES/63/244 (2009) and A/RES/67/167 (2013).

[120] *Treaty-specific guidelines regarding the form and content of periodic reports to be submitted by States parties under article 44, paragraph 1 (b), of the Convention on the Rights of the Child*, CRC/C/58/Rev.2 (2010). The common core should not exceed 60–80 pages (para. 7) and the treaty-specific report should not exceed 60 pages (para. 11).

[121] There are additional *Guidelines on the Form and Content of Reports to be submitted by States Parties to the International Human Rights Treaties*, HRI/GEN/2/Rev.6 (2009).

contain 'all information relating to the implementation of the Convention and its...Optional Protocols'.[122]

What, then, did the UN Committee on the Rights of the Child have to say about the progress states have made in complying with Article 3? Given the status of the primacy of best interests as a substantive right, an interpretive legal principle and a rule of procedure, the Committee's *Concluding Observations* contain frequent references to it, expressing disquiet where a State Party's report provides insufficient evidence to enable it to assess the status of the principle in the country.[123] Recent *Concluding Observations* often point states to *General Comment 14* and its very specific requirements in terms of Article 3(1).[124] Doubtless, states that reported before it was issued may feel a little aggrieved that they were being judged on the basis of criteria unpublished at the time they reported.

The UN Committee welcomed the inclusion of the best interests principle in States Parties' constitutions. On occasion, a specific constitutional provision, like that in Turkey, empowering the Supreme Court to annul any decision that does not take account of the child's best interests, is singled out for special mention.[125] However, the Committee has not been slow to point out that constitutional recognition alone is not enough and has sometimes applauded constitutional recognition at the same time as criticising the failure to publicise and apply the principle.[126]

Unsurprisingly, legislation according primacy – or in some cases, paramountcy[127] – to the child's best interests meets with the approval of the Committee and it expresses disquiet over the absence of such provision[128] or of attempts to provide a lesser alternative. So, for example, the Russian Federation comes in for criticism over its legislation referring

---

[122] *Treaty-specific guidelines*, para. 11.
[123] See for example, *Concluding Observations* on Congo, CRC/C/COG/CO/2–4 (2014), para. 30.
[124] See for example, *Concluding Observations* on Germany, CRC/C/DEU/CO/3–4 (2014), para. 27 and *Concluding Observations* on Portugal (2014), CRC/C/PRT/CO/3–4 para. 28.
[125] *Concluding Observations* on Turkey, CRC/C/TUR/CO/2–3 (2012), para. 30.
[126] *Concluding Observations* on Guatemala, CRC/C/GTM/CO/3–4 (2010), para. 43.
[127] *Concluding Observations* on Egypt, CRC/C/EGY/CO/3–4 (2011), para. 36.
[128] *Concluding Observations* on Bahrain, CRC/C/BHR/CO/2–3 (2011), para. 32; *Concluding Observations* on China, CRC/C/CHN/CO/3–4 (2013) para. 31; *Concluding Observations* on the Republic of Korea, CRC/C/KOR/CO/3–4 (2012), para. 32;'*Concluding Observations* on the Syrian Arab Republic, CRC/C/SYR/CO/3–7 (2012), para. 35; and *Concluding Observations* on Tuvala, CRC/C/TUV/CO/1 (2013), para. 25.

to the 'legitimate interests of the child',[129] as does Seychelles for its reference simply to 'the interests of the child'.[130] Mention of the principle in some legislation, but not across the board also causes the Committee concern.[131] On numerous occasions, the Committee emphasises that legislation acknowledging the best interests principle is not enough in itself and it has expressed concern over a lack of public awareness of it and insufficient understanding of it by traditional, community or religious leaders.[132] In addition, there is particular disquiet where the lack of understanding is on the part of the very people whom one might expect to have, if anything, a heightened appreciation of the principle, like judicial and administrative authorities and civil servants[133] and professionals working with or representing children.[134]

Given the status of best interests as an interpretative legal principle, it is not surprising that the Committee is concerned where legislation leaves its meaning vague,[135] the process by which it is determined is unclear[136] or where there are inadequate guidelines and procedures for implementing the primacy of best interests at a policy level and in programmes.[137] Specific examples of failing to take due account of the best interests

---

[129] *Concluding Observations* on Russia (2014), CRC/C/RUS/CO/4-5, para. 26(a). Similar criticism is found in the *Concluding Observations* on Armenia, CRC/C/ARM/CO/3-4 (2013), para. 20, and on Uzbekistan, CRC/C/UZB/CO/3-4 (2013), para. 22.

[130] *Concluding Observations* on Seychelles, CRC/C/SYC/CO/2-4 (2012), para. 36.

[131] *Concluding Observations* on Belgium, CRC/C/BEL/CO/3-4 (2010), para. 33; *Concluding Observations* on the Czech Republic, CRC/C/CZE/CO/3-4 (2011), para. 32; *Concluding Observations* on Finland, CRC/C/FIN/CO/4 (2011), para. 27; *Concluding Observations* on Germany, CRC/C/DEU/CO/3-4 (2014), para. 26; *Concluding Observations* on Guyana, CRC/C/GUY/CO/2-4 (2013), para. 26; *Concluding Observations* on the Netherlands, CRC/C/NDL/CO/3 (2009), para. 28; *Concluding Observations* on Vietnam, CRC/C/VNM/CO/3-4 (2012), para. 31.

[132] *Concluding Observations* on Guinea-Bissau, CRC/C/GNB/CO/2-4 (2013), para. 26, and *Concluding Observations* on Namibia, CRC/C/NAM/CO/2-3 (2012), para. 32.

[133] *Concluding Observations* on Australia, CRC/C/AUS/CO/4 (2012), para. 31; *Concluding Observations* on Egypt, CRC/C/EGY/CO/3-4 (2011), para. 36; *Concluding Observations* on Bahrain, CRC/C/BHR/CO/2-3 (2011), para. 32; *Concluding Observations* on Nicaragua, CRC/C/NIC/CO/4 (2010), para. 38.

[134] *Concluding Observations* on Azerbaijan, CRC/C/AZE/CO/3-4 (2012), para. 32, and *Concluding Observations* on Madagascar, CRC/C/MDG/CO/3-4 (2012), para. 25.

[135] *Concluding Observations* on Togo, CRC/C/TGO/CO/3-4 (2012), para. 33; *Concluding Observations* on Monaco, CRC/C/MCO/CO/2-3(2013), para. 24.

[136] *Concluding Observations* on Portugal: CRC/C/PRT/CO/3-4 (2014), para. 27; *Concluding Observations* on Spain, CRC/C/ESP/CO/3-4 (2010), para. 27.

[137] *Concluding Observations* on Luxemburg, CRC/C/LUX/CO/3-4 (2013), para. 24; *Concluding Observations* on Sao Tome and Principe, CRC/C/STP/CO/2-4 (2013), para. 25.

principle include the allocation of resources,[138] children in conflict with the law[139] and in asylum, immigration and refugee situations.[140]

Simply recognising the primacy of the child's best interests in legislation is not regarded by the UN Committee as sufficient if it is not respected and applied across the community[141] and in in judicial and administrative proceedings and decisions.[142] Nor is legislative recognition enough if, in fact, other interests, including those of parents,[143] other adults[144] or institutions,[145] take priority over the interests of the child. In this respect, traditional norms can present a challenge to the full implementation of the principle.[146]

Many of the general concerns expressed in respect of Article 3(1) have a direct bearing on the implementation of Article 3(2) and 3(3). Thus, for example, if there is widespread ignorance of, or inadequate procedures implementing, the best interests principle, that may affect the whole system of child protection. However, the UN Committee took the opportunity, in numerous *Concluding Observations*, to highlight concerns over the provision of alternative care for children deprived of their family.[147] Specific concerns include how the decision to place the

---

[138] *Concluding Observations* on Austria, CRC/C/AUT/CO/3-4 (2012), para. 26:
[139] *Concluding Observations* on Albania, CRC/C/ALB/CO/2-4 (2012), para. 29; *Concluding Observations* on United Kingdom, CRC/C/GBR/CO/4 (2008), para. 26.
[140] *Concluding Observations* on: Canada, CRC/C/CAN/CO/3-4 (2012), para. 34; *Concluding Observations* on Australia, CRC/C/AUS/CO/4 (2012), para. 31, the *Concluding Observations* on Denmark, CRC/C/DNK/CO/4 (2011), para. 34; *Concluding Observations* on Germany, CRC/C/DEU/CO/3-4 (2014), para. 26 and the *Concluding Observations* on the United Kingdom, CRC/C/GBR/CO/4 (2008), para. 26.
[141] *Concluding Observations* on Guinea, CRC/C/GIN/CO/2 (2013), para. 38.
[142] *Concluding Observations* on Cyprus, CRC/C/CYP/CO/3-4 (2012), para. 23; *Concluding Observations* on Kuwait, CRC/C/KWT/CO/2 (2013), para. 31; *Concluding Observations* on Loa People's Democratic Republic, CRC/C/LAO/CO/2 (2011), para. 28; *Concluding Observations* on Myanmar, CRC/C/MMR/CO/3-4 (2012), para. 37; *Concluding Observations* on Singapore, CRC/C/SGP/CO/2-3 (2011), para. 31.
[143] *Concluding Observations* on Russian Federation, CRC/C/RUS/CO/4-5 (2014), para. 26(c).
[144] *Concluding Observations* on Liberia, CRC/C/LBR/CO/2-4 (2012), para. 35.
[145] *Concluding Observations* on Holy See, CRC/C/VAT/CO/2 (2014), para. 29. See, Ioana Cismas, 'The Child's Best Interests and Religion: A Case Study of the Holy See's Best Interests Obligations and Clerical Child Sexual Abuse', Chapter 18 in this volume.
[146] *Concluding Observations* on Yemen, CRC/C/YEM/CO/4 (2014), para. 31.
[147] *Concluding Observations* on Andorra, CRC/C/AND/CO/2 (2012), para. 26; *Concluding Observations* on Bosnia and Herzegovina, CRC/C/BIH/CO/2-4 (2012), para. 31; *Concluding Observations* on Ukraine, CRC/C/UKR/CO/3-4 (2011), para. 29.

child in out-of-home care is taken,[148] failure to assess the child's emotional and psychological needs,[149] the management of alternative care,[150] the monitoring and evaluation of foster care, the number of alternative care facilities and their monitoring,[151] and the number and suitability of staff in institutions providing alternative care.[152]

E Conclusions

As one of the four general principles of the UN Convention on the Rights of the Child, Article 3 is of pervasive effect. Yet it continues to present challenges; challenges identified by the drafters and continuing today relating to the meaning of key terms employed and the interaction between the child's best interests and other rights and interests.

Long before the Convention was proposed, domestic legal systems had struggled with precisely what was meant by 'the best interests of the child'. In *General Comment 14*, the United Nations Committee on the Rights of the Child sought to offer clarification by providing a non-exhaustive list of the elements that may be relevant to making a best interests determination and elaborating on each in some detail. But there have been many attempts to formulate what are often known in domestic law as 'welfare checklists' and they have brought their own problems.

Does *General Comment 14* offer anything more? Arguably, it does – and for two reasons. First, the Committee's formulation of the elements to be considered in assessing the child's best interests is more comprehensive than many domestic checklists. Second – and crucially – *General Comment 14* provides guidance on the mechanics of making a best interests determination, requiring the use of a multidisciplinary team of suitably qualified professionals and a transparent, objective process complete with child-friendly procedural safeguards. When it offers its *Concluding Observations* on country reports, the Committee applies this systematic approach in its analysis and recommendations.

Article 3(2) introduces another key term, 'well-being'. For lawyers, at any rate, it may be even more ambiguous than 'best interests' since it

---

[148] *Concluding Observations* on Denmark, CRC/C/DNK/CO/4 (2011), para. 34.
[149] *Concluding Observations* on Russian Federation, CRC/C/RUS/CO/4–5 (2014), para. 26(b).
[150] *Concluding Observations* on Thailand, CRC/C/THA/CO/3–4 (2012), para. 35.
[151] *Concluding Observations* on South Africa: CRC/C/15/Add.122 (2000), para 25.
[152] *Concluding Observations* on Japan, CRC/C/JPN/CO/3 (2010), para. 39.

has less of a pedigree in domestic legal systems, there is no legal definition of its content and it has attracted little attention from legal scholars. The extensive discussion of the term in the social science literature focusses on its ambiguity and the inadequacy of the indicators used to evaluate it. Therein lies the key to understanding 'well-being'. Rather than being a test to be applied in the decision-making process, well-being is an outcome that may be amenable to measurement. In the course of its work on the Millennium Development Goals, UNICEF has produced a range of well-being performance indicators, some directed at child protection, and a number of states have responded to the UN Committee's call to establish national standards for child well-being.

The second main challenge facing Article 3 relates to the prioritisation of rights: that is, where the best interests of the child rank, when set alongside other rights. The 'primacy v paramountcy' debate dominated discussions of Article 3(1) at the drafting stage. Again, the debate was not new then and it continues today. It arises when the best interests of the child come into conflict, either with other rights of that child, like the right to have his or her views taken into account, or with the rights of others, whether adults or other children. Again, the UN Committee sought to clarify what it means to accord primacy to the child's best interests, settling on the formulation that these interests 'have high priority and [are] not just one of several considerations'.[153]

It is fair to say that the challenges facing Article 3 have not been resolved, if, by resolution, one means that the terms used are now certain and that the priority to be accorded to different rights is uncontentious. That is not, however, a flaw in Article 3. It is simply a reflection of the reality that children's lives are infinitely varied. In that context, individualised decision-making requires the nuanced application of a range of flexible criteria. That process will always be more difficult than simply employing a bright line rule but, if the price for ensuring tailor-made solutions, suited to the circumstances of the individual child, is a degree of unpredictability, then it is a price worth paying. Similarly, balancing rights is not always an easy task, but it is one with which legal and administrative systems are familiar. That task can be discharged more equitably, effectively and transparently if adequate

---

[153] *General Comment 14*, para. 39.

procedural safeguards are put in place. The UN Committee has provided considerable and valuable guidance on both the criteria for decision-making and the process by which decisions should be made. It now falls to states to draw on that guidance in meeting their obligations under Article 3 and the chapters that follow explore their progress in doing so.

2

The Best Interests of the Child: A Gateway to Children's Rights?

URSULA KILKELLY

A   Introduction

The requirement that the child's best interests should inform decisions made about the child is a well-established legal principle. The principle has been used to guide decision-making in family law for decades and it is contained in family law statutes in many jurisdictions around the world. The principle has been subjected to rigorous and critical analysis by scholars like Goldstein, Freud and Solnit[1] and Mnookin[2] who identify it as a vague, indeterminate and subjective standard. Despite these concerns, the enactment of the United Nations Convention on the Rights of the Child (CRC) enshrined the principle in binding international human rights law[3] and, according to the Committee on the Rights of the Child, the best interests principle, set out in Article 3 of the CRC, is one of the general principles of the children's rights Convention. Parker,[4] Eekelaar,[5] Herring[6] and others

---

[1] J. Goldstein, A. Freud and A. Solnit, *Beyond the Best Interests of the Child* (New York: Free Press, 1973), *Before the Best Interests of the Child* (New York: Free Press, 1979), and *In the Best Interests of the Child* (with S. Goldstein, New York: Free Press, 1996).

[2] See for example R.H. Mnookin, 'Child-Custody Adjudication: Judicial Functions in the Face of Indeterminacy' (1975) 39 *Law & Contemporary Problems* 226.

[3] Adopted and opened for signature, ratification and accession by General Assembly resolution 44/25 of 20 November 1989 entry into force 2 September 1990, in accordance with article 49.

[4] S. Parker, 'The Best interests of the Child – Principles and Problems' (1994) *International Journal of Law and the Family* 26.

[5] J. Eekelaar, The Interests of The Child and the Child's Wishes: The Role of Dynamic Self-Determinism (1994) 8 *International Journal of Law and the Family* 42.

[6] See for example J. Herring, 'The Welfare Principle and the Rights of Parents' in A. Bainham and M. Richards, *What Is a Parent? A Socio-legal Analysis* (Oxford: Hart Publishing, 1999).

have engaged with the principle in the context of the CRC, assessing its role in the determination of family law matters including custody, adoption and alternative care.

Most scholarship, although critical of the best interests principle, has accepted its value and sought ways to remedy any flaws so that its potential to advance the interests and position of children can be maximised.[7] Few question the connection between the best interests principle and children's rights and ask whether an approach predicated on what is in the best interests of the child can indeed further implementation of the rights of the child more generally. A rare voice here is Cantwell who questions the use of the best interests principle as a 'trump card' and asks whether this provision, among others, takes children's rights too far away from its human rights origins.[8]

Against this backdrop, this chapter proposes to critique the best interests principle as a provision of the Convention on the Rights of the Child. In doing so, the basis for the approach of the Committee on the Rights of the Child's – framing Article 3(1) as a right, a rule of procedure and an interpretive principle – is analysed and its legitimacy examined. The chapter goes on to outline with reference to original research on children's rights advocacy whether in fact the principle has additional value, namely as a gateway to children's rights when used within this broader policy context.

B   Article 3 of the CRC and the Guidance of the Committee on the Rights of the Child

Although the best interests of the child was included in the 1959 Declaration on the Rights of the Child,[9] it was not until 1989 that it was enshrined in binding international law as a free-standing

---

[7] See for example B. Bennett Woodhouse, 'Child Custody in the Age of Children's Rights: The Search for a Just and Workable Standard' (1999) 33(3) *Family Law Quarterly* 815.

[8] Cantwell, N. (2011) 'Are Children's Rights Still Human?' in A. Invernizzi and J. Williams (eds.), *The Human Rights of Children From Visions to Implementation* (Farnham: Ashgate, 2011), pp. 37–60.

[9] Under Principle 1 of the Declaration, which proclaims the child's right to special protection, the Declaration requires that in the enactment of laws for this purpose the best interests of the child shall be the paramount consideration. *Proclaimed by General Assembly Resolution 1386(XIV) of 20 November 1959.*

principle. According to Article 3(1) of the Convention on the Rights of the Child:

> In all actions concerning children, whether undertaken by public or private social welfare institutions, courts of law, administrative authorities or legislative bodies, the best interests of the child shall be a primary consideration.[10]

Accounts of the drafting process indicate that although there was controversy surrounding the question of whether the best interests should be 'paramount' or 'primary' (the latter was adopted as a compromise position[11]), the meaning of the concept seems 'either to have been taken for granted or considered unimportant'.[12] Alston concludes that the lack of discussion about the principle stems from the drafters' familiarity with the phrase from its 'extensive usage in the domestic law of many countries'.[13] He notes during the drafting process a similar lack of discussion of the potential of the principle clashing with other Convention provisions, which appears not to have been anticipated.[14]

The adoption of Article 3(1) can thus be said to have been largely uncontroversial in the Convention's drafting process. It is perhaps related that the provision has been criticised for enshrining a weak standard insofar as it prefers the requirement to treat the child's best interests as a 'primary' rather than a 'paramount' consideration. However, this can arguably be justified by the sheer scope of the provision, which applies 'in all actions concerning children'. In this way, enshrining the principle in the CRC reflects the extension of the principle beyond the boundaries of national family law into the realm of international human rights law. As the Committee on the Rights of the Child explains, the Article 3(1) obligation falls not only on state bodies but on the whole range of bodies and groups – including civil society and the private sector – whose actions or services impact on children.[15] According to Alston, this is a 'very significant extension' of the principle whose origins lie in the areas

---

[10] Adopted and opened for signature, ratification and accession by General Assembly resolution 44/25 of 20 November 1989, entry into force 2 September 1990 in accordance with article 49.

[11] P. Alston, 'Best Interests Principle: Towards a Reconciliation of Culture and Human Rights' (1994) *International Journal of Law and the Family* 1, 12–13.

[12] Ibid., 10–11.   [13] Ibid., at 11.   [14] Id.

[15] Committee on the Rights of the Child, *General Comment No. 14 (2013) on the right of the child to have his or her best interests taken as a primary consideration (art. 3, para. 1)* CRC/C/GC/14, para. 12.

of family law and divorce.[16] Notwithstanding the status of the CRC as an instrument of international law, the principle enshrined in Article 3 purports to extend beyond the strictly legal context.

The Committee on the Rights of the Child has identified Article 3(1) as one of the four general principles for interpreting and implementing all the rights of the child in the Convention.[17] It has been identified as 'a dynamic concept that requires an assessment appropriate to the specific context' and so even though the best interests of the child is referred to in several other Convention provisions, it is Article 3(1) that represents the 'best interests principle', as it has become known. It is interesting to note that the reference to the best interests of the child varies in the way it is used in other provisions. For instance, Article 9(1) provides that a child shall only be separated from his/her parents *inter alia* where such separation is necessary for the best interests of the child. The formulation differs slightly in provisions dealing with liberty and procedural guarantees in the criminal context however. Here, Article 37(c) provides that every child deprived of liberty shall be separated from adults 'unless it is considered in the child's best interest not to do so'. Similarly, Article 40(2)(b)(iii) provides for the presence of parents at court hearings in criminal matters 'unless it is considered not to be in the best interest of the child'. Different again is its use in Article 18, which states with respect to parents that '[t]he best interests of the child will be their basic concern'.

Central to the General Comment of the Committee on the Rights of the Child on the best interests principle is the presentation of Article 3 (1) as 'a right, a principle and a rule of procedure'.[18] The Committee first presents Article 3(1) as a substantive right meaning that it involves

> [t]he right of the child to have his or her best interests assessed and taken as a primary consideration when different interests are being considered in order to reach a decision on the issue at stake, and the guarantee that this right will be implemented whenever a decision is to be made concerning a child, a group of identified or unidentified children or children in general.[19]

---

[16] Alston, 'Best Interests Principle', 4.
[17] Committee on the Rights of the Child, *General Comment No. 5* (2003) on the General Measures of implementation of the Convention on the Rights of the Child, para. 12; and *General Comment No. 12* (2009) on the right of the child to be heard, para. 2.
[18] *General Comment No. 14*, para. 6.   [19] Ibid., para. 6(a).

According to the General Comment, Article 3(1) 'creates an intrinsic obligation for States, is directly applicable (self-executing) and can be invoked before a court'.[20]

In terms of Article 3(1) as a principle, the Committee's guidance is that '[i]f a legal provision is open to more than one interpretation, the interpretation which most effectively serves the child's best interests should be chosen.'[21] Importantly, although without elaboration, the General Comment indicates that the rights in the Convention and its Optional Protocols 'provide the framework for interpretation'.[22]

Finally, the General Comment indicates that the best interests principle also operates as a 'rule of procedure'. In this regard, the Committee has indicated that '[w]henever a decision is to be made that will affect a specific child, an identified group of children or children in general, the decision-making process must include an evaluation of the possible impact (positive or negative) of the decision on the child or children concerned.'[23]

The Committee has indicated that

> [a]ssessing and determining the best interests of the child require (sic) procedural guarantees. Furthermore, the justification of a decision must show that the right has been explicitly taken into account. In this regard, States parties shall explain how the right has been respected in the decision, that is, what has been considered to be in the child's best interests; what criteria it is based on; and how the child's interests have been weighed against other considerations, be they broad issues of policy or individual cases.[24]

It is implicit in the way in which this guidance has been framed by the Committee on the Rights of the Child that it is seeking to assert the rights credentials of the best interests principle. But in taking this approach, is the Committee attempting to remedy the lack of rights-focus in Article 3(1) or is it merely reflecting its position as a provision in the Convention on the Rights of the Child?

The Committee's use of language in the General Comment, in its expression of the best interests principle as a substantive right, is a forceful articulation of the principle from a rights perspective. This is augmented further by the manner in which the objective of the General Comment is explained. In addition to strengthening the understanding and application of what the Committee describes as 'the right of children

---

[20] Id. [21] Ibid., para. 6(b). [22] Ibid. [23] Ibid., para. 6(c). [24] Ibid.

to have their best interests assessed and taken as a primary consideration', the overall objective of the General Comment is explained as 'to promote a real change in attitudes leading to the full respect of children as rights holders'.[25] More specifically, this is indicated to have implications for the following:

(a) The elaboration of all implementation measures taken by governments;
(b) Individual decisions made by judicial or administrative authorities or public entities through their agents that concern one or more identified children;
(c) Decisions made by civil society entities and the private sector, including profit and non-profit organizations, which provide services concerning or impacting on children;
(d) Guidelines for actions undertaken by persons working with and for children, including parents and caregivers.[26]

In summary, the inclusion of the best interests of the child and its elaboration by the Committee on the Rights of the Child, predominantly in its General Comment, suggests that Article 3(1) can deliver more rights-based decision-making, designed to further implementation of the Convention. However, the legitimacy of the Committee's approach demands acceptance of the best interests principle as a children's rights principle. The next section of the chapter interrogates the basis for this approach by proceeding to analyse whether, as the Committee suggests, the best interests principle is a right, an interpretive principle and a rule of procedure.

C The Best Interests Principle as a Right

The first focus of this critique of the best interests standard stems from the question of whether 'this notion of the child's best interest, conceived at a time when the child was perceived as more object than subject, retains its raison d'être within the context of rights'.[27] The argument posited is that the best interests principle is borne more out of and belongs to an approach to children's treatment that is paternalistic,

---

[25] Ibid., para. 12.   [26] Ibid.
[27] R. Joyal, 'The Notion of the Best Interest of the Child: Its Place in the United Nations Convention on the Rights of the Child' paper presented to DCI/ICJ Conference in Siracusa 1990, 2, in Alston, 'Best Interests Principle', 18.

determined by adults, rather than rights-based, child-led and viewing the child as a rights-holder.[28] Does the best interests principle 'belong' in a human rights convention?

In terms of examining this further, in line with Article 31 of the Vienna Convention on the Law of Treaties,[29] it is useful to first look at the text of Article 3(1) in order to assess its content. As noted above, Article 3(1) requires that in all actions concerning children the best interests of the child must be a primary consideration. It is immediately apparent that Article 3(1) is one of only very few substantive CRC provisions that does not contain the word 'right'. It is not framed in the manner of most of the Convention's other provisions, in a way that articulates the substantive right or that makes clear that the child is the holder of the right being articulated. A review of other, more typical CRC provisions highlights how distinct Article 3(1) actually is. For example, Article 6 of the CRC provides that States Parties shall recognise that every child has the inherent right to life, Article 9 provides that States Parties shall respect the right of the child to maintain personal relations and direct contact with parents and under Article 31 States Parties recognise the right of the child to rest and leisure. A host of other provisions refer invariably but explicitly to 'the right of the child…' in some form. It can be argued that the unusual formulation of Article 3(1) reflects its position at the start of the Convention – in the 'umbrella' as it has been called – among the provisions dealing with the general interpretation (Article 1), application (Article 2) and implementation (Articles 4 and 5) of the Convention.[30]

Regardless of where it is situated in the Convention, a plain reading of the text does not support the view that Article 3(1) contains a right. At the same time, the interpretive rules of the Vienna Convention require the meaning of treaty provisions to be determined in their context and in light of the object and purpose of the Convention as a whole.[31] Reading Article 3(1) in light of the Convention as a whole undoubtedly bolsters the argument for presenting Article 3(1) as a rights principle, underpinned by the child's status as a rights-holder.

---

[28] B. Bennett Woodhouse, '"Out of Children's Needs, Children's Rights": The Child's Voice in Defining the Family' (1993) 8 *BYU Journal of Public Law* 321, 323.
[29] Vienna Convention on the Law of Treaties, Signed at Vienna 23 May 1969, Entry into force: 27 January 1980.
[30] Alston, 'Best Interests Principle', at 11.
[31] See Article 31(1) of the Vienna Convention.

It is perhaps this approach that justifies the Committee's insistence that Article 3(1) is a rights-based principle of the Convention.

The second question relating to the rights credentials of Article 3(1) is whether, like other Convention provisions, it contains an obligation; again this is disputable. Alston notes that Article 3(1) 'does not seek to impose specific duties' on states,[32] but rather it makes provision for a general requirement to ensure that 'all actions' are informed by consideration of what is in the child's best interests. Admittedly, the provision contains the word 'shall', reflective of a duty, but the difficulty is the absence of clarity as to who is the duty bearer. Compared to other provisions, it is remarkable that Article 3(1) makes no reference to 'States Parties', given that other CRC provisions, with limited exceptions, impose an explicit duty on States Parties to recognise, respect or take measures to protect or implement the rights of the child. Again there is some wriggle room created by the fact that Article 3(1) includes reference to 'public or private social welfare institutions, courts of law, administrative authorities or legislative bodies', clearly bodies for which the state has responsibility. Indeed, it is even arguable that by detailing specific national bodies – courts of law, etc. – is not only equivalent to the reference to 'states parties' in other provisions, but in fact the precise pinpointing of the duty bearer gives added strength, clarity and reach to Article 3(1) that other provisions do not have.

The Committee on the Rights of the Child has addressed the implementation of the best interests principle and has recommended that the principle be enshrined in domestic legislation.[33] According to General Comment No 5, '[e]very legislative, administrative and judicial body or institution is required to apply the best interests principle...by systematically considering how children's rights and interests are or will be affected by their decisions and actions'.[34] Combined with the Committee's guidance in General Comment No. 14, this is a clear articulation of the duty flowing from Article 3(1) even though the Committee's conflation of 'rights and interests' might prove problematic in some (namely court) settings. The imprecision of what the best interests principle involves raises its ugly head here – for instance, does the Committee's guidance provide clarity for administrative bodies challenged to apply

---

[32] Alston, 'Best Interests Principle', 15.
[33] Committee on the Rights of the Child, *General Comment No. 5* (2003) on the General Measures of implementation of the Convention on the Rights of the Child, para. 22.
[34] Ibid., para. 12.

Article 3 in their decision-making? Recent research undertaken into the implementation of children's rights in social services decision-making suggests that this is still very difficult to conceptualise.[35]

In conclusion, then, an analysis of the text of Article 3(1) reveals that it contains neither a child's right nor a duty bearer equivalent to other provisions in the CRC. On a purely textual level, the stark comparison between the formulation of Article 3(1) and almost all other CRC provisions obscures the children's rights meaning to be found in the provision. At the same time, it is true that read in the context of the Convention's object and purpose, notably the concept of the child as rights-holder, Article 3(1) must be said to have the same aim as other provisions of the CRC, namely to advance the rights of the child.

Assuming we can get around the problem of language, the obvious next question is what precise right Article 3 protects. According to the Committee in General Comment No 14, Article 3(1) 'gives the child the right to have his or her best interests assessed and taken into account as a primary consideration in all actions or decisions that concern him or her'. And so, in truth, this is not a substantive right but a procedural right or as the Committee describes it, a rule of procedure. The next section addresses this concept.

D Article 3(1) as a Procedural Rule

According to the Committee on the Rights of the Child, Article 3(1) reflects the best interests requirement as a procedural rule, designed to ensure that decision-making in matters that affect the child is informed by what is in the child's best interests. Significantly, it is to this concept that the critics of the best interests standard have turned in attempting to remedy its shortcomings by putting shape on the process of determining what is in a child's best interests. In this regard, scholars like Eekelaar[36] and Bennett Woodhouse[37] have sought to infuse the best interests principle with the child's voice in order to ensure that it operates as a 'fair and just' principle to advance children's rights. The Committee favours this approach too, reading Article 12 together with Article 3 so that both provisions work in

---

[35] U. Kilkelly and N. Kennan, 'Child-friendly Public Services: A Consultation', unpublished research conducted in 2015 for the Irish Ombudsman for Children.
[36] Eekelaar, 'The Interests of The Child and the Child's Wishes', 42.
[37] Woodhouse, 'Child Custody in the Age of Children's Rights', 832.

tandem for children's rights.[38] More generally, however, the Committee has developed the concept as a procedural rule by identifying the elements that must be taken into account in the determination of the child's best interests. Among what is described as an 'inexhaustive' and 'non-hierarchical list', the Committee includes: the child's views, the child's identity, maintaining family relations, the child's protection and care, education and health.[39] According to the Committee, the value of drawing up such a list is to provide guidance to 'the state or decision-maker in regulating specific areas affecting children such as family, adoption and juvenile justice laws'.[40] Its view is that 'the ultimate purpose of the child's best interests should be to ensure the full and effective enjoyment of the rights recognized in the Convention'.[41]

Notwithstanding that such an approach reflects the holistic reading of the Convention's provisions, in line with the general approach to treaty interpretation, the fact remains that all the elements to be taken into account in determining what is in a child's best interests comprise the substantive rights protected in other CRC provisions. Would a rights-based approach to decision-making, where all Convention rights are weighed in the balance, not be preferable or does Article 3 bring added value here? According to the Committee, Article 3(1) is one of the four general principles of the Convention and as such, its status is as a principle for interpreting and implementing all the rights of the child. Is its value then that it constructs a test that requires legislative and other bodies to weigh the child's rights (listed elsewhere in the Convention) in the balance – a test that the Committee says will be unique depending on the circumstances of each individual child?[42] If this is its true value, then Article 3's great importance is as a rule of procedure, a mechanism for weighing the child's rights, for enabling the effective delivery of all rights to children. But, is this not the purpose of Article 4 – the duty to take all appropriate measures to implement the CRC? And what about those situations in which the child's best interests patently clash with the child's rights? There are many, but participation in non-therapeutic research that furthers the (general)

---

[38] See Committee on the Rights of the Child, *General Comment No. 14*, paras. 43–45 and Committee on the Rights of the Child, *General Comment No. 12 The Right of the Child to be Heard (2009))* CRC/C/GC/12, paras. 70–72.
[39] See Committee on the Rights of the Child, *General Comment No. 14*, para. 50.
[40] Ibid., para. 51.   [41] Ibid.   [42] Ibid., para. 24.

child's right to health but cannot be said to be in the interests of the individual child concerned poses one example.[43]

The Committee's General Comment on Article 3(1) clearly details the mechanism by which the best interests principle can be applied. It is worth noting, however, that the Committee was not the first international body to address this issue. The Guidelines on child-Friendly justice adopted by the Council of Europe in 2010 articulated a decision-making process for the application of the best interests principle that is based on children's rights and respect for human dignity.[44] According to the Guidelines, [i]n assessing the best interests of the involved or affected children:

a. their views and opinions should be given due weight;
b. all other rights of the child, such as the right to dignity, liberty and equal treatment should be respected at all times;
c. a comprehensive approach should be adopted by all relevant authorities so as to take due account of all interests at stake, including psychological and physical well-being and legal, social and economic interests of the child.[45]

This approach to the application of the best interests principle arguably sets out a clearer, rights-based framework for such decision-making. At the same time, both instruments illustrate the challenge of framing best interests decision-making in a manner that is compliant with children's rights. The fit is an uncomfortable one.

E Article 3(1) as an Interpretive Tool

The third element of Article 3(1) as described by the Committee on the Rights of the Child is the best interests of the child as an interpretive principle. Unfortunately, the Committee says very little about the concept in its General Comment, although it appears to be suggesting that Article 3(1) is a lens through which children's rights can be implemented and interpreted. Whether such a powerful interpretive status should be

---

[43] See generally S. Gove, 'On the Limits of Parental Proxy Consent: Children's Right to Non-participation in Non-Therapeutic Research' (2003) 1 *Journal of Academic Ethics* 349.
[44] Guidelines of the Committee of Ministers of the Council of Europe on child-friendly justice *(Adopted by the Committee of Ministers on 17 November 2010 at the 1098th meeting of the Ministers' Deputies).*
[45] See Guideline III. B. 2

handed to any provision is unclear; whether it should be granted to a provision whose rights basis is uncertain is even more problematic.

F   Article 3(1) as a Gateway to Children's Rights

While this chapter touches on just a few of the relevant issues, it illustrates that there are clearly legitimate questions to be asked as to whether the best interests principle 'belongs to' children's rights. Judged against the goal of furthering implementation of children's rights, strictly defined, the contribution is not entirely clear. Research into children's rights advocacy shows, however, that the lines between children's interests and rights remain blurred and in this context the best interests principle can act as a gateway to children's rights, including as a means of increasing the reach of children's rights into domestic law. The final section of this chapter offers some reflections on this issue, drawing on empirical research undertaken into the implementation of children's rights[46] and children's rights advocacy.[47]

Increasing the Reach of Children's Rights in Domestic Law

Although the broad and vague nature of the best interests principle makes it difficult to measure its implementation in practice, it is possible to measure the extent to which it is incorporated into national law and policy.[48] Studies are beginning to show the progress made in the implementation of children's rights into national law[49] and what emerges from the research is an understanding that children's rights are better protected, at least in law if not also in practice, in countries that have given legal status to the CRC in some form.[50] Whilst the best interest principle has been widely incorporated in legislation, for example, awareness of the CRC was perceived to be crucial in ensuring

---

[46] L. Lundy, U. Kilkelly, B. Byrne and J. Kang, *The UN Convention on the Rights of the Child: A Study of Legal implementation in 12 Countries* (London: UNICEF, 2013).

[47] This (as yet unpublished) research on children's rights advocacy was funded by the Atlantic Philanthropies in Ireland. For more information see www.advancingchildrensrights.com.

[48] U. Kilkelly and L. Lundy, 'Children's Rights in Action: Using the UN Convention on the Rights of the Child as an Auditing Tool' (2006) 18 *Child and Family Law Quarterly* 331, 336–337.

[49] Lundy, Kilkelly, Byrne and Kang, *The UN Convention on the Rights of the Child*.

[50] Ibid., pp. 107–108.

that it was applied in a way that was compliant with the Convention.[51] In this way, the best interests principle is leading the way towards greater implementation of the CRC.

To illustrate this, a study undertaken for UNICEF UK found that legislative implementation of the CRC in the twelve countries studied most commonly involved the best interests principle. Although it was most common for such states to have incorporated the Article 3(1) principle into laws on adoption, custody and access, progress is starting to be made with the incorporation of the principle into laws on youth justice, health law and immigration. With respect to youth justice, the study found that the principle can now be found in the laws of Spain, South Africa, Ireland and in some Australian territories.[52] Norway and Sweden are examples of countries where the best interests principle has been applied to legislation in the area of immigration.[53] In Norway, this was considered to be 'a particularly important achievement given that competing public interest considerations make it difficult to advocate for children's rights in the area of immigration'.[54] The research also found that the incorporation of the CRC had led to the acceptability of this approach. Here, it appears that the strong support enjoyed by the best interests principle facilitates its widespread application into national laws, not only in areas where it is familiar, but in other more challenging areas. This 'gateway' potential of the best interest principle – where it acts as the thin end of the human rights wedge for children – is considered further later in this chapter.

Although noted as positive that the best interests principle is gaining widespread support at national level, it is still moot whether this will lead to greater implementation of the CRC. The UNICEF study shows that although the best interests principle has become widely accepted as a core principle in legislation affecting children, nevertheless the acceptance of a child rights-based approach is neither explicit nor automatic in such cases.[55] Similarly, states that have incorporated the best interests principle into legislation were not necessarily consistent with a rights-based approach to legislation (at least) suggesting the absence of symmetry between the

---

[51] Ibid., p. 102.
[52] Ibid., pp. 31–21 (Australia); p. 52 (Ireland); p. 65 (Spain) and p. 90 (South Africa).
[53] Ibid., p. 59 (Norway) and p. 95 (Sweden).   [54] Ibid., p. 59.
[55] L. Lundy, U. Kilkelly and B. Byrne, 'Incorporation of the United Nations Convention on the Rights of the Child in Law: A Comparative Review' (2013) 3 *International Journal of Children's Rights* 442.

best interests principle and a children's rights standard in practice.[56] For instance, in the case of Germany, the UNICEF study found that 'concepts of "need", well-being and best interests continue to be granted greater priority on the political agenda than child rights'.[57] However, Ireland's experience is that this is a gradual scale – from welfare/ to best interests to rights – and here the CRC-basis of the best interests principle was found to strengthen the case for its incorporation, along with the Article 12 (right to be heard) requirement, into the Irish Constitution. From a legal position where the welfare of the child was subject to the rights of parents,[58] to one where the best interests of the child is recognised in the Constitution as the paramount consideration in decision-making in a wide range of family law matters, Ireland has come a long way.[59] The fact that the wording used in the new Article 42A inserted into the Irish Constitution was drawn directly from Article 3(1) highlights the potential influence of the CRC in this context. It is important too that this reform was accompanied by a similar provision concerning the Article 12 principle and a more general constitutional expression of children as rights holders.[60] Here it is precisely because Article 3(1) is a provision of the CRC that its acceptability was unquestioned.

The Best Interests Principle as a Gateway to Children's Rights

Change is brought about using multiple strategies and approaches, captured under the broad heading of children's rights advocacy. Here, the concept of the best interests of the child as a gateway to the rights of the child is key. Opposition to children's rights – to the language of rights and to the concept of children as rights holders – is not uncommon, indeed it is circulating quite openly now in many countries among the public, among professionals and among decision-makers

---

[56] On this point also see J. Williams, 'General Legislative Measures of Implementation: Individual Claims, "Public Officer's Law" and a Case Study on the UNCRC in Wales'(2012) *International Journal of Children's Rights*, 20: 224, 226.

[57] Lundy, Kilkelly, Byrne and Kang, *The UN Convention on the Rights of the Child*, p. 45.

[58] E. Carolan, 'The Constitutional Consequences of Reform: Best Interests after the Amendment' (2007) 10(3) *Irish Journal of Family Law* 9, pp. 10–12.

[59] U. Kilkelly (2015), 'Children's Rights in Ireland: Ireland's Relationship with the CRC' in S. Egan (ed.) *International Human Rights: Perspectives from Ireland* (Dublin: Bloomsbury publishing,) p. 209, at p. 218.

[60] Ibid., p. 218

in parliaments and the courts.[61] Where opposition to children's rights is not overt, apathy, ignorance or simply a preference for an alternative emphasis – on child-centredness or equity – can be found.[62] As the UNICEF study noted in relation to Australia for example:

> Those working with and for children choose language such as "child-centred" in preference to the language of rights, and there is still public anxiety surrounding human rights.[63]

This opposition to rights means that those charged with children's rights advocacy must find ways to persuade decision makers about the value and importance of a rights-based approach to children's issues, when the legally binding obligations created by the CRC are ignored. In this context, the merit of Article 3 is, perhaps, that it *does not* mention rights – here it presents itself as the rights decoy. Research into children's rights advocacy in Ireland indicates that the best interests principle is sometimes the common bond between professionals and disciplines – everyone may have their own nuanced understanding of what it means, but they are clear nonetheless that it reflects a common purpose – of focus on the child, of child-centred decision-making. In this context, those working with children's rights report welcoming Article 3 generally as a way of promoting a child focus in a particular area, although they differed as to how useful Article 3 was given its wide scope for interpretation[64] and they showed some skill, when chameleon-like, they had to alter their colours depending on who they were trying to convince.

A second element to the concept of the best interests principle as a 'gateway' to children's rights is that without rights language, the child's best interests appears as a conciliatory gesture with its softer language reaching out to those to whom rights are not acceptable whatever the basis of that position. Those (politicians, judges, professionals) with whom it is not possible to discuss children's rights may discuss children's interests, may be persuaded by a focus on what the child's needs, may find the language of Article 3 more acceptable than the uncompromising language of rights. That is not to say that interests should ever replace rights – there is no Convention on the Interests of Children

---

[61] An illustration of the issues is found here. S. Kilbourne, 'US Failure to Ratify the U.N. Convention on the Rights of the Child: Playing Politics with Children's Rights' (1996) *Transnational Law & Contemporary Problems* 6: 437.
[62] Lundy, Kilkelly, Byrne and Kang, *The UN Convention on the Rights of the Child*, p. 106.
[63] Ibid., p. 35.   [64] Ibid., p 101.

– or that the flexibility and vagueness of the best interests principle is to be preferred to the clarity, respect and dignity that rights convey. However, research on children's rights advocacy shows that the best interests principle enables conversations to begin – with discussion of interests leading to rights as understanding evolves and knowledge is gained and relationships are developed.

As one NGO told us: 'by maintaining a child-centred, child's best interest approach, it's extremely helpful'.[65] This can be particularly important when advocating in areas like immigration where the language of rights can be uncommon. The fact that children's rights are frequently ignored or contested in these areas means that the best interests principle can be a less controversial way to place an emphasis on children here. Returning to Article 3, the breadth of the provision – which applies widely to 'all actions concerning children' including decision-making where the child is indirectly as well as directly affected – is really key. Here we can see how real progress can be made in advancing the rights of children by introducing the best interests principle into laws on youth justice and immigration and asylum, where consideration to the substantive rights of children might simply be too big a political challenge.

G Conclusion

In conclusion, then, a textual analysis of Article 3(1) does not reveal strong rights credentials even though an holistic interpretation of the provision can help the provision to be read in line with its CRC object and purpose. By contrast, the development of a decision-making framework that conveys Article 3(1) as 'a rule of procedure' is an important implementation tool although its added value is not entirely clear. What is clear, however, is that the different formulation and wide acceptance of the best interest principle enables it to be used widely. When connected to the Convention's other provisions, it can act as a gateway to children's rights, where advocacy leads to greater acceptance and understanding of rights. Sometimes this has to start with Article 3, but then it moves onward and upward from there.

---

[65] This quotation is from the CEO of a large children's organisation. See U. Kilkelly, A. O'Connell, S. Field and N. Kennan, *Advancing Children's Rights: Capturing the Learning of Atlantic Philanthropies' Grantees in Ireland*, unpublished research report, 2014, p. 17.

3

Conflict between Human Rights and Best Interests of Children: Myth or Reality?

JANYS M. SCOTT

A   Introduction

The United Nations Convention on the Rights of the Child (UNCRC) provides a touchstone for children's best interests. If the treatment of children does not conform to the UN Convention then a state that is party[1] to this Convention is defaulting on its commitment to children. Article 3(1) provides:

> In all actions concerning children, whether undertaken by public or private social welfare institutions, courts of law, administrative authorities or legislative bodies, the best interests of the child shall be a primary consideration.

The best interests of the child are thus key to the UNCRC. Article 3 continues with an obligation on States Parties to ensure the child such protection and care as is necessary for his or her well-being, taking into account the rights and duties of his or her parents, legal guardians, or other individuals legally responsible for him or her, and to this end, to take all appropriate legislative and administrative measures.[2] A child is not to be separated from his or her parents against their will, except where competent authorities determine that separation is necessary for the best interests of the child, and even then States Parties must respect the rights of the child who is separated from one or both parents to maintain personal relations and direct contact with both parents on a regular basis, except if it is contrary to the child's best interests.[3] Special protection should be afforded to a child temporarily or permanently deprived of his or her family

---

[1] All UN member states, save the United States, are parties. See Introduction, note 20.
[2] Article 3(2).   [3] Article 9.

environment[4] and when it comes to adoption the best interests of the child should be the paramount consideration.[5]

The European Convention on Human Rights (ECHR) represents a wide consensus between nations[6] about basic rights and freedoms that are to be enjoyed by all citizens, and that includes children. Children are, however, limited in their capacity to participate in any political or legal process and that has led to a fear that their interests have been overlooked, because adult voices are louder and more strident. When the ECHR seeks to protect the individual against state interference, and that interference relates to the family and to protection of children in the family, the concern may be that the insistence of adults that all is well leads to the neglect of children. There have, undoubtedly, been cases where such anxieties have been expressed,[7] but it is demonstrable that the European Court of Human Rights and national courts have been keen to see the ECHR interpreted and implemented in a manner that is consistent with the UNCRC. The ECHR is a 'living instrument'[8] to be interpreted in the light of present day conditions. One such condition is wide international consensus in relation to the rights of children, as expressed in the UNCRC.

B Protecting Children

Convention rights under the ECHR are not merely negative. They impose positive obligations on states in relation to, for example, the prohibition of torture. This sounds melodramatic, but is highly relevant to the protection of children. Article 3 reads: 'No one shall be subjected to torture or to inhuman or degrading treatment or punishment.'

The article does not, perhaps, go as far as Article 3(2) of the UNCRC in treating protection and care as necessary for a child's well-being, but it is certainly not inconsistent with the demands of Article 3(2).

The United Kingdom fell foul of Article 3 of EHCR when Dumfries and Galloway Regional Council (as it then was) failed to protect a child and her siblings from physical and sexual abuse at the hands of their stepfather.[9] In 1976, at the age of sixteen the young person concerned

---

[4] Article 20.   [5] Article 21.   [6] The Convention is currently in force in 47 states.
[7] See, for example, the dissenting judgment of Judge Bonello in *EP v Italy* (2001) 31 EHRR 17, discussed below.
[8] *Tyrer v United Kingdom* (1979–80) 2 EHRR 1.
[9] *E v United Kingdom* (2003) 36 EHRR 31.

had run away from home and attempted suicide. She complained that her mother's cohabitee hit her and shouted at her. Two months later her younger sister ran away from home, alleging that the cohabitee had tried to rape her. He was arrested and charged with indecent assault of the two girls. He entered certain guilty pleas and went home. He was ultimately placed on two years' probation with a condition that he lived somewhere else, but was seen at the house two or three times, apparently 'just leaving'. The eight children remained at home. None of them were referred to the children's hearing until there were problems with school attendance. In 1988 the applicant and two of her siblings reported that there had been a continuing history of abuse. The European Court of Human Rights upheld a complaint under Article 3. The local authority failed to recognise the risks and had failed to monitor the man's conduct. The lack of investigation and communication had contributed to the damage suffered by the applicant.

This case was an example of the failure to protect children's rights under existing domestic law, but the ECHR and the Court have influenced the development of the law in relation to protection of children from degrading treatment or punishment. It was the Court in the *Campbell and Cousins* case[10] that upheld the objection of two parents to corporal punishment in school. The case was decided by reference to the parents' convictions, but the Court recognised that the mere threat of treatment prohibited by Article 3 of the ECHR would amount to a breach of that Convention. In *Costello-Roberts v United Kingdom*[11] there was recognition that the state's obligation to protect children from degrading treatment or punishment extended into private schools.

The duty of the state to protect children was recently re-affirmed in *O'Keeffe v Ireland*[12] where the Grand Chamber of the Court was concerned with the failure of Irish State in the 1970s to put in place an adequate framework for the protection of children attending schools run by the Catholic Church. The judgment states:

> In sum, having regard to the fundamental nature of the rights guaranteed by art. 3 and the particularly vulnerable nature of children, it is an inherent obligation of government to ensure their protection from ill-treatment, especially in a primary education context, through the adoption, as necessary, of special measures and safeguards.[13]

---

[10] *Campbell and Cousins v United Kingdom* (1982) 4 EHRR 293.
[11] (1995) 19 EHRR 112.   [12] (2014) 59 EHRR 15.   [13] Ibid., para. 146.

The Court held (by a majority) that it was an inherent positive obligation of government in the 1970s to protect children from ill-treatment, and that this obligation had not been fulfilled by the Irish State. The judgment refers to the development of recognition of children's rights by the United Nations, and in particular to Article 19 of the UNCRC, which requires the state to protect the child from maltreatment by parents or others responsible for the care of the child. Unease was expressed in a dissenting opinion by a minority of the court that the majority were in effect applying current standards of practice retrospectively. One concurring opinion[14] referred to the developing recognition of the rights of the child, affirmed rights of special protection for children, but acknowledged the need to avoid interpretation of the ECHR in a manner which brought within its scope new elements that were not there when the Convention was drafted.

Baroness Hale of Richmond (now Deputy President of the UK Supreme Court) displays a keen awareness of the UNCRC in her judgments.[15] In *R (Williamson) v Secretary of State*[16] the House of Lords was considering a claim by Christian parents and teachers whose religious belief led them to seek to establish schools where moderate corporal punishment was permitted. The court rejected the claim to manifest such a belief. Interference with the parents' rights was, in the language of Article 9(2) of the ECHR 'necessary in a democratic society' for the protection of the rights and freedoms of children. Baroness Hale made express reference to Article 3 of the UNCRC requiring the best interests of children to be a primary consideration in justification of the proposition that the state was entitled to give children protection by banning all corporal punishment in schools.

C Protecting Family Life

Children are as much entitled to respect for their family life as are adults. Article 8 of the ECHR applies equally to both. Article 8 provides that:

---

[14] That of Judge Ziemele.
[15] See for example judgments of Baroness Hale in *Re E (Children) (Abduction: Custody Appeal)* [2011] UKSC 27, [2012] 1 AC 144; *ZH (Tanzania) v Home Secretary* [2011] UKSC 4, [2011] 2 AC 166; *R (SG) v Secretary of State for Work and Pensions* [2015] UKSC 16, [2015] 1 WLR 1449; mentioned below.
[16] [2005] UKHL 15, [2005] 2 AC 246.

1. Everyone has the right to respect for his private and family life, his home and his correspondence.
2. There shall be no interference by a public authority with the exercise of this right except such as is in accordance with the law and is necessary in a democratic society in the interests of national security, public safety or the economic well-being of the country, for the prevention of disorder or crime, for the protection of health or morals, or for the protection of the rights and freedoms of others.

Public authorities seeking to protect children from harm may well find themselves interfering with family life. Such interference will fall within the exception in Article 8(2) if it is in accordance with the law, in furtherance of a legitimate aim and 'necessary in a democratic society'. This allows for action that serves a pressing social need and is based on reasons that are relevant and sufficient. The action must be proportionate to the aim. There is no conflict between this article and Article 9 of the UNCRC, which permits separation of a child and parents where this is in accordance with applicable law and procedures and is necessary for the best interests of the child.

Consistent with the need to protect children, the European Court of Human Rights has been markedly reluctant to castigate authorities that take emergency measures to protect children. In landmark cases such as *Johansen v Norway*[17] the Court has declined to criticise removal into care. Such measures are regularly held to be within the margin of appreciation afforded to member states. The Court has been disapproving of removal of babies at birth, which has been regarded as a particularly harsh step, and only justified as a proportionate measure in exceptional circumstances.[18] It has not, however, proscribed removals that are necessary to ensure protection of the child.

Even when the original judgment about the necessity for removal transpires to be mistaken, the court will not hold that there has been a violation of the Article 8 right to family life.[19] However the court is clear that what follows is a positive duty to take measures to facilitate family reunion as soon as reasonably feasible, which begins to weigh on the responsible authorities with progressively increasing force, 'subject

---

[17] (1997) 23 EHRR 33. The court were critical of the subsequent deprivation of access and or parental rights.
[18] See *K and T v Finland* (2001) 31 EHRR 18; *P, C and S v United Kingdom* (2002) 35 EHRR 31.
[19] *AD v United Kingdom* (2010) 51 EHRR 8.

always to its being balanced against the duty to consider the best interests of the child'.[20] Thus where a risk assessment is required, but delayed, or the wrong risk assessment is conducted, or there is a delay after a risk assessment concludes that a child should be returned, there is a violation of Article 8.[21] Where a child had marks on her legs thought to be consistent with sexual abuse it was not a violation of her right to respect for family life to detain her in hospital, but it was a violation not to investigate promptly. A dermatologist who was eventually consulted was able to advise that the marks were the result of a rare skin disease.[22] It is quite clear that the ECHR is a challenge to poor practice. Family life is treated as valuable in the interests of children, and rightly so.

The approach under the ECHR is thus child focussed. The European Court of Human Rights is supportive of professionals seeking to protect children from harm, provided they act proportionately, but is critical of those who then fail children by not conducting prompt and appropriate investigations, to establish whether the initial concerns are justified. On the other hand, there is a cogent argument based on Article 3 of the UNCRC for a much more positive model for child protection that prioritises early support and assistance for carers, as opposed to the safety net of late intervention when harm is imminent or has actually occurred.[23]

D Protecting Future Relationships

It is unsurprising that the law applies a severe test before a child's relationship with his or her family may be permanently severed. Neither in England, nor Scotland, has it been possible to take a child from his or her birth family simply on the basis that he or she would be better off being brought up in another family.[24] Social engineering has never been permitted. The ECHR reinforces the point. It is no surprise to find the European Court of Human Rights saying:

> The Court reiterates that in cases concerning the placing of a child for adoption, which entails the permanent severance of family ties, the best

---

[20] *K and T v Finland* (2003) 36 EHRR 18.   [21] *AD v United Kingdom* (2010) 51 EHRR 8.
[22] *MAK v United Kingdom* (2010) 51 EHRR 14.
[23] See, Alison Cleland, 'A Long Lesson in Humility? The Inability of Child Care Law to Promote the Well-Being of Children', Chapter 7 in this volume.
[24] See, for example, *A and B v C* 1977 SC 27, at 31; *Re SB (Children) (Care Proceedings: Standard of Proof)* [2009] UKSC 17, [2010] 1 AC 678, at paras. 6 and 7.

interests of the child are paramount. In identifying the child's best interests in a particular case, two considerations must be borne in mind: first, it is in the child's best interests that his ties with his family be maintained except in cases where the family has proved particularly unfit; and second, it is in the child's best interests to ensure his development in a safe and secure environment. It is clear from the foregoing that family ties may only be severed in very exceptional circumstances and that everything must be done to preserve personal relations and, where appropriate, to "rebuild" the family. It is not enough to show that a child could be placed in a more beneficial environment for his upbringing. However, where the maintenance of family ties would harm the child's health and development, a parent is not entitled under Article 8 to insist that such ties be maintained.[25]

The structure of the law in Britain is consistent with these principles. The Adoption and Children (Scotland) Act 2007 was subjected to scrutiny by the Supreme Court in *S v L*[26] when a parent complained that the possibility that consent to adoption could be dispensed with on the ground that 'the welfare of the child ... requires the consent to be dispensed with' was not compliant with the ECHR Article 8 respect for family life. The Court held that the word 'requires' imposed a high test, namely that dispensation with consent was necessary, not merely desirable or reasonable. Decisions taken under this provision should be compatible with Article 8, as explained by the European Court of Human Rights. There is a similar decision from the Supreme Court in an English case, *In re B (A Child) (Care Proceedings: Threshold Criteria)* where a child was placed in local authority care with a view to adoption.[27] Her parents had a loving relationship with the child, but were fundamentally dishonest, manipulative and antagonistic to care professionals on whose expertise they would have to rely if the child was to live with them. The care order was compatible with Article 8. Both these decisions refer to the rights of the child in terms of the UNCRC. In the latter case, *In re B*, Lord Neuberger stresses that although the child's interest in an adoption case are 'paramount' in UK legislation and in Article 21 of the UNCRC, a court must never lose sight of the fact that those interests include being brought up by the natural family, ideally natural parents, or at least one of them.[28]

---

[25] *YC v United Kingdom* (2012) 55 EHRR 33, at para. 134.
[26] [2012] UKSC 30, 2013 SC (UKSC) 20.   [27] [2013] UKSC 33, [2013] 1 W.L.R. 1911.
[28] [2013] UKSC 33, [2013] 1 W.L.R. 1911, at para. 104.

Given the serious nature of adoption it is only right that the highest standard of professional consideration is applied by all those concerned. The Court of Appeal in England made this quite clear in the case of *Re B-S (Children)*.[29] The President of the Family Division, giving the judgment of the court put the matter like this:

> We have real concerns, shared by other judges, about the recurrent inadequacy of the analysis and reasoning put forward in support of the case for adoption, both in the materials put before the court by local authorities and guardians and also in too many judgments. This is nothing new. But it is time to call a halt.[30]

The essentials outlined by the President, Sir James Munby, are first of all proper evidence that addresses all the options that are realistically possible, with an analysis of the arguments for and against each option. Adoption orders should be granted only when the evidence drives the court to the conclusion that nothing short of adoption is appropriate. There needs to be 'analysis of the pros and cons' and a 'fully reasoned recommendation' if the requirements of Article 8 of the ECHR, and indeed the Article 6 requirement of a fair hearing, are to be met. The second essential is an adequately reasoned judgment. A judge considering an order that involves adoption must carry out a proportionality analysis. Adoption is to be viewed as a last resort and should be justified as such. There has to be a 'global, holistic evaluation', where all the options are evaluated, weighing their positives and negatives. This must be more than 'formulaic window dressing'.

The frustration of the Court of Appeal in the *B-S* case was quite clear. The judges were demanding high standards, commensurate with the severity of what is at stake for the child. The effect may not have been quite what the court intended. On 10 November 2014, the Telegraph newspaper reported that the number of children put forward for adoption in England had almost halved. Why? Was this because social workers and others involved in placing children had their confidence undermined? Or was it that on deeper consideration and proper analysis they realised they had been placing children for adoption when the best interests of those children lay with their birth families? We simply do not know.

Scotland has not, at least yet, had a '*Re B-S* revelation'. It is not clear whether this is because Scotland is managing the Article 8 issues,

---

[29] [2013] EWCA Civ 1146, [2014] 1 WLR 563.   [30] Para. 30.

or ignoring them. In *Midlothian Council v M*[31] a mother had set about reforming her life, in order to resume care of her baby girl. A social worker presented a seriously misleading report to a children's hearing from which the mother was absent. The hearing then supported the local authority plan for adoption and reduced the mother's contact to once every two months. The local authority compounded the error by starting permanence proceedings in the wrong court, preventing any review of the decision on contact for a period of six months. The mother complained that what had occurred violated the Article 8 rights of her and the child. The Inner House did not comment. They sustained the permanence order with authority to adopt on welfare grounds. The role afforded to Article 8 in Scottish cases can be difficult to discern. Lady Smith, giving the opinion of the Extra Division in *S, Petitioners*[32] held that Convention considerations had no part to play in deciding whether grounds for adoption were established. The Inner House comment on *B-S* was that it was concerned with deficiencies in first instance decision-making in another jurisdiction. In *Application by Fife Council*[33] an Extra Division concluded that the sheriff had met the requirements of *B-S* and Article 8, albeit neither had received a mention in the sheriff's judgment. It is difficult to find a refusal of a permanence application in Scotland.

In neither jurisdiction does the law, or the practice, prioritise the interests of adults over the interests of children. England demands high professional standards in the interests of children. Scotland may, in some cases, be excusing a less rigorous approach on the basis of the child's welfare. The motivation in both places is entirely consistent with the requirements of Article 21 of the UNCRC, which requires the best interests of the child to be the paramount consideration in relation to adoption. Article 8 of the ECHR should drive the best possible practice, yet provide a safety net for children if professionals fall short, but striking the balance in this area is one of the most difficult challenges of the European Convention. Matters are rendered more complex by the tension in the UNCRC between the child's right to an identity under Article 8, the right not to be separated from parents under Article 9 and the welfare provisions of Articles 3 and 21.[34]

---

[31] [2013] CSIH 71, 2014 SC 168.
[32] [2014] CSIH 42, 2014 Fam LR 23, at paras. [29] and [30].   [33] [2015] CSIH 74.
[34] See Brian Sloan, 'Primacy, Paramountcy and Adoption in England and Scotland', Chapter 11 in this volume.

The problem can be illustrated by the case of *EP v Italy*[35] where a child and her mother arrived in Italy from Greece. The mother was diagnosed as suffering from a psychological disorder that manifest itself in a 'vicarious hypochondriac obsession' centred on the little girl. The mother was denied contact with the child over a period of seven years, at the end of which the child was declared free for adoption. The majority in European Court of Human Rights had little difficulty in holding that this was a violation of both the Article 6 right to a fair trial within a reasonable time and the Article 8 right to respect for family life. There is a powerful dissenting judgment from Judge Bonello who said:

> The core question, in my view, should have been: did this unfortunate child have a right to a normal family and a happy home once her mother became unable to provide her with those basic minima? Saying, as the majority did, that the child's adoption was wrong is tantamount to saying that this particularly wretched child did not, for reasons undisclosed, deserve a normal family life. The Court does not dispute that adoption is the next best thing to a family life with a natural parent. The conclusion that the majority underwrote was, in substance, that since the applicant's daughter could not have the best (the mother had manifestly failed to provide that), she was not entitled to the next best either. It seems that the mother's ability to wreck all the child's chances in life had to be total. In the Court's view, the fact that she was unable to give her child happiness conferred on her the right to ensure that no one else should.[36]

There is no doubt that neither mother, nor child, were well served in this case, but the child was ultimately adopted. The mother did not 'wreck all the child's chances'. The solution was not to withhold an adoption order. The court awarded the mother a sum in respect of her non-pecuniary damages. While the value of family life cannot be measured in monetary terms, recognising the harm arising from a violation by damages may encourage good practice. It also indicates that recognising a parent's ECHR rights need not mean damaging a child's interests.

E Protecting Welfare

The European Court of Human Rights has been quite explicit about what should happen where there is conflict between the rights of a parent and the rights of a child. This is most clearly expressed in *Yousef v Netherlands*[37] where a father was prevented from asserting a legal

---

[35] (2001) 31 EHRR 17.   [36] Para. O-I 13.   [37] (2003) 36 EHRR 20

relationship with his daughter because he had not married the mother. When the mother died one of her brothers became the child's guardian and the child went to live with another brother. The father saw the child once every three weeks. He wanted recognition of his paternity so he could have his daughter live with him, but the domestic courts had found that her best interests would be served by being brought up as a member of her uncle's family, in which she had lived since her mother's death. The judgment states:

> The Court reiterates that in judicial decisions where the rights under Art.8 of parents and those of a child are at stake, the child's rights must be the paramount consideration. If any balancing of interests is necessary, the interests of the child must prevail.

Case after case has asserted the paramountcy of the welfare of the child. *R and H v UK*[38] confirms that 'in all decisions concerning children their best interests must be paramount'. *Pontes v Portugal*[39] says that the interest of the child 'doît passer avant tout autre considération'.[40] One could go on citing similar passages and statements.

The European Court of Human Rights has gone so far as to prevent enforcement of a judgment secured by a parent under the Hague Convention on the Civil Aspects of International Child Abduction in *Neulinger v Switzerland*.[41] This was a case that took years to determine. The father finally succeeded in securing an order for his son's return from Switzerland to Israel, only to find that the European Court of Human Rights held that this would be a violation of the boy's Article 8 rights as it would uproot him from the place he had lived since the age of two and likely to cause him significant mental disturbance. He was by then aged about seven. The case raised significant consternation as it was thought that the European Court had gone too far and undermined the Hague Convention.[42] In fact, the decision turns on the fact that Hague cases should result in a rapid return to the country of habitual residence, which is viewed as being in the interests of the child. This case had gone wrong due to inordinate delay, but it is significant that it was the ECHR that allowed the welfare of the child to prevail.

---

[38] (2012) 54 EHRR 2.
[39] (App no 19554/09), unreported, cited in *S v L* [2012] UKSC 30, 2013 SC (UKSC) 20.
[40] See *S v L* [2012] UKSC 30, 2013 SC (UKSC) 20, paras. 37 and 74.
[41] (2012) 54 EHRR 31.
[42] See *In re E (Children) (Abduction: Custody Appeal)* [2011] UKSC 27, [2012] 1 AC 144.

On the UK domestic front, in *ZH (Tanzania) v Home Secretary*[43] the Supreme Court allowed an appeal by a mother seeking asylum, on the ground that a decision to deport her taken without regard to the need to safeguard and promote the welfare of her child would not be 'in accordance with the law' for the purposes of the ECHR Article 8(2). The most relevant national and international obligation, to which the Home Secretary should have regard under Article 8 of the ECHR when taking such a decision, was identified as being that in Article 3(1) of the UNCRC.[44]

It does however remain a fact that in some areas the ECHR does not go as far as the UNCRC in serving the best interests of children. This emerged in the recent decision of the UK Supreme Court in *R (SG) v Secretary of State for Work and Pensions*.[45] The cap placed on a claimant's benefit entitlement is, according to three justices of the Supreme Court, inconsistent with affording the best interests of the child primary consideration in terms of Article 3 of the UNCRC, but it is not, according to the majority, a violation of the ECHR. However, this is a long way from saying that the ECHR is adverse to the interests of children.

F Protecting Participation in Decision-Making

The right to respect for family life under Article 8 of the ECHR includes procedural safeguards. While the right to a fair hearing is set out in the ECHR Article 6, the European Court of Human Rights has taken the right to be involved in the decision-making process as an aspect of Article 8. This can be traced back at least as far as the challenge in *W v United Kingdom*[46] where there was a complaint about the lack of remedies for parents whose children had been taken into local authority care. Since then this has been a theme running through the Court's decisions.[47]

The Court held that parents must be 'involved in the decision-making process, seen as a whole, to a degree sufficient to provide them with the requisite protection of their interests'. The procedural implications of Article 8 are quite different from the substantive issues relating to

---

[43] [2011] UKSC 4, [2011] 2 AC 166.
[44] [2011] UKSC 4, [2011] 2 AC 166, *per* Baroness Hale of Richmond at para. 23.
[45] [2015] UKSC 16, [2015] 1 WLR 1449.   [46] (1988) 10 EHRR 29.
[47] See, for example, *McMichael v United Kingdom*(1995) 20 EHRR 205 and *Jucius and Juciuvienè v Lithuania* (2009) 49 EHRR 3,

interference in family life. They are about ensuring that the decision-maker has the best and most accurate information in order to make the best decisions. This will often mean hearing from the person whose conduct is said to be causing problems for the child, but as Baroness Hale of Richmond said in *Principal Reporter v K*:[48]

> If decisions are then made on an inaccurate factual basis the child is doubly let down. Not only is the everyday course of her life altered but she may be led to believe bad things about an important person in her life. No child should be brought up to believe that she has been abused if in fact she has not, any more than any child should be persuaded by the adult world that she has not been abused when in fact she has.

A possible requirement for intervention cannot be pre-judged. It is not generally in the interests of a child to exclude a parent from the process of taking decisions. Where parents have been excluded then there have been misunderstandings leading to unwarranted removals of children as occurred in *TP v United Kingdom*[49] where the local authority had a video of an interview with a child, but failed to take steps to allow the mother to see the video. This meant they only discovered after the child had been in care for a year that the person she was referring to in the video was not the mother's boyfriend, leading to the child being, belatedly, returned home. The case illustrates that the procedural rights under the Convention are as much for the benefit of children as adults.

The UNCRC has been effective in promoting international consensus on the need to allow children themselves to express views, in compliance with Article 12, but less successful in encouraging legal representation of children. The General Assembly of the United Nations considered access to justice for children themselves during its 25th Session on 16 December 2013. The Report of the United Nations High Commissioner for Human Rights noted that access to justice referred to the ability to obtain a just and timely remedy for violations of rights, including rights under the UNCRC.[50] The right to an effective remedy has been identified by the UN Committee on the Rights of the Child as an implicit requirement of the Convention.[51] So far as Scotland is concerned, in 2014 the Scottish Alliance for Children's Rights reported that there was a lack of legal assistance for children in domestic proceedings.[52]

---

[48] [2010] UKSC 56, 2011 SC (UKSC) 91. [49] (2002) 34 EHRR 2.
[50] A/HRC/25/35, para. 4 [51] CRC/GC/2003/5, para. 24.
[52] *State of Children's Rights in Scotland* (Edinburgh: Together, Scottish Alliance for Children's Rights, 2014).

So far, it has fallen to the ECHR to spearhead representation for children. The right to a fair trial under Article 6 of the ECHR persuaded the Inner House of the Court of Session that a child should have free legal representation at a children's hearing where this was required in the interests of justice so he or she could present an effective case.[53] Progressed has stalled since then. In 2011 the rules for assessing eligibility for legal aid changed. The Scottish Legal Aid Board is required to take into account the financial circumstances of anyone with a duty to support the child, unless this was 'unjust and inequitable'. The Children and Young People (Scotland) Act 2014 requires the Scottish Ministers to keep under consideration whether there are any steps they could take which might secure better or further effect in Scotland of the UNCRC requirements, and if they consider it appropriate to do so, take any of the steps identified by that consideration.[54] Addressing effective rights of legal representation is one area for their consideration.

G Conclusions

A dispassionate examination of cases under the ECHR should label the proposition that there is a conflict between the rights of children given expression by the UNCRC and human rights under the ECHR, in general, a myth. Arguments based on the ECHR have regularly drawn on the UNCRC as reflecting international consensus on the rights that should be afforded to children. The two Conventions are not coterminous, but they overlap. Careful balancing of competing interests may be required but both the ECHR and the UNCRC require consideration of the best interests of children as at least a primary consideration. The perceived conflict may be the result of difficulty in determining where children's best interests lie.

The ECHR does, however, pose a challenge to inadequate professional practice. It is based on the proposition that children and families deserve better. The same message can be derived from the UNCRC. This means there are difficult decisions to make when practice is poor. When this occurs it is not the fault of either Convention. The imperative is good practice. We should be rising to the standard expected by both Conventions.

---

[53] *S v Miller* 2001 SC 977.   [54] Children and Young People (Scotland) Act 2014, s. 1(1).

4

Final Appeal Courts and Article 3 of the United Nations Convention on the Rights of the Child: What Do the Best Interests of the Particular Child Have to Do with It?

MARK HENAGHAN[*]

A Introduction

A final appellate court sets the tone for a country's entire legal system, especially because their decisions are binding on the courts below them. In order to reach a final appeal court, the issues in question, which have already been fiercely contested, frequently include a fundamental conceptual difference pertaining to the interpretation of key legal principles. Cases about the welfare and best interests of children are no exception.

There has been a significant amount of debate about the correct determination of a child's best interests in decisions about (or affecting) children and whether the child's interests should be a paramount consideration or a primary one.[1] This chapter argues that such debates focus on overly linguistic interpretations of international treaties/conventions, domestic legislation, and case law and do not actually advance the position of individual children in family law cases.

Instead, this chapter focuses on the importance of judges in final appellate courts better incorporating the welfare and best interests of

---

[*] Thank you to Ruth Ballantyne (Professional Practice Fellow, Faculty of Law, University of Otago, Dunedin, New Zealand) for her invaluable research and editorial assistance with this chapter.
[1] See Jon Elster 'Solomonic Judgments: Against the Best Interest of the Child' (1987) 54 *University of Chicago Law Review* 1, John Eekelaar 'Beyond the Welfare Principle' (2002) 14 *Child and Family Law Quarterly* 237, Jonathan Crowe and Lisa Toohey 'From Good Intentions to Ethical Outcomes: The Paramountcy of Children's Interests in the Family Law Act' (2009) 33 *Melbourne University Law Review* 391, John Eekelaar 'The Role of Best Interests Principle in Decisions Affecting Children and Decisions About Children' (2015) 23 *International Journal of Children's Rights* 3.

each individual child in his or her particular familial and social circumstances into their judicial decisions. Decision-making that is truly in the best interests of children is less about whether a child's interests should be paramount, or primary, or something in-between, and actually about considering the particular child and his or her way of seeing the world.

To this end, this chapter provides a detailed examination of a variety of different types of decisions about and affecting children that have previously reached final appellate courts in the United Kingdom, the United States, Canada, Australia, and New Zealand involving issues of relocation, parental rights, fundamental principles of justice, deportation, extradition, and the Hague Convention on the Civil Aspects of International Child Abduction (the 'Hague Convention').[2] This examination illustrates that the particular children who are the subject of the proceedings, or who are significantly affected by the decisions are, barring three notable exceptions,[3] largely absent from the analysis carried out by judges in final appellate courts around the world. Generalisations about what is best for children have replaced the best interests of the specific child and what is important to *that* child. This is in direct contravention of Article 3(1) of the 1989 United Nations Convention on the Rights of the Child (the 'UN Convention'),[4] which states:

> In all actions concerning children, whether undertaken by public or private social welfare institutions, courts of law, administrative authorities or legislative bodies, the best interests of the child shall be a primary consideration.[5]

Article 3(1) of the UN Convention is concerned about the best interests of *the* individual child, rather than with the best interests of children generally. To properly meet their obligations under the UN Convention, final appellate court judges need to personalise each of their determinations to the life of the individual child whom the decision is about.

---

[2] Hague Convention on the Civil Aspects of International Child Abduction, 25 October 1980, in force 1 December 1983, HCCH 28.

[3] See *ZH (Tanzania) v. Secretary of State for the Home Department* [2011] UKSC 4, [2011] 2 AC 166 per Lady Hale (on behalf of the majority); *Baker v. Canada (Minister of Citizenship and Immigration)* [1999] 2 SCR 817 per L'Heureux-Dubé J. (on behalf of the majority); and *Secretary for Justice v. HJ* [2006] NZSC 97, [2007] 2 NZLR 289 per Elias C.J..

[4] United Nations Convention on the Rights of the Child, 20 November 1989, in force 2 September 1990, 1577 UNTS 3.

[5] Article 3(1) of the United Nations Convention on the Rights of the Child, 20 November 1989, in force 2 September 1990, 1577 UNTS 3.

B Relocation Cases and the Particular Child in Final Appellate Courts

Relocation cases, where one parent wants to take the parties' child to live elsewhere against the wishes of the other parent, feature prominently in decisions from final appellate courts. Such cases are particularly difficult because there is little room for compromise. Final appellate courts traditionally provide a variety of adult-focused responses to what is deemed to be in the best interest of children in relocation cases. None of the relocation cases that fell to be determined by the relevant final appellate court considered the rich tapestry of the particular child's life, despite the fact that the relocation dispute was directly about the child. Rather, the courts dealt in generalisations.

Whilst this is somewhat understandable, given that the role of final appellate courts is to provide guidance to lower courts as to how to decide similar cases, by providing general answers to questions about the best interests of a particular child, final appeal courts suggest that the particular child's circumstances and point of view are not central to their decisions. In some instances what is best for a particular child in their particular circumstances may well align with generalisations as to what is best for children in such circumstances. However, this will not always be the case and such an approach runs the risk of failing to consider the fundamental uniqueness of each child. Ignoring an individual child's feelings, aspirations, and concerns about the proposed relocation, or only giving such matters superficial consideration, makes a mockery out of the claim that the decision is based on the best interests of the child. Judges should not pretend to be contemplating the best interests of the particular child, when what they are really doing is making a decision based on what is presupposed to be the fairest result between the parents who are in dispute over where the child lives.[6]

Canada

Like other final appellate courts, the Canadian Supreme Court has experienced difficulty in determining the best interests of children in relocation cases and applying a sufficiently individualised, child-focused

---

[6] For more information about fairness between the interests of parents see John Eekelaar 'Beyond the Welfare Principle' (2002) 14 *Child and Family Law Quarterly* 237, 238.

approach. Instead, in *Gordon v. Goertz*,[7] an international relocation case concerning a young female child whose mother wanted to relocate with her from Canada to Australia, the Court suggested the adoption of a preference in favour of the primary carer in relocation cases. This is premised on the generalisation that it is best for children to remain with their primary caregivers and that such caregivers know the most about their children's interests. As McLachlin C.J. said (on behalf of the majority):

> The judge will normally place great weight on the views of the custodial parent, who may be expected to have the most intimate and perceptive knowledge of what is in the child's interest.[8]

Express preferences about what is usually best for children in relocation cases do not harm a best interests approach *per se*, so long as the individual child's needs and circumstances in terms of the relocation are still closely examined to ensure that the general preference aligns with that particular child's interests. However, such preferences run the risk of effectively ignoring the particular child involved in the case or inappropriately prioritising adult interests. McLachlin C.J. was acutely aware of this issue and for that very reason disavowed the introduction of a more directive presumption in favour of a primary caregiver parent being able to determine where a child will live, saying that such a presumption in favour of a 'custodial parent may be criticized on the ground that it tends to shift the focus from the best interests of the child to the interests of the parents'.[9] Such presumptions may provide more certainty and predictability, but at a significant cost to the interests of individual children in relocation cases. In denouncing the introduction of a legal presumption in relocation cases, McLachlin C.J. rightly states:

> [T]he ultimate and only issue when it comes to custody and access is the welfare of the child whose future is at stake. The multitude of factors that may impinge on the child's best interest make a measure of indeterminacy inevitable. A more precise test would risk sacrificing the child's best interests to expediency and certainty.[10]

However, despite the detailed discussion in the case of the different possible approaches and the importance of focusing on the best interests

---

[7] *Gordon v. Goertz* [1996] 2 SCR 27. [8] Ibid., para. 36. [9] Ibid., para. 46.
[10] Ibid., para. 20. The minority (led by L'Heureux-Dubé J.) argued for the introduction of a presumption in favour of primary caregivers in relocation cases. See *Gordon v. Goertz* [1996] 2 SCR 27, paras. 132–142.

of the particular child, very little information is provided in the decision about the particular child. We know that she was seven years old at the time of the Supreme Court hearing,[11] and that she had been spending more time with her father than her mother since her parents separated.[12] However, we know little of the details of the child's daily life, what she is interested in, or how she feels about the proposed relocation.

The majority ultimately decided that the mother could relocate to Australia with the child and that the father could have contact with the child in both Australia and Canada. However, it is impossible to determine whether this outcome was in the best interests of this particular child given we know so little about that particular child's interests.

Australia

The High Court of Australia has at times also focused on the importance of the interests of the primary caregiver in relation to those of the child. In *AMS v. AIF*,[13] a case about a nine-year-old boy whose mother wanted to relocate with him from Perth to Darwin, Kirby J. said that the best interests of the child 'cannot be viewed in the abstract separate from the circumstances of the parent with which the child resides'.[14] Kirby J. expanded upon these sentiments further in *U v. U*,[15] a international relocation decision about a young female child whose mother wanted to relocate home to India from Australia with the child, where he said that 'significant effects on the mother's emotional, residential, economic, employment and personal life have an inevitable impact on the happiness and best interests of the child'.[16] Kirby J. later emphasised the importance of the primary parent's ability to enjoy freedom of movement, and stated that 'Courts, exercising such discretions, should not ignore the disproportionate burden typically cast upon women by their being effectively immobilised as the custodial/residence parent'.[17]

Interestingly, both cases failed to discuss in detail the particular interests of the two individual children involved in the relocation decisions. There was no mention about what the children's lives might be like if

---

[11] Ibid., para. 59. [12] Ibid., para. 3. [13] *AMS v. AIF* [1999] HCA 26.
[14] Ibid., para. 144. The High Court ultimately determined that the mother did not have to provide a compelling reason for her desire to relocate from Perth to Darwin and the case was sent back to the Family Court for final determination.
[15] *U v. U* [2002] HCA 36. [16] Ibid., para. 143.
[17] Ibid., para. 146. This case was also remitted back to the Family Court for final determination as a result of the trial judge failing to separately evaluate each parent's proposal.

they were to relocate to Darwin and India, respectively. Their personal interests and views were totally absent from the decisions.

New Zealand

The New Zealand Supreme Court also failed to properly take into account the particular interests of two children (aged six and eight) in *Kacem v. Bashir*.[18] The case was primarily about the importance for a child in having both parents involved in their upbringing and whether this principle should be given priority when deciding what is best for children in an international relocation decision. The court unanimously agreed that the involvement of both parents was not more important than other principles pertaining to the welfare and best interests of children. They disagreed over whether, in determining that the mother was not permitted to relocate from New Zealand to Australia, the Court of Appeal had given undue priority to the principle of both parents' involvement to the extent that this principle had been turned into a presumption. The majority held that the Court of Appeal had created an inappropriate presumption, whereas the minority found that the Court of Appeal had merely prioritised the importance of the involvement of both parents on the facts of the particular case.

In terms of the best interests of the children in the case, Tipping J. was careful to point that the unique interests and circumstances of the children concerned have to be taken into account in relocation cases. As Tipping J. said, '[e]verything will depend on an individualised assessment of how the competing contentions should be resolved in the particular circumstances affecting the particular children'.[19] However, despite this statement, there was very little discussion about the children's daily life and how things looked from the children's point of view. There was some evidence that the children wanted to move to Australia with their mother, but this was not given any substantial weight by the Court. The Supreme Court ultimately decided that it was best for the children to remain living in New Zealand because the children were settled in New Zealand and the mother was deemed to be capable of overcoming her personal difficulties of living in New Zealand in isolation from her family who were in Australia. It is hard to ascertain if this decision was

---

[18] *Kacem v. Bashir* [2010] NZSC 112.   [19] Ibid., para. 24.

made in the best interests of the children because so little information is provided about the children's interests.

C Parental Rights Cases and the Particular Child in Final Appellate Courts

Cases about parental rights feature prominently in decision of final appellate courts around the world. Such cases frequently involve disputes over whether a child should live with their biological parents or with other possible parental figures (including grandparents or foster parents). Despite the fact that the best interests of children are supposed to be the paramount consideration in determining cases about whom a child lives with, these cases can be particularly adult-focused as a result of biological parents feeling as though they have a greater right to raise their children than other people, even in difficult circumstances.

United Kingdom

The most cited common law case on the paramountcy principle is the House of Lords decision in *J v. C*.[20] This case revolved around who a ten-year-old boy should live with, his biological parents in Spain (who had given up the child when he was a baby due to financial circumstances), or his foster parents in the United Kingdom who had looked after the child for most of his life. The child's biological parents had attempted to have the child returned to them when he was four years old, but the matter had been stalled for two years due to unacceptable bureaucratic reasons. By the time the case reached the House of Lords, the ten-year-old child had spent the vast majority of his life in the United Kingdom with his foster parents. This made it virtually impossible for the child to be returned to his biological parents.

The decision contains a significant amount of discussion about whether biological parents have absolute rights to raise their children in such circumstances and what it means for the best interests of children to be a paramount consideration. Lord MacDermott states that for the child's interests to be first and paramount 'that must mean more than that the child's welfare is to be treated as the top item in a list of items

---

[20] *J v. C* [1969] 1 All ER 788.

relevant to the matter in question'.[21] To Lord MacDermott, the paramountcy principle connotes:

> [A] process whereby, when all the relevant facts, relationships, claims and wishes of parents, risks, choices and other circumstances are taken into account and weighed, the course to be followed will be that which is most in the interests of the child's welfare [...] That is the first consideration because it is of first importance and the paramount consideration because it rules on or determines the course to be followed.[22]

It is notable that this oft-quoted statement of principle actually focuses on parents' wishes and does not mention the child's point of view. This is also reflected in the decision itself where the child's individual views are not discussed in any real detail, and the majority of the judges do not discuss the child's interests, feelings, and aspirations at all. Lord Donovan makes the best attempt at analysing the child's life when he states:

> The boy was born here nearly 11 years ago and has been with the foster parents ever since, with the exception of some 18 months in 1960 to 1961. He speaks little or no Spanish. He regards the foster parents as his mother and father. He is happily integrated into their family and is on terms of close comradeship with their young son. He is about to commence his further education. If he is now sent to Madrid against his will it is inevitable that he will begin making comparisons between what he has come to, and what he has left behind; and a rankling sense of injustice and depression may result which will not only hinder his resettlement, but could easily prejudice his whole future.[23]

Ultimately, despite the lofty statements in the decision about the paramountcy of a child's best interests, the child at the centre of the dispute appears to have been primarily used as a means to the stating of judicial principles, rather than an end unto himself.

United States

The United States Supreme Court case of *Troxel v. Granville*,[24] was a dispute between two young girls' biological mother and grandparents. The paternal grandparents wanted to continue to spend time with their grandchildren regularly after the father committed suicide, as they had

---

[21] Ibid., at 820. [22] Ibid., at 821. [23] Ibid., at 835.
[24] *Troxel v. Granville* 530 US 57 (2000).

before the father's death. The mother had unilaterally limited the grandparents' contact to one short visit per month.

The Supreme Court was concerned that allowing the grandparents to have contact with the children against the wishes of the mother may interfere with parents' fundamental rights to raise their children. The majority decided that biological parents act in their children's best interests and denied the grandparents contact with their grandchildren. This is a traditionally adult-focused argument. The court also shied away from creating any kind of preference, presumption, or precedent as they made their finding entirely fact-specific,[25] and encouraged 'state courts to evaluate visitation statutes on a case-by-case basis'.[26] Stevens J. (in the minority) examined the issue more from the children's points of view and held that there was room to consider the impact on a child of parents arbitrarily making decisions 'that neither serve nor are motivated by the best interests of the child'.[27] There was no analysis in the decision at all as to how important the visits with the grandparents were for the particular children, or any other information about the children's daily lives. The children's ages are not even mentioned.

United Kingdom

In *Re KD (A Minor)*,[28] a young mother (who was fifteen years old at the time of the child's birth) argued for a fundamental right of access to her four-year-old child who was being placed for adoption. The House of Lords held that the best interests of the child overrode any fundamental right of access by a parent and that it was not in this child's interests to spend time with the mother. However, it was clear that the House of Lords disapproved of the mother's lifestyle and that this had influenced their decision. Lord Oliver noted that there had been 'a number of occasions upon which [the mother] allowed her interest in going out and meeting boyfriends to take priority over the interests of her child'.[29] Lord Oliver also said:

---

[25] Amanda Allison Catlin 'The Verdict Is in – or Is It?: The Constitutionality of the Texas Grandparent Visitation Statute in Doubt After Troxel v. Granville' (2002) 33 *Texas Tech University Law Review* 405, 405.

[26] Sara Elizabeth Culley 'Troxel v. Granville and Its Effect on the Future of Grandparent Visitation Statutes' (2001) 27 *Journal of Legislation* 237, 238.

[27] *Troxel v. Granville* 530 US 57 (2000), at 2074.

[28] *In Re KD (A Minor)* [1988] 1 AC 806.   [29] Ibid., at 814.

> It may be that there may come a time in the future when the mother may marry and settle down with a stable establishment into which [the child] could be received as a member of an integrated family, but it is not in the future but in the present that the decision about his future has finally to be made.[30]

The decision was clearly not about the well-being of the young child and indeed the child's interests are not discussed in a child-focused way. The decision seems to have been made almost entirely on the basis of adult issues, such as the court's disapproval of the mother's lifestyle.

D Fundamental Principles of Justice in Final Appellate Courts

In *Canadian Foundation for Children, Youth and the Law v. Canada (Attorney General)*,[31] a case about whether parents have a right to physically discipline their children, the majority of the Supreme Court of Canada held that the best interests of the child 'is not a principle of fundamental justice'.[32] On behalf of the majority, McLaughlin C.J. held:

> Society does not always deem it essential that the 'best interests of the child' trump all other concerns in the administration of justice. The 'best interests of the child', while an important legal principle and a factor for consideration in many contexts, is not vital or fundamental to our societal notion of justice, and hence is not a principle of fundamental justice.[33]

This may well be true in some circumstances because the interests of some members of society will not always trump all other interests, but it is concerning that that reasoning was used in relation to a case about the physical discipline of children by their parents. It is hard to believe that the use of legally sanctioned physical force against children for the purposes of parental discipline does not affect a fundamental principle of justice, especially because the protection of a person's bodily dignity is one of the oldest principles in common law history.[34] The minority rightly held that the legalisation of force against children reverted back

---

[30] Ibid., at 829.
[31] *Canadian Foundation for Children, Youth and the Law v. Canada (Attorney General)* [2004] SCC 4, [2004] 1 SCR 76.
[32] Ibid., para. 7.   [33] Ibid., para. 10.
[34] See *Tuberville v. Savage* 1669 1 Mod Rep 3, 86 ER 684; *Cole v. Turner* (1704) 6 Mod Rep 149, 90 ER 958; and *Fagan v. Metropolitan Police Commissioner* [1969] 1 QB 439.

to the inappropriate 'traditional legal treatment of children as the property or chattel of their parents or guardians'.[35]

Allowing the physical discipline of children by their parents is not child-focused in any way. To tell a small child that the use of physical force towards them by their parents, who are much bigger and stronger than the child, is in their 'best interests' is a hollow and unacceptable argument.

E   Deportation, Extradition, Hague Convention Cases, and the Particular Child in Final Appellate Courts

Deportation, extradition, and Hague Convention cases are classified as decisions that 'affect' children, rather than decisions 'about' children. In such cases, the best interests of the child are a primary rather than paramount consideration.[36] The best interests of the child can be outweighed by other adult-focused considerations. Deportation cases, which involve sending people away from a country for a variety of (usually) immigration reasons, have a significant impact on the children of those deported individuals. Children are similarly affected by extradition cases, where individuals who have committed certain criminal offences, are removed from one country to face criminal charges in another. Hague Convention cases that focus on returning children (except in limited circumstances) who have been removed from their habitual residence by one parent without the consent of the other parent can also have a significant impact on children. In all of these types of cases the best interests of the child is not paramount, but rather, is deemed to be a primary consideration.

In most of the decisions about deportation, extradition, and the Hague Convention final appellate courts have not incorporated the interests of the particular children who will be affected by their decisions into their decisions in any meaningful way, or sometimes not at all. Many of these cases prioritise adult considerations over the best interests of the children concerned. However, there are three notable exceptions to this where courts in different parts of the world have properly considered the best

---

[35] *Canadian Foundation for Children, Youth and the Law v. Canada (Attorney General)* [2004] SCC 4, [2004] 1 SCR 76, para. 225.

[36] In *ZH (Tanzania) v. Secretary of State for the Home Department* [2011] UKSC 4, [2011] 2 AC 166, para. 25 Lady Hale said that where decisions are made that indirectly affect a child the child's interests are a primary consideration rather than a paramount one.

interests of the particular children involved. It is instructive to contrast the adult-focused approach with that according priority to the best interests of the child. The following two sections provide a more detailed examination of these two different positions.

Adult-Focused Considerations Prioritised Over the Best Interests of the Particular Child

Where other adult-focused interests are at stake, the best interests of children quickly take a back seat. For example, in the Supreme Court of the United Kingdom in *BH v. Lord Advocate*,[37] the parents of six children (aged between one and fourteen years old) who were British citizens were extradited from the United Kingdom to the United States to face charges pertaining to the importation of chemicals used to manufacture methamphetamine, despite the fact that it would have been possible for their trial to have been held in Scotland. Political and purely adult-focused issues such as the United Kingdom's treaty obligations with the United States were central to this decision.[38] Lord Hope found that the extradition of the parents was a 'tragedy, especially for the children',[39] and acknowledged the following:

> It is obvious that the children's interests will be interfered with to at least some degree by the extradition of either parent. If both parents are to be extradited the effect on the family life of the children will be huge. The weight to be given to their best interests lies at the heart of the issue whether the extradition of both parents, or either of them, would be proportionate.[40]

However, Lord Hope did not otherwise consider the interest of the children or provide detailed information about the particular impact it would have on these particular children.

In *Zoumbas v. Secretary of State for the Home Department*,[41] the best interests of two children (aged two and seven years old) were given little consideration by the Supreme Court of the United Kingdom when the Court decided to deport their parents who were from the Republic of Congo, despite the fact that both children had been born in the United Kingdom and the parents had lived there for the previous twelve years.

---

[37] *BH v. Lord Advocate* [2012] UKSC 24.   [38] Ibid., paras. 55 and 58.
[39] Ibid., para. 72.   [40] Ibid., para. 1.
[41] *Zoumbas v. Secretary of State for the Home Department* [2013] UKSC 74.

The Court acknowledged, 'it was in the best interests of the children that they and their parents stayed in the United Kingdom so that they could obtain such benefits as health care and education which [...] might be of a higher standard than would be available in the Congo'.[42] However, because the children 'were not British citizens' the Court said they had no right to enjoy these privileges.[43]

A True Prioritisation of the Best Interests of the Particular Child

Three cases (two majority judgments by a final appellate court, and one separate judgment by an individual judge in a final appellate court) from different parts of the world stand out for the detailed ways in which they considered the best interests of particular children in decisions affecting those children.

In *ZH (Tanzania) v. Secretary of State for the Home Department*,[44] the decision was about the deportation of a woman from Tanzania who was a mother to two female children (aged eleven and thirteen years old). The mother had been living illegally in the United Kingdom for fourteen years. However, her children were both British citizens because their father was from the United Kingdom.

In deciding not to deport the mother, the Supreme Court of the United Kingdom, led by Lady Hale, rightly explains that in deportation cases it is easier for political interests to outweigh the interests of the child when a parent's presence in the country poses a specific risk to others (such as if they have been involved in criminal activity).[45] However, where the parent's presence poses 'a more general threat to the economic well-being of the country' it is more likely that a child's invested interest in their parent not being deported will prevail.[46]

In this case, Lady Hale (on behalf of the majority) considered what was in the children's best interests from the two children's particular points of view. Part of this involved 'discovering the child's own views'.[47] To that end, there was a letter from the children's school and a youth worker setting out the children's views.[48] It was also noted that

---

[42] Ibid., para. 24.
[43] Ibid., para. 24. In is important to note that the children in *ZH (Tanzania) v. Secretary of State for the Home Department* [2011] UKSC 4, [2011] 2 AC 166 (as discussed below) were British citizens.
[44] *ZH (Tanzania) v. Secretary of State for the Home Department* [2011] UKSC 4, [2011] 2 AC 166.
[45] Ibid., para. 28.   [46] Id.   [47] Ibid., para. 34.   [48] Ibid., para. 37.

immigration authorities should hear directly from children affected by deportation decisions who wish to express a view.[49]

The fact that the children were British citizens, and had educational and social links with the United Kingdom was also given particular emphasis.[50] As Lady Hale observed it is 'very different' for children 'who have lived here all their lives and are being expected to move to a country which they do not know and will be separated from a parent whom they also know well'.[51] Lady Hale also rightly acknowledged that it 'should not be taken for granted' that children's interests are the same as their parents,[52] and noted that the children should not be blamed for the mother's behaviour.[53]

Likewise, in *Baker v. Canada (Minister of Citizenship and Immigration)*,[54] the Canadian immigration authorities sought to deport a woman from Jamaica who was a mother of four Canadian children (aged between seven and fourteen years old),[55] claiming that the mother would be a 'tremendous drain on [the] social welfare systems for (probably) the rest of her life'.[56] The mother had lived in Canada illegally for eighteen years and had been diagnosed with paranoid schizophrenia. All of the children were Canadian citizens. Two of the children lived with the mother after spending some time in foster care and two lived with their father.

The Supreme Court of Canada ultimately held that the mother should not be deported. L'Heureux-Dubé J. (on behalf of the majority) held that 'emphasis on the rights, interests, and needs of children and special attention to childhood are important values that should be considered' in such cases, and that the children's interests had not been sufficiently taken into account in the immigration authority's decision to deport the mother.[57] In a clear example of the best interests of children in action, L'Heureux-Dubé J. said:

> I conclude that because the reasons for this decision do not indicate that it was made in a manner which was alive, attentive, or sensitive to the interests of Ms. Baker's children, and did not consider them as an important factor in making the decision, it was an unreasonable exercise of the power conferred by the legislation, and must, therefore, be overturned.[58]

---

[49] Id.   [50] Ibid., para. 31.   [51] Id.   [52] Ibid., para. 37.   [53] Ibid., para. 33.
[54] *Baker v. Canada (Minister of Citizenship and Immigration)* [1999] 2 SCR 817.
[55] The mother also had four children back in Jamaica. See *Baker v. Canada (Minister of Citizenship and Immigration)* [1999] 2 SCR 817, para. 5.
[56] Ibid., para. 5.   [57] Ibid., para. 73.   [58] Id.

Likewise, Elias C.J. also illustrated her understanding of the best interests of the children in action in the New Zealand Supreme Court case of *Secretary for Justice v. HJ*.[59] This was a Hague Convention case where the two children (aged seven and six years old), who had been born and living in Australia had been brought to New Zealand by their mother four years earlier without their father's consent. The children were deemed to be 'well settled' in New Zealand, which is one of the possible exceptions (to which judicial discretion applies) to the principle of immediately returning the child to their habitual residence.[60]

The majority of the Supreme Court held that in exercising their discretion in this regard the Court had to balance the best interests of the child with the clear policy of return under the Hague Convention. They also indicated that if a parent concealed a child from the other parent in the country absconded to, enforcing the Hague Convention's return policy would prevail over the child's best interests, even if the child was well settled into the new country. Elias C.J. did not agree with the majority's analysis and held that the exceptions to return are designed to protect the best interests of children. The only consideration once a ground to refuse return had been made out is the 'primary and paramount consideration' of the 'welfare and best interests of the children affected'.[61] Elias C.J. applied this approach to the individual children and particular facts of the case in a child-focused way and emphasised how well settled the children were in New Zealand after a disrupted life in Australia. Elias C.J. found that the 'disruption inevitable in the return of children who are now settled would be greatly exacerbated for these children'.[62]

F   Conclusion

Final appellate courts have traditionally used the 'best interests of the child' principle to justify adult preferences, based on adult values. It is difficult, if not impossible, to gain any real understanding of the particular children's world from such decisions. Children are not heard nor seen in such decisions that are about them or 'affect' them, even though the decisions are supposed to be made in their best interests. Three cases provide a welcome exception to this trend, in the context of decisions

---

[59] *Secretary for Justice v. HJ* [2006] NZSC 97, [2007] 2 NZLR 289.
[60] Ibid., para. 1. See also s. 106(1)(a) of the Care of Children Act 2004.   [61] Ibid., para. 24.
[62] Ibid., para. 30.

affecting children where the children's best interests are supposed to be a primary consideration, rather than a paramount one. In the relevant parts of these three decisions the individual circumstances and perspectives of these particular children are taken into account and given overriding weight.[63] This is a clear step in the right direction.

Courts at all levels need to engage altogether more closely with the particular child involved in relevant cases and consider the issues involved in the case from the individual child's point of view. As Atticus Finch said in *To Kill a Mockingbird* 'You never really understand a person until you consider things from his point of view [...] until you climb into his skin and walk around in it.'[64] Whilst it is not physically possible to walk around in another person's skin, in determining the best interests of a child in a particular case, judges should put aside their own personal views of what is best for children generally, or what is best for the adults involved, and look at the facts before the court from the child's point of view alongside the child's individual circumstances. This is the only way for the courts to truly give effect to Article 3(1) of the UN Convention.

---

[63] See *ZH (Tanzania) v. Secretary of State for the Home Department* [2011] UKSC 4, [2011] 2 AC 166, per Lady Hale (on behalf of the majority); *Baker v. Canada (Minister of Citizenship and Immigration)* [1999] 2 SCR 817, per L'Heureux-Dubé J. (on behalf of the majority); and *Secretary for Justice v. HJ* [2006] NZSC 97, [2007] 2 NZLR 289, per Elias C.J..

[64] Harper Lee, *To Kill a Mockingbird* (London: Arrow Books, 2010), p. 33.

PART II

Confronting the Challenges of Article 3

5

Two Dimensions of the Best Interests Principle: Decisions About Children and Decisions Affecting Children

JOHN EEKELAAR

A Introduction

Article 3(1)[1] of the UN Convention on Children's Rights may be embodied in domestic law in a number of ways. It could be by enacting the provision directly, or by following it in a variety of legislative or administrative instruments. Whatever way it is done, decision-makers will need to consider the interests of children alongside any other considerations that may legitimately be taken into account in the matter. Given the well-known problems about the 'indeterminacy' of the best interests principle, it is not surprising that the way children's interests are factored into such decisions has caused much discussion, in particular with regard to the 'weighting', or prioritization, to be given to those interests vis-à-vis other relevant interests.

The purpose of this chapter is to seek to introduce some stability into the decision-making process in this context by suggesting a way in which the reasoning should be structured. It does not therefore speculate about what children's interests are, or about the degrees of weight to be given to them in specific situations, although the structure of the reasoning will affect the latter.

The suggestion is that, when the best interests principle falls to be considered, a distinction should be drawn between decisions that are directly about children and decisions that affect children indirectly. In the latter case, the *focus* of the decision-maker should be on reaching the 'best' solution *to the issue to be decided* rather than on what outcome would be

---

[1] United Nations Convention on the Rights of the Child, 20 November 1989, in force 2 September 1990, 1577 UNTS 3, Article 3(1), which provides that 'In all actions concerning children, whether undertaken by public or private social welfare institutions, courts of law, administrative authorities or legislative bodies, the best interests of the child shall be a primary consideration.'

best for the child. The child's interests are relevant, and are *a* 'primary' consideration, though there may be others. If it is thought that the 'best' solution to the issue in question is seriously detrimental to the child's interests, it may need to be modified or even abandoned. But that is not inevitable because the nature of that outcome may be so important that it must be achieved notwithstanding its detrimental effect on the child's interests. In the former case, the focus should be on seeking the *best outcome for the child*. This requires a holistic examination of a wide range of possible outcomes, and, subject to weighing other relevant interests, choosing what is best for *this* child in *these* circumstances. So, in contrast to decisions indirectly affecting children, where the interests of the child appear among 'other considerations', in this case the interests other than those of the child are among the 'other' considerations. Hence, while the best outcome for the child could be modified in the light of those other interests if they are sufficiently grave, it would be hard to contemplate any decision that would inflict harm on the child's interests. As will be seen later, there can be circumstances where it is not so easy to draw this distinction, but these are relatively rare and do not, it is suggested, undermine the value of making it.

The distinction was made by Baroness Hale in *ZH (Tanzania) (FC) v Secretary of State for the Home Department*,[2] a deportation case, where she contrasted 'decisions which directly affect the child's upbringing, such as the parent or other person with whom she is to live' with 'decisions which may affect her more indirectly, such as decisions about where one or both of her parents are to live'.[3] She remarked that in the former case ('direct' measures) the best interests were to be the 'determining' consideration, but in the latter ('indirect' measures), (only) 'a primary' consideration. But she does not elaborate on this, merely saying that the best interests must be considered 'first', but could be outweighed.[4]

The Committee on the Rights of the Child made a similar distinction in its General Comment No. 14 (2013):

> Thus, the term "concerning" refers first of all, to measures and decisions directly concerning a child, children as a group or children in general, and secondly, to other measures that have an effect on an individual child, children as a group or children in general, even if they are not the direct targets of the measure.[5]

---

[2] [2011] UKSC 4.   [3] Ibid., para. 25.   [4] Paras. 26, 33.
[5] Committee on the Rights of the Child, *General Comment No. 14: The Right of the Child to Have his or her Best Interests Taken as a Primary Consideration*, UN Doc CRC/C/GC/14 (2013), para. 19.

But the Committee does not explore the implications of this distinction, and paragraph 39 of the Comment obscures it by saying that all cases would have to be considered 'individually' and on a 'case-for-case' basis.

The matter is complicated by the structure of Article 8 of the European Convention on Human Rights. While this makes no mention of the best interests principle, the European Court of Human Rights has for many years taken the line that 'where the rights under Article 8 of parents and those of a child are at stake, the child's rights must be the paramount consideration. If any balancing of interests is necessary, the interests of the child must prevail'.[6] But the reasoning under the Convention follows the same structure whether the decision is directly about children or affects them only indirectly, namely, that the child's right to respect for family and private life (which includes assessment of his best interests) can be infringed only if justified in accordance with the Article 8 criteria.

This could be seen as requiring an investigation in both types of cases into what constitutes the child's best interests, and then deciding whether they are outweighed by other interests. It will be argued that that does not follow for cases indirectly affecting children. In those cases the Convention can be followed by determining the best solution *to the main issue for decision*, weighing it against the child's interests, and then subjecting the result to the Article 8 test (that is, whether its impact on the child's right to respect for family and private life is justified under the test).

B Decisions Directly about the Child

The proper structure of the reasoning appropriate in such cases was explained by the English Court of Appeal in *re G*,[7] which concerned the granting of a care order and an appeal from it.

> The judicial exercise should not be a linear process whereby each option, other than the most draconian, is looked at in isolation and then rejected because of internal deficits that may be identified, with the result that, at the end of the line, the only option left standing is the most draconian and that is therefore chosen without any particular consideration of whether there are internal deficits within that option.

---

[6] *Yousef v The Netherlands* [2002] ECHR 716, para. 73; see also *YC v United Kingdom* Application No 4547/10) [2012] FLR 332; *Johansen v Norway* (1997) 23 EHRR 33, para. 78.

[7] *Re G* [2013] EWCA Civ 965, paras. 49 and 50, per MacFarlane LJ.

The linear approach, in my view, is not apt where the judicial task is to undertake a global, holistic evaluation of each of the options available for the child's future upbringing before deciding which of those options best meets the duty to afford paramount consideration to the child's welfare.

So the decision-maker must keep an open mind about the eventual outcome until all options are considered: it may, for example, be possible to combine elements of different options in a unique solution.[8] Examples can be found in both 'private law' cases (for example, between parents, or parental figures),[9] and 'public' law cases involving state intervention. So in *re B-S (Children)*,[10] the Court of Appeal recommended the need for an 'analysis of pros and cons' perhaps set out in a form of 'balance sheet' when deciding whether to make an adoption order for a child in care. The caution that even if this process is followed, an adoption order should be made only 'exceptionally' and 'as a last resort' expresses only a combination of an understanding that maintaining family relationships, which would be severed by adoption, could be beneficial to the child and appreciation of the important 'other' interests at stake, particular of the parents. In *Flintshire County Council v Mrs LD and Mr GJ*,[11] where the issue was whether children with 'special needs' should remain in long-term fostering or be placed for adoption, the Circuit Judge referred to the need to make a 'holistic' evaluation of the children's welfare, and listed ten factors relevant to the decision.[12] In *Bradford County Council v M and others*,[13] where the children had been found to have suffered non-accidental injury, the Circuit judge went through all the options available in detail, observing that he had 'weighed each option and considered the internal positives and negatives; I have compared them side by side'.

---

[8] In *re B (A Child)* [2013] UKSC 33, Lady Hale gave an example of 'a case where the mother was slowly starving her baby to death because she could not cope with the colostomy tube through which the baby had to be fed, but solutions were found which enabled the child to stay at home'. (para. 197).

[9] See *In the matter of K (children) HN and DW and GK and Wiltshire County Council* [2014] EWCA Civ 1195 [31], a contact dispute where the same court said that 'nothing less' than a comparative analysis of the benefits and detriments of each option would do.

[10] [2013] EWCA Civ 1146, para. 36.   [11] [2014] EWCC B17 (Fam)   [12] Para. 64.

[13] [2014] EWCC B4 (Fam) para. 183. See also *In the Matter of E* [2014] EWCC B1 (Fam) for a routine example of a judge considering all the alternatives.

C Decisions Indirectly Affecting Children

International Cases

In child cases involving conflicts between jurisdictions, the UK courts can decide whether to make an order enforcing a decision of a foreign court or resulting in a child leaving the United Kingdom for another jurisdiction under Council Regulation (EC) No 2201/2003 (Brussels IIR)[14] or The Hague Convention on Child Protection 1996, and under the Hague Convention on the Civil Aspects of Child Abduction of 1980.[15]

Under Brussels IIR, primary jurisdiction is in principle seen to lie with the state in which the child has habitual residence at the time of the proceedings, and the subsequent provisions work out the implications of this position. As Rob George explains, under Brussels IIR, 'the idea is simply that orders about residence or contact, say, which are made in State A (which is the child's original country of habitual residence), should be automatically recognized and enforced by a court in State B (to which the child lawfully relocates or visits after the order is made), so long as both states are either signatories to the Convention or members of the European Union'.[16] However, recognition is not required 'if such recognition is manifestly contrary to the public policy of the Member State in which recognition is sought taking into account the best interests of the child'.[17] Further, by way of exception and under certain conditions, the court having jurisdiction may transfer a case to a court of another Member State if this court is better placed to hear the case.[18] In cases of wrongful removal or retention of a child, the Regulations require that the child be returned without delay in accordance with the Hague Child Abduction Convention of 1980, except in specific, duly justified cases.

In these cases the decision is not directly about the child, but about which decision about the child is to be followed. Of course it affects the child indirectly. A court is not bound to undertake a detailed investigation into the child's interests before making its decision, but need not make an order if this would be 'manifestly contrary to the public

---

[14] Council Regulation (EC) No 2201/2003 (Brussels IIR), 27 November 2003, in force 1 August 2004, JO L 338 of 23.12.2003.
[15] Convention on the Civil Aspects of Child Abduction (Hague XXVIII), 25 October 1980, in force 1 December 1983, HCCH, No. 25.
[16] R. George, 'Children in Cross-Border Situations' in J. Eekelaar and R. George (eds.), *Routledge Handbook of Family Law and Policy* (London: Routledge, 2014), p. 406.
[17] Article 23(1).   [18] Article 50.

policy ... taking into account the best interests of the child'. So, in *Re S (Brussels II: Recognition: Best Interests of Child) (No 1)*[19] Holman J. recognized a Belgian judgment under the Regulation, saying:

> I have frankly said that in my view it is not an order which was in his best interests, but I am quite unable to conclude that it is so contrary to his best interests that it would be actually contrary, let alone manifestly contrary, to some English principle of public policy to enforce it.[20]

In *re N*,[21] Holman J. decided that he was bound to follow a Spanish order, and was prepared to return the child to Spain without a 'full welfare inquiry' because:

> there is no evidence that it would be damaging to (the child) to the point of being manifestly contrary to public policy.[22]

The best interests principle clearly operates in a very different way than it does in the decisions about children considered earlier. The principle operates in a similar way under the Hague Child Abduction Convention of 1980. This Convention requires the return of a child who has been wrongfully removed in breach of rights of custody held by a person in the jurisdiction in which the child had been habitually resident 'forthwith' to that jurisdiction where the application for return is made within twelve months of the wrongful removal unless there is a 'grave risk that his or her return would expose the child to physical or psychological harm or otherwise place the child in an intolerable position'.[23] Hence the European Court of Human Rights has held that the right to family life of a father who had made a timely application for the return of his child was infringed when the Slovakian Constitutional Court barred the child's return on the ground that the return would not be in the child's best interests.[24]

If more than a year has passed since the removal, the child must still be returned unless 'now settled in his new environment'. Hence once the child is 'settled', the courts can decide the matter according to their assessment of the child's best interests. So if an application for return is made *within* the twelve-month period, the primary focus is on whether the removal is wrongful in terms of the Convention. The best interests of

---

[19] [2003] EWHC 2115 (Fam), [2004] 1 FLR 571; approved in *re L (A Child)* [2012] EWCA Civ 1157.
[20] Para. 32.   [21] [2014] EWHC 749 (Fam).   [22] Para. 53.
[23] Hague Convention 1980, Articles 12 and 13.
[24] *López Guió v Slovakia* [2014] ECHR 558.

the particular child are to be taken into account, but only in the narrow manner specified by the Convention. If the application is made *after* that period, and the child has settled in the new environment, the decision becomes one directly about the child, and Convention policy is one among any other relevant considerations. It would need to carry much weight to overcome the best interests of the child, but could do so.[25]

Custodial Sentencing

In *HH v Deputy Prosecutor of the Italian Republic*,[26] Lord Judge explained that in making sentencing decisions:

> ... the starting point ... involves an evaluation of the seriousness of the crime or crimes and the criminality of the offender who committed them or participated in their commission and a balanced assessment of the countless variety of aggravating and mitigating features which almost invariably arise in each case. In this context the interests of the children of the offender have for many years commanded principled attention, not for the sake of the offender, but for their own sakes, and the broader interests of society in their welfare, within the context of the overall objectives served by the domestic criminal justice system. Sadly the application of this principle cannot eradicate distressing cases where the interests even of very young children cannot prevail.[27]

The recognition that the 'starting point' involves the application of penal policy illustrates that this is the primary focus of the decision. However, other matters, like the interests of affected children, are also 'on the agenda', but will often be outweighed even if seriously affected. So even in South Africa, where the Constitution directs that 'a child's best interests are of paramount importance in every matter concerning the child'[28] the Constitutional Court has stated that:

> The children will weigh as an independent factor to be placed on the sentencing scale only if there could be more than one appropriate sentence ..., one of which is a non-custodial sentence. For the rest, the approach merely requires a sentencing court to consider the situation of children when a custodial sentence is imposed and not to ignore them.[29]

---

[25] See the comments by the Inner House of the Court of Session in *In the Petition of JP and FM* [2014] ScotCS CSIH 19, para. 33
[26] [2012] UKSC 25   [27] [2012] UKSC 25, para. 131.
[28] South African Constitution, Section 2 (Bill of Rights) Article 2, s. 28(2).
[29] *S v M* (2008) 3 SA 232 (Constitutional Court).

Deportation and Extradition Cases

Similar problems have arisen in deportation and extradition cases.[30] Section 55 of the Borders, Citizenship and Immigration Act 2009 provides that, in relation among other things to immigration, asylum or nationality, the Secretary of State must make arrangements for ensuring that those functions 'are discharged having regard to the need to safeguard and promote the welfare of children who are in the United Kingdom'. Applying this in the deportation case, *ZH (Tanzania) (FC) v Secretary of State for the Home Department*,[31] Lord Kerr said:

> Where the best interests of the child clearly favour a certain course, that course should be followed unless countervailing reasons of considerable force displace them. It is not necessary to express this in terms of a presumption but the primacy of this consideration needs to be made clear in emphatic terms. What is determined to be in a child's best interests should customarily dictate the outcome of cases such as the present, therefore, and it will require considerations of substantial moment to permit a different result.[32]

This treats a deportation decision as if it were a decision directly about a child.[33] There were conflicting views about this in the combined extradition cases reported as *HH v Deputy Prosecutor of the Italian Republic*.[34] Lord Judge drew an analogy between extradition and domestic sentencing practice (discussed earlier), thereby indicating that in extradition the issue should be approached as a decision indirectly affecting a child,[35] whereas Lord Kerr took the opposite view.[36] Lord Wilson thought the matter of more theoretical than practical significance, but concluded that the structure of Article 8 favoured Lord Kerr's position.[37]

---

[30] For a detailed account of UK cases see Ayesha Christie, 'The Best Interests of the Child in UK Immigration Law', *Nottingham Law Journal* 22 (2013) 16–40.

[31] [2011] UKSC 4.

[32] Para. 46. This approach has been adopted subsequently, so, for example, in *EV (Philipinnes) and Ors v SSHD* [2014] EWCA Civ 874 where, it having been found that the children's education was best served by them remaining in the UK, the Court of Appeal decided that this was outweighed in this case by the need to maintain immigration control. See also *Deron Peart v SSHD* [2012] EWCA Civ 568; *Miguel Nesta Cover v SSHD* [2014] UKUT 376 (IAC), para. 25.

[33] Jane Fortin, 'Are the Best Interests of the Child Really Best?' *Modern Law Review* 74 (2011) 947–61 expresses concern about using the best interests principle in this way on the grounds of its indeterminacy.

[34] [2012] UKSC 25.   [35] See especially paras. 130–2.   [36] Para. 144.   [37] Para. 153.

Subsequent cases have, however, tended towards Lord Judge's position. For example, in a deportation case Laws LJ sought to rephrase the best interests principle as proclaiming the best interests of the child to be 'of substantial importance' rather than 'a primary consideration',[38] which would not be possible if the decision was directly about a child. It has also been said that in such cases there is no need for a court to be proactive in seeking to assess the child's best interests,[39] and that, provided those interests were considered as a separate matter, there was no need to reach any decision about what was in the child's best interests.[40]

In *Hines v London Borough of Lambeth*[41] the issue was whether a mother had a right to receive housing assistance. If she did not, she would be forced to return to Jamaica, which might have the effect of depriving the child of the right of residence in the EU to which he had a right.[42] The housing authorities decided that she was ineligible for housing assistance because she was subject to immigration control. The reviewer did not consider it unreasonable for the father to look after the child in the event of the mother leaving the UK. Her appeal failed. The court decided that the child living with his father (thus fulfilling his citizenship rights) would not 'so seriously [to] impair his quality and standard of life that he would be effectively forced to leave the UK' if the mother left.[43] The court did not seek first to decide what was best for the child, and then weigh that against the policies behind the appealed decision. Rather, the child's interests were considered solely to ascertain whether they would be so seriously compromised that the decision, which was in other respects thought appropriate, should be modified or abandoned. It was held that they were not.

---

[38] *SS (Nigeria) v Secretary of State for the Home Department* [2013] EWCA Civ 550 Para. 44.
[39] *Hamidreza Azimi-Moayed and 3 others v SSHD* [2013] UKUT 197 (IAC) para. 12. 'Where that evidence gives no hint of a suggestion that the welfare of the child is threatened by the immigration decision in question, or that the best interests of the child are undermined by such action, there is simply no basis for any further judicial exploration or reasoned decision on the question.'
[40] *In the Petition of NB* [2014] CSOH 66.
[41] [2014] EWCA Civ 660. See also *EV (Philippines) v Secretary of State for the Home Department* [2014] EWCA Civ 874, para. 58 (Lewinson LJ).
[42] Case C-34/09 *Gerardo Ruiz Zambrano v Office National de L'Emploi* [2011] Grand Chamber Judgment of 8 March 2011 (*Zambrano*).
[43] Para. 24.

D The European Convention on Human Rights

The European Court of Human Rights has stated that 'where the rights under Article 8 of parents and those of a child are at stake, the child's rights must be the paramount consideration'[44] and *Neulinger and Shuruk v Switzerland*,[45] a case concerning the Hague Child Abduction Convention 1980, extended the principle saying that the issue was whether 'a fair balance between the competing interests at stake – those of the child, of the two parents, *and of public order* – has been struck, within the margin of appreciation afforded to States in such matters . . . bearing in mind, however, that the child's best interests must be the primary consideration'[46] and that 'their best interests must be paramount'.[47] Since interference in those interests infringes a child's right to family life, the structure of the Convention implies that, in either type of decision affecting a child, the child's best interests should be ascertained and followed unless compromising them is permissible if 'in accordance with the law and [is] necessary in a democratic society in the interests of national security, public safety or the economic well-being of the country, for the prevention of disorder or crime, for the protection of health or morals, or for the protection of the rights and freedoms of others'.

Accordingly, in *Neulinger and Shuruk v Switzerland*,[48] where a mother and child argued that their Article 8 rights were breached by an order of the Swiss Federal Appeal court that the child be returned to Israel pursuant to an application under the Hague Child Abduction Convention 1980, the European Court of Human Rights held that the domestic courts should have 'conducted an in-depth examination of the entire family situation and of a whole series of factors, in particular of a factual, emotional, psychological, material and medical nature, and made a balanced and reasonable assessment of the respective interests of each person, with a constant concern for determining what the best solution would be for the abducted child in the context of an application for his return to his country of origin'.[49] The Court concluded that it was 'not convinced that it would be in the child's best interests for him to return to Israel' and held that the infringement was not justified.

By stating that it was necessary first to decide what the child's interests were and then whether departing from them was justifiable under Article 8,

---

[44] *Yousef v The Netherlands* [2002] ECHR 716, para. 73; see also *YC v United Kingdom* Application No 4547/10) [2012] FLR 332; *Johansen v Norway* (1997) 23 EHRR 33, para. 78.
[45] 41615/07 [2010] ECHR 1053.   [46] Ibid., para. 134.   [47] Para. 135.
[48] 41615/07 [2010] ECHR 1053.   [49] Para. 139.

the European Court of Human Rights treated a determination under the Hague Abduction Convention as if it were a decision *about* a child. But it is a decision about the appropriate jurisdiction to decide those interests, which should therefore be chosen unless that would create a grave risk of exposing the child to physical or psychological harm or otherwise place him in an intolerable situation. That does not require an initial determination of the best outcome for the child. This can be reconciled with Article 8 by considering whether the interference with the child's Article 8 rights occasioned by the decision to return the child without the full application of the best interests test could nevertheless be justified under that Article. It is quite possible that they could.

E   Ambiguous and Contestable Instances

I have argued that the structure of the reasoning process follows the characterization of the decision. Usually the characterization will be straightforward, but there will be ambiguous or contestable cases. For example, in England, a Head Teacher may exclude a child from school for a 'serious breach, or persistent breaches, of the school's behaviour policy; or where a pupil's behaviour means allowing the pupil to remain in school would be detrimental to the education or welfare of the pupil or others in the school'.[50] As Ferguson and Webber point out,[51] this allows exclusion to take place without regard to the excluded child's welfare at all. That would infringe Article 3(1). However, for more serious exclusions (for example, if permanent or lead to lengthy periods off school) the school's governing body must consider 'the interests and circumstances of the excluded pupil', which is a weak reference to the child's best interests.[52] But is the decision directly about the child, or primarily about protecting others? Since the matter would only have arisen out of concerns over threats to the interests of the school community, these processes could be seen as directed at safeguarding those interests in ways that indirectly impact on the potentially excluded child. On the other hand, once the process starts, the decision seems to be about what to do with that child. Decision-makers need to choose which characterization best reflects the process as the way the child's interests

---

[50] Department for Education, Department for Education, *Exclusion from maintained schools, Academies and Pupil referral units in England* (DFE-00001-2015, 2015)
[51] School Exclusion and the Law: A Literature Review and Scoping Survey of Practice (Oxford: University of Oxford, 2015) 18–19.
[52] Exclusions and Reviews Regulations 2012, Reg. 6(3)(a).

are set against other interests will depend on which characterization is adopted. The legislation and guidance seems to indicate it should be the former.

Sometimes the two processes follow very closely. An English court cannot make a care order regarding a child unless the child is at risk of 'significant' harm 'due to the care he has received and would receive if the order was not made, not being what a reasonable parent would provide'.[53] Rather than seeking the best outcome for the child, this decision is focused more directly on the parents' qualities and behaviour, although with significant indirect consequences for the child. However, if the risk of significant harm is found, the decision becomes one directly about the child, and the court must make a holistic evaluation of all options now available to it.[54]

An example of potentially ambiguous characterization occurs in 'relocation' cases. These could be perceived as the obverse side of extradition cases. Extradition cases concern decisions whether or not to *order* a parent's removal from the jurisdiction in the light of its indirect impact on a child. Relocation cases concern whether or to *allow or restrain* a parent from leaving the jurisdiction with the child, and how this decision should be affected by its impact on the child. Rob George[55] has shown that, although the court in *Poel v Poel*[56] correctly expressed its reasoning in terms of the best interests of the child, the language of Winn and Sachs LJJ led some later cases to represent the decision as one about the reasonableness about a parent's wish to relocate, thus moving the focus of the decision from the child to the parent, so that 'the English courts were saying that international moves which were reasonable for the parent should not lightly be stopped'.[57] This approach was confirmed in *Payne v Payne*.[58] George describes how this shift from seeing the decision as being about a child to a decision substantially about a parent was resisted in UK cases of shared care and 'internal' relocation, which continued to be focused on the child and where a broad welfare analysis was accordingly likely to be applied, and rejected in New Zealand, where in *Payne* it was considered 'inconsistent with the wider all-factor child-centred approach required under New Zealand law'.[59]

---

[53] Children Act 1989, s. 31. [54] See *Re G* [2013] EWCA Civ 965.
[55] *Relocation Disputes: Law and Practice in England and New Zealand* (Oxford: Hart Publishing, 2014), pp. 31ff.
[56] [1972] 1 WLR 1469. [57] George, op. cit., p. 35. [58] [2001] EWCA Civ 166.
[59] George, op. cit., p. 52.

F Conclusion

Making the distinction between decisions directly about children and decisions indirectly affecting them introduces a structure into the decision-process that can make decisions, especially those falling into the second category, more stable. It does not however eliminate indeterminacy of the standard. Should this be a matter of concern? We can ask whether it should always be the object of the legal process to provide clear and predictable outcomes. In fact, many of the most characteristic tasks of legal reasoning involve resolving indeterminate issues. Has X taken reasonable care? Was Y reasonably foreseeable? Was Z's behaviour unconscionable? Has a proper balance been struck between freedom of speech and personal protection? Jeremy Waldron has described the processes by which these matters are dealt with in legal systems as 'forms of argumentative thoughtfulness'.[60] Legal sources (precedents, standards) provide points of departure and frameworks within which reasoned discussion takes place. This also accurately describes the operation of the best interests principle. It does not matter that it does not point to determinate results in all, or even in most, cases. It would be alarming if it did, because that would suggest that relationships involving children and children's interests needed to constantly conform to community rules. The best interests principle, which incorporates the need to have regard to the child's perspective, opens the way for evaluating the effects of social rules on particular children and for creative solutions that go beyond such rules. The process is mandated by the law, and the process overseen by the law. It takes place within a mass of policies and interests that are not necessarily identical with those of the child in question, but which are also the legitimate concern of the law. The law therefore needs to adopt a defensible basis upon which to relate the children's interests to those other interests, and to structure the way that is done. I have tried to suggest how this could be improved.

---

[60] Jeremy Waldron, 'Thoughtfulness and the Rule of Law', (2011) *British Academy Review* Issue 18 (2011) p. 4. See also http://papers.ssrn.com/sol3/papers.cfm?abstract_id=1759550.

6

A Developmental Equality Model for the Best Interests of Children

NANCY E. DOWD

Article 3 of the United Nations Convention on the Rights of the Child (UNCRC)[1] and its core standard of serving the 'best interests of the child' is closely interlinked with its Article 2 guarantee of equality and non-discrimination for all children.[2] The best interests of children are the interests of all children in growth, support, development and becoming adult citizens who maximize their own potential as well as contribute to the community and the broader society. The universal language of Article 3, then, must be read in conjunction with the strong guarantee in Article 2 that ensures attention to outcomes and opportunities for all children.

One way in which the concept of best interests takes on real meaning is to link it to a developmental measure. This ensures that best interests are normatively nuanced, as well as individually meaningful. So, for example, the needs of an infant and a teenager are quite different in terms of the structures and policies that maximize developmental opportunity and potential.[3] If a particular child has developmental or physical disabilities, that child has needs that also may require different support structures to maximize development.[4]

---

[1] United Nations Convention on the Rights of the Child, 20 November in force 2 September 1990, 1577 UNTS 3 [hereafter UNCRC].

[2] Article 2 (1). Also critical to equality rights is Article 4, which requires states to implement all rights in the Convention but states in particular, 'With regard to economic, social and cultural rights, States Parties shall undertake such measures to the maximum extent of their available resources.'.

[3] This is reflected in common developmental stages and indicators used to evaluate children and to provide guidance to parents. See, e.g., Centers for Disease Control and Prevention, Developmental Milestones, available at www.cdc.gov/ncbddd/actearly/milestones/ (last accessed August 15, 2015).

[4] This is recognized in Article 23 of the UNCRC. Such differential needs are also the foundation of American legislation including the Individuals with Disabilities Education Act, 20 U.S.C. §§ 1400 *et seq.*

American law has increasingly recognized the value of the developmental perspective. The United States Supreme Court has cited to developmental scholarship as the basis for a series of decisions on punishment of juvenile offenders, reasoning that the state's consequences should take account of youth brain development to determine both culpability and the potential for rehabilitation.[5] At the same time, in the reproductive realm, the Court has recognized the maturity of youth to make decisions about contraceptives and abortion.[6] American state courts also commonly incorporate developmental insights when framing custody and parenting plan orders, recognizing the different needs of children at various ages and stages, and therefore the need for flexible and supportive arrangements that meet developmental needs over time.[7]

This chapter argues that this progressive use of interdisciplinary research to incorporate a developmental perspective nevertheless requires attention to persisting inequalities among children.[8] The developmental lens, I argue, must be adjusted to serve developmental equality. Otherwise, well-meaning 'neutral' measures to foster development replicate subordination by failing to address the enormous developmental challenges placed in the path of children who are the objects of inequality. It is critical that a developmental perspective, essential to meaningful best interests, should incorporate developmental equality, meaning that each child should have the same opportunity to maximize their developmental capabilities. The developmental perspective must incorporate what we know of inequalities that persist among children.

The equality principle of Article 2, then, is the trigger to infuse Article 3 best interests with developmental perspectives that serve all children. The purpose of this developmental equality lens is twofold: (1) to identify

---

[5] *Roper* v. *Simmons*, 543 U.S. 551 (2005); *Graham* v. *Florida*, 560 U.S. 48 (2010); *Miller* v. *Alabama*, 567 U.S. —, 132 S.Ct. Rep. 2455 (2012).
[6] *Bellotti* v. *Baird*; 443 U.S. 622 (1979); *City of Akron* v. *Akron Center for Reproductive Health*, 462 U.S. 416 (1983); *Hodgson* v. *Minnesota*, 497 U.S. 419 (1990); *Carey* v. *Population Services International*, 431 U.S. 678 (1977).
[7] For example, the Florida custody statute includes developmental considerations as a factor to craft parenting plans. Florida Statutes Chapter 61.13(3)(s)(2015).
[8] This chapter draws on my prior work on African American boys. Nancy E. Dowd, 'Unfinished Equality: The Case of Black Boys,' (2013) 2 *Indiana Journal of Law and Social Equality* 36–61; Nancy E. Dowd, 'What Men? The Essentialist Error of The End of Men,' (2013) 93 *Boston University Law Review* 1203–36. The theoretical model of this chapter is developed in greater detail in my article in progress, 'Developmental Equality,' and my book in progress, *Equality Reimagined: The Case of Black Boys* (New York: New York University Press).

risks and challenges that must be immediately addressed, but more importantly, (2) to trigger an obligation by the state to eliminate its role in supporting, directly or indirectly, identifiable challenges that create or exacerbate developmental inequality for children that perpetuate their potential for, or reality of, subordination.[9]

In this chapter I frame the concept of developmental equality and show how it can be used to impose concrete obligations for the state, consistent with the purposes of Articles 2 and 3 and the affirmative obligations of Article 4. In other words, the Convention by its terms provides the mechanism for implementation of the theory, because of its goals of achieving children's equality as well as maximizing their developmental potential. In the United States, the failure to ratify the Convention means that while this UNCRC analysis may be persuasive authority, additional and different strategizing is necessary to implement a litigation strategy or a proactive public policy.[10] Those strategic and theoretical issues are not explored here but are part of a larger project to implement developmental equality.[11]

In the first part of the chapter I briefly explore the ecological perspective on child development, a broadly accepted developmental model, and its relation to best interests. In the second part, I consider the limitations of a 'neutral' ecological perspective, using as my example data about the life course of African American boys from birth to age eighteen years. In the third part, I suggest how to shift the lens to one of developmental equality, using the theoretical models of Cynthia Garcia Coll and Margaret Beale Spencer.[12] While linked to the experience of children of color in the United States, these models are valid starting points, I would argue, for similar explorations of inequalities among children in other countries. I conclude with what I suggest could be the benefit of the developmental equality perspective, and what obligations it should trigger for the state.

---

[9] This model might also inform our perspective on how race, gender and class privilege is generated and replicated. See, e.g., Peggy McIntosh, 'White Privilege and Male Privilege: A Personal Account of Coming to See Correspondences Through Work in Women's Studies,' in Margaret L. Anderson & Patricia Hill Collins (eds.), *Race, Class and Gender*, 9th edition (Boston: Cengage Learning, 2013), pp. 74–78; Barbara J. Flagg, '*Was Blind But Now I See*': *White Racial Consciousness and Law* (New York: New York University Press, 1993).

[10] On the failure of the US to ratify the UNCRC, see, Barbara Bennett Woodhouse, *Hidden in Plain Sight: The Tragedy of Children's Rights from Ben Franklin to Lionel Tate* (Princeton: Princeton University Press, 2010), pp. 6–13.

[11] Dowd, *Equality Reimagined* (in progress).   [12] See infra part C.

A The Ecological Perspective

The best interests standard necessarily requires a developmental perspective in order to meaningfully implement the standard. Children are dynamic, moving targets in terms of their needs and necessary support, as well as their competence and capability.[13] This is recognized in the most fundamental way by familiar developmental charts that identify physical, mental, cognitive, and social skills, as well as labeling different stages in a more general way.[14] Based on those charts that distill multidisciplinary research, particularly neuroscience research, the most critical periods of neurological development are in infancy, 0–3 years, and in adolescence.[15] Within those periods change is dramatic. So, for example, some of the developmental hallmarks at six months are sitting up with support, rolling over, and saying two syllable words.[16] At three years they are climbing, running, going up and down stairs; understanding simple words, communicating well; and exhibiting a range of emotions.[17] At adolescence, developmental goals include separation from parents and greater interest in peer relationships, more future orientation and independent work habits, and dealing with sexuality,[18] and at the same time experiencing incomplete brain development, identity development and maturation, creating a perfect storm of risk, including lack of judgment, susceptibility to peers, and separation from parents.[19]

---

[13] Woodhouse, *Hidden in Plain Sight*, 24–27, 111, 127–32.

[14] Centers for Disease Control, Developmental Milestones, available at: www.cdc.gov/ncbddd/actearly/milestones/ (last accessed August 15, 2015).

[15] For the importance of birth (and pre-birth) to age three, see data at Zero to Three, National Center for Infants, Toddlers and Families, www.zerotothree.org; for adolescence, see data at National Institute of Mental Health, *The Teen Brain: Still Under Construction* at www.nimh.nih.gov/health/publications/the-teen-brain-still-under-construction/index.shtml?utm_source=LifeSiteNews.com+Daily+Newsletter&utm_campaign=2c0fa9560b-LifeSiteNews_com_Intl_Full_Text_12_18_2012 (last accessed August 15, 2015).

[16] Child Development Milestone Chart, available at https://s-media-cache-ak0.pinimg.com/736x/12/7c/6e/127c6effd2170ff8c987ffb289628040.jpg (last accessed August 15, 2015).

[17] Center for Disease Control, *Important Milestones, Your Child at 3 years*, available at: www.cdc.gov/ncbddd/actearly/milestones/milestones-3yr.html (last accessed August 15, 2015).

[18] Center for Disease Control, *Teenagers (15–17 Years Old)*, available at www.cdc.gov/ncbddd/childdevelopment/positiveparenting/adolescence2.html (last accessed August 15, 2015).

[19] Mark Fondacaro, 'Why Should We Treat Juvenile Offenders Differently? It's Not Because the Pie Is Half Baked' in Nancy E. Dowd (ed.), *A New Juvenile Justice System: Total Reform of a Broken System* (New York: New York University, 2014), pp. 129–138.

A child does not move through these stages in isolation; rather, they function within an ecology. Uri Bronfenbrenner's ecological model captures the complex pieces of this interaction, with his identification of microsystems, mesosystems, exosystems and macrosystems, and the interconnections between elements of each level, and each level with each other.[20] Microsystems are those that most immediately and directly affect the child, including family, school, peers, and neighborhood. Mesosystems are the next level of the ecology that interact with those most direct connections, including, for example, the workplace and school systems or structures. Exosystems are the systemic levels that impact on children and their parents, including the educational system, political system, religious organizations, health care systems, and the courts and legal system. Finally, the macrosystem is the mix of ideas, principles, biases, and theories that drive the systemic level and impact through various levels to the child.

The component pieces of the ecology may act functionally or dysfunctionally within each level and between levels. For example, a child may have a highly supportive and positive family situated within a dangerous neighborhood, or linked to a failing school or even a single inadequate teacher. On the other hand, a child may have a family that is internally dysfunctional but the other direct microsystems reinforce positive outcomes and provide support for developmental outcomes. A good example of this is home nursing visiting programs that ensure that very young mothers are provided with support and education to care for newborns.[21] Another example would be programs supporting father involvement for young or low-income fathers who might otherwise drop out of their children's lives because the meso and exosystems fail to provide structural or ideological support for non-marital fatherhood.[22]

---

[20] Uri Bronfenbrenner, *The Ecology of Human Development: Experiments by Nature and Design* (Cambridge: Harvard University Press, 1979). The following paragraph describes Bronfenbrenner's model.

[21] U.S. Department of Health and Human Services, Administration for Children and Families, *Home Visiting Evidence of Effectiveness*, available at: http://homvee.acf.hhs.gov/Implementation/3/Early-Intervention-Program-for-Adolescent-Mothers-/39/1 (last accessed August 15, 2015)

[22] Programs based on empirical data are critical, see, e.g., Constance M. Dallas, 'Paternal Involvement of Low Income AA Fathers With Children in Multiple Households', University of Illinois at Chicago, College of Nursing, Research, available at www.nursing.uic.edu/research/paternal-involvement-low-income-aa-fathers-children-multiple-households (last accessed August 15, 2015).

This model also makes clear the interaction of macrosystem ideas on direct microsystem functioning. An ideological system that views families as private and problems within families or with children as personal responsibilities tends towards a lack of support services for families. Differences, especially economic ones, are viewed as a product of personal choices. On the other hand, an ideological system of solidarity and mutual support is often reflected in institutional supports for families grounded in the belief that providing supports for children and their families provides long-run benefits to the social good. Law is a mechanism that reflects ideological beliefs and norms, and functions throughout the systems to reinforce values and beliefs.[23]

In a well-functioning ecology, the immediate actors at the micro level are systemically supported, and this provides essential structural and cultural support to the child, and to those who most directly influence her well-being. If, for example, families and neighborhoods mutually reinforce positive development, this provides a secure and stimulating context in which children can grow, and be ready to begin school. On the other hand, if systems are in conflict, it creates stress, or even trauma, either directly to the child or indirectly, through the lack of support of their most essential interactions.[24] So, for example, if work and family exosystems for parents (employment demands, the availability of high-quality child care, income support where needed) are in conflict, making it difficult for parents to provide time and quality nurture to their children, that impacts on parental and family dynamics, and thus on the child.[25]

The macrosystem of ideas and ideologies are critical to how the entire ecosystem works, and law is a critical component of the macrosystem that also implements and effects critical players at each level of the ecosystem. A system of mutual support and solidarity, for example, supports the concept that all children are our children, and to provide

---

[23] Barbara Bennett Woodhouse, 'Ecogenerism: An Environmental Approach to Protecting Endangered Children' (2005) 12 *Virginia Journal of Social Policy and Law* 409–47; Woodhouse, *Hidden in Plain Sight*, pp. 31–32.

[24] For rich descriptions of dysfunction, see Clare Huntington, *Failure to Flourish: How Law Undermines Family Relationships* (New York: Oxford University Press, 2014); Katheryn Edin and Timothy J. Nelson, *Doing the Best I Can: Fatherhood in the Inner City* (Chicago: University of Chicago Press, 2013).

[25] See, e.g., Nancy E. Dowd, '(Re)constructing the Framework of Work and Family' (2010) 16 *Washington and Lee Journal of Civil Rights and Social Justice* 333–348.

for each child in a child-centered, individually appropriate way.[26] A system dominated by ideas of private responsibility and non-intervention in families, on the other hand, may provide little support and rationalize inequalities as privately created rather than publically structured.[27]

B Limitations of the Ecological Perspective

The ecological perspective is enormously important to understanding development contextually, identifying the important factors in development, and how systems and structures impact in the life of individual children and communities. If the child at the center of this inquiry is a neutral child, a generic child, the model if used in that way may unintentionally exacerbate or perpetuate inequalities.

An example of this is the case of African American boys from ages 0–18. In prior work focusing on this group, defined by race and gender, I have presented a detailed demographic portrait.[28] Rather than being supported to achieve their developmental potential, they are set up to fail, to be subordinated as adults, by virtue of poverty, lack of education, and involvement in the criminal justice system. Three critical statistics substantiate this powerful negative picture: one in three is born in poverty;[29] one in two will not graduate from high school;[30] and one in three will be incarcerated in their lifetime; and if they come from a lower socioeconomic status, the risk is doubled.[31]

These stark statistics are devastating to the life circumstances of black boys. And as recent events continue to demonstrate, they also run the risk of simply not surviving their childhood, of becoming another statistic in an ongoing pattern of racialized violence whether public (police) or private.[32]

---

[26] Barbara Bennett Woodhouse, *The Ecology of Childhood: Small Worlds in Peril* (New York: New York University Press, forthcoming 2016).
[27] Id.; see also Woodhouse, *Hidden in Plain Sight*, pp. 29–47.
[28] Dowd, Unfinished Equality, 45–59.   [29] Ibid., at 45.   [30] Ibid.   [31] Ibid.
[32] Beginning with the death of Trayvon Martin, there have been highly publicized deaths and injuries of young black men particularly as a result of police shootings that have been captured in videos and pictures. This visual evidence vividly shows the persistence and lethality of racism at its most violent. These tragedies are the tip of the iceberg. While they seem to have begun to move consciousness, they undeniably also demonstrate the daily risks of life for that begin even for quite young black boys, and increase with age.

A remarkable amount of social science research, until recently, has responded to these patterns with the question 'What is wrong with African American boys?' Or the variant, 'What is wrong with African American families? Communities?' Within the developmental literature, the focus has long been on the causes of 'deviance' and risky behaviors.[33] As critics have noted, this ignores the structural factors that impact on the lives of black boys. Indeed, the very norms against which children of color have been measured are white norms: virtually all child development theory and research has been either exclusively or predominantly focused on white children.[34] As one scholar put it, 'even the rat was white'.[35]

A focus on the child that does not take race and gender into account when those factors trigger structural and cultural challenges and differential supports means the wrong questions are asked. Policy aims at 'fixing' what is deemed a deviation from the norm, rather than uncovering why structures, institutions and policies continue to replicate inequality. Instead, if there is evidence of discrimination, as the voluminous data and significant social science literature on implicit bias, stereotypes, and structural discrimination substantiate, then the developmental model itself must be reframed to take that into account. In order to achieve children's developmental equality, we must use a model that is raced and gendered in order to identify the structural and cultural barriers that children face and that must be eliminated.[36]

Although I have used the American example of African American boys, the phenomenon of inequalities among children is by no means limited to the USA. One prominent European example is Roma or Romani children, who have been the focus of significant efforts to improve their life circumstances in the face of devastating demographics that defy normative developmental possibilities.[37] Roma children are

---

[33] See Margaret Beale Spencer, 'Revisiting the 1990 *Special Issue on Minority Children*: An Editorial Perspective 15 Years Later' (2006) 77(5) *Child Development*, 1149–1154.

[34] Cynthia Garcia Coll, Gontran Lamberty, Renee Jenkins, Harriet Pipes McAdoo, Keith Crnic, Barbara Hanna Wasik, & Heidie Vazquez Garcia, 'An Integrative Model for the Study of Developmental Competencies in Children,' (1996) *Child Development* 1891–1914, at 1893–95.

[35] Robert V. Guthrie, *Even the Rat Was White: A Historical View of Psychology*, 2nd ed. (New York: Allyn and Bacon, 2009).

[36] This also suggests that such a model would expose how privilege is conferred on white children in the USA; by failing to include racial identity and racial/gender context in current models, it ignores how children acquire a sense of self that replicates hierarchies.

[37] Lilla Farkas, Report of Experts in the Non-Discrimination Field, *Report on Discrimination of Roma Children in Education* (Utrecht: European Commission,

subordinated in almost every developmental demographic: they experience a high poverty rate, including suffering from hunger; many do not go to school, even as compared with other impoverished children, and they are often segregated in schools.[38] Roma children, their families, and their communities suffer intense discrimination that transcends national borders.[39] Another example of inequality is the treatment of children of Muslim immigrants, whether the children are themselves immigrants or citizens. For example, these children have been the object of discrimination in France and Sweden.[40] The movement of Muslim immigrants throughout the EU, and into the EU zone, continues to trigger strong reactions that inevitably entangle children.[41] Yet another example is the segregated educational treatment of Palestinian Arab children in Israel.[42]

The litany of examples of discrimination among children unfortunately is a long list. Added to that would be a global comparison that finds disadvantage and exploitation concentrated along race, gender and class lines.[43] The persistence of those patterns, I would argue, should generate a shift in our developmental lens in order to achieve the goal of

---

Directorate-General for Justice, 2014):http://ec.europa.eu/justice/discrimination/files/roma_childdiscrimination_en.pdf

[38] Id., pp. 5, 6 and 11.   [39] Ibid., pp. 12–15.

[40] 'In Sweden, the Land of the Open Door, Anti-Muslim Sentiment Gains a Foothold,' *New York Times*, 2 January 2015, available at www.nytimes.com/2015/01/03/world/in-sweden-the-land-of-the-open-door-anti-muslim-sentiment-finds-a-foothold.html?_r=0 (last accessed August 15, 2015); Alessandria Masi, 'France's Secularism is Driving Young Muslims Out of School, Work and French Culture,' International Business Times, 21 January 2015 available at www.ibtimes.com/frances-secularism-driving-young-muslims-out-school-work-french-culture-1789258 (last accessed August 15, 2015).

[41] This is evident in a photo essay on the Mediterranean immigration crisis; Alan Taylor, 'The Mediterranean Migrant Crisis: Risking Everything for a Chance at a Better Life', *Atlantic*, 11 May 2015, www.theatlantic.com/photo/2015/05/the-mediterranean-migrant-crisis-risking-everything-for-a-chance-at-a-better-life/392957/ (last accessed August 15, 2015).

[42] Zama Coursen-Neff, 'Discrimination Against Palestinian Arabic Children in Israel' (2015), available at www.theatlantic.com/photo/2015/05/the-mediterranean-migrant-crisis-risking-everything-for-a-chance-at-a-better-life/392957/https://www.hrw.org/news/2005/05/01/discrimination-against-palestinian-arab-children-israeli-education-system (last accessed August 15, 2015).

[43] See, e.g., UNICEF, *The State of the World's Children 2006: Excluded and Invisible*, available at www.unicef.org/sowc06/pdfs/sowc06_fullreport.pdf; Children's Defense Fund data on American children, available at www.childrensdefensefund.org. See also the United Nations' Millenium Development Goals, available at www.un.org/millenniumgoals/ (last accessed August 15, 2015).

children's equality. Where inequalities exist among children, Article 2 should trigger examination of the developmental consequences of those inequalities and the role of the state in perpetuating inequality, in order to ensure that children's Article 3 best interests are served in maximizing their developmental potential. Where there are demonstrable differences in children's developmental outcomes that fall along race, gender and/or class lines, a developmental lens informed by the consequences of those developmental challenges should be used to not only counter the effects of discrimination, but more importantly, to trigger obligations and responsibilities to dismantle those structures in the ecology that generate those disproportionate challenges, and implement systems that support children's equal development.

In the following section, I present two models that can be used to adjust the developmental lens to a developmental equality lens, the work of Cynthia Garcia Coll and Margaret Beale Spencer.

Dealing with the Limitations: Shifting the Lens

To incorporate the perspective of children of color and to acknowledge that a neutral developmental perspective ignores critical differences among children that are constructed by structural and cultural factors that the state may create, implement, or foster, it is essential to use a developmental lens that is explicitly raced and gendered, to determine how those factors impact development. Using this lens should focus on the role of the state and should mandate the end of the state creating differential developmental challenges for children. In place of dismantled structures of subordination, the state should create egalitarian ones.

This is a dramatically different approach than that fostered under typical risk/resilience models commonplace in public health policy making. In those models, policy focuses first on children with demonstrated problems, then those who are at risk, and then all children (primary, tertiary, and secondary interventions).[44] The risk/resilience model is important because it is responsive to current realities. But it does not necessarily target structural, state-created or state-supported

---

[44] For the public health model, see generally Institute for Work and Health, available at www.iwh.on.ca/wrmb/primary-secondary-and-tertiary-prevention (last accessed August 15, 2015); Centers for Disease Control and Prevention, Public Health Approach to Violence Prevention www.cdc.gov/violenceprevention/overview/publichealthapproach.html (last accessed August 15, 2015).

factors that create or exacerbate risk. It may focus, for example, on interventions for children in poor neighborhoods with low-functioning schools, but it does not trigger actions about poverty and its neighborhood, family, and individual consequences, and institutional manifestations in schools.

Using the two models I describe later, a developmental equality approach would identify the factors that create developmental challenges that significantly contribute to differential developmental outcomes along lines of race, gender and class. Developmental equality would require the state to do something about identified barriers and challenges to development, as well as to provide the supports for every child to reach their developmental potential. The models therefore provide a measurable metric to impose state responsibility for children's equality.

Margaret Beale Spencer

Margaret Beale Spencer

(1) RISK CONTRIBUTORS
Self Appraisal Processes:
Social-cognition dependent
(In response to stereotypes & biases)

Race
(e.g., ethnicity/color bias)

Sex (Female: e.g., perceptions of femininity/Male: e.g., need for instrumentality)

SES
(e.g., poverty; school & neighborhood quality; family dynamics)

Physical status
(e.g., early maturing)

Biological characteristics
(e.g., temperament; physiological processes)

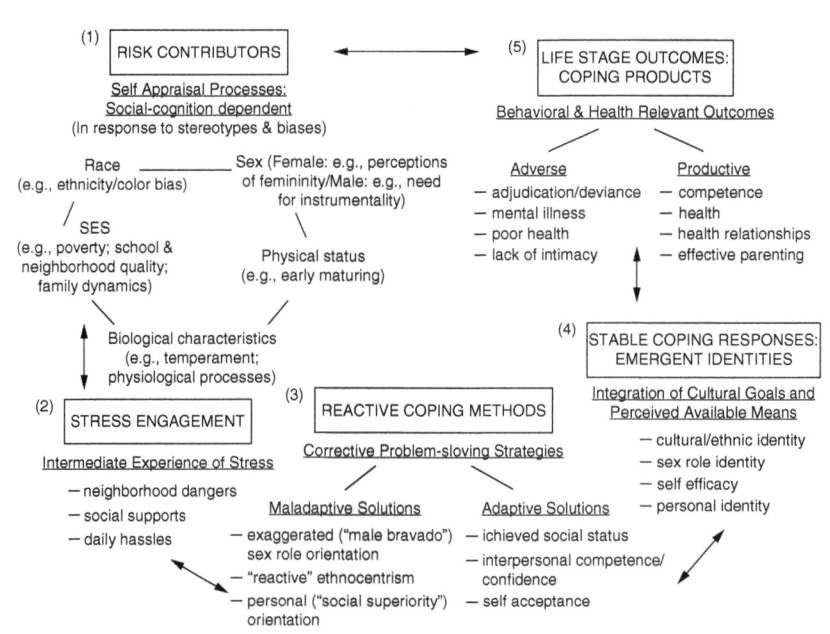

(2) STRESS ENGAGEMENT
Intermediate Experience of Stress
– neighborhood dangers
– social supports
– daily hassles

(3) REACTIVE COPING METHODS
Corrective Problem-sloving Strategies

Maladaptive Solutions
– exaggerated ("male bravado") sex role orientation
– "reactive" ethnocentrism
– personal ("social superiority") orientation

Adaptive Solutions
– ichieved social status
– interpersonal competence/ confidence
– self acceptance

(5) LIFE STAGE OUTCOMES: COPING PRODUCTS
Behavioral & Health Relevant Outcomes

Adverse
– adjudication/deviance
– mental illness
– poor health
– lack of intimacy

Productive
– competence
– health
– health relationships
– effective parenting

(4) STABLE COPING RESPONSES: EMERGENT IDENTITIES
Integration of Cultural Goals and Perceived Available Means
– cultural/ethnic identity
– sex role identity
– self efficacy
– personal identity

Figure 6.1 The phenomenological variant of ecological systems theory (PVEST).

Margaret Beale Spencer's model,[45] the phenomenological variant of ecological systems theory (PVEST), captures the individual's experience and engagement with the ecology within which the child develops, from the perspective of children of color.[46] The model captures individual responses within structural factors that operate at the micro-, meso-, exo- and macro-levels of the ecological model. Each of the key aspects of the model interact with each other, in a dynamic process of development and identity formation; this happens not in a linear progression, but rather interactively. The five major subdivisions in the model are: risk contributors; stress engagement; reactive coping methods (to stresses), which can be adaptive or maladaptive; stable coping response/emergent identities; and life stage outcomes/coping products, which can be adverse or productive.

Risk contributors included in the model are described as self-appraisal processes dependent on social cognition, so responses to stereotypes and biases. Inherent in this part of the model is that identity characteristics trigger risk. The risk factors Spencer includes are: race, sex, SES (socioeconomic status), physical status (level of maturity/age/perceived maturity) and biological characteristics, like temperament. Within this category, then, are distilled factors that alone or in combination generate risk for the child. The inclusion of race, gender, and SES distills a wealth of information that indicates these characteristics generate the risk of adverse situations and stresses that may confront the child. Recognition and validation of this part of the model is critical to its use as a guiding lens to achieve developmental equality. As long as these factors are identifiable risks, then they should trigger evaluation of structural and

---

[45] The graphic model is from Margaret Beale Spencer, David Dupree, and Tracey Hartman, 'A Phenomenological Variant of Ecological Systems Theory: A Self Organization Perspective in Context,' (1997) 9:4 *Development and Psychopathology*, 817–833, at 819.

[46] The description of Spencer's model in this segment is based on Margaret Beale Spencer Suzanne Fegley and Gregory Seaton, 'Understanding Hypermasculinity in Context: A Theory-driven Analysis of Urban Adolescent Males' Coping Responses' (2004) 1(4) *Research in Human Development* 229–257; Margaret Beale Spencer, Margaret B., Suzanne G. Fegley, and Vinay Harpalani, 'A Theoretical and Empirical Examination of 'Identity as Coping: Linking Coping Resources to the Self Processes of African American Youth,' (2003) 7(3) *Applied Developmental Science* 181–188; Margaret Beale Spencer, Blanch Dobbs, & Dena Phillips Swanson, 'African American Adolescents: Adaptational Processes and Socioeconomic Diversity in Behavioural Outcomes,'(1988) 11 *Journal of Adolescence* 117–137; Margaret Beale Spence and Carol Marstrom-Adams, 'Identity Processes among Racial and Ethnic Minority Children in America' (1990) 61(2) *Child Development* 290–310.

cultural factors that foster that risk, and the responsibility to dismantle that toxic ecology while building a supportive ecology.

Risks in this model identify what may cause harm or pose challenges. Spencer links this to two pieces of the model: stresses that create situations that must be dealt with by the child, and overall life stage outcomes, where risk can generate either positive or negative outcomes. The link to stress engagement in the model includes neighborhood dangers, social supports, and daily hassles. This captures individual interaction with the microsystems of family, neighborhood, peers, and schools that are most direct for children and youth. The model includes both positive and negative factors, recognizing that even if there are neighborhood dangers, such as a high rate of violence or minimal health care in the event of illness, family and neighborhood can also provide social support. The experience of stress is a common phenomenon of development; the accumulation of stressors, however, is harmful to development. This part of the model also incorporates the wealth of data on microaggressions, that is, the daily insults that persist in the lives of children and adults of color, as well as the culture of negative images and messages in media and the general culture. It captures the cost of that particularly for children, as well as the development of social supports to counter those messages particularly in families, community, and religious organizations.

Risks are also linked to overall life stage outcomes, meaning behavioral and health outcomes, which may be mediated by the response to stressors, the development of solidified identities, and their effect at each developmental stage. It is important to note that this links psychological and developmental well-being to physical/health well-being. But Spencer's model also suggests that the risk factors impact life stage outcomes. These can be positive or negative outcomes, but importantly, these are stages, so they may be positive for one stage, negative for another, or some combination. Positive outcomes include competence, health, healthy relationships, and effective parenting. Adverse outcomes include adjudication/deviance, poor health, lack of intimate relationships, and mental illness. These life stage outcomes, the products of this experiential process, are themselves generated by, and generate, coping responses, as well as being affected by risk factors. This complex interaction is critical to understanding the impact of structural and cultural factors on development, and therefore the essential role of the state in facilitating the positive development of each child. What Spencer's model clearly demonstrates is how the risk factors generate developmental challenges and potential adverse outcomes because of race, gender and class, and therefore should trigger the state's obligation not to create or be complicit in creating those challenges, and to affirmatively intervene to ensure positive development.

How the dynamic works in specific situations is illustrated in the parts of the model that deal with reactions to stressful situations, and the emergence of a stable identity, including stable coping methods. This part of the model captures the process of development, in the sense of the movement of children and youth through experiences where they experiment, make mistakes, learn and grow, but that very process is highly dependent on the ecology and what responses it reinforces and what consequences flow from experience. In addition, it is affected by the perception of one's context, whether one can recover from mistakes or if one will be judged as fitting within a stereotype. If deviance and conformity to a negative stereotype is assumed, then outcomes that lead to lack of achievement, high rates of discipline and school suspension, and harsh justice system involvement are predictable.

Spencer sees reactive coping strategies as problem solving strategies, ones that ultimately work and those that do not. Adaptive strategies are achieved social status, interpersonal competence, and self acceptance. Maladaptive strategies are exaggerated sex role orientation (male bravado); 'reactive' ethnocentrism, and personal 'social superiority' orientation. What is interesting about the maladaptive categories is that each of these strategies, according to Spencer, is likely to generate behavior and systemic response to that behavior that is highly negative. Spencer and others have noted the cycle of hypervigilence of young men of color, generating a hypermasculine response, likely to trigger more oppressive responses from police, teachers, and community members.[47]

This is apparent when looking at the final part of the model, stable coping responses. The outcome of positive coping methods/problem solving is the solidification of a positive identity that can contribute to positive life outcomes, despite ongoing risks. The aspects identified here are 'integration of cultural goals and perceived available means', including cultural/ethnic identity, sex role identity, personal identity, and self-efficacy. This part of the model encapsulates robust recent scholarship exploring the affirmative development of children of color, and in particular, African American boys. What this scholarship includes is the

---

[47] Victor Rios, *Punished: Policing the Lives of Black and Latino Boys* (New York: New York University Press, 2011).

complex process of achieving positive development in the fact of the risk factors and challenges that Spencer identifies, but also focuses on the positive process of development for children of color because of the strength of their families and communities. There is much to be gained by drawing on these strengths particularly to suggest how white families can move toward supporting development of their children without replicating hierarchy. And in the process of identifying what developmental equality would look like, it provides a vision of that outcome, unencumbered by the need for parents to protectively arm their children to survive the current developmental gauntlet.

Spencer's model is particularly focused on individual level interaction with systemic factors, and reminds us of how this intersects with all of the layers of the ecology. Her work has been focused on reducing the consequences of risk and facilitating supportive resilience and success, but this model can be applied to require the identification and removal of challenges, triggering a responsibility of support until the demographic data indicate developmental equality, a place that would remove not only the three stark factors mentioned earlier, but others as well that indicate challenges to the development of every child to their maximum potential.

Cynthia Garcia Coll

Spencer's model particularly captures the individual child's experience in the developmental process of structural and cultural discrimination that creates developmental challenges. Garcia Coll focuses on the same dynamic, but even more strongly captures what is happening in the ecology structurally and culturally. Garcia Coll's model,[48] the integrative model for the study of developmental competencies in minority children, is grounded like Spencer's in Bronfenbrenner's ecological model.[49]

---

[48] The graphic model is drawn from Cynthia Garcia Coll et al., 'An Integrative Model for the Study of Developmental Competencies in Minority Children', at 1896.

[49] This section is based on Garcia Coll's model as described in Cynthia Garcia Coll and Laura A. Szalacha, 'The Multiple Contexts of Middle Childhood' (2004) *The Future of Children*, 14(2), 80–97; Cynthia Garcia Coll, and K. Magnuson,'Cultural Differences as Sources of Developmental Vulnerabilities and Resources: A View from Developmental Research' (2000) in *Handbook of Early Childhood Intervention*, (Jack P. Phonkoff and Samuel J. Meisels, eds.) (Cambridge: Cambridge University Press 2000) 94–114; Cynthia Garcia Coll et al., 'An Integrative Model for the Study of Developmental Competencies in Minority Children'; Cynthia Garcia Coll, 'Developmental Outcomes of Minority Infants: A Process-Oriented Look into Our Beginnings' (1990) 61:2 *Child Development*, Special Issue on Minority Children, 270–289.

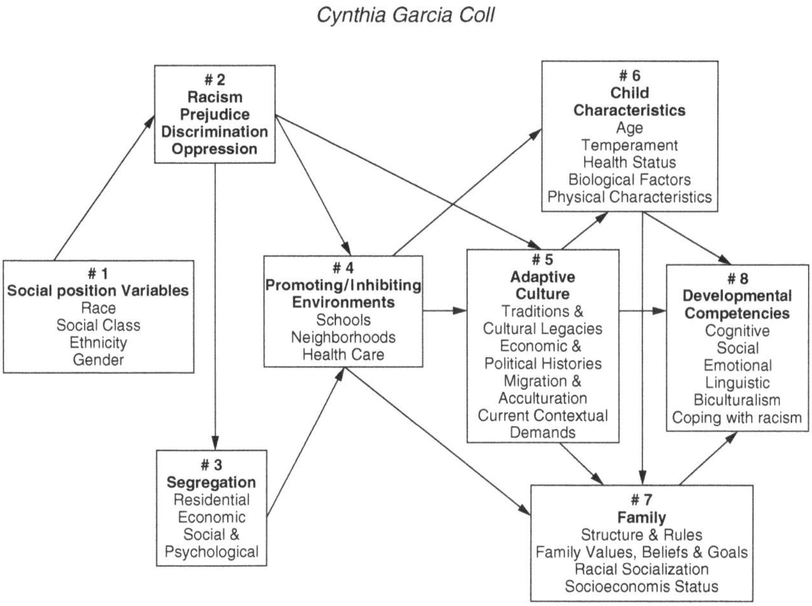

A DEVELOPMENTAL EQUALITY MODEL   127

Cynthia Garcia Coll

Figure 6.2 Integrative model for the study of developmental competencies in minority children.

Garcia Coll's model has eight component parts: social position; oppression factors (racism, sexism, prejudice, oppression); segregation; promoting or inhibiting environments; adaptive cultures; family; child characteristics; and developmental competencies. These are conceptualized in an interactive but linear fashion: each of the factors has an impact on developmental capacities. The first three factors create developmental challenges or hurdles; then a variety of pieces of the ecology can help or hurt in meeting those challenges, along with the individual characteristics of the child, resulting in achieving normative developmental categories or having an impact on those categories. Rather than focusing on the individual dynamic, Garcia Coll's model is particularly helpful in identifying the systemic and cultural dynamics. Her model also identifies the critical supportive role of families and communities, and the development of cultural adaptations to confront and deal with the developmental challenges wrought by inequality.

The first three parts of Garcia Coll's model develop the factors that impact on development based on social position. Included within the social position variable is race, social class, ethnicity and gender.

The relevance of these factors, as with Spencer's similar risk variables, is that these factors generate challenges. Again, this suggests the necessity of monitoring the challenges generated by these factors to ensure children's equality. The next two factors expand on particular ways social position impacts children. The second factor includes racism, prejudice, discrimination, and oppression. These categories attempt to encompass the dynamic of inequality inclusively rather than, for example, limiting it to 'discrimination', a term that has in the USA tended to be narrowly construed.[50] Garcia Coll links this second factor not only to the characteristics of the child, but also to its impact on the development of adaptive cultures. Families and communities respond and react in ways to promote the well-being of their children as impacted by these forces in their lives. Her third factor, segregation, encompasses the importance of spatial characteristics for children, including residential, economic, and social/psychological segregation. These three factors (social position, the dynamic of inequality, and segregation) distill rich scholarship of inequality and point to important factors that generate structures that reinforce cultural norms of inequality.

At the next phase, Garcia Coll focuses on promoting and inhibiting environments, specifically schools, neighborhoods and health care. In addition to the role of the state with respect to the factors that create social position (versus a society where each child is equally valued and supported irrespective of social position), here she identifies two critical systems, schools and health care, that impact on children's development, as well as neighborhoods. Neighborhoods can also be conceptualized as a system heavily influenced by state action, in terms of their ability to promote or inhibit child development. Garcia Coll sees these promoting or inhibiting environments interacting with the child and their particular characteristics apart from social position (age, temperament, physical characteristics, health status, biological characteristics), as well as the child's family and its characteristics (structure and roles; values, beliefs and goals; SES; racial socialization). Family and child also interact directly with each other.

Promoting or inhibiting environments also interact more broadly with communities, affecting what Garcia Coll calls adaptive cultures, meaning the cultural response to promoting development, or inhibiting it based on social position factors. Within the category of adaptive cultural

---

[50] See, e.g., *Washington v. Davis*, 426 U.S. 229 (1976).

response she includes traditions and cultural legacies, economic and political histories, migration and acculturation, and current cultural demands. One of the strongest implications of Garcia Coll's research is paying attention to the actions and beliefs of communities of color and immigrant communities and understanding their actions as adaptive responses to support their children, rather than constructing them as negative or deviant.

The end result of these complex reactions, triggered by social position and context, fed by the interaction of promoting and inhibiting environments and adaptive cultures, as well as specific characteristics of particular children and families, are developmental outcomes, identified as cognitive, social, emotional, linguistic, bicultural and coping with racism. Included with the familiar and normative 'neutral' developmental categories are developmental competencies fostered by communities and families and also necessary to children of color – linguistic competency, the ability to function in their culture and majority culture, and the ability to deal with a context of ongoing racism.

Garcia Coll's model is especially helpful to identifying the structural pieces that intersect to affect children, their families, and communities that are implemented institutionally in those systems that affect children most. These are institutions that are created and sustained by the state. Therefore, the state is implicated in this model, and this should trigger state responsibility to dismantle challenges and support families and communities as well as provide promoting environments for all children to reach their developmental capacities.

Together, Spencer and Garcia Coll provide concrete theoretical and practical frameworks for developmental equality. These models can be used to identify concrete metrics to measure not only conventional measures of normative development, but to measure whether developmental support is provided for all children. They also incorporate developmental factors that matter for all children: race or ethnicity, gender and class. Such a modification of the developmental model is critical to make equality meaningful for all children.

D   Conclusion

The embrace of the developmental model in implementing the best interests of the child is an important positive step to link legal rules and public policy outcomes to a multidisciplinary model aimed to best support children and youth. In an era where children's inequalities remain, and where those inequalities fall along lines of race, gender and class, it is essential that the model itself recognize the developmental challenges created by those identity factors alone and in combination. It is also essential that these aspects of identity be affirmatively supported. This model can provide a mechanism to trigger more responsibility on the part of the state to dismantle those challenges and provide support for all children to reach their developmental capacity.

7

A Long Lesson in Humility? The Inability of Child Care Law to Promote the Well-being of Children

ALISON CLELAND

'life is a long lesson in humility'

J.M. Barrie, The Little Minister

A Introduction

This chapter considers the nature of current child protection laws and analyses their ability to provide the care and protection necessary for the well-being of children, as required by Article 3(2) of the United Nations Convention on the Rights of the Child.[1] Article 3(2) requires that 'States Parties undertake to ensure to the child such protection and care as is necessary for his or her well-being, taking into account the rights and duties of his or her parents, legal guardians, or other individuals legally responsible for him or her'.

The threshold criteria currently used widely are misconceived. The use of the concept of 'significant harm' delivers a high legal test for state intervention in families. The circumstances of most children do not meet the legal test and state intervention comes very late. Investigation and assessment results in decisions to monitor rather than to support families.

The adversarial nature of the legal interventions mandated by the model brings increased conflict between families and the state. This is stigmatising and counter-productive and makes co-operation and safe outcomes for children unlikely.

The late intervention, legalistic model of child protection prevents child protection systems from providing support services to families, to

---

[1] United Nations Convention on the Rights of the Child, 20 November 1989, in force 2 September 1990, 1577 UNTS 3.

assist them to keep their children safe. The model requires child protection services to use the bulk of their resources to investigate concerns about possible child abuse, to assess risks and to monitor families. This diverts resources from family support.

The effects of the model as currently constructed have been disastrous for children and young people. The operation of the laws have brought additional trauma with few discernible benefits. For indigenous children in particular, the laws have demonstrably failed to deliver care that promotes well-being. The state takes children into care, but fails to ensure an environment in which they can thrive.

The chapter concludes with preliminary suggestions for reframing child protection laws using an ecological approach. Current threshold criteria should be replaced with a central concept of children's well-being. Legally authorised actions should be aimed at supporting the child in his or her family and community and providing services to improve children's well-being.

B The Late Intervention, Legalistic Model

Those interested in the well-being of children are depressingly familiar with the inevitable enquiries that follow deaths of children due to non-accidental injury. Many such enquiries have taken place over the years in Aotearoa New Zealand,[2] Australia,[3] Canada and the United Kingdom.[4] Often, the enquiries paint a picture of children and families who were known to child protection agencies.[5] The question is asked: why

---

[2] See, e.g., *Final report on the investigation into the death of James Whakaruru 1994–1999* (Wellington: Office of the Commissioner for Children, 2000); C. Kiro, *Report of the Investigation into the Deaths of Saliel Jalessa Aplin and Olympia Marisa Aplin* (Wellington: Office of the Commissioner for Children, 2003).

[3] In most Australian jurisdictions (not Tasmania), Child Death Review Teams conduct official enquiries into child deaths to improve understanding of the circumstances, see e.g., *ACT Children and Young People Death Review Committee, Annual Report 2013–14* (Canberra: Australian Capital Territory, 2014).

[4] See, e.g., Lord Laming *The Protection of Children in England: A Progress report*, HC 330 (London: The Stationery Office, 2009).

[5] For example, James Whakaruru was seen 40 times by health professionals, before he died at the age of 5: see, *Final Investigation into the death of James Whakaruru*, n2. Victoria Climbié was known to 3 housing agencies, 4 social services departments, 2 child protection teams, 1 specialist child protection centre and was seen by two hospitals before she died aged 8: see, *The Victoria Climbié Inquiry: Report of an Inquiry by Lord Laming* (Cm5730, London, Stationery Office, 2003). Baby Peter Connolly's name was on the child protection register and he was known to Child and Young

did the 'system' not protect the children by removing them from the dangerous homes in which they lived?

There are two responses to that question. First, the system did not protect children because professionals were doing what they were mandated to do: to watch and wait. The current structure of child protection laws requires investigation then, in most cases, inaction. The threshold criteria for intervention, grounded in the central concept of 'significant harm', are very high; the situations of most children will not meet them.

Second, many children who died have not, in fact, been known to child protective services.[6] This raises the question: are the current systems for assessing and monitoring risky families doing the job children need them to do?

'Significant Harm' Mandates Late Intervention

Aotearoa New Zealand, Australia, Canada and the UK (both Scotland and England), use different iterations of 'suffering or likely to suffer serious or significant harm', as the threshold criteria for substantial state intervention in families.

In Aotearoa New Zealand, one of the child care principles in the Children, Young Persons and Their Families Act 1989 (CYPF Act 1989) is that a child or young person should be removed from his family or extended family only if there is a serious risk of harm.[7] A court may find that a child or young person[8] is in need of care and protection (and thus subject to removal) if he or she is being, or is likely to be, harmed, ill-treated, abused or seriously deprived.[9] Other grounds refer to serious impairment or neglect.[10]

People Services, a Teaching Primary Care Trust, 3 hospitals, the police, two schools, a Family Welfare Association and a Housing Association before he died aged 17 months: see, *Haringey Local Safeguarding Children Board Serious Care Review Child 'A'* (Department of Education, October 2010).

[6] In New Zealand, in 1996–2000, 19 per cent of those who died were known to child protective services: M. Connolly and M. Doolan, *Lives Cut Short* (Wellington: Dunmore Publishing for the Office of the Children's Commissioner, 2007). In the ACT, 20.9 % of the children who died in 2008–2013 were known to child protection services: *ACT Children and Young People Death Review Committee 2nd Annual Report* (Canberra, Australian Capital Territory, 2013).

[7] CYPFA 1989, s. 13(e).   [8] Up to age 17, CYPF Act 1989, s. 2(1).
[9] CYPF Act 1989, s. 14(1)(a).   [10] CYPF Act 1989, s. 14(1)(b), (c), (h).

In Australia, intervention is triggered if a child[11] 'is in need of protection'. The thresholds across the states and territories use different formulae, but the key concept of serious or significant harm is consistent. The Australian Capital Territory legislation refers to abuse 'that has caused or is causing significant harm' to well-being or development.[12] Legislation in Victoria uses 'has suffered, or is likely to suffer, significant harm as a result of physical, sexual or emotional abuse.[13]

An English court cannot make a care or supervision order in respect of a child[14] unless satisfied that he or she 'is suffering, or is likely to suffer, significant harm'.[15] In Scotland, the first ground on which a child[16] may be referred to a children's hearing[17] is he or she 'is likely to suffer unnecessarily, or the health or development of the child is likely to be seriously impaired, due to a lack of parental care'.[18] In both jurisdictions, there is also provision for emergency orders that allow children to be removed from their families. The threshold criteria for these orders are suspicion (for assessment orders) or reasonable belief (for protection orders) that a child 'is suffering, or is likely to suffer, significant harm.'[19]

Agencies of the state are authorised to intervene in a child's family only where there are – at least – suspicions that the child may be suffering 'significant harm'. The primary functions of the state agency, therefore, are to investigate, to gather evidence of harm and to carry out a risk assessment. This is not the place to explore the inadequacies of risk assessment in child protection matters.[20] It is clear, however, that the

---

[11] Most states and territories define a child subject to state investigation and reporting as under the age of eighteen years; in Victoria, the definition is up to sixteen years and, in New South Wales, up to fifteen years.

[12] Children and Young People Act 2008 (ACT), s. 342.

[13] Children, Youth and Families Act 2005 (VIC) s. 162(1).

[14] For the purposes of care or supervision order, a child is under the age of seventeen years, or under sixteen years if married – Children Act 1989, s. 31(3).

[15] Children Act 1989, s. 31(2).

[16] Generally a person under the age of sixteen years, Children's Hearings Scotland Act 2011, s. 199(1).

[17] The primary decision-maker in respect of care and protection matters in Scotland is not the court, but a panel of trained lay people, forming a children's hearing. For discussion of the history and philosophy of children's hearings, see E.E. Sutherland, *Child and Family Law*, 2nd edn (Edinburgh: Thomson/W.Green, 2008), paras. 10-001–10-034.

[18] Children's Hearings (Scotland) Act 2011, s. 67(2)(a).

[19] Children Act 1989, ss. 43(1), 44(1) and Children's Hearings (Scotland) Act 2011, ss. 36(2)(a), 38(2).

[20] For analysis of some of the issues involved, see: N. Parton 'Child Protection and Safeguarding in England: Changing and Competing Conceptions of Risk and their Implications for

taking of active steps to safeguard a child's well-being will come only after a long process establishing that a child is suffering or likely to suffer significant harm.

The 'significant harm' threshold for intervention is high. In *Re L (Care: Threshold Criteria)*.[21] Hedley J said:[22]

> society must be willing to tolerate very diverse standards of parenting, including the eccentric, the barely adequate and the inconsistent ... it was not the provenance of the state to spare children all the consequences of defective parenting.

The fact that the judgment did not focus on the harm to the child, but rather on the parenting, led Keating to note[23] 'one begins to fear that the very concept of significant harm itself is in the process of being ratcheted up'.

In *Re M*[24] a child had been assaulted but there was a finding of no significant ill-treatment, as there were no physical signs of abuse. Ward LJ referred to the balance that the legal framework attempted to achieve, between protecting children from harm and protecting parents and families from state intervention. He emphasised that the criteria for state intervention were high and that compulsory intervention should be used as a last resort.[25]

In Aotearoa New Zealand, a declaration that a child is in need of care of protection can be made if there is a serious risk of harm.[26] This is the gateway to possible assistance for children and families. Discussing the standard to be met for a declaration, the court has stated:

> [i]t can be expected that there will be a high threshold that must be crossed before the intrusive remedy of declaration under CYPF Act, which gives the Department custodial powers and the ability to send children to foster homes, is granted.[27]

Cases considering whether the harm or likelihood of harm is severe enough to justify state intervention are not concerned with identifying

---

Social Work' (2011) 41 *British Journal of Social Work* 854–875; E. Keddell, 'The ethics of predictive risk modeling in the Aotearoa/New Zealand child welfare context: Child abuse prevention or neo-liberal tool?' (2014) *Critical Social Policy* published online at http://csp.sagepub.com/content/early/2014/07/23/0261018314543224.

[21] [2007] EWHC 3527 (Fam), [2007] 1 FLR 2050.   [22] Ibid., para. 50.
[23] Discussing the threshold criteria from *Re L* as they were used in a later case: H. Keating 'Care Commentary, *Re MA*: the significance of harm' (2011) 23(1) CFLQ 115–127, p. 121.
[24] [2009] EWCA Civ 853.   [25] Ibid., para. 54.
[26] CYPF Act 1989, s. 67; grounds for the declaration are in s. 14.
[27] *P v Department of Child Youth and Family Services* [2008] NZFLR 898 at [58].

the needs of a particular child. They are concerned with providing reasons that will justify overcoming the rights of carers to look after their children in the way they wish: '[I]t is difficult to see how the reasons for taking a child away from her family for the indefinite future can be "relevant and sufficient" if they rely on unproven allegations'.[28]

The Children Act 1989, places local authorities under a duty to promote the upbringing of children in need by their families.[29] The Children, Young Persons, and Their Families Act 1989 contains the principles that, in respect of a child in need of care and protection, assistance and support should, wherever practicable, be provided to enable the child or young person to be cared for and protected within his or her family, whanau, iwi and family group.[30] Family autonomy and civil liberties present the courts with powerful additional lenses through which to view child protection evidence. The result is severe limitation of the circumstances in which a child will be found to be suffering or likely to suffer significant harm.

Legalistic Processes Are Counter-Productive

The application of the 'significant harm' test makes it less likely that children's best interests will be a paramount consideration. The activities of professionals who could provide supports to families to improve the children's well-being are geared towards evidence gathering and assessment. Jack, analysing the child protection model used in England, has noted:

> Therapeutic and welfare orientations have been replaced by the 'forensic gaze' of the child protection system...[t]he daily routine of most area team child-care social workers is now dominated by such tasks as 'risk assessment', the collection of 'evidence' and the surveillance of children considered to be 'at risk of abuse'.[31]

Tomison makes the same point in relation to Australia: '[u]nder a legalistic framework, developing a legal response has pervaded child protection practice and usurped the therapeutic needs of the child and family'.[32]

---

[28] *Re P* [2009] 1 AC 11 at [78].   [29] Children Act 1989, s. 17(1)(b).
[30] CYPF Act1989, s. 13(d).
[31] G. Jack, 'Discourses of Child Protection and Child Welfare' (1997) 27 *British Journal of Social Work* 659–678, p. 663
[32] A. M. Tomison 'A History of Child Protection: Back to the Future' (2001) 60 *Family Matters* Spring/Summer (Australian Institute of Family Studies) available at https://aifs.gov.au.

Gupta[33] stresses the fact that all social work practice takes place in the context of an adversarial legal system. She notes that: '[t]he dominant political discourse is one of blaming poor families for their poverty and related difficulties, and there is much evidence to suggest that challenging this discourse is not a feature of social work assessments.'[34]

The legal criteria for intervention support that dominant discourse. The deficit approach condemns households who are deprived in myriad ways. The risk factors that may trigger investigation are closely associated with the results of poverty and, in particular, the results of colonialism on indigenous families.[35]

State agencies assess the adequacy of parenting in emotional and material terms and the effects on families can be devastating. Dale[36] notes that investigations inevitably will be conducted in crises, resulting in strong emotions in families. Other research has indicated a broad range of negative emotions for families, associated with investigations, including fear[37] and powerlessness.[38] Cooper et al note that those drawn into the system 'frequently find the whole experience traumatic, and sometimes more traumatic than the abuse itself'.[39]

The process of proving that the threshold criteria have been met usually involves the attaching of culpability to carers. This is especially true in cases of alleged neglect,[40] which is defined in terms of failure of carers. For example: '[n]eglect is the failure to provide the child with the basic necessities of life such as food, clothing, shelter, medical attention

---

[33] A. Gupta 'Significant Harm: The Application of the Law in Practice with Vulnerable Children' in R. Sheehan and J. Ogloff (eds.) *Working Within the Forensic Paradigm: Cross-Discipline Approaches for Policy and Practice* (Abingdon: Routledge, 2015).

[34] Ibid., p. 163.

[35] For discussion of the phenomenon in settler colonial states, see A. Armitage, *Comparing the Policy of Aboriginal Assimilation: Australia, Canada and New Zealand* (Vancouver: UBC Press, 1995), particularly chapters 3 (Aboriginal Peoples), 5 (First Nations) and 7 (New Zealand).

[36] P. Dale, 'Like a Fish in a Bowl: Parents' Perceptions of Child Protective Services' (2004) 13 *Child Abuse Review* 137–157, 144–145.

[37] G. Dumbrill, 'Parental Experiences of Child Protection Intervention: A Qualitative Study' (2006) 30 *Child Abuse & Neglect* 27–37.

[38] D. Yatchmenoff, 'Measuring Client Engagement from the Client's Perspective in Non-Voluntary Child Protective Services' (2005) 15 *Research on Social Work Practice* 84–96.

[39] A. Cooper, R. Hetherington and I. Katz, *The Risk Factor: Making the Child Protection System Work for Children* (Demos Open Access, www.demos.co.uk, 2003), p. 13.

[40] See, e.g., J. Sykes 'Negotiating Stigma: Understanding Mothers' Responses to Accusations of Child Neglect' (2011) 33 *Child and Youth Services Review* 448–456, available at www.sciencedirect.com.

or supervision, to the extent that the child's health and development is, or is likely to be, significantly harmed'.[41]

In his research with lawyers and social workers involved in child neglect cases, Dickens[42] notes that these cases were of long-standing with no previous action taken. Consequently, when cases were brought to court, lawyers looked for a 'catapult' to persuade the court to make a care order. This would be a change in circumstances or a specific incident and until this arose, there would be delay and inaction.

It is not only the court process itself that is adversarial and damaging to a meaningful relationship between social services and families. Most jurisdictions allow emergency protection processes, under which a child may be removed from a home for a short period of time. Masson's work on emergency protection[43] found that most families were known to social services and, again, that there were long-standing child protection concerns. Agreements with the families (usually to have the child cared for elsewhere) were made to avoid court proceedings and because of the substantial shift of power that successful proceedings represented, parents were compelled to enter the agreements. As one social worker in her study observed, '[m]ost families can be persuaded and it may be that it is a bit of an arm up the [back] job'.[44] Social workers in the study also noted that the parents' failure to meet the expectations in the agreement could be used to show lack of cooperation and therefore the necessity of a formal order.

Under existing child protection regimes, it is unlikely that families and state agencies can ever work together in a beneficial way that will promote children's well-being. In situations that are judged to be high risk, social workers find working in partnership extremely difficult: 'it was only in cases where the risk factors were low and perceptions about the abuse were shared that a full partnership was achievable'.[45] Carrying out risk assessments, particularly in more serious cases, militates strongly against the development of any meaningful working relationship between families and agencies.

To keep children safe and to improve their lives requires that state agencies work with families and support them to improve their parenting.

---

[41] Victoria State Government, Department of Human Services, available at www.dhs.vic.au.
[42] J. Dickens, 'Child Neglect and the Law: Catapults, Thresholds and Delay' (2007) 16 *Child Abuse Review* 77–92.
[43] J. Masson 'Emergency Intervention to Protect Children: Using and Avoiding Legal Controls' (2005) 17(1) *Child and Family Law Quarterly*, 75–96.
[44] Ibid., at 82.
[45] M. Bell, 'Working in Partnership in Child Protection: The Conflicts' (1999) 29 *British Journal of Social Work* 437–455 at 447.

The atmosphere of judging, blaming and criticism that is an inevitable result of child protection investigations, together with the trauma experienced by the families as a result of the process, makes is very unlikely that the families who need help to keep their children safe will be prepared to work with state agencies. If the only circumstances in which work that promotes well-being can be done are low risk, the question is: should the point of engagement not be much earlier in the child's life – and with consent?

Inability to Intervene Early

Promoting the health and development of children requires early social services support and preventive work with their families. This is important, difficult work that will, by its nature, take time and considerable resources. Unfortunately, the operation of the legalistic model for investigation and assessment swallows up the bulk of resources available.

The relationship between a child protection system and the ability of agencies to provide supportive services is apparent from a comprehensive study of child welfare programmes in the USA in the 1980s.[46] The study considers the effects on the welfare programmes, once investigation and assessment becomes a priority. It concludes: '[t]he increased demand for child protection has driven out all other child welfare services'.[47]

Acknowledgement of the reality that child protection prevents child welfare work can also be seen in the *Every Child Matters: Change for Children* initiative.[48] The overall aim was to focus more on prevention, while continuing to protect children who needed it. A public health approach is adopted, using risk factors 'to design particular intervention programmes and to reorient mainstream services'.[49]

An additional requirement, to assess and monitor more families earlier, has been imposed on social services.[50] At the same time, the

---

[46] S.B. Kamerman and A.J. Kahn, *Social Services for Children, Youth and Families in the United States* (New York: The Annie E Casey Foundation, 1989).
[47] Ibid., pp. 7–8.
[48] Department of Education and Skills, *Every Child Matters: Change for Children* (London, 2004) available at www.education.gov.uk.
[49] N. Parton and D. Berridge 'Child Protection in England' in N. Gilbert, N. Parton and M. Skivenes, *Child Protection Systems* (Oxford: Oxford University Press, 2011) at 65.
[50] For analysis of the issues, see N. Parton, '"From Dangerousness to Risk": The Growing Importance of Screening and Surveillance Systems for Safeguarding and Promoting the Well-Being of Children in England' (2010) 12(1) *Health, Risk and Society* 51–64.

requirement to investigate and assess for 'significant harm' continues. While that threshold remains, there will be few resources to undertake meaningful child welfare work.

Social service agencies in Australia and Aotearoa New Zealand have legal duties to respond to 'notifications'.[51] In Australia, in 2013 to 2014, there were 304,097 notifications and 54,438 substantiations.[52] In Aotearoa New Zealand, for year 2014 to 2015 (June), there were 150,905 notifications and 16,472 substantiations.[53] In the USA, states' responses to reports of child maltreatment may differ, but all report to the National Child Abuse and Neglect Data System. For financial year 2013, approximately 2.1 million reports were screened in as appropriate for a child protection response.[54] One fifth of the children investigated were found to be victims of abuse or neglect.

Even more significant than the number of notifications, is their increase over time. In Australia, between 1977 and 1978 and 1993 and 1994, the numbers increased by 5000 per cent. A major reason for this was the introduction of mandatory reporting in most states during the 1970s.[55] The numbers dropped somewhat between 2009 and 2011, but the upward trend continued thereafter.[56] Similar vast increases occurred in the USA, where mandatory reporting is also used: in 1994, there were just short of 2 million maltreatment reports and by 2007, that figure was 3.2 million.[57] The increases are not confined to systems with mandatory reporting: notifications in Aotearoa New Zealand more than doubled between 2006 and 2011.[58]

---

[51] A notification is a contact with the relevant social services agency that contains allegations of abuse of or harm to a child.

[52] Australian Institute of Health and Welfare, *Child Protection Australia, 2013–2014* (Canberra: Australian Institute of Health and Welfare, 2015), at p. 17.

[53] Provided on the Child, Youth and Family website, www.cyf.govt.nz.

[54] U.S. Department of Health and Human Services, Administration for Children and Families, Children's Bureau *Child Maltreatment 2013*, available from www.acf.hhs.gov/programs/cb/research-data-technology/statistics-research/child-maltreatment.

[55] For an overview, see, B. Mathews, *Mandatory Reporting Laws for Child Sexual Abuse in Australia: A Legislative History* (Sydney: Royal Commission into Institutional Responses to Child Sexual Abuse, Commonwealth of Australia, 2014).

[56] Australian Institute of Health and Welfare, *Child Protection Australia, 2013–2014* (Canberra: Australian Institute of Health and Welfare, 2015), at p. 27.

[57] U.S Department of Health and Human Services, Administration on Children, Youth and Families *Child Maltreatment 2007* (Washington DC:U.S. Government Printing Office, 2009), p. 5. Note that this is the total number of reports. Some will not be screened in for a child protection response.

[58] P. Tapp and N. Taylor 'Protecting the Family' in M. Henaghan and B. Atkins (eds.) *Family Law Policy in New Zealand*, 4th edn. (Wellington: LexisNexis NZ, 2013), p. 104.

It is obvious that the scope of child protection investigations under the present system is almost limitless. Huge amounts of resources, representing a large portion of state budgets for child and family support, are consumed by child protection investigations, assessments and monitoring. Realistically, the remaining resources cannot deliver the early intervention services required. Cooper et al, analysing the English system, found more and more resources were being focused on high-risk situations and crises, stifling prevention and support for families.[59] To retain resources to deliver early preventive and support services to children and families, the legal framework of child protection law will require to be redrawn.

C The Effect of the Current Child Protection Model

The effects of the operation of the late intervention model have been disastrous for the children and young people. Systemic racist outcomes and extremely limited life chances have been the legacy of state care.

Systemic Racism

The model used to identify and investigate families is fundamentally racist in its application and outcomes. Disproportionality of children in state care in Canada is very marked: 30 to 40 per cent are Aboriginal, despite their making up less than 6 per cent of Canada's children.[60] In Australia in 2014, Aboriginal and Torres Strait Islander children were 9.2 times more likely than non-indigenous children to be in out-of-home care.[61] In Aotearoa New Zealand in 2015, 59 per cent of children in out of home placements were Māori.[62] Māori make up 14.9 per cent of the population.[63]

---

[59] A. Cooper, R. Hetherington, I. Katz, *The Risk Factor: Making the Child Protection System Work for Children* (Demos Open Access, www.demos.co.uk, 2003), at pp. 10–11.
[60] C. Blackstock, N. Trocmé and M. Bennett, 'Child Welfare Response to Aboriginal and Non-Aboriginal Child in Canada: A Comparative Analysis' (2004) 10(8) *Violence Against Women* 901–916.
[61] Child Family Community Australia, *Child Protection and Aboriginal and Torres Strait Islander children* (CFCA Resource Sheet, 2015), available at www.aifs.gov.au
[62] Māori are the indigenous people of Aotearoa New Zealand.
[63] Statistics New Zealand, *2013 Census QuickStats about Māori* (Wellington: Crown Copyright, 2013), available at www.stats.govt.nz.

In England, children of mixed ethnicity are the largest group in state care and children of African and Caribbean origins are over-represented by a factor of 2:1.[64] In the USA, 15 per cent of all children are African American, but they account for 42 per cent of children in the state child welfare system; and 1 per cent of all children are First Nations children, but 2 per cent are in state care.

The statistics referred to are not directly comparable, but they present a picture of gross disproportionality in relation to state care of children. There are many interrelated circumstances that contribute to the picture[65] and this is not the place to review them comprehensively. Some particularly damaging factors that illustrate the scope and pervasiveness of racism, however, include: the application of cultural deficitism;[66] agencies that operate institutionally racist policies and practices that do not support kin care;[67] and lack of cross-cultural competence, resulting in social work decisions that investigate indigenous and minority ethnic families more readily and remove children more frequently.[68]

Poor Outcomes for Children and Young People: 'It's like a hole in your heart that can never heal'[69]

The current child protection legislation is based on a deficit model that targets and punishes families who live with multiple stressors,

---

[64] J. Thoburn, A. Chand and J. Procter, *Child Welfare Services for Minority Ethnic Families: The Research Reviewed* (London: Jessica Kingsley, 2005), p. 29.

[65] For example, A.M. Hines, K. Lemon, P. Wyatt, J. Merdinger 'Factors Relating to the Disproportionate Involvement of Children of Color in the Child Welfare System: A Review and Emerging Themes' (2004) 26 *Child and Youth Services Review*, 507–527, available at www.sciencedirect.com in relation to the USA; the significant disadvantages experienced by African American families because of poverty are highlighted.

[66] Discussed in R. Barn, 'Race, Ethnicity and Child Welfare: A Fine Balancing Act' (2007) 37 *British Journal of Social Work* 1425–1434, at 1429.

[67] See R. B. Hill, 'Institutional Racism in Child Welfare' (2004) 7 *Race and Society* 17–33, for analysis of the phenomenon in the USA.

[68] Y. E. Lu, J. Landsverk, E. Ellis-Macleod, R. Newton, W. Ganger, I. Johnson 'Race, ethnicity and case outcomes in child protective services' (2004) 26 *Children and Youth Services Review*, 447–461 available at www.sciencedirect.com.

[69] *Bringing Them Home: Report of the National Inquiry into the Separation of Aboriginal and Torres Strait Islander Children from Their Families* (Canberra: Commonwealth of Australia, 1997), confidential evidence 162, Victoria, available at www.humanrights.gov.au.

the most significant of which is poverty. Indigenous families and communities are affected disproportionately by these stressors; it is inevitable that they will be drawn into the state system more often. Where the result of state intervention is the removal of indigenous children from their families, the damage is profound.

A generation of Aboriginal children were taken from their homes from the 1940s to the early 1970s under assimilationist legislation. The report of the national inquiry into the results of the legislation[70] makes grim reading. Grief, loss and suffering suffuse the report. The effects on the children included: psychological trauma due to separation from primary carers; loss of cultural knowledge, indigenous identity, and connections with land; and dehumanisation as a result of institutionalisation. There were also severe effects on the families and communities.

In Canada, until the 1950s, children between ages six and fifteen years were sent to residential schools under the Indian Act. As Armitage notes[71], at the peak of 'child protection' through education, one third of all First Nations children were in these schools: '[i]n some communities, this meant that all its children were removed'.[72] In Aoteraoa New Zealand, the Child Welfare Act 1925 resulted in large numbers of Māori children being removed from their families by the state.[73] Dissatisfaction with state child care practices increased, as the supposedly benign 'child rescue' model under the Children and Young Persons Act 1974[74] separated more and more Māori children from their families and communities.

Colonialism sought to erase the unique cultural identity of indigenous peoples. Child protection laws added another layer of trauma. The removal of any child from his or her community will be traumatic and damaging. For indigenous children, the effects are far more profound. The well-being of indigenous children is inextricably linked to their knowledge of their cultural heritage and identity. The

---

[70] *Bringing Them Home*, above.
[71] A. Armitage, *Comparing the Policy of Aboriginal Assimilation: Australia, Canada and New Zealand* (Vancouver: UBC Press, 1995).
[72] Ibid., p. 108.
[73] M. Doolan and M. Connolly, 'Care and Protection: Capturing the essence of our Practice', www.practicecentre.cyf.govt.nz.
[74] For detailed discussion see B. Dalley, *Family Matters: Child Welfare in 20th Century New Zealand* (Auckland: Auckland University Press, 1998).

damaging effects are intergenerational[75] and continue long after overtly racist policies are withdrawn.[76]

Indigenous children have been damaged most severely, but outcomes for all children in state care are extremely poor.[77] The abuse of children while they were in state care has become a modern scandal, with historical claims being lodged in all jurisdictions. This is the ultimate betrayal of those whom the system was mandated to protect. Children who have been in care are far less likely to attain educational qualifications; this reduces their employment chances and results in many living in poverty.[78] Care leavers are at severe risk of becoming homeless.[79] Those in care and leaving care very often have mental health problems and drug and alcohol addictions.[80] Most unconscionable is the high correlation between state care and incarceration. If the parenting abilities of the state were subjected to risk assessment and measured against the 'significant harm' criteria, they would be labelled inadequate and dangerous; decisions to remove children from its care would undoubtedly follow.

D An Ecological Approach to Child Care Law Reform: To ask 'How is the child?'...rather than 'Do we have a case?'[81]

Child care laws must be reformed, removing existing threshold criteria. In deciding what should replace them, an ecological approach to child

---

[75] S. R. Silburn, S. R. Zubrick, D. M. Lawrence, et al., 'The Intergenerational Effects of Forced Separation on the Social and emotional Wellbeing of Aboriginal Children and Young People' (2006) Family Matters 75, available at www.aifs.gov.au.

[76] H. Douglas and T. Walsh, 'Continuing the Stolen Generations: Child Protection Interventions and Indigenous Peoples' (2013) 21 International Journal of Children's Rights 59–87.

[77] For a review of material from Australia, the UK and the USA, see P. Mendes and B. Moslehuddin 'From Dependence to Interdependence: Towards Better Outcomes for Young People Leaving State Care' (2006) 15 Child Abuse Review 110–126.

[78] See e.g., P.J. Pecora, R.C. Kessler, K. O'Brien, et al., 'Educational and Employment Outcomes of Adults Formerly Placed in Foster Care: Results from the Northwest Foster Care Alumni Study' (2006) 28 Children and Youth Services Review 1459–1481.

[79] See, e.g., G. Mallon, 'After Care, Then Where? Outcomes of an Independent Living Program' (1998) 77 Child Welfare 61–78.

[80] See, e.g., J. Neale, Drug Users in Society (Basingstoke: Palgrave Macmillan 2001); a third of heroin users in the Glasgow study were previously in state care.

[81] E. G. Khoo, U. Hynönen and L. Nygren 'Child Welfare or Child Protection: Uncovering Swedish and Canadian Orientations to Social Intervention in Child Maltreatment' (2002) 1 Qualitative Social Work 451–471 at 466.

protection and child well-being may help us. Bronfenbrenner[82] proposed an ecological approach to human development, studying the interaction of the human organism with various systems. This approach has been applied to child abuse, both in respect of its etiology[83] and its relationship with community violence.[84] The ecological analysis identifies four 'systems': macrosystem (societal beliefs and values); exosystem (social structures that impact a child's immediate environment); microsystem (child's family); and ontogenic development (child's own abilities, characteristics).

Studies comparing 'child protection' systems and 'child welfare systems'[85] found that they had different macrosystems. The liberal, narrowly focused child protection models in Canada and Australia had macrosystems that valued the free market and limited, targeted intervention in families. Child protection was risk dominated and forensic and considered only ontogenic development – damage to the child – and the microsystem – characteristics and risk factors in the immediate family. The child welfare models in Sweden and Norway had macrosystems that valued extensive, publicly funded systems and widely available, preventive services for families. Child welfare services were aimed at the exosystem – developing communities, reducing poverty and tackling the difficulties arising from low socio-economic status of communities – as well as the microsystem of family functioning.

We can see that late intervention child protection laws prevent the child care system from considering and addressing the macrosystem and exosystem that profoundly affect the well-being of children. How could a law be framed to encourage and enable this? The central concept of 'significant harm' could be replaced with that of the 'well-being of children'. Instead of duties to look for evidence of significant harm, social services agencies would have legal obligations to assess what services and supports could enhance the abilities of families and communities to safeguard their children's well-being. This would refocus child care law,

---

[82] U. Bronfenbrenner, 'Towards an Experimental Ecology of Human Development' (1977) 32(7) *American Psychologist* 513–531.
[83] J. Belsky, 'Child Maltreatment: An Ecological Integration' (1980) 35(4) *American Psychologist* 320–335.
[84] D. Ciccetti and M. Lynch, 'Towards an Ecological/Transactional Model of Community Violence and Child Maltreatment' (1993) 56 *Psychiatry* 96–117.
[85] Khoo, Hynönen and Nygren 'Child Welfare or Child Protection'; B.H. Kojan and B. Lonne, 'A Comparison of Systems and Outcomes for Safeguarding Children in Australia and Norway' (2012) 17 *Child and Family Social Work* 96–107.

policy and services on the exosystem that so profoundly influences the health and welfare of children. Even if this were possible within existing neo-liberal macrosystems, the success of the measures would ultimately depend on the skills of social service professionals and society's belief in the necessity of their work. It may be too much to hope that child care law reform could bring with it a renewed respect for our much-maligned social workers.

PART III

Best Interests and Bestowing Parentage

8

Serving Best Interests in 'Known Biological Father Disputes' in the United Kingdom

LESLEY-ANNE BARNES MACFARLANE

A 'Known Biological Father Disputes' and Best Interests

Introduction

In recent decades, the increased availability of assisted reproduction has conferred upon many groups, couples and individuals new procreative freedoms and choices. As a consequence, the paradigms of family life are rapidly evolving, but the essential questions remain the same: 'Who is my parent? Is this my child?'[1] When known individuals (rather than anonymous donors) provide eggs, sperm or embryos to those otherwise unable to conceive, several adults might assert their parenthood in respect of any child born – on biological[2] or psychological grounds.

During the last fifteen years or so, UK courts have decided a small but steadily growing number of cases brought by men who, having provided sperm to a female couple, are seeking recognition of their status in respect of the child, or children, subsequently conceived.[3] In such cases, sperm has typically been provided through an informal arrangement in which it has been agreed that all adults involved would assume a parental role of some sort. While the lesbian couple (one of whom is the

---

[1] *A & Ors (Human Fertilisation and Embryology Act 2008)* [2015] EWHC 2602, para. 3, per Sir James Munby.

[2] The term 'biological parent' is used in this chapter as a generic term for: (i) men who have provided sperm to the child's biological mother, including those who have done so in a non-sexual arrangement (these men are also the genetic parent); (ii) the child's gestational mother who is often, although need not always be, the genetic mother.

[3] See, e.g., *X v Y*, 2002 SLT 161; *Re M (Sperm Donor Father)* [2003] Fam Law 94; *B v A, C, D (acting by her Guardian)* [2006] EWHC 2 (Fam); *B (Role of Biological Father)* [2007] EWHC 1952 (Fam); *T v T (Shared Residence)* [2010] EWCA Civ 1366; *MA v RS (Contact: Parenting Roles)* [2011] EWHC 2455 (Fam); *A v B & C (Lesbian Co-Parents: Role of Father)* [2012] EWCA Civ 285; *Re G (Children) (Children: Sperm Donors: Leave to Apply for Children Act Orders)* [2013] EWHC 134 (Fam); *DB v AB (Contact: Alternative Families)* [2014] EWHC 384 (Fam); *JB v KS* [2015] EWHC 180 (Fam).

gestational[4] mother) normally provide the child's primary care, the terms 'multiple-parenting' or 'co-parenting' have sometimes been used in reference to such arrangements.[5] The proceedings raised in the event that these arrangements break down have yet to acquire a homogenous label and nomenclature itself is a sensitive issue.[6] Although the phrase 'known donor dispute' persists in legal discourse, the judiciary has increasingly discouraged the use of the word 'donor', deeming it 'belittling and disrespectful to all concerned, most importantly the child'.[7] This chapter analyses the extent to which the child's best interests are the central focus in resolving these disputes. Accordingly, the term 'known biological father' is preferred[8] since it is submitted that it is an accurate and inclusive way of characterising such cases with reference to the child involved.

Article 3 and UK Law: Challenges

Article 3(1) of the United Nations Convention on the Rights of the Child ('the Convention') provides that in 'all actions concerning children' the 'best interests of the child shall be a primary consideration'.[9] The Article has been indirectly incorporated into UK law. In legislation regulating family proceedings, the 'welfare' (the synonym for 'best interests' found in UK legislation) of the child concerned is described as 'the paramount' rather than 'a primary' consideration.[10] This means that all other considerations are secondary to the overriding issue of what serves the child's best interests. Consequently, disputes between two – or

---

[4] That is, the woman who carries and gives birth to the child, whether or not the eggs used are hers.

[5] See, e.g., *Different Families: A Guide for Gay Dads*, Stonewall web-publication, 2010, pp. 19-24: www.stonewall.org.uk/sites/default/files/A_Guide_for_Gay_Dads__1_.pdf; *A v B & C (Lesbian Co-Parents: Role of Father)* [2012] EWCA Civ 285; *X v Y*, 2002 SLT 161, paras. 11-37.

[6] See, e.g., Alan Brown, 'Re G; Re Z (Children: Sperm Donors: Leave to Apply for Children Act Orders): Essential "biological fathers" and invisible "legal parents"' (2014) 26(2) *CFLQ* 237-252.

[7] *JB v KS* [2015] EWHC 180 (Fam), para. 40, per Hayden J. See, e.g., also *A v B & C (Lesbian Co-Parents: Role of Father)* [2012] EWCA Civ 285, para. 48, per Black LJ.

[8] See, e.g., Alan Inglis, 'Children and same sex parents' (2015) 11 *SLT* 53-56 at 53. Other terms, e.g., 'surrogate known father', have also been suggested: Andrew Bainham and Stephen Gilmore, *Children: The Modern Law*, 4th ed., (Bristol: Jordans, 2013), p. 128.

[9] UN Convention on the Rights of the Child (adopted 20 November 1989, entered into force 2 September 1990) 1577 UNTS 3.

[10] Children Act 1989, s. 1(1); Children (Scotland) Act 1995, s. 11(7)(a).

more – adults about parental entitlements can only be decided with reference to whether endorsing any parental role will enhance or be detrimental to the child's welfare.

The United Nations Committee on the Rights of the Child ('the Committee') recently outlined the comprehensive nature of the Article 3 obligation as embodying 'a right, a principle and a rule of procedure based on an assessment of all elements of a child's ... interests in a specific situation'.[11] The Committee also directed that State Parties include those family circumstances 'that make each child unique'[12] in best interest assessments. Recognition of diverse parenting paradigms is gradually becoming more common across a breadth of jurisdiction, some of which have already enacted legislation regulating multiple parenthood.[13] However, in each of the UK legal systems, the premise that children have two parents[14] underpins the statutory framework regulating family life and family disputes.

In the absence of explicit statutory provision for multiple-parented children, courts have determined known biological father disputes with reference to the 'one legal principle in play',[15] namely the paramountcy of the child's welfare. Yet such cases have proved challenging for the judiciary, principally for two reasons. The first of these concerns defining adult roles and responsibilities within the context of a distinct, and relatively novel, construct of parenthood and parenting. The second relates to the development of a consensus in judicial approach, particularly since the precedents regarding the best interests of children in more conventionally comprised families are of limited assistance.

In Section B of this chapter, it is observed that the legislation governing the taxonomy of the parent-child relationship has long been complex, fragmented and, at times, ambiguous. It is demonstrated that the restrictive provisions found in statute increasingly contrast with

---

[11] General Comment No. 14 On The Right of the Child to Have his or her Best Interests Taken as a Primary Consideration UN Doc CRC/C/GC/14, s I(A), V, para. 46.

[12] General Comment No. 14, ibid., paras. 48–9.

[13] For example, British Columbia's Family Law Act 2013, ss. 29–31, allows for three or more legal parents; California's Family Code, § 7612(c) provides that 'In an appropriate action, a court may find that more than two persons with a claim to parentage ... are parents if the court finds that recognising only two parents would be detrimental to the child'.

[14] Traditionally, mother and father (Births and Deaths Registration Act 1953, s. 1; Registration of Births, Deaths and Marriages (Scotland) Act 1965, s. 14).

[15] *DB v AB (Contact: Alternative Families)* [2014] EWHC 384 (Fam), at para. 29, per Holman J.

more inclusive contemporary judicial trends – particularly in known biological father disputes. Such disputes do not fit established two-parent norms, nor does the scheme governing the allocation of legal parenthood in the Human Fertilisation and Embryology Acts[16] provide adequately for them. An overview of evolving judicial rationale is provided in Section C where the underlying (and familiar) logic of decisions made regarding the child's best interests is discussed. However, certain inconsistencies in approach and terminology are also noted in known biological father precedent. It is argued that these inconsistencies are inevitable for jurisdictions, like the UK, in which the precise meaning and applicability of the term 'parent' is itself unclear and where there is a dearth of legal provision for multiple-parented children. Section D offers concluding observations and proposals for reform.

B 'Who Is My Parent? Is This My Child?'[17]

Competing Conceptions of Parenthood

Questions about the precise meaning of 'parent' have long confounded legislators, politicians, judges and academics. The law concerning parenthood is the equivocal product of decades (and in some instances centuries) of piecemeal legislative policy. The word 'parent' frequently refers to a child's biological mother and father, both of whom are commonly named on the birth certificate. Nonetheless, 'parent' is a term inconsistently used across a range of statutes,[18] many of which are directed towards ensuring a restrictive interpretation of the term for a particular purpose.[19] Courts, instead, consider questions of parenthood comprehensively, having regard to the welfare of the child concerned and to evolving social norms. In her oft-cited judgment in *Re G* in 2006, Lady Hale, currently Deputy President of the UK

---

[16] Human Fertilisation and Embryology Acts 1990 and 2008 (both extending throughout the UK), hereinafter referred to as the 1990 and 2008 Act(s)/legislation.

[17] *A & Ors (Human Fertilisation and Embryology Act 2008)* [2015] EWHC 2602, para. 3, per Sir James Munby.

[18] See, e.g., Education (Scotland) Act 1980, s. 135; Children (Scotland) Act 1995, s. 15(1); Adoption and Children Act 2002, ss. 52(6), 52(9), 52(10); Education Act 1996, s. 576.

[19] For different senses in which the term 'parent' is used, see, e.g., Adoption and Children Act 2002, s. 52; Education (Scotland) Act 1980, s. 135.

Supreme Court, approached the subject of contemporary parenthood in a most inclusive manner:

> There are at least three ways in which a person may be or may become a natural parent ... The first is genetic parenthood ... The second is gestational parenthood ... The third is social and psychological parenthood.[20]

According to this definition, a child may have (or acquire) several parents. Yet 'natural parents' and 'natural parenthood' are neither precise medical nor legal categorisations. Such individuals need not be biologically related to the child, nor does statute necessarily empower natural parents to exercise any parental role. Thus, Lady Hale's pragmatic and child-focused definition of what it means to be a parent within the reality of twenty-first century family life is not borne out fully in wider law.

Within the uneven legal landscape, a longstanding distinction has been drawn between bearing the status of being a parent, on one hand, and the possession of parental authority, on the other hand.[21] The former status, sometimes described as being a 'legal parent',[22] creates a lifelong relationship, while the latter – having parental authority[23] – invests in the individual concerned the legal responsibilities and rights necessary to parent a child throughout childhood. These categories, and the distinction between them, were perhaps more unambiguous historically when parental status was a simple matter of lineage.[24] However, in contemporary law, this is not always the case. Where a child is conceived with

---

[20] *Re G (Children) (Residence: Same-sex Partner)* [2006] UKHL 43, per Baroness Hale of Richmond, paras. 33–35.

[21] See Elaine E Sutherland, *Child and Family Law*, 2nd ed. (Edinburgh: W Green, 2008), pp. 203–257, 357–403; Alexander B. Wilkinson and Kenneth McK Norrie, *The Law Relating to Parent and Child in Scotland*, 3rd ed. (Edinburgh: W Green, 2013), pp. 71–97; Bainham and Gilmore, *Children: The Modern Law*, pp. 111–136, 159–162.

[22] The term 'legal parent' has grown in use in the UK in recent years with reference to (often legally created, as opposed to naturally evolving) family dynamics. Broadly speaking, 'legal parenthood gives a lifelong connection between a parent and a child, and affects things like nationality, inheritance and financial responsibility': Human Fertilisation and Embryology, A Code of Practice: Guidance Note 6, para. 6.3, Version 4.0: www.hfea.gov.uk/399.html#guidanceSection3937).

[23] 'Parental authority' is called 'parental responsibility' in s. 3(1) of the (English) Children Act 1989 and 'parental responsibilities and rights' in the Children (Scotland) Act 1995, ss. 1–2.

[24] Whether proved of presumed: Family Law Reform Act 1969, s. 26; Law Reform (Parent and Child) (Scotland) Act 1986, s. 5. Where the child's mother and father were unmarried, establishing a legal parent-child relationship between father and child was (and to a lesser extent still can be) a more onerous process: Family Law Reform Act 1987; Children (Scotland) Act 1995, ss. 3–4. For further reading, see note 21.

reproductive assistance, statutory provisions often override biology by stipulating that neither of the child's legal parents need be genetically related to the child. In most cases, parental authority flows as a direct consequence of legal parenthood, but it might also be imposed by courts upon a wide range of individuals where to do so serves the welfare, or best interests, of the child concerned. Generally, those holding parental authority either live, or have contact, with the child concerned. Orders for parental authority are broadly analogous in English and Scottish law,[25] although some procedural differences exist.[26]

Thus, while a predominant two-parent legal tradition endures, UK law is capable of bestowing upon multiple adults, concurrently, the power to participate in raising a child. Also, many adults fulfil a parenting role – describing themselves, and being described by others, as a 'parent' – without possessing any formal legal entitlement. The UK government made a Declaration, upon ratifying the Convention in 1991, that it would recognise as parents 'only those persons who, as a matter of national law, are treated as parents'.[27] It is nonetheless worth observing the Committee's all-encompassing view on parenthood with reference to best interest considerations. In *General Comment No. 14* the value accorded to family ties, whether formalised or not, was emphasised. 'Parents' may include 'biological, adoptive or foster parents ... members of the extended family or community ... and persons with whom the child has a strong personal relationship'.[28]

Yet, where a dispute arises in UK courts in which several adults assert parental entitlement on genetic, gestational, social and/or legal grounds, questions about the classification and labelling of 'parents' quickly become those of hierarchy. How should the title and/or authority of being a 'parent' in law be apportioned (if at all) among the various models of parenting and parenthood? The question for the court remains: what serves the child's best interests? Answering this question generates particular difficulties when it is addressed (as it is in known

---

[25] Children Act 1989, s. 8(1)(b); Children (Scotland) Act 1995, s. 11(2).

[26] In Scotland, anyone 'with an interest' (including a known biological father) may seek an order for parental authority (Children (Scotland) Act 1995, s. 11(3)(a)(i). In England, those who do not possess the requisite standing must generally seek the court's permission to apply for an award of parental authority (Children Act 1989, ss. 4, 8–11).

[27] UN Treaty Collection, Chapter IV, Human Rights, Convention on the Rights of the Child, UNTS 1577: https://treaties.un.org/pages/viewdetails.aspx?src=treaty&mtdsg_no=iv-11&chapter=4&lang=en.

[28] General Comment No. 14, ibid., para. 59–60.

biological father disputes) in the context of the existing social and legal opacity of the term 'parent'.

Statutory Particulars versus Judicial Generalities

The Human Fertilisation and Embryology Acts of 1990 and 2008 regulate the provision of licensed fertility services throughout the UK. The welfare of any child who may be conceived is not the paramount/primary consideration.[29] Rather, the twin priorities of the legislative framework are reproductive choice and the acquisition of the status of 'legal parenthood'.[30] The legislation provides that the child's gestational mother is the central parental figure. By virtue of carrying the child and giving birth, she will always be recognised as the child's legal mother – irrespective of whether donor eggs or embryos were used.[31]

Where a man merely donates sperm through a licensed clinic, he will not be recognised as the legal father of any child conceived.[32] In those circumstances, if the gestational mother has no partner, any child she conceives will have only one legal parent (i.e., herself).[33] Alternatively, if she is in a relationship, then regardless of the child's genetic parentage, the legislation allows, by agreement, her spouse, civil partner, boyfriend or girlfriend to be treated as the other legal parent of the child.[34] A 'legal parent' in terms of the 1990 and 2008 Acts is placed in the same position as any other legally recognised 'parent' but, in some cases, may still require to obtain parental authority using other statutory

---

[29] Clinics are required to take account generally of the welfare of any child conceived or affected by that child's birth and to provide counselling/general information etc: see 1990 Act, ss. 13(5), 13(6)–(6A); HFEA Code of Practice, 1 April 2015, chapter 8.3.

[30] See note 22 for a definition of legal parenthood.

[31] 1990 Act, s. 27(1); 2008 Act, s. 33(1). The terminology used in respect of all adults is that they are 'to be treated as' the 'mother', 'father' or 'parent' of the child conceived (2008 Act, ss. 33(1); 35(1); 36; 42; 43(c)).

[32] 2008 Act, s. 41(1); 1990 Act, Sch 3, para. 5.

[33] The gestational mother and the known biological father could agree that, as the child's genetic father, he is also recognised as the child's legal father: see 1990 Act Sch 3, para. 5(3).

[34] 2008 Act, ss. 35–40; 42–47; s. 48(1); 48(2). Unless it is shown that the gestational mother's husband, wife or civil partner does not consent to the licensed fertility treatment then he or she will become the second legal parent. Thus, presumed consent to a spouse's/civil partner's fertility treatment creates a(n artificial) legal parent-child relationship. If the gestational mother's partner is not her civil partner or spouse, then he/she will be treated as the second legal parent only by adhering to the 'agreed fatherhood' or 'agreed female parenthood' conditions.

provisions.[35] The provisions enabling two women, jointly, to become legal parents were introduced by the 2008 Act. Here, the terminology is gender-neutral: the legislation characterises the gestational mother's partner as the 'second woman ... parent', rather than child's second mother.[36]

In the reported known biological father cases, however, the legal and factual matrices are often more complex, since reproductive assistance has normally been provided without the involvement (and without the statutory regulation relating to) a licensed clinic. Instead, a private transaction has taken place between biological father and gestational mother – and her female partner. Due to the dearth of statutory regulation of such 'Do It Yourself' (DIY) insemination arrangements, the allocation of legal parenthood is problematic. The 2008 Act allows the gestational mother's spouse/civil partner to become the child's other legal parent in non-clinic cases.[37] However, the Act provides no mechanism whereby the gestational mother's boyfriend or girlfriend might be recognised as the child's other legal parent if a licensed facility is not involved. In that eventuality, where the 1990 and 2008 legislation is silent, genetic truth can be expected to prevail: the known biological father might then expect to be viewed as the father. He will not, however, possess legal authority to parent unless (employing alternative statutory provisions) he marries the mother, is named on the birth certificate, has signed a parental agreement with the child's mother or is awarded parental authority by a court.[38]

Known biological fathers, therefore, generally raise legal proceedings to apply for an award of parental authority and/or contact in a climate of considerable ambivalence. In terms of biology, or genetics, these men are the fathers of the child(ren) concerned – they might have regular contact with their offspring and be referred to in the family as 'daddy'.[39]

---

[35] See, e.g. Children (Scotland) Act 1995, ss. 3(1)(d); 3A; 4A; Children Act 1989, s. 4ZA(1), both statutes providing for the acquisition of parental authority by legal parents who are unmarried/not civil partners through birth registration or formal agreement.

[36] Section 43(c); s. 45(1).   [37] 2008 Act, ss. 35; 42.

[38] Children Act 1989, ss. 4(1)(a); 4(1)(b); 4(1)(c); Children (Scotland) Act 1995, ss. 3, 4, 11. The case law is fact-specific, e.g., in *A v B & C (Lesbian Co-Parents: Role of Father)* [2012] EWCA Civ 285, the known biological father possessed parental authority because he had, for cultural/religious reasons, gone through a marriage ceremony with the gestational mother.

[39] See, e.g., *MA v RS (Contact: Parenting Roles)* [2011] EWHC 2455 (Fam), para. 21, per Hedley J. The father's partner, known to the children as 'Addy', was the second applicant

Yet, from the cases decided, it appears relatively rare for them to be the child's legal parent. Nor can they apply to be recognised as such if the mother's female partner is already the child's second legal parent[40] in terms of the 2008 Act. Regardless of the intricate statutory provisions focused on the acquisition of legal parenthood, all three adults (the gestational mother, her female partner and the child's biological father) might easily be encompassed by Lady Hale's definition of 'natural parenthood'. Her inclusive approach, characterising each adult involved using the vocabulary of parenthood, has gathered momentum among the judiciary. Thus, in *DB v AB (Contact: Alternative Families)*,[41] in 2014, Holman J began his judgment simply by stating that the child concerned had:

> two mothers and one father ... Mrs AB, who is his genetic mother and the person who carried and gave birth to him, and her civil partner, Mrs CB. His genetic father is Mr DB.[42]

An Emerging Picture of Parenthood in Known Biological Father Disputes

Despite undermining the general two-parent ethos of legal policy, this inclusive judicial approach seems entirely consistent with the Article 3(1) obligation to consider family disputes with reference to the individual child's perspective and his or her best interests in 'specific'[43] circumstances. In the closing paragraphs of his judgment in *DB v AB*, Holman J remarked that a father is 'another person in [the child's] life with other interests and experiences to offer', for, he opined, which child 'does not benefit from more love rather than less love'?[44] This judicial perspective is not new. In 2012, Lord Justice Thorpe, sitting in the Court of Appeal, observed in another known biological father case that:

> It is generally accepted that a child gains by having two parents ... [i]t does not follow from that that the addition of a third is necessarily disadvantageous.[45]

---

in the case brought against the female couple (making a total of four adult litigants). The evidence, at para. 21, 'establish[ed] a parenting role for all four adults'.

[40] Section 45(1) also provides that 'Where a woman is treated by virtue of section 42 or 43 as a parent of the child, no man is to be treated as the father of the child.'
[41] [2014] EWHC 384 (Fam), ('*DB v AB*').   [42] *DB v AB*, para. 3.
[43] General Comment No. 14, ibid., para. 46.   [44] Ibid., para. 37.
[45] *A v B (Contact: Alternative Families)* [2012] 1 WLR 3456, para. 24, per Thorpe LJ.

Such comments deepen the chasm between restrictive statutory regulation of parenthood and the increasingly flexible approach of the judiciary. At one end of the spectrum, the 1990 and 2008 Acts empower both of the child's legal parents to circumvent 'the normal rules of genetic parentage automatically and with little consideration of the best interests, or welfare, of the child conceived'.[46] At the other, UK courts rely on the language of welfare when enabling the child's biological father to offer an alternative family construct – one involving more than two parents.[47] This embroils the judiciary in precisely what statute sought to prevent: private family disputes among a range of adults, each with an arguable factual or legal parental claim. In other words the judiciary has picked up a gauntlet that the UK Parliament never intended to throw down.

The emerging picture of parenthood – and of contemporary family life – from the case law is clearly one that includes known biological fathers. The willingness of courts to endorse fatherhood in such cases has been criticised as undermining 'fatherless families', particularly in the wake of the joint female parenthood provisions in the 2008 Act.[48] Yet, even when a child is settled in a 'two-parent lesbian nuclear family',[49] the judiciary routinely stress the 'real benefits' in the child having a 'proper knowledge of ... and some relationship with'[50] his or her biological father. As in other family disputes, opposition from the primary carer(s) is generally insufficient to break established views about

---

[46] Brenda Hale, 'New families and the welfare of children' (2014) 36(1) *JSWL* 26–35 at 28.

[47] See, e.g., *Re G (Children) (Children: Sperm Donors: Leave to Apply for Children Act Orders)* [2013] EWHC 134 (Fam) in which the court took into consideration the underlying two-parent/lesbian parenting provisions in the 2008 Act but nonetheless granted both known biological father applicants leave to apply for contact orders. The orders would, in turn, be granted if in the best interest of the children concerned. For further discussion about welfare-based debate surrounding the provisions of the 1990 and 2008 Acts. See Chapter 9 by Kenneth McK Norrie in this volume.

[48] Here it is worth noting that the 2008 Act amended s. 13(4) of the 1990 Act to remove the reference to the 'need ... for a father', instead inserting reference to the 'need ... for supportive parenting'. See also Leanne J. Smith, 'Clashing symbols? Reconciling support for fathers and fatherless families after the Human Fertilisation and Embryology Act 2008' (2014) 22(1) *CFLQ* 46–70; Aleardo Zanghellini, 'Av B and C [2012] EWCA Civ 285 – heteronormativity, poly-parenting, and the homo-nuclear family' (2012) 24(2) *CFLQ* 475–486 at 475.

[49] *A v B (Contact: Alternative Families)*, [2012] EWCA Civ 285, para. 27, per Thorpe LJ.

[50] *DB v AB (Contact: Alternative Families)* [2014] EWHC 384 (Fam), assuming always, at para. 38 per Holman J, that there is 'nothing to disqualify' the father from exercising contact from a child safety etc. perspective.

the advantages of a positive father-child relationship.[51] Nonetheless, every family (however comprised) is different and the decisions of family courts are fact-specific and welfare-driven. Developing a judicial consensus in determining the precise nature and scope of each parental role has thus proved particularly difficult. There are relatively few reported decisions to date and existing precedent about the best interests of children in more conventional families provides limited assistance.

C Developing a Judicial Consensus

Broad Consensus on Broad Issues

The customary best interests considerations common to private family actions are, then, clearly evident in known biological father judgments. So, for example, the status quo[52] is a factor of importance, as is the conduct of the parties involved[53] and the ascertainable wishes of the child (ren).[54] Children able to express a view are, routinely, found capable of understanding 'entirely' the composition of their own family – and of being comfortable with the role each adult plays in their upbringing.[55] In *T v T (Shared Residence)*, Black LJ noted the findings in evidence that, while the three adults litigating:

> may be very concerned about issues of status such as who could and should be classed as "the parents" ... those matters are not ... of particular concern to the children ... labelling is an issue for or, more accurately, between the parents and adults.[56]

---

[51] For example, *Re S (Parental Responsibility)* [1995] 2 FLR 648; *White v White* 2001 SC 689. This approach is also compatible with precedent about the 'right to respect for ... private and family life' (Article 8(1) of the European Convention on Human Rights ETS Nos 5 and 155). See *G v Netherlands* (1993) 16 EHRR CD38; *Kroon v The Netherlands* (1995) EHRR 263; *Soderbach v Sweden* (2000) 29 EHRR 95; *Anayo v Germany* (2012) 55 EHRR 5.

[52] In in *R v E (Female Parents: Known Father)* [2010] 2 FLR 383, the court endorsed the existing living arrangements whereby the child had been settled in England, living with both female parents, for seven years (the known biological father lived in America).

[53] See *MA v RS (Contact: Parenting Roles)* [2011] EWHC 2455 (Fam) in which the adults' mutual hostility was noted to have impacted negatively upon the children's best interests.

[54] See English Welfare checklist in Children Act 1989, s. 1(3) and Scottish Welfare test in Children (Scotland) Act 1995, s. 11(7)(b).

[55] See, e.g., *MA v RS (Contact: Parenting Roles)* [2011] EWHC 2455 (Fam), at paras. 21, 30, per Hedley J; *T v T (Shared Residence)* [2010] EWCA Civ 1366. For recent research about this, see Susan Golombok, *Modern Families: Parents and Children in New Family Forms*, (Cambridge: Cambridge University Press, 2015), pp. 192–218.

[56] *T v T (Shared Residence)* [2010] EWCA Civ 1366, para. 13, per Black LJ.

Some broad areas of consensus have emerged concerning the endorsement and exercise of parental roles. Where the female couple exercise residential care of the child(ren) for the majority of the time, the known biological father is not generally acknowledged as a parent of equivalent standing.[57] Nevertheless, minimal awards of 'identity contact', merely enabling the child to appreciate his or her heredity, are uncommon among the judgments to date.[58] In some cases, the court has endorsed a role akin to that of a 'distant avuncular'[59] relative for the biological father. In others, where the dispute concerns children living in what might be described as a 'three parent, two homes regime',[60] courts have shown willingness to invest known biological fathers with parental authority.[61] Such an award empowers these fathers to make various important parental decisions, for example, about their child's education or health, jointly with the female (usually also the 'legal') parents. Yet, developing a deeper consensus in respect of the finer points of decision making, and establishing a common lexicon of terms, in known biological father cases continues to be problematic.

Lack of Consensus in Detail – and in Terminology

At first instance in *A v B (Contact: Alternative Families)*, Jenkins J cautioned 'against the use of stereotypes from traditional family models'.[62] A number of factors have been proposed to which reference might be made in determining what arrangements might serve the child's best interests in known biological father cases. These include, for example, ranking adult/'parental' entitlement according to time spent with the child. Even this exercise is not without difficulty. In the Court of Appeal in *A v B (Contact: Alternative Families)*, Thorpe LJ observed that, were the adults in the life of the child concerned to be placed in such a

---

[57] In, e.g., *MA v RS (Contact: Parenting Roles)* ibid, the court drew a clear distinction between the roles of the female couple as primary carers and the role of the biological father and his partner.

[58] See, e.g., *A v B (Contact: Alternative Families)*, [2012] EWCA Civ 285; *MA v RS (Contact: Parenting Roles)* [2011] EWHC 2455 (Fam).

[59] *Re B (Role of Biological Father)*[2007] EWHC 1952 (Fam), at para. 28, per Hedley J who also stressed, at para. 29, that the purpose of contact was not to give the father in that case 'parental status'.

[60] *A v B (Contact: Alternative Families)*, [2012] EWCA Civ 285, at para. 45, per Black LJ, citing Jenkins J at para. 41.

[61] See, e.g., *T v T (Shared Residence)* [2010] ibid; *MA v RS (Contact: Parenting Roles)*, ibid.

[62] [2011] EWHC 2290 (Fam), para. 8.

hierarchy, the full-time nanny – and none of the parties litigating – might well be the child's primary 'parent'.[63]

Another factor suggested is reliance on the nature of the adults' prior relationship and/or terms of any 'co-parenting' discussions, or agreement reached, by the parties at the outset.[64] While this might seem superficially just, the nature of adults' prior relationships (i.e., whether platonic or sexual) surely should not dictate the nature any future relationship with their children? Nor, as Hedley J said in *Re P (Contact)*, should the intentions of parents-to-be (perhaps expressed long before the child's birth) rule out certain considerations about what might serve their child's best interests many years later.[65] In the end, what it is most 'likely to be important, in deciding what is in the child's best interests [is] to identify' in each case, and endorse, 'the source of the child's nurture, stability and security'.[66]

Further, the breadth of vocabulary that has emerged in recent years in attempts to characterise and regulate these family structures is in itself indicative of an absence of judicial consensus. In *B v A, C, D*, Dr Sturge, a Consultant Child and Adolescent Psychiatrist, gave evidence about 'just how deep rooted concepts and language are in relation to families'.[67] She went further, observing that 'the law, in a sense, pre-empts ways of understanding new family structures'.[68] Similar observations have been made in other cases by the judiciary. In *A v B (Contact: Alternative Families)*, Black LJ said that:

> new ways of family life [are] evolving but [have] not yet crystallised and that there [is] not even the language to accommodate them.[69]

---

[63] *A v B (Contact: Alternative Families)*, [2012] EWCA Civ 285, para. 30.
[64] For example, in *Re P (Contact)*, [2011] EWHC 3431 (Fam), Hedley J, acknowledged, at para. 5, that, 'in a case like this we are in what is still new territory in defining the roles of the various parties in the context of parenting' but said that, unlike the gestational mother and her partner, the known biological father and his partner 'have never been, nor did they ever intend to be, resident parents'.
[65] Ibid, at para. 8, Hedley J also noted in the same para. that having regard to an agreement made at the outset did not negate the court's ability to override that if such an agreement no longer represented what was 'right for those children in that case'.
[66] *A v B (Contact: Alternative Families)*, [2012] EWCA Civ 285, para. 45, per Black LJ.
[67] *B v A, C, D (acting by her Guardian)* [2006] EWHC 2 (Fam), evidence of Dr Sturge, para. 57.
[68] Ibid.
[69] *A v B (Contact: Alternative Families)*, [2012] EWCA Civ 285, at para. 37, per Black LJ quoting herself in *Re G (Residence: Same-Sex Partner)* [2005] 2 FLR 957, paras. 33–34.

Although the Court of Appeal ruled that the 'the only principle [to be applied] is the paramountcy of child's welfare',[70] Black LJ acknowledged that, 'despite the passage of time, courts continue to struggle to evolve a principled approach' to cases of this sort.[71] The struggle is an inevitable consequence of long-established, restrictive, statutory policy concerning who, or what, is a 'parent', and the lack of explicit statutory provision for multiple-parented children. In responding to the 'prompt of a minority' bringing such cases, family courts are 'in the vanguard of change.'[72]

The judiciary has on occasion made reference to social research,[73] and the vocabulary that has sprung up within, and around, such litigation is compendious. It includes, for example, describing such families as 'different',[74] 'unconventional' or 'alternative',[75] 'new',[76] 'core' with additional 'identified male parents',[77] 'two-parent lesbian nuclear family'.[78] Parents and parenthood have, similarly, been characterised (and re-characterised) in an assortment of ways – 'biological and psychological' parenthood, 'invisible' and 'essential' parents',[79] 'genetic', 'gestational', 'social' and 'natural' parents,[80] 'core' and 'secondary parents'.[81] Further, questions have been posed which read like modern-day riddles to which the current law offers no clear or constant answer:

---

[70] Ibid., para. 23, per Thorpe LJ.   [71] Ibid., para. 38.
[72] *B v A, C, D (acting by her Guardian)* [2006] EWHC 2 (Fam), para. 32.
[73] For example, in *B v A, C, D*, ibid., Dr Sturge referred to the social research in her evidence.
[74] *Different Families: A Guide for Gay Dads*, Stonewall web-publication, 2010: www.stonewall.org.uk/sites/default/files/A_Guide_for_Gay_Dads__1_.pdf.
[75] For example, *A v B (Contact: Alternative Families)*, ibid.; *DB v AB (Contact: Alternative Families)*, ibid.
[76] Brenda Hale, 'New families and the welfare of children' (2014) 36(1) *JSWL* 26–35.
[77] *A v B (Contact: Alternative Families)*, [2012] EWCA Civ 285, paras. 23; 41–42.
[78] Ibid., para. 27.
[79] Alan Brown, '*Re G; Re Z (Children: Sperm Donors: Leave to Apply for Children Act Orders)*: essential "biological fathers" and invisible "legal parents"', ibid., 237–252.
[80] *Re G (Children) (Residence: Same-sex Partner)* [2006] UKHL 43, per Baroness Hale of Richmond, paras. 33–35. See also Leanne J Smith, 'Principle or pragmatism: Lesbian parenting, shared residence and parental responsibility after *Re G (Residence: Same-Sex Partner)*' (2006) 18(1) *CFLQ* 125–137.
[81] *MA v RS (Contact: Parenting Roles)* [2012] 1 FLR 1056 per Hedley J at para. 16–17, in which he referred to 'secondary parenting' and a parental role of 'secondary capacity'. However, this was later disapproved of by Thorpe LJ in the Court of Appeal in *A v B (Contact: Alternative Families)*, ibid, at para. 30, who said that he 'would not endorse the concept of principal and secondary parents' and that he would 'certainly not categorise [biological fathers] as ... secondary parent[s]'.

for example, 'can a father who shows interest and commitment be a father and not a parent?'[82]

This emerging and varied vocabulary has done nothing to clarify the nature of the issues at stake. The language has grown steadily more opaque during the last decade. This has had the effect, on one hand, of rendering unreliable the application of existing legal concepts about family life[83] while, on the other, providing nothing fixed or certain to replace them. The statutory requirement that the child's best interests are the paramount consideration is certainly a flexible requirement but, as Sutherland observes elsewhere in this volume, 'the price of flexibility is a degree of uncertainty'.[84] While there is undoubtedly an underlying, and familiar, logic to decisions made in known biological father disputes, the judicial narrative lacks conceptual consistency. This is concerning for, as Sir James Munby (President of the Family Division) recently observed, the issues being determined are those of 'the most fundamental gravity and importance ... to any child, to any parent, never mind to future generations and indeed to society at large'.[85]

D Conclusions: Reform

Since 2004, UK statutes have bestowed a range of rights and remedies upon adults in intimate relationships other than heterosexual marriage.[86] This process of reform has produced a variety of new legal terms and statuses.[87] Notwithstanding extensive provision for adult relations, insufficient attention has been devoted to the growing diversity within the

---

[82] *B v A, C, D (acting by her Guardian)* [2006] EWHC 2 (Fam), at para. 57, per Black LJ citing Dr Sturge.
[83] *In re P and L (Contact)* [2012] 1 FLR 1068, Hedley J observed in, para. 5, that such families are 'still new territory' to the law, noting that conventional models would not work and that 'a distinct concept of parenting and parental roles' would be necessary.
[84] See Elaine E Sutherland, 'Article 3 of the United Nations Convention on the Rights of the Child: The Challenges of Vagueness and Priorities', chapter 1 of this volume, at p. 22.
[85] *A & Ors (Human Fertilisation and Embryology Act 2008)* [2015] EWHC 2602, para. 3.
[86] See, e.g., the Civil Partnership Act 2004 (UK-wide legislation); Family Law (Scotland) Act 2006. In 2014, the Marriage and Civil Partnership (Scotland) Act 2014 and the Marriage (Same Sex Couples) Act 2013 each came into force enabling same-sex couples to marry throughout the UK.
[87] For example, 'Civil Partner' (Civil Partnership Act 2004, s. 1); 'Cohabitant' (Family Law (Scotland) Act 2006, s. 25); 'Domestic interdicts', the new s. 18A amendment introduced by the Family Law (Scotland) Act 2006, s. 31(3), to the Matrimonial Homes (Family Protection)(Scotland) Act 1981.

sphere of family life. Increasing reproductive freedom has generated new – and 'by no means unusual'[88] – multiple-parenting structures. These, in turn, require the amendment of existing law and/or the introduction of new legal structures if the child's best interests are to be served.

Certain steps towards reform are proposed. Firstly, public consultation is required on the question of who, or what, ought to be considered in contemporary family life and society to be a 'parent'– and of the legal consequences that should attach to parental status. If law is to meet the needs of society then legal policymakers must clearly identify and reflect in statute what those needs are. Secondly, the approaches adopted by jurisdictions[89] already legislating for multiple-parenting should be studied. Thirdly, in view of current trends in assisted reproduction, the regulatory framework of the 1990 and 2008 Acts should be amended to provide more comprehensively for the allocation of 'legal parenthood' in private ('DIY') insemination cases. Also, the legislation[90] should enable, in appropriate cases, the registration of more than two adults as a child's 'legal parent'. Finally, in terms of current statute, gestational mothers can, by formal agreement,[91] share their parental authority with another adult, namely their child's father, a step-parent[92] or their female partner. These agreements were designed to enable co-parenting by adults who live in a permanent family relationship with a child and his or her mother. Consideration should now be given to extending the use of such parental agreements to all relevant adults in families in which a child has two female parents and a known biological father.

---

[88] *Re P* [2011] EWHC 3431 (Fam), per Hedley J at para. 5.   [89] See note 12.

[90] This would also require amendment of related legislation, such as the Births and Deaths Registration Act 1953 and the Registration of Births, Deaths and Marriages (Scotland) Act 1965.

[91] Children (Scotland) Act 1995, s. 4 ('Acquisition of parental rights and responsibilities by natural father'); s. 4A ('Acquisition of parental responsibilities and parental rights by second female parent by agreement with mother'); Children Act 1989, s. 4 ('Acquisition of Parental Responsibility by father'), s. 4ZA(b) ('Acquisition of parental responsibility by second female parent'). In both England and Scotland any such agreement must be made in the prescribed statutory form and formally registered before it has effect (1995 Act, s. 4(2); 1989 Act s. 4(2)).

[92] This step-parent provision only exists in English legislation: the 1989 Act, s. 4A(a) states that, if the mother's ex-partner also retains parental authority, 'both parents may by agreement with the step-parent provide for the step-parent to have parental responsibility for the child'.

9

Surrogacy in the United Kingdom: An Inappropriate Application of the Welfare Principle

KENNETH MCK. NORRIE

A Introduction

The proposition has been well explored in the literature that the 'best interests' test in child law is uncertain of application, vague, and even meaningless on its own.[1] The focus on the child's best interests can often obscure the reality of the dispute before the court (which is frequently caused by a clash of adult interests); it can blind us to the reality of the deeply paternalistic assumptions underpinning the principle;[2] and it can divert attention from important social policies in relation to children in general to the understandable desire to improve the lot of the particular child whose fate is in the hands of the court. For these reasons, and others, it is important to keep in mind that Article 3 of the UN Convention on the Rights of the Child – at any rate, as manifested in domestic legislation – is not a principle of ubiquitous application that will govern every legislative, judicial or administrative decision that has

---

[1] See Nicholas Bala 'Judicial Discretion and Family Law Reform in Canada' (1986) 5 *Canadian Journal of Family Law* 15; Laura Dupaix, 'Best Interests Revisited: In Search of Guidelines' (1987) 3 *Utah Law Review* 651; Jonathan Montgomery 'Rhetoric and Welfare' (1989) 9 *Oxford Journal of Legal Studies* 395; Stephen Parker 'The Best Interests of the Child: Principles and Problems' (1994) 8 *International Journal of Law and the Family* 26; Helen Reece, 'The Paramountcy Principle: Consensus or Construct?' (1996) 49 *Current Legal Problems* 267; John Eekelaar, 'Beyond the Welfare Principle' (2002) 14 *Child and Family Law Quarterly* 23; Elsje Bonthuys 'The Best Interests of Children in the South African Constitution' (2006) 20 *International Journal of Law and Policy and the Family* 23.

[2] As Kilkelly points out, the concept of children's 'rights', foundational of most other articles in the UN Convention on the Rights of the Child, is noticeably absent from Article 3: Ursula Kilkelly, 'The Best Interests of the Child: A Gateway to Children's Rights?'; Chapter 2 in the present volume.

the potential to affect any child.[3] When courts fail to remember this and seek to apply the welfare principle to an issue that in domestic law is not governed by that principle, the end result is a distortion of the law and a deviation from doctrinal principle that risks subverting the Rule of Law itself. In this chapter, I seek to illustrate this point through an examination of one narrow issue: the treatment by the English courts of the statutory conditions for the making of a parental order after a surrogacy arrangement, and in particular the statutory time limit for the making of such an order.

B Making a Parental Order

Section 54 of the Human Fertilisation and Embryology Act 2008[4] allows the court to make what it (rather unhelpfully) calls a 'parental order': this transfers parenthood from a surrogate mother to a commissioning couple, but only if various conditions are satisfied, including that the applicants be a couple, that one of them is the genetic parent of the child and that the existing parents consent.

The requirement in s. 54(2) that the applicants be a couple raised a potential problem in *A v P*[5] for, while the application itself had been made by a couple, unfortunately one of them died before the application could be dealt with. The court held that the order could be made in favour of the survivor. Now, as a matter of strict statutory interpretation this decision is unobjectionable, for the requirement is not that the order be made in favour of two people, but that the application be made by two people. The policy justification for limiting parental orders to couples was not explored, though an underpinning assumption that joint parenting is better for children than single parenting is the obvious (if not the only plausible) explanation.[6] It may be noted that no such assumption is manifested in the adoption legislation in either Scotland or England and Wales, where sole adoption applications have long been permitted.

---

[3] See further John Eekelaar, 'Two Dimensions of the Best Interests Principle: Decisions About Children and Decisions Affecting Children'; Chapter 5 in the present volume. This proposition underlay the UK Supreme Court's decision in *Rhodes v OPO* [2015] UKSC 32.

[4] For a discussion of other complexities created by the UK's human fertilisation and embryology legislation, see Lesley-Anne Barnes Macfarlane, 'Serving Best Interests in Known Biological Father Disputes in the UK'; Chapter 8 in the present volume.

[5] [2011] EWHC 1738 (Fam).   [6] See *Re Z (A Child)* [2015] EWFC 73.

Another condition, contained in s. 54(4), requires that the child has its home with both applicants both at the time the application was made and at the time the order is made. This also proved problematical in *A v P*, because by the time the order came to be made, after the death of one of the applicants, it could no longer be said that the child had his home with that deceased applicant. The court, however, held that the condition could be found to be satisfied if it were interpreted expansively, as required by s. 3 of the Human Rights Act 1998. Theis J held that to refuse the order in this case would amount to an interference in the family life that had been established between the child and the surviving applicant, with whom he had lived all of his short life. The judge found reinforcement in this conclusion in Article 8 of the UN Convention on the Rights of the Child, which protects the child's right to identity. The same judge made a parental order in favour of a commissioning couple who had actually separated, holding that the children had homes with each of the couple, and with no one else.[7]

The condition that has generated most judicial discussion is that in s. 54(8), which provides that the court must be satisfied that no money or other benefit, other than reasonable expenses, has been given or received for or in consideration of the making of the order, the granting of any consent, the handing over of the child or the making of any arrangements in respect of the surrogacy agreement. But this prohibition on payments is explicitly qualified by the words 'unless authorised by the court'. The courts have proved ready to authorise payments that would otherwise amount to an unlawful infringement of this provision:[8] indeed, in no reported case has the court refused to authorise such payments. The authorities were reviewed by Hedley J in *Re X and another (Children) (Parental Order: Surrogacy)*[9] where he said that the court must ask itself three questions: '(1) was the sum paid disproportionate to reasonable expenses? (2) Were the applicants acting in good faith and without 'moral taint' in their dealings with the surrogate mother? (3) Were the applicants party to any attempt to defraud the authorities?'

---

[7] *A v X* [2015] EWHC 2080. It is worth noting that had the couple been unmarried they might have faced difficulty in establishing that they were in an 'enduring family relationship' (as required by s. 54(2)(c)). Does the welfare of the child demand the making of a distinction between married and unmarried couples, or demand that the statutory distinction be ignored?

[8] A review of the case law may be found in A.B. Wilkinson and K. McK. Norrie, *The Law Relating to Parent and Child in Scotland*, 3rd edn (Edinburgh, W. Green, 2013) para. 4.35.

[9] [2009] Fam 71.

If the answers were 'no' to each of these questions then payments should be authorised whenever the welfare of the child requires that the order be made. It may be noted in passing that the judge examined the child's welfare only *after* the issue of authorisation had been dealt with: this indicates a (doctrinally sound) understanding that the condition in s. 54(8) is a condition-precedent, failure to satisfy which would render the making of the order incompetent – and an examination of the child's welfare irrelevant.[10]

While these authorisations are clearly within the terms of the Act, and so constitute no challenge to the rule of law, the fact that commercial surrogacy has been effectively permitted by this means is entirely inconsistent with the otherwise strong prohibition of that practice in the Surrogacy Arrangements Act 1985.[11] Few would question that the making of the order even when the child has been paid for may well be in the best interests of the child involved, but that rather misses the point of the prohibition, which can only achieve its aims if general social policy is not allowed to be trumped by individual cases. Given the dangers of international surrogacy in particular, but also with surrogacy in general, there are obvious reasons why a parental order should be available only in highly constrained (and non-commercial) circumstances. These reasons tend to relate to the protection of children – and parents – in general. The prohibition on payments beyond reasonable expenses serves the function of reducing the risk that the practice of surrogacy will become a means of buying (and, of course, selling) babies – but when you have a baby who has been bought, its own best interests may well be to allow the purchasers to obtain their parental order. Twenty years ago Lord Weir in the Court of Session identified a 'clash of two principles' – the 'social evil of trafficking in children' and 'the duty of the court in an individual case ... [to] safeguard and promote the welfare of the child'.[12]

---

[10] It is to be noted that the Human Fertilisation and Embryology (Parental Orders) Regulations (2009 SI 2010/985) do not contain any equivalent to s. 34 of the Adoption and Children (Scotland) Act 2007. This explicitly provides that the court may make an adoption order even although the applicants have committed the criminal offence in s. 72 (making payments in consideration of the adoption of the child). Nor is there any provision in the English adoption legislation allowing an adoption to be made in the face of commission of an offence under s. 92 of the Adoption and Children Act 2002 but in *A, B v A Local Authority, C* [2014] EWHC 4816 (Fam) Keehan J held that the absence of any prohibition on making an adoption order meant that he could do so.

[11] The prohibition is so strong that even firms of solicitors charging for legal advice as to the effects of the Act might be caught: see *JP v LP* [2014] EWHC 595 (Fam).

[12] *C v S* 1996 SLT 1387 at 1399.

He went on: 'The risk of [child-trafficking] is a real one nowadays in view of the marked decline in the number of babies now available for adoption. And the resort to the practice of surrogacy seems likely to exacerbate the problem. It is therefore of importance that the court should be careful not to lose sight of this principle of public policy.' One cannot help but be left deeply uncomfortable with the ease with which the social policy of discouraging the buying of children – a policy that is virtually unquestioned in relation to adoption – is cast aside in the surrogacy situation by the understandable desire of judges to authorise unlawful payments as a means of satisfying the condition precedent for making a parental order that is in the interests of the individual child before the court. The dangers of this policy in the context of adoption are adverted to in Whitecross's contribution to the present volume.[13] It remains speculation whether the courts would be quite so ready to subvert sound general policy in the adoption situation for the sake of individual children though there are a small number of cases in which adoptions have been permitted following unlawful payments.[14]

C Time Limits: *Re X (A Child) (Surrogacy: Time Limit)*[15]

The cases previously discussed may all be justified by established rules of statutory interpretation, as modified by the Human Rights Act 1998. *Re X (A Child)*, however, goes very much further and amounts to a judicial repealing of one of the conditions in s. 54, for no better reason than that its application would have denied the particular child the order that (the judge said) was necessary for its welfare. Section 54(3) of the Human Fertilisation and Embryology Act 2008 provides that for a court to make a parental order after a surrogacy arrangement 'the applicants must apply for the order during the period of six months beginning with the day on which the child is born'. The Act quite deliberately uses the imperative 'must' and the obvious interpretation of this is that a parental

---

[13] See, Richard W. Whitecross, 'Article 3 and Adoption in and from India and Nepal'; Chapter 12 in the present volume.

[14] In *A, B v A Local Authority, C* [2014] EWHC 4816 (Fam) an adoption order was made notwithstanding an unlawful payment, which the judge did not explicitly authorise (the police having investigated, and deciding to take no action); a decision to the same effect under the prior legislation is *Re C (A Minor) (Adoption: Illegality)* [1999] 2 WLR 202. But see *Re C (A Minor)* [1993] 1 FLR 87 where the adoption application was refused in face of an unlawful payments.

[15] [2014] EWHC 3135 (Fam).

order is simply not available after the child reaches the age of six months: the application becomes then incompetent. So, indeed, it was stated (if *obiter*) in a number of earlier decisions.[16]

However, in *Re X (A Child)*, Sir James Munby, President of the Family Division of the English High Court, sitting as a judge of first instance, was faced with an application for a parental order in respect of a child who was almost three. The reason the applicants had not applied earlier was that they were unaware of the 2008 Act that permitted parental orders to be made at all. The child had been born in India, handed over to the commissioning couple, and the surrogate mother and her husband signed a document relinquishing all parental responsibilities and parental rights. Both the surrogacy arrangement and the relinquishing document were lawful under Indian law. The child was brought to the UK by the commissioning couple and had lived with them ever since.[17] Their application for a parental order ought to have been dismissed as incompetent, but instead Munby P allowed it to proceed on the basis that the word 'must' in s. 54(3) did not mean 'must'. If it does not mean 'must', then either s. 54(3) as a whole has no meaning, or any application after the statutory six-month period will be heard only if it satisfies judicially created conditions, yet to be revealed to us. How did Munby P reach this unexpected result?

He pointed out, first, that the Parliamentary debates were silent as to why the six-month time limit had been included in the legislation.[18] This is true, though it is not unusual for a provision to be enacted without being explicitly debated and it is a leap of logic to conclude from the fact that no reason for the prohibition was offered in the parliamentary process that there was no reason for the prohibition. He then pointed out that the Parental Orders regulations[19] require the court to make the welfare of the child its paramount consideration. This is also true, but the welfare test in adoption only applies once the conditions precedent for the making of the order have been satisfied – once the application is

---

[16] *Re X (Children) (Parental Order: Foreign Surrogacy)* [2009] EWHC 3030, per Hedley J at [12]; *J v G* [2013] EWHC 1432, per Theis J at [29]. It was a matter of concession in *JP v LP & Others* [2015] EWHC 595 (Fam).

[17] Actually, the facts were marginally more complicated since the couple had separated and lived apart for some time before being reconciled.

[18] At [17].

[19] N. 10. These import s.1 of the Adoption and Children Act 2002 for England and Wales and s.14 of the Adoption and Children (Scotland) Act 2007 for Scotland: each of these provisions makes the welfare of the child the court's paramount consideration.

shown to be competent, in other words – and that must be so in this context also: in other words the welfare of the child cannot determine the very competency of an action relating to the child.[20]

Munby P then explored how the higher courts have dealt with statutory time limits expressed as imperatives, and he pointed to *Regina v Soneji*[21] where the House of Lords rejected the traditional distinction between 'mandatory' and 'directory' requirements in favour of a purposive approach to interpretation of such requirements. He held, without much evidence, that the purpose of the surrogacy legislation was to enhance the child's welfare and concluded that it could not have been within Parliament's intention that an order that would enhance a child's welfare was absolutely not available in any circumstances outwith the time limit.[22] Interestingly he felt able to come to this conclusion without relying on the ECHR but he held additionally that if he were wrong on the point of pure statutory interpretation he would have decided the same way via the ECHR. His decision to allow an application out of time has subsequently been followed on a number of occasions and indeed an application has not since been rejected on the basis of being out of time.[23]

Let us pause for a moment to consider just exactly what Munby P has done here. First, he has implicitly rejected an analysis of the conditions in s. 54 that sees them all as competency-determining conditions precedent. This approach allows him to ignore the decision of the Supreme Court in *Re B (A Child)*,[24] which had held that welfare considerations are not relevant at the 'threshold' stage of the inquiry: he is able therefore to bring in the welfare of the child at the stage of interpreting what the provision means. Second, he has constructed the limitations contained in s. 54 as being for the benefit of the individual child rather than as a means of furthering any generalised social policy of keeping surrogacy within constrained – and benign – circumstances. A purposive approach to statutory interpretation, however, depends for its validity on a robust exploration and identification of the *purpose* and judicial assertion simply will not do. It is wrong to assume that any statutory provision

---

[20] A point made in another context by the present writer in 'Children's Hearings, Relevant Persons and the Welfare of the Child' (2014) Greens Family Law Bulletin 128/4, the argument in which was adopted by the Court of Session in *T v Locality Reporter* 2015 Fam LR 2.
[21] [2006] 1 AC 340. [22] At [55].
[23] See *AB v CT* [2015] EWFC 12; *A v X* [2015] EWHC 2080. And in *Re A (A Child)* [2015] EWHC 911 the application was made a full eight years late.
[24] [2013] UKSC 33.

in which a child is the central element has a purpose of enhancing that child's welfare. It is at the very least arguable that the various limitations to the making of a parental order in s. 54 have as their major purpose the pressing social need to protect the surrogate mother from exploitation (both financial and emotional) and to ensure that a child's legal status is clarified and settled as early in the child's life as possible. Other obvious purposes serve the adults' interests too, by ensuring that a parental order is available only when the surrogacy arrangement behind it has been carried out to the satisfaction of all parties, so that there can be a 'speedy consensual regularisation of the legal parental status of the child's carers'.[25] Section 54 appears in a Part of the 2008 Act headed 'Parenthood in Cases Involving Assisted Reproduction'. Parenthood is an issue that very directly affects children but it needs to be remembered that it is not exclusively about children. Parenthood affects parents too. If this is so, then the very fact that there are statutory limitations on when a parental order may be made inevitably means that sometimes the order will not be available, even in circumstances in which it is undeniably in the best interests of the child to make the order – for the justification of the limitation may be traced to the needs of the parents.

The end result of *Re X (A Child)* is that the best interests of an individual child have been used – and remember Munby P explicitly said he comes to this conclusion by means of statutory interpretation and not by application of the ECHR – not just to rewrite a statute but to repeal a statutory provision. This is 'crossing the Rubicon'[26] that separates the interpretative and the legislative functions. As such it is a decision that could not have been reached by application of the Human Rights Act 1998 which allows judges to read down statutory provisions that are inconsistent with the ECHR, but only when doing so does not go against the grain of the legislation.[27] To interpret 'the order must be applied for within six months' to mean 'the order may also be applied for after six months' goes very much against the grain of the limitation, by allowing

---

[25] This was the purpose identified by Eleanor King J in *JP v LP and Others* [2014] EWHC 595 (Fam) at [30].

[26] In Lord Steyn's famous phrase in *Ghaidan v Mendoza* [2004] UKHL 30 at [49].

[27] Though Munby P said, obiter and *per incuriam*, that he would have reached the same conclusion in this case via the ECHR, when asked subsequently to utilise the interpretative power in s. 3 of the Human Rights Act to disregard the condition that a parental order required two applicants, he refused to do so on the ground that this went beyond interpretation and into the forbidden realms of judicial legislation: *Re Z (A Child)* [2015] EWFC 73.

judges to ignore it. If Munby P is correct, the end result would be that judges could use the best interests of the child to achieve not only ends that are not otherwise permitted, but also those ends that are explicitly forbidden by Parliament. Given the protean nature of the best interests principle this is, to say the least, a startling proposition.

This decision also illustrates the anchorless nature of the welfare principle, for the judge has invoked it to achieve a purpose that *he* conceived necessary but which is certainly not 'necessary' in the sense of being an imperative.[28] The judge may have been right to say that '[the child's] best interests plainly demand'[29] a mechanism to be applied that transferred parenthood from the surrogate parents to the commissioning couple. But that would take us nowhere if the law provided no such mechanism: any court from a jurisdiction that did not have within its range of orders an order that would achieve transference of parenthood could not invent one simply on the basis of the child's welfare: nor should a judge in the UK, where parental orders are available, ignore their requirements for competency simply on that basis. And this is especially so when, as in the UK, the law does indeed provide a perfectly satisfactory mechanism to transfer parenthood even when a parental order is not available: adoption. Now, Munby P did not explore very thoroughly why an adoption order would not achieve everything the child required to satisfy his or her best interests. He states[30] that it is 'plainly in X's interests for the commissioning parents, with ... whom he has lived for almost all of his short life, to be recognised in law as his legal parents, now and for his entire life' – an assessment that is clearly within the remit of the judge. He goes on (with rather more absolutist language than was, surely, necessary): 'it cannot ... be in his interests for the surrogate parents to retain any form of legal right or responsibility in relation to him'. Be that as it may, his conclusion that this required a parental order is a leap of logic: all that was needed was an order that achieved a transference of parenthood. Munby P does recognise that there are two ways of achieving this – a parental order or an adoption order – but he asserts that 'Adoption is not an attractive solution given the commissioning father's existing biological relationship with X'.[31]

---

[28] The phrase 'welfare requires' where it appears as a ground to dispense with parental consent to adoption was held by the Supreme Court to import a test of 'necessity': *S v L* 2012 SLT 961.
[29] At [7].   [30] At [77].   [31] At [7].

Yet the very existence of the availability of adoption means that the authorities Munby P relied upon to justify this departure from the natural meaning of 'must' can be clearly distinguished, because they all involved situations in which there was no alternative. So for example in *Adesina v Nursing and Midwifery Council*[32] the statutory provision in question required an appeal against a decision to strike a person off from their professional register to be brought within twenty-eight days: the appellant was two days out of time and the Court of Appeal (though finding in the circumstances of the case that she had no good reason for delay and so could not now appeal) held that the twenty-eight-day day limit could not in all cases be regarded as absolute. But in that case there was no alternative: either the struck off nurse could appeal or she could not, and if she could not the consequences were devastating. But with s. 54 of the 2008 Act, there is an alternative. If the parental order is not available because the conditions precedent for its making have not been satisfied it does not mean that the child will be left parentless: it simply means that the parties would need to apply for the near-identical order that would achieve for the parent-child relationship everything that is in the law's gift. A parental order was not available in the Scottish case of *C v S*[33] because the surrogate mother changed her mind and withheld her consent; the commissioning couple therefore sought and obtained an adoption order instead and there is no sense in which this outcome can be regarded as devastating to either the applicants or the child. (It might have been devastating for the mother).

Why, then, might it be that an adoption order was not held to satisfy the child's best interests in *Re X (A Child)*, which demanded instead a parental order? Munby P does not explain, but the question was explored by Theis J in *AB & CD v CT*.[34] The facts in that case were substantially similar to those in *Re X (A Child)*, except that it involved a British (same-sex) couple living in Australia who had taken the children from India to Australia before deciding to emigrate to the UK as a family, where they then applied for an adoption order, by which time the children were over three years old. There were other deeply troubling issues in the case: it was unclear whether the surrogate mother was married or not, which would affect whether the biological father (one

---

[32] [2013] EWCA Civ 818. [33] 1996 SLT 1387.
[34] [2015] EWFC 12. See also Russell J's examination of the point in *Re A (A Child)* [2015] EWHC 911 at [56]–[69], and Munby P's discussion in *Re Z (A Child)* [2015] EWFC 73 at [16] and [36].

of the commissioning couple) was recognised as father without the 2008 Act and whether the mother's husband had to consent to whatever order the commissioning couple sought. The mother, though signing a legal document giving up her parental rights in highly legalistic terms (which included references to case law but did not amount to consent to a transference of parenthood itself) had, worryingly, signed that document by thumb print since she was illiterate; and now she could not be found.

After making the adoption application, the commissioning couple then found out about the case of *Re X (A Child)* and they asked for the adoption proceedings to be stayed to allow them to make an application for a parental order.

Now, the reason for the delay in applying for the parental order was again sheer ignorance, compounded by the fact that when the surrogacy arrangement was made – and given effect to – the parties were living in Australia and the UK courts would have no jurisdiction. Theis J explored rather more thoroughly than Munby P had done in the earlier case why making a parental order rather than insisting on adoption was so clearly in the interests of the children that the statutory provision could be judicially ignored/expanded/altered. Theis J held that 'the applicants and the children ... will suffer ... *immense and irremediable prejudice* ... if this application is stopped in its tracks'.[35] 'The applicants' legal relationship with the children', she went on, 'would be significantly different from what they had intended'.[36] This is factually not true. At the time of the surrogacy arrangement, the applicants had intended to use the Australian courts to transfer parental responsibility away from the mother to them. After they moved to the UK, their intention changed to one to seek an adoption order and transfer thereby full parenthood from the mother to them. Even if their 'intent' was not directed to one legal order or another, their intent to create a secure and stable family relationship that would be recognised by the law in all respects and for all purposes is achieved by either an adoption order or a parental

---

[35] At [40] (emphasis added).
[36] I do not have time to address here the deeply problematical use of 'intent' to determine either who a child's parents are or what order affecting parenthood should be made. See Gillian Douglas, 'The Intention to be a Parent and the Making of Mother' (1994) 57 *Modern Law Review* 636; Kirsty Horsey, 'Challenging Perceptions: Legal Parenthood and Surrogacy' (2010) 22 *Child and Family Law Quarterly* 449. The Supreme Court of California famously used intention to resolve a parenthood dispute in *Johnson v Calvert* 851 P (2d) 776 (1993).

order, and the legal relationship created thereby is not 'significantly different' depending upon which order is made. Theis J goes on to state that 'there are positive benefits to the applicants and the children in allowing this application to proceed',[37] but what these benefits are – over and above those inherent in an adoption order – are not obvious.[38] The applicants had argued that there is a difference between an adoption order and a parental order: the former creates a presumption in law that the child is treated as if the biological child of the adopters; the latter does not involve that presumption and proceeds on the assumption[39] that one of the applicants is the biological parent. This of course ignores the fact that adoption by a genetic parent has always been possible in law[40] (if less common now that step-parents do not need to include the natural parent in their application[41]). The applicants also argued that an adoption order is designed for a child who already exists, while a parental order is designed for a child whose conception and birth have been planned and commissioned by the parents. This is factually true but does not, it seems to me, change the very nature of the order nor its legal effects. All it amounts to, as Theis J recognised, is that adoption is designed for one situation while parental orders are designed for another[42]: yet since they substantially overlap (both effect a transference of parenthood, neither can be revoked,[43] and the effects of both will last for the lifetime of the subject of the order)[44] the use of one when the other is not (for whatever reason) available seems an entirely satisfactory outcome for all concerned. Or at the very least, it does not seem so

---

[37] At [40].
[38] Russell J in *Re A (A Child)* [2015] EWHC 911 drew attention to the child's right of identity which, she asserted, could only be fully protected by a parental order rather than an adoption order. This ignores the fact that both orders change the legal reality, and neither order completely reflects the genetic reality.
[39] It is a condition required by s. 54(1)(b): one wonders how absolute?
[40] In Scots law, see Adoption and Children (Scotland) Act 2007, s. 30(1)(d).
[41] This amendment was made in Scotland when s. 97 of the Children (Scotland) Act 1995 amended the then extant Adoption (Scotland) Act 1978.
[42] See also *Re A (A Child)* [2015] EWHC 911 where at [68] Russell J said this: 'The very existence of parental orders is a testament to the decision of Parliament that adoption orders do not befit children born through surrogacy. Parliament provided parental orders to be the legal remedy designed for surrogacy situations and it is a contrivance to use adoption as an alternative solution unless there is no other option within the court's discretion'. The time limit, in other words, is discretionary.
[43] See *G v G* [2013] 1 FLR 286.
[44] 'The effect of a parental order is the same as an adoption order': per Theis J in *A v P* [2011] EWHC 1738 at [30].

outrageously unsatisfactory that it creates 'immense and irremediable prejudice' to either the child or the commissioning parents such as to justify a radical rewriting of a statutory rule.[45]

D Conclusion

These decisions illustrate the dangerous subjectivity of 'welfare'. One of the few facets of welfare that we can be unshakeably confident about is that children's welfare is protected by having a secure upbringing by people unchallengeably recognised in law as their parents: this may be equally achieved by either an adoption order or a parental order. Even if there may be some emotional benefit to the child in being the subject of an order that recognises that they were planned and that they have a genetic connection with one of their (legal) parents over an order that does not imply the former and need not involve the latter, that benefit is so marginal and so speculative that it does not justify rewriting an unambiguous statutory provision. Our concern for the welfare of an individual child has been misused in this case. The danger is that if the requirement in s. 54(3) can be interpreted out of existence if the child's welfare demands it, what is to prevent the other requirements in s. 54 from being ignored for the same reason? If the limitations in s. 54 are even partly designed to protect the surrogate mother, then to ignore them runs the risk of causing her 'immense and irremediable prejudice'.

We can live with some of the expansive interpretations of the limitations in s. 54 discussed above, but only because – like not requiring the mother's consent if she cannot be found – doing so involves, as we have seen, no violence to the terms of the statute.[46] And Munby P himself refused to ignore (or disapply) the requirement in s. 54(1) that the application be made by a couple, notwithstanding that it was in the child's interests to have the relationship with the

---

[45] In *A v P* at [30] Theis J lists some practical disadvantages in seeking an adoption order if a parental order is refused. But these were not substantive disadvantages and could have been avoided by seeking the correct order first. More substantive policy limitations to the availability of adoption are listed by Russell J in *Re A (A Child)* [2015] EWHC 911 at [69].

[46] See *R v T* [2015] EWFC 22. Courts have a habit of referring to 'dispensing' with the mother's consent in this circumstance (see *Re D (Minors) (Surrogacy)* [2013] 1 All ER 962), but this is not appropriate: if the mother cannot be found then her consent is simply not needed and there is no need to dispense with that consent.

genetic father (who was acting alone) regularised.[47] But his decision in *Re X (A Child)* invites challenge to every other condition in s. 54 including, for example, the requirement for parental consent. What would Munby P's response be if the mother were explicitly withholding her consent? There is no statutory basis for dispensing with parental consent, just as there is no statutory basis for extending the time limit, and it would surely be unacceptable to ignore that requirement in order to ensure that the commissioning couple become the child's parents even if the mother refuses, and adoption is not available because there is no ground upon which to dispense with parental consent.[48] What if the surrogate mother became pregnant by sexual intercourse?[49] What if the mother's consent was given within six weeks of the birth and she then died?[50] What if there was no genetic connection with either of the applicants[51] but in all other respects the commissioning couple do everything the statute asks for and it is in the interests of the child to regularise the relationship between him and her and the commissioning couple? Few of these conditions precedent to the making of a parental order trace their justification to the welfare of the child, but if any is to be dropped then it is surely for Parliament to do so. In sum, the cases discussed in this chapter illustrate, in my view, the fact that the focus on the child's best interests has blinded the courts to the requirement to follow statutory language, which risks disrupting the balance of interests struck by Parliament through all the limitations in s. 54.

Best interests is not a trump card, a grundnorm, a high level principle. In domestic legal systems it is a statutory rule that needs to be interpreted consistently with other – equally valid – statutory rules. The Rule of Law demands no less. The best interests principle in international law,

---

[47] *Re Z (A Child)* [2015] EWFC 73. The same judge subsequently held the rule to be unjustifiably discriminatory: see *Re Z (a Child)* [2016] EWHC 1191.

[48] Admittedly, this example becomes circular since one of the grounds for dispensing with consent is the child's welfare: Adoption and Children Act 2002, s. 52(1)(b); Adoption and Children (Scotland) Act 2007, s. 31(3)(d). Parental consent was refused in *C v S* 1996 SLT 1387 and *Re MW (Adoption: Surrogacy)* [1995] 2 FLR 789.

[49] It is a condition in s. 54(1)(a) of the 2008 Act that the mother becomes pregnant by artificial means. Do we really believe that this is designed to promote the child's welfare, or that welfare is affected by the mechanism through which sperm is inserted into the child's mother?

[50] It is a condition in s. 54(7) that consent be given after six weeks. How absolute is that time limit?

[51] This condition is found in s. 54(1)(b).

encapsulated by Article 3 of the UN Convention on the Rights of the Child, is an aspiration and a guide to state action: it is an important reminder that judicial, legislative and administrative bodies should always keep children at the forefront of their attention. It is no more than that and treating it otherwise denies state legislatures the power to adopt good social policy, compromising thereby the welfare of children in general by favouring the individual child.

10

Baby Switching: What Is Best for the Baby?[*]

TRYNIE BOEZAART

A Introduction

In biblical times King Solomon drew his sword to establish who the real parent was. A recent case of baby switching in South Africa uncovered disturbing facts relating to babies being handed over to the 'wrong' mothers while in neonatal care. In this case, eighteen months elapsed before the truth was discovered and in the absence of Solomon's sword, a legal process has since been started to establish the best interests of the children involved with the view to guide the process accordingly.[1] What might make this case unique is that it is the only known case where babies of different genders were switched.

This chapter will consider the best interests of the child where the negligence of hospital staff has led to babies being handed over to mothers with whom they have no genetic bond. The reported cases in South Africa will provide a factual background for this discussion. The chapter will also identify problematic issues relating to the balancing of children's rights and parental responsibilities and rights as they relate to the acquisition and termination of parental responsibilities and rights in this particular context. The case law in other jurisdictions

---

[*] This material is based on work supported financially by the National Research Foundation (NRF). Any opinions, findings and conclusions or recommendations expressed in this material are those of the author and therefore the NRF does not accept any liability with regards thereto.

[1] *Centre for Child Law v. NN, NS, Presiding Officer, Children's Court, District of Boksburg and MEC of Health, Gauteng*, case no 32053/2014 (GNP). Professor Ann Skelton, the Director of the Centre for Child Law at the University of Pretoria, was appointed curator ad litem for the children on 26 May 2014. She submitted her report on 23 March 2015. The court thereafter postponed the case until June 2015 for an expert opinion on indigenous traditions and practices. On 16 November 2015 the court made an order along the lines proposed by the curator ad litem granting full parental responsibilities and rights to the care-giving parents through the operation of the de facto adoption principle. Unfortunately the reasons for this order have to date (21 September 2016) not been given.

will be briefly mentioned while the international law will be dealt with more thoroughly. The relevance and influence of culture on the application of the best interests of the child principle will be considered because it might be relevant in some instances.

B The South African Experience

The South African law reports revealed two cases besides the one already mentioned. The first reported case dates back prior to the 1996 Constitution[2] indicating that baby switching is not a new phenomenon or symptomatic of an over-burdened and under-resourced health system.[3] In this case, two baby boys were switched in the Tygerberg hospital. Both couples involved were married parents. The father that brought the application to court to claim their biological child back (after two years) had his doubts all along. In this instance the baby that was brought to Mrs Petersen the day after she gave birth had a name tag around his foot bearing the surname 'Kruger'. When she made inquiries, the Petersen and Kruger boys were presented to her and she had to choose which child was hers. Sadly she chose the 'wrong' child.

In the second reported case, the babies were switched at the Nigel hospital but the matter was heard after the institution of the new constitutional dispensation.[4] The error was discovered eighteen months after the switch and the parents decided to keep the children handed to them at the hospital. They instituted actions in delict (tort) for damages based on the cost of psychological treatment, travelling costs to visit the

---

[2] It should be noted that the rights of biological parents are common law rights in South Africa (SA) and not fundamental rights in the sense that they are constitutional rights. Parental care is a constitutional right of the *child*, but so is family care: s. 28(1)(b) of the Constitution of the Republic of South Africa, 1996 (hereinafter referred to as the Constitution). This was the case under the Interim Constitution of 1993 as well and the court duly referred to these children's rights (provided for in s. 30) in *Clinton-Parker v. Administrator, Transvaal; Dawkins v. Administrator, Transvaal* 1996 2 SA 37 (W) 64B. In the USA an individual's right to nurture his or her offspring is a fundamental right guaranteed in the Constitution: C. G. Baunach, 'The role of equitable adoption in a mistaken baby switch' (1992–1993) 31 *University of Louisville Journal of Family Law* 501 at 509.
[3] *Petersen v. Kruger* 1975 4 SA 171 (C).
[4] *Clinton-Parker v. Administrator, Transvaal; Dawkins v. Administrator, Transvaal* 1996 2 SA 37 (W).

biological children and general damages for emotional shock and psychiatric injury. No mention was made of the pre-constitutional case in this matter and Judge Navsa described the case as 'unique in our legal history'.[5]

What should be noted is that after spending approximately the same time in the care of the non-biological parents, the outcomes in these two instances were exactly the opposite. In the first case the babies were returned to their biological parents, while in the second the children were brought up by the non-biological/psychological parents. Although the one case was decided in a constitutional dispensation, both these cases were decided before the Children's Act 38 of 2005 took effect. This is significant because with the backing of the Constitution this Act embodies the shift from parental rights to children's rights. The Act introduced the concept 'parental responsibilities and rights',[6] the notion of shared parenting[7] and mandated or implied mediation in specific instances.[8]

Judging from the surnames in the two cases just discussed, it may be assumed that the babies were not Black. In the most recent case, the babies were Black, which raises the issue of adherence to customary law and indigenous practices because South Africa recognises that common law and customary law run parallel under the supremacy of the Constitution.[9] This is an additional factor that needs to be explored in this context. In the recent case under discussion, all the parents involved were unmarried and their initial views on the future of the parent-child relationships varied. A team of psychologists employed at the Child, Adolescent and Family Unit of the hospital was working with the mothers and the children according to a treatment plan when a curator ad litem was appointed to investigate all issues pertaining to the children and determine what is in the best interests of the two children in this matter.

---

[5] At 40E.
[6] See the definition in s. 18(2) of the Children's Act 38 of 2005. Before the Act the common law used the concept 'parental power' or 'parental authority'. See *WW v. EW* 2011 6 SA 53 (KZP) paras. 19–28 for an explanation of the similarities and differences between these concepts.
[7] See ss. 18, 22 and 23.
[8] Mandated in s. 21 (parental responsibilities and rights of unmarried fathers) and 33 (parenting plans) and implied in s. 22 (parental responsibilities and rights agreements).
[9] Constitution, s. 8. See s. 211(3) that the courts *must* apply customary law when applicable, subject to the Constitution and any legislation that specifically deals with customary law. See also *Mthembu v. Letsela* 1997 2 SA 936 (T) 944B-C.

C Baby Switching in Other Jurisdictions

While the media in South Africa was scrutinising and reporting on every fact as it was revealed in the recent baby switching case, some coverage was also given to a similar incident in France.[10] It took a very brief search on the Internet to find many more cases on several other continents.[11] Cloud[12] and Kaufer's consulting firm even opined that one out of every 1,000 infant transfers in hospitals is a mistake![13]

The most frequently cited case is perhaps *Mays v. Twigg*.[14] In this case, two baby girls were switched in 1978 and the Twiggs discovered this ten years later when the child they raised died of a congenital heart condition. A legal battle ensued in which the Twiggs initially sought a declaration that Kimberley Mays was their biological daughter but in the end lost all when the court decided that they were a source of insecurity and a danger to the family relationship that the child was in.[15] The best interests of the child took centre stage in reaching this decision.[16]

---

[10] J. Lichfield 'French families sue clinic and staff for €12m over suffering caused by cot blunder that saw baby girls swapped at birth', *The Independent*, 3 December 2014, available at www.independent.co.uk/news/world/europe/french-families-sue-clinic-and-staff-for-€12m accessed on 5 December 2014. In this case, the changelings were ten years old before the mistake was revealed. In February 2015, the court in Grasse ordered the clinic to pay €400,000 to each of the girls, €300,000 to three of the parents, and €60,000 each to three siblings: 'France baby-swap families win damages', *BBC News*, 10 February 2015, available at www.bbc.com/news/world-europe-31350550 accessed on 10 February 2015.

[11] See the cases referred to by T. R. Crane, 'Mistaken baby switches an analysis of hospital liability and resulting custody issues' (2000) 21 *Journal of Legal Medicine* 109–124 and the table of cases provided by N. L. Segal *Someone Else's Twin: The True Story of Babies Switched at Birth* (New York: Prometheus Books, 2011), pp. 101 and 169–171, on the frequency of baby-switching incidents.

[12] 'Where do they belong? How Callie and Rebecca were switched remains a mystery. Will there be a fight over both their future and their past?' *Time*, 17 August 1998, at p. 62 in J. L. Foote, 'What's best for babies switched at birth? The role of the court, rights of non-biological parents and mandatory mediation of the custodial agreements' (1999) 21 *Whittier Law Review* 315.

[13] C. R. Mabry, 'The tragic and chaotic aftermath of a baby switch: Should policy and common law, blood ties, or psychological bonds prevail?' (1999–2000) 6 *William and Mary Journal of Women and the Law* 1 at 50; M. D. Ginsberg 'How much anguish is enough? Baby switching and negligent infliction of emotional distress' (2010–2011) 13.2 *DePaul Journal of Health Care Law* 255 at 255–256.

[14] 543 So 2d 241 (Fla Dist Ct App 1989).

[15] *Twigg v. Mays* 1993 WL 330624 at 2 (Fla Cir Ct 1993).

[16] See also *Moore v. Pope* 396 SE 2d 243 (Ga Ct App 1990) overruled by *Pope v. Moore* 403 SE 2d 205 (Ga 1991) where the boys were four when the switch was discovered.

Some jurisdictions enacted legislation to address care/custody disputes and curtail the acrimony when non-biological parents were involved in a parent-child relationship. Although these legislative measures were not specifically adopted to cater for baby switching, they did address issues that were likely to surface. In these statutes the best interests of the child was adopted as the standard to be applied[17] and the status of this and other norms involved should be evaluated in the course of reaching any decision.

D   An International Benchmark

Convention on the Rights of the Child 1989

It is fitting that the United Nations Convention on the Rights of the Child (CRC) is first in line when an international standard has to be found in dealing with these issues.[18] The CRC is renowned for the fact that it recognises the child's status as a rights-holder. The child has individual rights that have to be protected by the state. Implicit in this premise is the acknowledgement that it is possible for parents to act contrary to the child's well-being. The children's rights clause in the South African Constitution was based on this Convention and it has found its way into legislation in South Africa.[19] The Constitutional Court has in the past relied on the CRC in the development of South African law.[20]

The Preface of the CRC articulates the importance of 'family' for the well-being of children without providing a definition. Consensus has been reached that the definition should be broad.[21] However, the pivotal

---

[17] See, e.g., the Tennessee Code Annotated s. 36-6-101(a)(1) (1991) and the Oregon statute (Or Rev. Stat s. 109.119 (1997) that acknowledge the rights of any person in a parent-child relationship very explicitly. However, these statutes are criticised for *inter alia* threatening children's well-being and stability: W. C. Duncan, 'The legal fiction of de facto parenthood' (2010) 36 *Journal of Legislation* 263 at 269–271.

[18] UN, General Assembly, 20 November 1989, in force 2 September 1990, 1577 UNTS 3. SA ratified the Convention on 16 June 1995.

[19] See, for example, s. 28(2) of the Constitution, the Children's Act 38 of 2005 and the Child Justice Act 75 of 2008.

[20] For example, in *S v. M (Centre for Child Law as* amicus curiae) 2008 3 SA 232 (CC) paras. 16–17.

[21] It is a concept in transition: G. Van Bueren 'The international protection of family members' rights as the 21st century approaches' (1995) *Human Rights Quarterly* 732 at 734.

role of parents in caring for the child[22] and family relationships in establishing the child's identity[23] are mentioned as substantive provisions. The role of tradition and cultural values is also acknowledged in the Preface with respect to the development of the child.[24]

Article 3 of the CRC addresses cases of this nature in each subsection thereof. Article 3(1) firstly dictates the standard to be applied, namely 'the best interests of the child'. This is the standard that both the hospital, whether a public or private facility, and the court have to adhere to in dealing with the matter. Secondly, this standard has to be applied '[i]n all actions concerning children' without any exceptions made to accommodate over-burdened or undeveloped systems. Thirdly, 'the best interests of the child *shall* be a primary consideration'.[25] The word 'shall' is in the imperative. Fourthly, the best interests standard is not merely a consideration, but it is a 'primary' consideration and therefore first in line when considering all the relevant factors.[26]

Article 3(2) provides for the duty of States Parties in relation to the parent-child relationship. This subsection acknowledges the importance of the 'rights and duties' of the parents, legal guardians and other individuals in the care and protection of the child. It is taken further in Article 5 where the role of the extended family is included in guiding the child in accordance with the child's evolving capacities. This subsection also requires an appropriate legislative framework in dealing with these issues.[27]

Finally Article 3(3) dictates the required level of service to be delivered, particularly in the areas of health and safety. The adherence to norms and standards are a must in all state and private neonatal units. This subsection also requires sufficient and suitably qualified staff performing their duties under competent supervision.[28] In dealing with baby switching, Article 3 should also be read with Article 24(1) which affords children the highest standard of medical care attainable.

---

[22] Art. 7(1) and as primary caregivers: art. 18. See also art. 9 that a child has the right to live with his or her parent and maintain contact with them if separation is inevitable. Art. 10 deals with family reunification in the same vein.
[23] Art. 8(1).   [24] See footnotes 95–107 and accompanying text.   [25] Own emphasis.
[26] The best interests standard is also applied when adoption is considered: Art. 21, i.e., formal adoptions.
[27] R. Hodgkin and P. Newell *Implementation Handbook for the Convention on the Rights of the Child*, 3rd edn, (Geneva: Unicef, 2007) 41.
[28] In line with the Committee on the Rights of the Child *General Comment No. 7* 2005 CRC/ GC/7/ Rev 1 para. 23.

Whenever the system fails the children and baby switching occurs, a formal investigation should be undertaken and preventative measures should be enforced.[29]

The CRC emphasises that the child who is capable of forming his or her own view has the right to express that opinion freely.[30] States Parties have to ensure that the child's view is given due consideration in the judicial and administrative proceedings which are inevitable upon making the discovery.[31] It should be a factor in establishing the best interests of the child, but the fact that it is mentioned separately highlights the importance thereof. In cases where baby switching occurred, a curator (or guardian) ad litem should be appointed to establish and reveal all the facts on which a final decision regarding the child's best interests is based. This curator ad litem will probably play an important role in protecting another right afforded to children in the CRC that is important in the context of baby switching, namely the child's right to privacy.[32]

African Charter on the Rights and the Welfare of the Child 1990

The African Charter on the Rights and the Welfare of the Child (ACRWC)[33] is a very important regional document. It recognises the child's privileged position in the African society and it highlights the unique and challenging circumstances children are exposed to on the continent.[34] In this Charter the family unit enjoys special protection[35] and the parent-child relationship is respected.[36] The parents are the primary care-givers but are also obliged to put the best interests of the child first at all times.[37]

In line with these sentiments, the ACRWC in Article 4(1) expresses the best interests of the child in stronger terms than the CRC. The best interests of the child are not termed merely as *a* primary consideration, but as *the* primary consideration.[38] It states very clearly that this standard

---

[29] In line with the Committee on the Rights of the Child *General Comment No. 5* 2003 CRC/GC/2003/5 paras. 45–47 and *General Comment No. 7* 2005 CRC/GC/7/Rev 1 para. 13.
[30] Art. 12(1). [31] Art. 12(1) read with 12(2). [32] Art. 16.
[33] OAU Doc CAB/LEG/24.9/49 (1990). [34] Preface. [35] Art. 18(1).
[36] Art. 19(1). See also art. 19(2) on maintaining contact with the parents.
[37] Art. 20(1)(a): 'ensure that the best interests of the child are their basic concern at all times'.
[38] On the fact that the ACRWC increases the level of protection for children when compared to the CRC in a number of important respects, see F. Viljoen, 'The African Charter on the Rights and Welfare of the Child' in T. Boezaart (ed.) *Child Law in South Africa* (Claremont: Juta, 2009) p. 331 at p. 342; T. Davel, 'The African Charter on the

applies '[i]n all actions ... undertaken by any person or authority' and therefore also applies to public and private hospitals and neonatal care. Article 14 should be read in conjunction with Article 4 on health-related matters and then children are afforded the best attainable state of health.[39]

The ACRWC entrenches the right of the child to be heard in the same Article in which it deals with the best interests standard. Article 4(2) states:

> In all judicial and administrative proceedings affecting a child who is capable of communicating his/her own views, an opportunity shall be provided for the views of the child to be heard either directly or through an impartial representative as a party to the proceedings, and those views *shall* be taken into consideration by the relevant authority in accordance with the provisions of appropriate laws.[40]

Article 4(2) should be read with Article 7, because in the latter every child capable of communicating his or her views has the right to express his or her opinions freely in all matters and to disseminate those opinions subject to the restrictions of domestic law. Although the right to be heard provided for in terms of the ACRWC could seem more restricted than the scope of the right in the CRC, in some ways[41] the ACRWC is stronger than the CRC as it makes the consideration of children's views obligatory and specifies how children will be heard.[42]

The ACRWC urges States Parties in the Preamble to take 'into consideration the virtues of their cultural heritage, historical background and the values of African civilization'. Children are obliged to preserve African cultural values.[43] State Parties have to direct the education of children towards preserving and strengthening African morals, traditional values and cultures,[44] and promote children's participation in

---

Rights and Welfare of the Child, Family Law and Children's Rights' (2002) 35 *De Jure* 281 at 283. SA ratified the ACRWC on 7 January 2000.

[39] See Art. 24 that the best interests of the child is also the paramount consideration when dealing with adoption.

[40] Emphasis added.

[41] For example, that the representative must be impartial and that the child must be capable of communicating his or her views. See D. M. Chirwa 'The merits and demerits of the African Charter on the Rights and Welfare of the Child' (2002) 10 *International Journal of Children's Rights* 157 at 161.

[42] The child's right to privacy is protected in terms very similar to that of the CRC: Compare art. 10 of the ACRWC with art. 16 of the CRC.

[43] Art. 31(d).   [44] Art. 11(2)(c).

cultural activities.[45] The Preamble of the ACRWC also alludes to the negative impact of *inter alia* culture on the situation of children in Africa. It provides that 'any custom, tradition, cultural or religious practice' that is inconsistent with the rights, duties and obligations contained in the Charter must be discouraged to the extent that it is inconsistent.[46] The ACRWC furthermore contains an article dedicated to harmful social and cultural practices and the elimination thereof in specific instances.[47]

Other International Documents

The best interests of the child is a universally accepted standard in all the contested issues relating to children. Without providing a complete list, the best interests of the child standard is the benchmark in at least the following international and regional documents: the United Nations Declaration of the Rights of the Child 1959,[48] principle 2;[49] the Convention on the Elimination of all forms of Discrimination against Women 1979,[50] Articles 5(b) and 16(1)(d);[51] the European Convention on the Exercise of Children's Rights 1995,[52] Article 1(2); and the Convention on the Rights of People with Disabilities 2006,[53] Article 7(2).[54]

E The Acquisition of Parental Responsibilities and Rights in South African Law

In South Africa parental responsibilities and rights are acquired either automatically or by assignment. The holders of automatically acquired parental responsibilities and rights acquire *full* parental responsibilities and rights. In the case of assigned acquisitions the holder(s) may acquire either full or specific parental responsibilities and rights.[55]

---

[45] Art. 12(2).   [46] Art. 1(3).   [47] Art. 21.
[48] UN General Assembly, 20 November 1959, A/RES/1386 (XIV).
[49] '[T]he paramount consideration'.
[50] UN General Assembly, 18 December 1979, in force 3 September 1981, 1249 UNTS 13.
[51] Using the term 'paramount' instead of 'primary'. SA ratified the Convention on the Elimination of All Forms of Discrimination against Women on 15 December 1995.
[52] UN General Assembly, 25 January 1996, in force 1 July 2000, ETS 160.
[53] UN General Assembly, 13 December 2006, in force 3 May 2008, A/RES/61/106. SA ratified the Convention on 30 November 2007.
[54] '[A] primary consideration'.
[55] S. 18(1), read with ss. 19(1) and 20 of the Children's Act 35 of 2008.

If the couples involved in baby switching are married, the biological mothers and their husbands will be the holders of (full) parental responsibilities and rights.[56] Unmarried fathers also have the opportunity to acquire full parental responsibilities and rights and they do so by either being in a permanent life-partnership with the mother[57] or demonstrating their commitment towards the child in specific ways.[58] The position of unmarried fathers involved in baby switching is precarious because there is no way that they could have complied with the Act's requirements to acquire automatic parental responsibilities and rights. They either dedicated themselves to the wrong woman or to the wrong child. In one of the reported cases the couples involved were married,[59] but in the most recent case all the parents involved are unmarried. I hold the view that in such a case, the mothers retain parental responsibilities and rights. My view entails that parental responsibilities and rights do not cease to exist due to the fact that they are not exercised. All or some of their parental responsibilities and rights will only be terminated if the child turns eighteen years old, if they enter into a parental responsibilities and rights agreement with other interested party/parties,[60] by a court order[61] or if adoption takes place.[62]

The parent(s) caring for the switched babies will have to be granted parental responsibilities and rights by an adoption order,[63] which will have to be a formal adoption[64] or by assignment. However, it could be argued that formal adoption is not available at all due to the fact that the switched baby does not fit the definition of an adoptable child.[65] The parental responsibilities and rights may be assigned by a court upon application[66] or by concluding a parental responsibilities and rights agreement with the biological parent(s)[67] and either registering it with the Family Advocate or by making that agreement an order of court.[68] This agreement route, provided for in the Children's Act, is available to

---

[56] Ss. 19(1) and 20. This is not the case if the biological mother is an unmarried child (s. 19(2)) or a surrogate mother (s. 19(3)).
[57] S. 21(1)(a).
[58] That is by acknowledging paternity (s. 21(1)(b)(i)) and contributing to the child's upbringing (s. 21(1)(b)(ii)) and maintenance (s. 21(1)(b)(iii)).
[59] *Petersen v. Kruger.* [60] S. 22(1)(b) and comply with all the other requirements in s. 22.
[61] S. 28(1). [62] S. 242(1).
[63] S. 242(2) or appointment in the valid will of a sole guardian: s. 27. [64] S. 228.
[65] S. 230(3), over and above the fact that the process involved seems unsuitable because constitutional rights like dignity and privacy are at risk.
[66] S. 23 (contact and care) and s. 24 (guardianship). [67] S. 22(1).
[68] S. 22(4), which has to be in the best interests of the child, s. 22(5).

biological fathers as well as to any other person having an interest in the care, well-being and development of the child.[69] The parents who cared for the switched baby are thus perfectly suited to enter into such an agreement with the biological parents and it seems like an obvious choice in the baby switching cases. What is more, mediation takes on a very important role in constructing this agreement.[70]

In the South African Children's Act mediation is implied in reaching a compromise in parental responsibilities and rights agreements.[71] It is common knowledge that this form of alternative dispute resolution will eliminate some of the conflict and improve the chances of achieving what is best for the child. The advantages of mediation include the efforts of an unbiased mediator providing an opportunity to hear the child and focus on the future.[72] It creates the perfect space for both sets of parents to reach an agreement based on the child's best interests after which the court then finalises the issue in the same way that we deal with joint care (joint custody) in divorce proceedings.[73]

F De Facto Adoptions and Psychological Parenthood

The Children's Act's agreement route was not the curator ad litem's choice in the current baby switching case because it arguably applies only until the child reaches majority and does not deal with intestate succession. She explored the de facto adoption route and interestingly enough the Children's Act provides for de facto care-givers who otherwise would have had no parental responsibilities and rights to exercise the parental responsibilities and rights that are reasonably necessary to safeguard the child's health, well-being and development.[74]

De facto adoptions have been mentioned only a few times by the South African judiciary. In *Flynn v. Farr NO*[75] the Supreme Court of Appeal decided that a stepson could not rely on the fact that he was treated like a son to claim that he should share intestate in the inheritance with the offspring. The stepson passed away before the matter against the

---

[69] S. 22(1)(b).
[70] Foote, 'What's best for babies switched at birth?' Also see *MB v. NB* 2010 3 SA 220 (GSJ) para. 50 for the advantages of mediation in family law.
[71] L. de Jong, 'Child-Focused Mediation' in T. Boezaart *Child Law in South Africa*, p. 112 at p. 123 (mandatory in ss. 21 and 33).
[72] Foote, 'What's best for babies switched at birth?', and provides flexibility: 344.
[73] See *Krugel v. Krugel* 2003 6 SA 220 (T) para. 19 on the advantages of joint care arrangements.
[74] S. 32.   [75] 2009 1 SA 338 (SCA).

stepfather's estate was resolved and the Supreme Court of Appeal was not convinced that section 1(4)(e) of the Intestate Succession Act 81 of 1987 unfairly discriminated against persons that maintained close but informal relationships resembling parent-child relationships. In *MB v. NB*[76] the stepfather contemplated adopting the son, gave him his surname and shared in the decision to send the boy to a private school. Upon divorce the stepfather denied being liable for the school fees. The court decided that it was not necessary to decide whether this was a de facto adoption to reach the conclusion that the stepfather was obliged to pay the school fees. The stepfather created the impression that he was the father and he should be bound by his misrepresentation.

The latter case resembles 'equitable adoptions' recognised in some other jurisdictions. Ellis mentions cases where a Texas court recognised equitable adoptions or adoption (parentage) by estoppel in limited circumstances, which is where acts, promises and conduct (mis)led the child to believe that he or she is or will become an adopted or own child.[77] However, similar labels can have different meanings from the one jurisdiction to another.[78] In other instances the de facto parent is on the same footing as the biological parent and that resembles the agreement route just described.[79]

To acknowledge and formalise a de facto adoption found favour with the court in the baby switching case under discussion. This unfortunately implies terminating the parental responsibilities and rights of the biological parents by an order of the court. It is submitted that the circumstances and requirements of the de facto adoption should be restrictively defined in the order to curtail abuse thereof in other instances.

G Establishing the Best Interests

The best interests of the child is always the criterion if parental responsibilities and rights are assigned, whether by way of a court order or an

---

[76] 2010 3 SA 220 (GSJ) para. 22.

[77] M. D. Ellis, 'A need for clarity: Assisted reproduction and embryo adoption in Texas' (2014) 66:1 *Baylor Law Review* 164 at 167–168. See also J. A. Parness, 'Troxel revisited: A new approach to third-party childcare' (2015) 18:2 *Richmond Journal of Law and Public Interest* 227 at 233.

[78] As from state to state in the USA: Parness, 'Troxel revisited' at 233.

[79] Foote, 'What's best for babies switched at birth?', 338. Also note Baunach, 'The role of equitable adoption in a mistaken baby switch', 503, equating equitable adoption and de facto adoption in these particular instances.

agreement. The Children's Act provides a list of factors that must be taken into consideration when applying the best interests of the child standard.[80] It is the best interests of *all* the children involved, including the biological siblings/psychological siblings that have to be considered as well as the short-term and long-term best interests.[81] In these cases, where the babies were switched at birth, the following factors would probably stand out: the nature of the relationships,[82] the attitude of the parent(s),[83] the parent's capacity to provide for the child's needs,[84] the effect of separation on the child and the child's siblings[85] and the child's emotional security.[86]

The court will rely on the curator ad litem to assist it by investigating all the facts relating to the factors mentioned above and thus discovering what is in the child's best interests. The curator will provide the court with an objective and unbiased report. The curator ad litem will involve a team of experts because psychological and/or psychiatric assessment, individual counselling, psychotherapy and family therapy will be necessary.[87] Appointing a curator ad litem will also have other benefits such as preventing the child from having to attend mediation sessions and providing the child with a safe space to air his or her views.[88]

The South African Constitution raised the best interests standard to a principle of paramountcy.[89] Every child has the right to have his or her best interests considered to be of paramount importance in every matter concerning him or her.[90] This means that children are afforded a specific right, which guarantees the paramountcy of their best interests. Like all the other specific rights of children, this best-interest right is a fundamental right endorsed in the Bill of Rights in the Constitution.

---

[80] S. 7(1).
[81] *Implementation Handbook for the Convention on the Rights of the Child*, p. 38.
[82] S. 7(1)(a)(ii).   [83] S. 7(1)(b).   [84] S. 7(1)(c).   [85] S. 7(d).
[86] S. 7(h). See also subss. 7(e), 7(f)(ii), 7(g), 7(k) and 7(n).
[87] Mabry, 'The tragic and chaotic aftermath of a baby switch', 48.
[88] Foote, 'What's best for babies switched at birth?', 348.
[89] S. 28(2): 'A child's best interests are of paramount importance in every matter concerning the child'. Cf s. 30(3) of the Interim Constitution, 1993, for a similar provision.
[90] Per Goldstone J. in *Minister for Welfare and Population Development v. Fitzpatrick* 2000 3 SA 422 (CC) para. 18: 'Section 28(2) requires that a child's best interests have paramount importance in every matter concerning the child. The plain meaning of the words clearly indicates that the reach of section 28(2) cannot be limited to the rights enumerated in section 28(1) and section 28(2) must be interpreted to extend beyond those provisions. It creates a right that is independent of those specified in section 28(1).' See also *Central Authority v. MR (LS Intervening)* 2011 2 SA 428 (GNP) paras. 13 and 26.

The right of the child to have his or her best interests considered to be of paramount importance is not the only (specific) constitutional right of the child at stake. Section 28(1) gives every child a right to family care, parental care or appropriate alternative care if removed from the family environment. Aspects of the content of this right refer to the law regarding parental responsibilities and rights.[91]

These rights, like all the other fundamental rights, have vertical and horizontal applications. These rights, like all other fundamental rights, are also not absolute, because the Constitution itself provides for the limitation of fundamental rights.[92] These rights, like all the other rights, will have to be demarcated and balanced with the rights of various other persons and groups.[93] Fortunately, the Constitutional Court has provided guidelines for this process.[94] The balancing process will have to discount the competing interests of both biological and psychological parents.

H The Role of Customary Law and Tradition

The Constitution promotes cultural diversity in South Africa.[95] In customary law a child 'belongs' to a family or family group. The extended family plays an important role in the rearing of a child.[96] Customary law favours communal or group rights above individual rights and the rules of affiliation, fostering and guardianship appear to serve the rights of others rather than the best interests of the child.[97] The parent-child

---

[91] See footnotes 55–62 and accompanying text.
[92] S. 36. See *S v. Lawrence; S v. Negal; S v. Solberg* 1997 4 SA 1176 (CC), paras. 142, 165 and 166; *De Reuck v. Director of Public Prosecutions, Witwatersrand Local Division* 2004 1 SA 406 (CC) para. 55.
[93] See *V v. V* 1998 4 SA 169 (C) 189 where Foxcroft J pointed out that 'situations may well arise where the best interests of the child require that action is taken for the benefit of the child which effectively cuts across the parents' rights'.
[94] It is a nuanced and contextual standard (*Christian Education South Africa v. Minister of Education* 2000 4 SA 757 (CC) para. 31) and does not trump other constitutional rights (*De Reuck v. Director of Public Prosecutions, Witwatersrand Local Division* para. 55). See also *S v. M* (Centre for Child Law as amicus curiae) 2008 3 SA 232 (CC) para. 25 and para. 15: 'that the courts must function in a manner which at all times shows due respect for children's rights'.
[95] See ss. 31, 30 and 15(3) of the Constitution.
[96] J. C. Bekker, 'Interaction between Constitutional reform and family law' (1991) *Acta Juridica* 1 at 2.
[97] R. T. Nhlapo, 'Biological and Social Parenthood in African Perspective: The Movement of Children in Swazi Family Law' in J. Eekelaar and P. Šarčević (eds.) *Parenthood in Modern Society* (1993) p. 35 at p. 47.

relationship entails a much broader concept because of the 'movement' of children in a family group.[98] Parenthood is more socially than biologically constructed.[99] Social parents are those that acquire their status as such when parental roles are split, delegated or transferred while the link with the biological parents remains intact. Adoption is not construed in this way because adoption involves the cessation of parental responsibilities and rights.[100] There is a strong notion that a man's rights to his own child can never lapse.[101]

Against this backdrop South African courts are obliged to develop customary law in line with the Constitution. In *Maneli v. Maneli* the court made it clear that development of both customary law and common law have to be consistent with promoting the best interests of the child as envisaged in the constitutional prescript of the paramountcy of the child's best interests.[102] The applicant and the respondent married after having first concluded a customary marriage. They then adopted an orphaned child in terms of Xhosa customary law[103] while not complying with the legislation pertaining to formal adoptions.[104] The parties later separated following a breakdown of the marriage and the child remained in the care of the applicant. After the separation the respondent argued that he was no longer obliged to maintain the child. His argument was based on the fact that he was neither the biological father nor had he legally adopted the child.[105]

Judge Mokgoatheng found that neither the Child Care Act nor the Children's Act repealed or modified the Xhosa customary law of adoption, and that the common law had to be developed to accommodate customary adoptions. He concluded that the respondent had a legal duty to maintain the child adopted in terms of customary law.[106]

---

[98] T. W. Bennet *Customary Law in South Africa* (Lansdown: Juta, 2004) p. 321.
[99] Nhlapo in *Parenthood in Modern Society*, pp. 36 and 47.
[100] Nhlapo in *Parenthood in Modern Society*, p. 37.
[101] Nhlapo in *Parenthood in Modern Society*, p. 41.
[102] 2010 7 BCLR 703 (GSJ) paras. 24, 39 and 44.
[103] Customary law adoptions are widely practiced by Xhosas in the Eastern and Western Cape provinces of SA. It entails the performance of Xhosa traditional rites and rituals to proclaim publicly that the adoptive parents have formally accepted parental responsibility for the child. Thereafter the child is regarded as a child of the adoptive parents: *Maneli v. Maneli* paras. 4 and 5.
[104] At that stage Chapter 4 of the Child Care Act 74 of 1983, this is now replaced by Chapter 15 of the Children's Act.
[105] Para. 8.
[106] Para. 43. Note that South African law also recognises adoptions according to customary law to the extent that the child is entitled to compensation in delict when a third party causes the death of the adoptive parent: *Metiso v. Padongelukfonds* 2001 3 SA 1142 (T).

Customary law therefore, on the one hand, stands firm on the acknowledgement of the biological ties and, on the other hand, also constructs social parenthood. Furthermore, family acceptance of a switched baby could make it more difficult for the psychological parents to give the child up to the biological parents. Rituals, which play an important role in various customs, could be used to enhance the outcome for all involved.[107]

I Concluding Remarks

In South Africa, the Children's Act provides a solution in cases where babies were switched. It perhaps provides the legislative guidance that Foote requested many years ago in the USA.[108] The answer depends on what is best for the children, the switched baby that was cared for as a child, the biological child and the sibling children in both families involved. The best interests might be a compromise between the best now and the best later. The 'advantage' that we have in baby switching is the fact that none of the parents can be blamed for the tragedy that the individuals have to deal with.

Some might argue that the best is the least detrimental alternative in this type of situation.[109] The least detrimental alternative approach employs three guidelines, namely the child's need for permanency/continuity, the child's sense of time and the court's inability to make accurate predictions regarding the child's long-term best interests.[110] I beg to differ. The best interests of the child standard provides the child-centeredness that is required. The emphasis is on the *child's* established relationship with the current care-givers/psychological parents; the trauma that separation would cause the *child*; the *child's* need to maintain bonds with extended siblings and family and the fact that the best interests of the *child* (and all the children involved) can only be estimated at this stage – as is the case in most care disputes.

The best for the baby might be to extend his or her family by adopting the shared parental responsibilities and rights model between the switched family and the own family. In my view, the quest for justice

---

[107] Even in customary law adoptions, see note 103.
[108] Foote, 'What's best for babies switched at birth?', 316.
[109] As was done in *P v. P* 2007 5 SA 94 (SCA) at p. 102 in a custody dispute.
[110] J. Goldstein, A. J. Solnit, S. Goldstein and A. Freud *The Best Interests of the Child: The Least Detrimental Alternative* (New York: Free Press, 1996) pp. 20, 41 and 46–7.

will rather be served by a mediated court approved agreement. However, the de facto adoption route also implies that not only biology establishes parent-child relationships and might therefor be a viable option.[111] All options should be considered carefully before deciding what is best.

---

[111] Also see Baunach, 'The role of equitable adoption in a mistaken baby switch', 512, arguing for 2 sets of parents, the biological and the psychological parents.

11

Primacy, Paramountcy and Adoption in England and Scotland

BRIAN SLOAN[*]

A Introduction

Article 3(1) of the United Nations Convention of the Rights of the Child ('UNCRC') requires children's 'best interests' to be 'a primary consideration' in actions concerning them. Article 21, however, mandates States that recognise the concept of adoption to ensure that 'best interests' 'shall be the paramount consideration'. English[1] and Scots adoption law have both moved from treating best interests as merely the 'first' consideration[2] to treating them as the 'paramount' consideration.[3] This ostensibly aligned both systems with the UNCRC, but raised issues regarding the child's relationship with her birth family, also protected by the Convention. This chapter analyses the relationship between 'primacy' and 'paramountcy' within the UNCRC, before considering the implications of the shift in the governing principle in domestic law.

B Primacy and Paramountcy in the UNCRC

Article 3(1) UNCRC provides that '[i]n all actions concerning children...the best interests of the child shall be a *primary* consideration' (emphasis added). Nevertheless, Article 21 provides that 'States Parties that recognize and/or permit...adoption shall ensure that the best

---

[*] This chapter is based on materials as at 19 October 2015. I am grateful for the comments of attendees at the Edinburgh colloquium, particularly Janys Scott QC, on an early draft. The usual disclaimer applies.
[1] Since adoption law is a partially devolved matter for the Welsh Government (see, e.g., Children and Families Act 2014 Explanatory Notes, at [41]), this chapter focuses on English Law *per se* (and Scots Law).
[2] Adoption Act 1976, s. 6 (England); Adoption (Scotland) Act 1978, s. 6 before amendment (Scotland).
[3] Adoption and Children Act 2002, s. 1 (England); originally Children (Scotland) Act 1995, s. 95, but see now Adoption and Children (Scotland) Act 2007, s. 14 (Scotland).

interests of the child shall be the *paramount* consideration' (emphasis added). While Unicef's *Implementation Handbook* regards the Article 3 principle as 'evident' in Article 21,[4] it acknowledges that Article 21 requires best interests to be more 'than simply "a primary" consideration as in [A]rticle 3'.[5] The United Nations Committee on the Rights of the Child ('the Committee') has said that 'the right of best interests is further strengthened' regarding adoption as compared to Article 3,[6] although it has used the word 'primary' regarding adoption.[7]

As ever, the question becomes what is meant by 'paramount' and 'best interests' or (in the broadly equivalent terminology of the English and Scots legislation) 'welfare'. In addition, as the *Handbook* emphasises, '[t]he Convention is indivisible and its articles interdependent', meaning that 'Article 21 should not be considered in isolation'.[8] As I have suggested elsewhere,[9] other provisions of the Convention might provide clues as to the meaning of 'best interests' under Article 21 (or Article 3). Welfare/best interests and their paramountcy are notoriously uncertain concepts[10] that have been interpreted narrowly by the English judiciary, an example being the assertion that '[i]t is only as a contributor to the child's welfare that parenthood assumes any significance'.[11] This is true notwithstanding the facts that those other Convention provisions are themselves qualified, and that the notion of indivisibility of rights is problematic where rights appear to conflict.[12]

---

[4] R. Hodgkin and P. Newell, *Implementation Handbook for the Convention on the Rights of the Child*, 3rd edn. (Geneva: Unicef, 2007), available at: www.unicef.org/publications/index_43110.html, pp. 35–36.

[5] Ibid., p. 295. See also Committee on the Rights of the Child, *General Comment No. 7 (2005): Implementing Child Rights in Early Childhood* (CRC/C/GC/7/Rev.1, 2006) at [36(b)].

[6] *General Comment No. 14 (2013) on the Right of the Child to have his or her Best Interests taken as a Primary Consideration (art. 3, para. 1)* (CRC/C/GC/14, 2013) at [38].

[7] *Consideration of Reports submitted by State Parties under Article 44 of the Convention – Concluding Observations: Tongo* (Third and Fourth Reports) (CRC/C/TGO/CO/3-4, 2012), at [48].

[8] Hodgkin and Newell, *Implementation Handbook*, p. 303.

[9] See, generally, B. Sloan, 'Conflicting Rights: English Adoption Law and the Implementation of the UN Convention on the Rights of the Child' (2013) *Child & Family Law Quarterly* 40–60.

[10] See, e.g., H. Reece, 'The Paramountcy Principle: Consensus or Construct?' (1996) 49 *Current Legal Problems* 267–304.

[11] *Re B (A Child) (Residence: Biological Parent)* [2009] UKSC 5 at [37] *per* Lord Kerr, giving the judgment of the court. See, historically, *J v. C* [1970] AC 668 at 710–11 *per* Lord MacDermott.

[12] See, e.g., Sloan, 'Conflicting Rights'.

The full terms of Article 21 might undermine the suggestion that a simple 'welfare' test is applicable since the article also requires that the adoption is 'permissible in view of the child's status concerning parents, relatives and legal guardians' and refers to the 'informed consent to the adoption' of relevant persons.[13] It has been said that the paramountcy principle contained in Article 21 is 'in one sense circumscribed by the legal necessities of satisfying legal grounds and gaining necessary consents',[14] and the relevance of consent to welfare is illustrated by the Committee's statement about the need to ensure both 'that the best interests of the child are of paramount consideration, and that the parents or legal guardians have given their informed consent to the adoption'.[15]

Other potentially countervailing UNCRC obligations include protecting a child's right, 'as far as possible,...to know and be cared for by...her parents',[16] respecting a child's right to her identity and 'family relations',[17] ensuring that 'a child shall not be separated from...her parents against their will, except when competent authorities subject to judicial review determine, in accordance with applicable law and procedures, that such separation is necessary for the best interests of the child',[18] and rendering 'appropriate assistance to parents and legal guardians',[19] who 'have the primary responsibility for the upbringing and development of the child',[20] 'in the performance of their child-rearing responsibilities'.[21] Overall, the *Implementation Handbook* regards the UNCRC as 'neutral about the desirability of adoption',[22] and the Committee has emphasised the need to consider 'the least intrusive intervention as warranted by the circumstances'.[23] Even where some form of intervention is necessary to secure a child's Convention rights, then, it does not necessarily follow that adoption is the most appropriate one notwithstanding Article 21.[24]

---

[13] UNCRC, Article 21(a).   [14] Hodgkin and Newell, *Implementation Handbook*, p. 296.
[15] Committee on the Rights of the Child, *Consideration of reports submitted by State Parties under Article 44 of the Convention – Concluding Observations: Belarus* (Third and Fourth Reports) (CRC/C/BLR/CO/3–4, 2011), at [48].
[16] UNCRC, Article 7(1).   [17] UNCRC, Article 8(1).   [18] UNCRC, Article 9(1).
[19] UNCRC, Article 18(2).   [20] UNCRC, Article 18(1).
[21] UNCRC, Article 18(2); see also UN General Assembly *Guidelines for the Alternative Care of Children* (resolution A/RES/64/142, 24 February 2010) Annex at [3].
[22] Hodgkin and Newell, *Implementation Handbook*, p. 294.
[23] *General Comment No. 13 (2011): The Right of the Child to Freedom from All Forms of Violence* (CRC/C/GC/13, 2011) at [54]
[24] See Sloan, 'Conflicting Rights'.

C England

Legislation

The Adoption and Children Act 2002 reflects the policy that adoption should be used as a means of finding a permanent home for more children who might otherwise 'drift' through state foster care.[25] Prima facie, section 1 of the 2002 Act implements Article 21 by making welfare the paramount consideration,[26] although the UK's 1994 Initial State Report to the Committee claimed that English Law already complied with that Article.[27] This was despite fact that under the Adoption Act 1976 (broadly similarly to Article 3) child welfare was merely the 'first' consideration.[28]

The 2002 Act applies an adoption-specific version of the 'welfare principle', requiring the court or adoption agency to treat the child's welfare 'throughout his life' as paramount.[29] There is an obligation to have regard to, *inter alia*, 'the child's ascertainable wishes and feelings' 'in the light of [his] age and understanding' (without formally requiring any child's consent to adoption),[30] 'the likely effect on the child (throughout his life) of having ceased to be a member of the original family and become an adopted person',[31] 'any of the child's characteristics' considered relevant,[32] 'any harm' the child 'has suffered or is at risk

---

[25] Secretary of State for Health, *Adoption: A New Approach*, Cm. 5017 (TSO, 2000). See, more recently, Children and Families Act 2014; Education and Adoption Bill 2015-16.

[26] Adoption and Children Act 2002, s. 1(2). See, e.g., Joint Committee on Human Rights, *The Adoption and Children Bill: As Amended by the House of Lords on Report*, HL 177/ HC 979 (HMSO, 2002); UK Government, *The Consolidated 3rd and 4th Periodic Report to UN Committee on the Rights of the Child* (2007), at [103]; See also UK Government, *The United Nations Convention on the Rights of the Child: How Legislation underpins Implementation in England* (2010), at [5.114]–[5.117]; see now HM Government, *The Fifth Periodic Report to the UN Committee on the Rights of the Child: United Kingdom* (2014).

[27] UK Government, *Initial Reports of State[ ] Parties due in 1994: United Kingdom of Great Britain and Northern Ireland* (1994), at [284]. The UK's view on compatibility as regards adoption was not apparently disputed by the Committee on the Rights of the Child: *Concluding Observations of the Committee on the Rights of the Child: United Kingdom of Great Britain and Northern Ireland* (CRC/C/15/Add.34, 1995), though cf. Committee on the Rights of the Child, *Consideration Of Reports submitted by State[ ] Parties under Article 44 of the Convention – Concluding Observations: United Kingdom of Great Britain and Northern Ireland* (Second Report) (CRC/C/15/Add.188, 2002), at [31] and B. Walsh, 'The United Nations Convention on the Rights Of The Child: A British View' (1991) 5 *International Journal of Law, Policy and the Family* 170–94, 192 fn. 42.

[28] Adoption Act 1976, s. 6.   [29] Adoption and Children Act 2002, s. 1(2).

[30] Ibid., s. 1(4)(a).   [31] Ibid., s. 1(4)(c).   [32] Ibid., s. 1(4)(d).

of suffering',[33] and 'the relationship which the child has with relatives' and relevant others (including *inter alia* their wishes and feelings).[34] The court or agency must 'at all times bear in mind that, in general, any delay in coming to the decision is likely to prejudice the child's welfare',[35] and the court must not make an order under the 2002 Act 'unless it considers that making the order would be better for the child than not doing so'.[36]

While there are links between the 2002 Act and Article 21, the UNCRC is given little or no analysis in several official documents.[37] This arguably reflects (alongside the absence of specific incorporation of the Convention in English Law) the difficulty in balancing the various requirements of the UNCRC throughout the adoption process, including Article 21 and Article 3.

English local authorities are obliged to apply for a 'placement order'[38] where *inter alia* the authority is 'satisfied that the child ought to be placed for adoption'.[39] The policy of securing more adoptions, pursued in spite of apparently mixed outcomes for children adopted out of care,[40] can also be seen *inter alia* from the adoption agency's power to place a child for adoption by virtue of the consent of a child's parents (with parental responsibility)[41] or her guardian, without the need for a court order.[42]

It is also significant that the 2002 Act explicitly applies a welfare standard to the issue of dispensing with parental consent to the adoption. Under the 1976 Act, if the relevant parent could be found and was capable of giving agreement,[43] it had to be shown that she was withholding consent 'unreasonably',[44] or had relevantly mistreated the child.[45]

---

[33] Ibid., s. 1(4)(e). [34] Ibid., s. 1(4)(f). [35] Ibid., s. 1(3). [36] Ibid., s. 1(6).
[37] Secretary of State for Health, *Adoption: A New Approach* Cm. 5017 (TSO, 2000); Adoption and Children Act 2002 Explanatory Notes; Department for Education, 'Statutory Guidance on Adoption' (2013), though cf. p. 7.
[38] Adoption and Children Act 2002, s. 21. [39] Ibid., s. 22.
[40] S. Harris-Short, 'Holding onto the Past: Adoption, Birth Parents and the Law in the Twenty-First Century' in R. Probert and C. Barton (eds.), *Fifty Years in Family Law: Essays for Stephen Cretney* (Cambridge: Intersentia, 2012), pp. 150–151; cf, e.g., J. Selwyn et al, *Beyond the Adoption Order: Challenges, Interventions and Adoption Disruption* (Department for Education, 2014).
[41] Adoption and Children Act 2002, s. 52(6).
[42] Ibid., s. 19; see also 'fostering for adoption', introduced by Children and Families Act 2014, s. 2.
[43] Adoption Act 1976, s. 16(2)(a). [44] Ibid., s. 16(2)(b).
[45] The mistreatment-based grounds were that the parent had 'persistently' failed without reasonable cause to discharge her parental responsibility (ibid., s. 16(2)(c)), and that she had abandoned, neglected, (s. 16(2)(d)) or persistently (s. 16(2)(e)) or seriously (s. 16(2)(f)) ill-treated, the child.

If consent is not forthcoming from parents with parental responsibility under the 2002 Act, by contrast, a court can dispense with the need for it (at the placement order stage or, if necessary, the final order stage) if 'the welfare of the child requires the consent to be dispensed with',[46] and public law adoption can proceed based on welfare alone provided either that relevant parents have at some stage consented to the process or that the criteria for state care, involving the child suffering or being likely to suffer, significant harm,[47] have been satisfied.[48] Procedural restrictions are also placed on parents' ability to withdraw their consent and/or oppose the making of the final adoption order.[49]

The prioritisation of adoptions has profound implications for the child's birth family and her relationship with them as protected by the UNCRC. It is nevertheless carried further in the Children and Families Act 2014 in light of continued concerns that adoption is not proceeding quickly enough.[50]

Judicial Approaches

As mentioned earlier, English courts have often utilised a narrow and individualistic conception of welfare when applying the 'paramountcy' principle to more general decisions about the upbringing of children,[51] and this approach continued in the early case law under the 2002 Act. In Re C (A Child) (Adoption: Duty of Local Authority),[52] although Arden LJ accepted that the Act imposed an 'extended meaning' of welfare because of the need to consider the long-term effect of acquiring a new legal family,[53] she considered that Parliament had intentionally prioritised the 'no delay' principle and felt unable to 'quarrel with that basic value judgment'.[54] In the present case, the priority was therefore 'finding a long-term carer for the child without delay',[55] even if that meant

---

[46] Adoption and Children Act 2002, s. 52(1)(b). Consent can also be dispensed with where 'the parent or guardian cannot be found or is incapable of giving consent': s. 52(1)(a).
[47] Children Act 1989, s. 31(2).   [48] Adoption and Children Act 2002, ss. 18, 21, 47.
[49] Ibid., s. 52(4), s. 47; see Sloan, 'Conflicting Rights', 56–57.
[50] See, e.g., B. Sloan, 'Adoption and Fostering as Means of Securing Article 6 Rights in England' (2015) 26(2) Stellenbosch Law Review 363–79.
[51] Cf., e.g., J. Herring, 'The Human Rights Act and the Welfare Principle in Family Law – Conflicting or Complementary?' (1999) 11 Child & Family Law Quarterly 223–236.
[52] [2007] EWCA Civ 1206. For a detailed analysis, see B. Sloan, 'Re C (A Child) (Adoption: Duty of Local Authority) – Welfare and the Rights of the Birth Family in "Fast Track" Adoption Cases' [2009] Child & Family Law Quarterly 87–103.
[53] [2007] EWCA Civ 1206 at [18] per Arden LJ.   [54] Ibid., at [17].   [55] Ibid., at [3].

adoption occurring without her father being assessed as a potential carer or being aware of her existence, given her mother's consent to the adoption.

Rather than reflecting the UNCRC's preference for care by birth parents, Arden LJ stated that the 2002 Act did not prioritise the birth family over the adoptive family simply because of their status.[56] It was later accepted that the Court of Appeal in *Re C* had prioritised 'the interests of the child as an individual'.[57] The cases were not always entirely consistent,[58] and in *Re P (Placement Orders: Parental Consent)*, it was emphasised that 'adoption, unlike other forms of order...is something with lifelong implications'.[59] Nevertheless, the English courts' early emphasis on quickly achieving a secure adoption may not have given sufficient weight to the various aspects of the UNCRC.

In *Re B (A Child) (Care Proceedings: Appeal)*,[60] however, Lord Neuberger noted and did not appear to disagree with my criticism of *Re C*.[61] Influenced by the UNCRC, he inspired a more rigorous approach to adoption, potentially introducing tension with government policy. He was anxious to assert that 'adoption of a child against her parents' wishes should only be contemplated as a last resort – when all else fails',[62] meaning that 'before making an adoption order...the court must be satisfied that there is no practical way of the authorities (or others) providing the requisite assistance and support'.[63] On his analysis, '[a]lthough the child's interests in an adoption case are "paramount"...a court must never lose sight of the fact that those interests include being brought up by her natural family, ideally her natural parents, or at least one of them'.[64]

The legacy of *Re B* is demonstrated by *Re B-S (Children) (Adoption Order: Leave to Oppose)* and the case law it produced by imposing exacting standards regarding local authorities' evidence and judicial reasoning *inter alia*.[65] While it is unclear that the courts' recent approach

---

[56] Ibid., at [15].
[57] *Re A (Father: Knowledge of Chilld's Birth)* [2011] EWCA Civ 273 at [39] *per* Black LJ.
[58] See, e.g., *Re A (A child) (Disclosure of Child's Existence to Paternal Grandparents)* [2006] EWHC 3065 (Fam).
[59] [2008] EWCA Civ 535 at [128].
[60] [2013] UKSC 33. See, generally, B. Sloan, 'Loving but Potentially Harmful Parents in the Supreme Court' (2014) 73 *Cambridge Law Journal* 28–31.
[61] [2013] UKSC 33 at [103].   [62] Ibid., at [104].   [63] Ibid., at [105].
[64] Ibid., at [104].
[65] [2013] EWCA Civ 1146; see, e.g., B. Sloan 'Adoption Decisions in England: *Re B (A Child) (Care Proceedings: Appeal)* and Beyond' (2015) 37 *Journal of Social Welfare and Family Law* 437–57.

has resulted in adoptions being refused where they would have been granted before *Re B*, and the Court of Appeal later 'emphasise[d], with as much force as possible, that *Re B-S* was not intended to change and has not changed the law',[66] the value of rigour in the adoption process should not be underestimated for the purposes of compliance with the UNCRC, even if its differing language and priorities causes difficulty. Whether a true meaning of 'paramountcy' or even 'primacy' can ever be deduced, a balance must be achieved between various UNCRC rights. The courts have made considerable efforts to do so, but the government's approach (reflected *inter alia* in the Children and Families Act 2014) raises questions.

D   Scotland

Legislation

It is claimed that the adoption of children looked after by the state in Scotland 'does not happen very often',[67] and the policy context of adoption in England and Scotland may therefore differ. This might be borne out by statistics, whatever the difficulties of comparisons.[68] In Scotland in the year ending July 2014, only 7.2 per cent of those leaving care were adopted (albeit that those subject to a permanence order but not adopted would be considered 'in care'),[69] as compared to the broadly equivalent figure of 17 per cent in England,[70] although the UK's fifth periodic report to the Committee emphasised that 'the number of adoptions has almost doubled since 2008 in Scotland'.[71]

Although the current Scots adoption law is in the Adoption and Children (Scotland) Act 2007, the paramountcy of welfare in adoption decisions dates from the Children (Scotland) Act 1995.[72] There was thus an intermediate period where welfare was paramount under the 1995 Act

---

[66] *Re R (A Child)* [2014] EWCA Civ 1625 at [44] *per* Sir James Munby.
[67] C. Kidner, *SPICe Briefing: Child Protection* (Scottish Parliament, 2012), p. 10.
[68] Department for Education, *Statistical First Release: Children looked after in England (including adoption and care leavers) year ending 31 March 2014* (2014), pp. 20–21.
[69] National Statistics, *Children's Social Work Statistics Scotland, 2013–14* (2015).
[70] Department for Education, *Statistical First Release*, pp. 10–11.
[71] HM Government, *The Fifth Periodic Report* at [50].
[72] Children (Scotland) Act 1995, s. 95, substituting a new s. 6 of the Adoption (Scotland) Act 1978.

but the old consent grounds (based broadly on the English 1976 Act) applied.[73] This suggests that paramountcy of child welfare and specific grounds for dispensing with consent are not necessarily inconsistent, although Macfarlane and Scott opined that the provisions were interpreted in *P v. Aberdeen City Council* such that there was 'no point to having any other ground for dispensing with a parent's agreement to adoption' and '[t]he only test...require[d] to be satisfied is the welfare test'.[74]

Under the 2007 Act, where a court or adoption agency is 'coming to a decision' relating to the adoption of a child,[75] it must 'regard the need to safeguard and promote the welfare of the child throughout the child's life as the paramount consideration'.[76] In doing so, it must 'have regard to all the circumstances of the case'[77] but also, 'so far as is reasonably practicable', 'in particular' to the value of a stable family unit in the child's development, the child's views, religious, racial, cultural and linguistic factors and the likely effect on the child, throughout her life, of making the order.[78] There must be consideration of 'whether adoption is likely best to meet the needs of the child or whether there is some better practical alternative'.[79] Similarly, '[t]he court must not make an adoption order unless it considers that it would be better for the child that the order be made than not'.[80] Many of these considerations are broadly consistent with the English 2002 Act, although the emphasis on an absence of delay appears less prevalent in Scottish legislation.[81] It is also noteworthy that the specific obligation to 'give due consideration to the child's religious persuasion, racial origin and cultural and linguistic background'[82] has been repealed in England.[83]

The Adoption Policy Review Group had recommended in 2005 that the consent dispensation grounds in Scotland be changed to reflect those in the English 2002 Act,[84] albeit acknowledging concerns that a

---

[73] Adoption (Scotland) Act 1978, s. 16.
[74] 2001 *Green's Family Law Reports* 127 at 131 (Editors' Note).
[75] Adoption and Children (Scotland) Act 2007, s. 14(1). [76] Ibid., s. 14(3).
[77] Ibid., s. 14(2). [78] Ibid., s. 14(4). [79] Ibid., s. 14(6). [80] Ibid., s. 28(2).
[81] Cf. Act of Sederunt (Sheriff Court Rules Amendment) (Adoption and Children (Scotland) Act 2007) SSI 2009/284; Act of Sederunt (Rules of the Court of Session 1994) SSI 1994/1443, ch. 67.
[82] Adoption and Children Act 2002, s. 1(5) (still applicable in Wales).
[83] Children and Families Act 2014, s. 3.
[84] Adoption Policy Review Group, *Adoption: Better Choices for our Children* (2005) at [3.23]–[3.24].

welfare test could conflate the question whether the adoption order should be made and whether consent should be dispensed with.[85] It therefore suggested that the 2002 Act's approach should be used but 'amended to reflect the "necessity test" in Article 8' of the European Convention on Human Rights.[86] 'Parent' for these purposes, somewhat similarly to the 2002 Act, means a parent who 'has any parental responsibilities or parental rights in relation to the child' or does not have them 'by virtue of a permanence order which does not include provision granting authority for the child to be adopted'.[87]

The original Adoption and Children (Scotland) Bill was amended so that the 'welfare requires' provision in section 31(3)(d) of the 2007 Act applies only where the parent has parental responsibilities or rights or is likely to be given them in the future,[88] and it cannot be said that the parent is 'unable satisfactorily' to discharge or exercise those rights or responsibilities and 'is likely to continue to be unable to do so'.[89] It has thus been described as 'a residual ground'.[90] In the English case of *Re Z (Adoption: Scottish Child Placed in England: Convention Compliance)*, however, it was opined that 's31(3)(d) is the counterpart of, and is almost identical to, s52(1)(b) ACA 2002'.[91] Donnelly describes the section 52 welfare ground as 'identical' to the Scots one, albeit 'within a very different structure'.[92]. Norrie identified potential difficulties with the new provisions as regards Articles 7, 8 and 9 of the UNCRC, though it is noteworthy that (as Scott points out)[93] he did not expressly mention Article 21.[94] In any case, Lord Glennie undermined the possible impact of the more nuanced dispensation provisions in *M* v. *R* by holding (with reference to *S* v. *L*) that the inability element did not apply where 'the discharge by the parents of their parental responsibilities and the

---

[85] See, e.g., *M* v. *R* [2012] CSOH 186 at [138] *per* Lord Glennie, albeit apparently reversing the stages.
[86] Adoption Policy Review Group, *Adoption* at [3.24].
[87] Adoption and Children (Scotland) 2007, s. 31(15).   [88] Ibid., s. 31(5).
[89] Ibid., s. 31(4).   [90] *S* [2014] CSIH 42 at [28] *per* Lady Smith.
[91] [2012] EWHC 2404 (Fam) at [10] *per* Mostyn QC.
[92] M. Donnelly, 'The Supreme Court and the Welfare Ground for Dispensing with Parental Consent to Adoption: ANS and Another v ML (Scotland)' [2014] *International Family Law* 110, 110.
[93] J.M. Scott, 'Welfare and the New Grounds for Dispensing with Parental Consent to Adoption – A Reply' 2009 *Scots Law Times* (News) 17, 18.
[94] K.McK. Norrie, 'Welfare and the New Grounds for Dispensing with Parental Consent to Adoption' 2008 *Scots Law Times* (News) 213, 215.

exercise by them of their parental rights is curtailed...by a supervision requirement and a condition of residence'.[95]

On Lord Reed's analysis, the grounds for dispensing with consent 'are specified in greater detail than in sec 52(1) of the 2002 Act',[96] and section 31(3)(d) is narrower in scope in the context than the equivalent ground in the 2002 Act. While it directs a court to consider the extent to which a parent can look after a child effectively (now or in the future) before dispensing with consent, it also underlines the fact that consent can in principle be dispensed with even where no such finding can be made.

It is noteworthy that a Scottish adoption order cannot be made in respect of a child aged twelve or over unless she consents (or the court is satisfied that she is incapable of consenting),[97] although consent is not a sufficient condition.[98] This more obviously gives effect to Article 12 of the UNCRC than does English Law (which contains no truly equivalent position).

Although similar welfare standards are apparently applied in England and Scotland, the details of the adoption process, and the implications of those standards, suggest some differences. Attaching authority for the child to be adopted to a Scottish 'permanence order' (rendering it more like a placement order in England) is a separate decision and 'the test for granting such authority is different from that for the making of a permanence order' *per se*.[99] It is at that latter stage that the test for dispensing with parental consent is applied,[100] and the test for making the order in the first place involves paramoutcy *inter alia*.[101]

The permanence order itself must at least vest the parental responsibilities as to the provision of guidance and regulation of the child's residence in the local authority,[102] and Mostyn QC described it as having 'many of the characteristics of a[n English] final care order'.[103] He nevertheless asserted that a permanence order (rather than what is now a compulsory supervision order) 'is more often sought where the case involves an older child where long term fostering, but not adoption, is the

---

[95] [2012] CSOH 186, at [72]. Cf. *East Lothian Council v. S* [2012] CSIH 3; *W v. Aberdeenshire Council* [2012] CSIH 37; *S v. City of Edinburgh Council* [2012] CSIH 95.
[96] [2012] UKSC 30 at [25]. [97] Adoption and Children (Scotland) Act 2007, s. 32(1).
[98] See, e.g., *X v. Y* 2015 Green's Family Law Reports 41.
[99] *Dumfries and Galloway Council* 2013 G.W.D. 31-628 at [32] *per* Sheriff Kenneth A. Ross.
[100] Adoption and Children (Scotland) Act 2007, s. 83. [101] Ibid., s. 84.
[102] Adoption and Children (Scotland) Act 2007, s. 81.
[103] [2012] EWHC 2404 (Fam), at [21].

plan',[104] but a Scottish Parliament-published briefing claims that permanence orders 'appear to have been used mainly as a prelude to adoption'.[105] It is interesting that the Adoption Policy Review Group stated that a permanence order 'would *also* be used as a pre-adoption order', implying that (unlike 'placement orders' in English Law) facilitating adoption was not necessarily intended as the main purpose of the new order.[106] The Group opined that '[t]o an extent', the English special guardianship order (allowing a non-parent to acquire parental responsibility and exercise it 'to the exclusion' of others without transferring parenthood)[107] 'has the same aim' as a permanence order, but also that 'Special Guardianship has more features in common with adoption'.[108]

A 'compulsory supervision order'[109] facilitates a care plan's implementation in Scotland,[110] and Mostyn QC described its predecessor (without reference to sources) as a 'common route for achieving a long term placement as part of an adoption plan' as a potential alternative to a permanence order.[111] A compulsory supervision order can include a range of measures[112] such as a requirement that the child should live in a particular place or that her movement should be restricted,[113] and specifies a local authority 'responsible for giving effect to the measures included in the order'.[114] The 'grounds' for referral to a Children's Hearing that can make them are broad (some being justice-related):[115] they include that 'the child is likely to suffer unnecessarily, or the health or development of the child is likely to be seriously impaired, due to a lack of parental care',[116] (which Mostyn QC described as 'very similar to the threshold test in s. 31(2) Children Act 1989'),[117] but also (for example) that 'the child has, or is likely to have, a close connection with a person who has carried out domestic abuse'.[118] There is generally an obligation to 'regard the need to safeguard and promote the welfare of the child throughout the child's childhood as the paramount consideration'.[119]

---

[104] Ibid., at [21].   [105] Kidner, *SPICe Briefing* p. 10.
[106] Adoption Policy Review Group, *Adoption* at [1.7] (emphasis added).
[107] Children Act 1989, s. 14C(1)(b).
[108] Adoption Policy Review Group, *Adoption* at [5.50].
[109] Children's Hearings (Scotland) Act 2011, s. 83.
[110] [2012] EWHC 2404 (Fam) at [20].
[111] [2012] EWHC 2404 (Fam) at [23] on a supervision requirement with conditions. Cf. Kidner, *SPICe Briefing* p. 10.
[112] Children's Hearings (Scotland) Act 2011, s. 83(1)(a).   [113] Ibid., s. 83(2).
[114] Ibid., s 83(1)(b).   [115] Ibid., s. 67(2).   [116] Ibid., s. 67(2)(a).
[117] [2012] EWHC 2404 (Fam) at [15].
[118] Children's Hearings (Scotland) Act 2011, s. 67(2)(f).   [119] Ibid., s. 25(2); cf. s. 26.

A 'no order' principle also applies.[120] Significantly, compulsory supervision orders do not themselves 'give any parental responsibilities or rights to the local authority or the foster carers' and they 'suspend, rather than remove, the rights of the birth parents to regulate residence, contact and, possibly, other matters',[121] even though they can ultimately facilitate adoption.

It was claimed in *Re Z* that what were previously supervision requirements (unlike permanence orders) are made by Children's Hearings that are less formal and where 'the evidence is perhaps less full and less stringently tested than would be the case south of the border'.[122] That said, it has also been claimed that '[t]he child protection and children's hearings systems operate on the basis of legal principles derived, in the main, from' UNCRC rights.[123] The 2011 Act apparently imposes 'an increased proceduralisation and specificity in the regulation of...children's hearings',[124] and if the relevant grounds for the compulsory supervision order are not accepted the case is referred to the sheriff for determination of whether they are established.[125] It will nevertheless be seen that, combined with judicial approaches to the 2007 Act, the findings that can ultimately facilitate adoption have caused concern in Scotland.

Judicial Approaches

The Supreme Court considered the Scots 2007 Act in *S* v. *L*,[126] the year before it considered the English 2002 Act in *Re B*. In *S* v. *L*, the birth mother of a child subject to adoption proceedings submitted that section 31(3)(d) of the 2007 Act was incompatible with the ECHR in allowing parental consent to be dispensed with where the child's welfare 'requires' it. In dismissing the claim, Lord Reed noted the 'paramountcy' requirement in Article 21 of the UNCRC,[127] but (unlike Lord Neuberger in *Re B*) did not consider its other requirements. He nevertheless concluded, with considerable reference to *Re P* and *YC* v. *United Kingdom* (where the European Court of Human Rights ruled that the 2002 Act was in

---

[120] Ibid., s. 28. [121] Adoption Policy Review Group, *Adoption* at [5.4].
[122] [2012] EWHC 2404 (Fam) at [23]. [123] Kidner, *SPICe Briefing* p. 5.
[124] J. McGhee, *Forty-four years on – Reflections on the Scottish Children's Hearings System* (Dublin: Law Society of Ireland, 2015), p. 4.
[125] Children's Hearings (Scotland) Act 2011, s. 93. [126] [2012] UKSC 30.
[127] Ibid., at [37]. See also *City of Edinburgh Council* v. *C* 2012 *Green's Family Law Reports* 132 at [89] *per* Sheriff Principal M.M. Stephen.

general compatible with the ECHR),[128] that the 2007 Act was also compatible with the ECHR because of the necessity implied by the word 'requires'. He did emphasise a requirement that 'nothing less than adoption will suffice'.[129] Nevertheless, Norrie has said that 's.31(3)(d) should be interpreted in such a way that it is not satisfied where the child's welfare would be served less well, *but still satisfactorily*, by a less drastic intervention than adoption'.[130] This suggestion might cause difficulties with the UNCRC's text, but the uncertainty of that text should be taken into account.

The European Court's remarks in *YC* to the effect that family ties should be severed only in very exceptional circumstances were, in Lord Reed's analysis in *S* v. *L*, 'not a legal test, but an observation about the rarity of the circumstances in which the compulsory severing of family ties will be in accordance with Art 8'.[131] He expressed concern about the delay that had occurred in the case including the amount of evidence presented, which might be something of a contrast to the current English emphasis on rigour following *Re B* and *Re B-S*, but might also be consistent with the emphasis on proper case management also visible in *Re B-S*.

In the later case of *S*, the Inner House of the Court of Session specifically opined that *Re B-S* 'was concerned with addressing deficiencies which the court identified as occurring regularly at the stage of first instance decision making in [England]', and did not consider that it 'adds anything of relevance in the present case to *In re B*'.[132] The Outer House was equally dismissive of *Re B-S*'s implications for Scotland in *West Lothian Council*, on the questionable basis that 'the Scottish legislation imposes the principal obligation to consider alternatives to adoption on the Adoption Agency rather than the court' and 'the Agency...shouldn't recommend adoption (or permanence with authority to adopt) unless other reasonable alternatives have been considered and rejected'.[133] *S* may be the only available Scottish judgment citing *Re B*, and neither it nor *S* v. *L* seems to have produced a flurry of case law equivalent to that seen in England following *Re B* and *Re B-S*. *S* may suggest a reluctance to

---

[128] [2012] 2 FLR 332.
[129] [2012] UKSC 30 at [43]; see also *M* v. *R* [2012] CSOH 186 at [137] *per* Lord Glennie.
[130] K. Norrie, 'The Welfare Ground for Dispensing with Consent to Adoption: The Supreme Court Decides' 2013 *Scots Law Times* (News) 117, 119.
[131] [2012] UKSC 30 at [44].   [132] [2014] CSIH 42 at [54].
[133] [2014] CSOH 73, at [68] *per* Lady Wise.

impose the kind of rigour in Scotland that has recently been seen in England, and there were also some remarks in *M* v. *R* that might undermine the 'last resort' principle. Lord Glennie there opined that if he refused the adoption orders the mother concerned 'would seek to resume contact with a view to making an application to take the children back'.[134] He asserted that '[w]hether or not such an approach would succeed is nothing to the point' whether consent should be dispensed with.[135] While he considered it 'unlikely' that the mother would succeed, he was primarily concerned that 'it would introduce disruption and uncertainty into the lives of the petitioners and the children'.[136] This reasoning does not obviously contribute to a firm conclusion on whether anything less than adoption would do, even if other aspects of the judgment are more adamant on that point.

Moreover, Donnelly claims that there is an 'absence of threshold criteria to be satisfied before the court decides whether to grant the adoption order'.[137] This concern, in one possible interpretation, means that neither *Re P* nor *YC* v. *UK* should have been followed in Scotland where an adoption order can be made without either parental consent or a finding that the threshold has been met, although she may be suggesting (perhaps implausibly) that *Re P* and *YC* should never be applied to the final adoption order hearing because the threshold has not been established literally at that hearing.[138] This would mean that they should never be so applied in either jurisdiction, even where the threshold has been found to be crossed at an earlier point by virtue of a care or placement order in England or a permanence or compulsory supervision order in Scotland. Similarly, Norrie has claimed that '[t]he requirement to satisfy other threshold criteria appears on the face of s. 52(1)(b) of the English legislation when [placement] orders are sought, but no such requirement to satisfy the "risk" conditions in other legislation appears in s. 31(3) of the 2007 Act and as such [it] fails to satisfy the ECHR requirement for legal certainty'.[139] It should be noted, however, that such criteria do not appear literally on section 52's face.[140] Procedural restrictions also mean that few parents who suffer the compulsory removal of

---

[134] [2012] CSOH 186 at [141].   [135] Ibid.   [136] Ibid.
[137] Donnelly, 'The Supreme Court and the Welfare Ground', 112. See also K.McK. Norrie, *The Law Relating to Parent and Child in Scotland*, 3rd edn. (Edinburgh: W. Green, 2013) at [21.60].
[138] Ibid.   [139] Norrie, 'The Welfare Ground', 122.
[140] Cf. Adoption and Children Act 2002, s. 21(2); Children Act 1989, s. 31(2).

their children actually have the opportunity to oppose the order and have their consent dispensed with at the final stage in England,[141] whereas adoption without a permanence order in Scotland (whatever the arguable difficulties with the compulsory supervision order only route) at least provides that opportunity.[142] It has also been seen that contested grounds must be established by a sheriff in the context of a compulsory supervision order, so that some formality in factual findings is key even there. All of this suggests that Donnelly and Norrie's views should be treated with caution, even if there is some resistance in the Scottish courts to imposing the *Re B-S* level of rigour there.

In any case, in *X* v. *Y*, it was said regarding step-parent adoption that '[t]here would...have to be some clear advantage in formalising the petitioner's relationship with the child in order to exclude the respondent from his life'.[143] In the English case of *Re P (A Child) (Adoption: Stepparent)*, the Court of Appeal held it wrong to say that every step-parent adoption case required a finding that 'welfare would be prejudiced significantly if the order were not made',[144] possibly suggesting a more cautious approach where consent is required at the final stage in Scotland as compared to England. It is therefore difficult to come to a firm conclusion on the similarities or differences in legislative and judicial approaches to adoption in England and Scotland.

Conclusion

It is probably easier to argue that the Adoption and Children Act 2002 and the Adoption and Children (Scotland) Act 2007 are compatible with the UNCRC than to do so about their predecessors, since both expressly treat child welfare as the 'paramount' consideration. While the mere use of that word does not itself guarantee compatibility in light of the UNCRC's other requirements, and there remain difficulties about the difference between 'paramount' and 'primary' or 'first', at least the judiciary in both jurisdictions largely appear to be appreciating the range of rights possessed by children and the need for rigour in relation to adoption, even if such appreciation is more evident in England.

---

[141] See, e.g., Sloan, 'Adoption Decisions in England'.
[142] Compare Adoption and Children (Scotland) Act 2007, s. 31(2)(7) and s. 31(2)–(6).
[143] 2015 *Green's Family Law Reports* 41 at [18] *per* Sheriff D. Kelly QC.
[144] [2014] EWCA Civ 1174 at [54] *per* McFarlane LJ.

12

Article 3 and Adoption in and from India and Nepal

RICHARD W. WHITECROSS

A   Introduction

Nepal has experienced an increase in intercountry adoption in recent years. Following the opening up of authorisation to arrange adoptions, the number of child centres offering children for adoption significantly increased after 2000. The emergence in the 1990s of new 'sender' countries, such as India and, more recently, Nepal and the troubling absence of well-implemented and enforced regulations on intercountry adoptions in and by sending countries is the focus of this chapter. It examines how India and Nepal interpret and apply Article 3. India ratified the UN Convention on the Rights of the Child (UNCRC) in December 1992 and has experienced significant political and economic changes, including its population exceeding one billion.[1] After ratifying the UNCRC, Nepal experienced a debilitating civil war between 1996 and 2006 and continues to suffer from political instability.[2] Underpinning this chapter is discussion of the extent to which the state can regulate intercountry adoption effectively. It is important to note that the chapter does not focus on the highly contentious issue of whether intercountry adoption contributes to the welfare of the child or increases their suffering. In looking at intercountry adoption from Nepal and India domestic adoption will be discussed for it is the preferred approach under the UNCRC and the Hague Convention on the Protection of Children and Co-operation in Respect of Intercountry Adoption 1993.[3]

---

[1] UN Convention on the Rights of the Child, 20 November 1989, in force 2 September 1990, 1577 UNTS 3 (hereafter UNCRC).
[2] A new constitution, replacing the interim constitution 2007, was brought in to effect on 20 September 2015. Riots broke out in areas of Nepal leading to interethnic violence and bloodshed.
[3] The Hague Convention on Protection of Children and Co-operation in Respect of Intercountry Adoption, 29 May 1993, in force 1 May 1995, 51 ILM 1134 (hereafter, the Hague International Adoption Convention).

B The Rise of Intercountry Adoption

From the early 1990s the number of intercountry adoptions began to accelerate.[4] Transnational or intercountry adoptions originated in the aftermath of World War II and the Korean War.[5] During the 1990s the list of 'sending countries' changed. The change in the 'sending countries' reflects a complex range of political, social and economic factors. Volkman notes that with the exception of South Korea, most of the 'sending countries', China, Russia, Guatemala, Ukraine, Romania, Vietnam, India and Cambodia all became active participants in intercountry adoption during the 1990s.[6] The same decade that saw the sending countries all sign the UNCRC.

Article 21 of the UNCRC is the basis of the regulatory framework for intercountry adoption ensuring that the 'best interests' of the child must be the 'paramount consideration' in any adoption system. In particular, intercountry adoptions should be subject to the same safeguards and standards applicable to domestic adoptions. Under the Optional Protocol on the sale of children, child prostitution and child pornography added to the UNCRC in 2000,[7] all contracting states are required to criminalise the improper inducement of consent and to introduce laws and state programmes to deter the sale of children.[8] In 1993, the Hague Intercountry Adoption Convention created a framework of standards and practices for intercountry adoption to achieve and further the goals of the UNCRC. Under the Hague Intercountry Adoption Convention, contracting states are required to implement the standards and practices set out by introducing governmental accreditation or approval of adoption facilitators. Specifically, contracting states are required to establish central authorities to oversee its requirements. Over the past two decades, sending and receiving states

---

[4] P. Selman, 'Trends in intercountry adoption: Analysis of data from 20 receiving countries, 1998–2004' (2006) 23(2) *Journal of Population Research* 183, at 183.

[5] See B. Tizard, 'Intercountry adoption: A review of the evidence' (1991) 32(5) *Journal of Child Psychology and Psychiatry* 743, at 743. UNICEF *Intercountry Adoption*, 31 July 2014, available at: www.unicwef.org/media/media_41918. Last accessed 6 July 2015.

[6] T.A. Volkman, *Cultures of Transnational Adoption* (Durham and London: Duke University Press, 2005) p. 1.

[7] Optional Protocol to the Convention on the Rights of the Child on the Sale of Children, Child Prostitution and Child Pornography, G.A.Res. 54/263, annex II, U.N. Doc. A/RES/54/263 (May 2000) (hereafter the Optional Protocol).

[8] Ibid., Arts. 3, 9–10.

have undertaken reforms of their intercountry adoption practices.[9] However, there are major challenges, as we will see illustrated by Nepal, to ensuring that regulatory systems are sufficient to ensure that intercountry adoptions are conducted in a manner that does serve the best interests of children.

Although UNCRC Article 21 and the Hague Intercountry Adoption Convention permit intercountry adoption, both emphasise the need to exhaust domestic adoption or fostering before placing a child for intercountry adoption. This preference for domestic adoption recognises the child's right to an identity that may be lost through intercountry adoption. As Yngvesson notes in her groundbreaking ethnographic study of intercountry adoptees, 'many are identified or have self-identified as ethnically or racially different from their adoptive parents'.[10] However, it is significant that UNICEF in 2005, then again in 2014, appears to favour intercountry adoption over in-country institutional care. In 2005, UNICEF stated that:

> For children who cannot be raised by their own families, an appropriate alternative family environment should be sought in preference to institutional care, which should be used only as a last resort and as a temporary measure. Inter-country adoption is one of a range of care options which may be open to children, and for individual children who cannot be placed in a permanent family setting in their countries of origin, it may indeed be that best solution. In each case, the best interests of the individual child must be the guiding principle in making a decision regarding adoption.[11]

The emphasis in this statement on the 'best interests' of the child as the 'guiding principle' underscores the centrality of this principle to the UNCRC and Article 3.

Best Interest Principle and Intercountry Adoption

UNCRC Article 3 sets out the principle that 'the best interest of the child' shall be a 'primary' consideration in 'all actions concerning children'.[12]

---

[9] For example, in the UK the Adoption (Intercountry Aspects) Act 1999, and, in Ireland, the Department of Health and Children, *Adoption Legislation: 2003 Consultation and Proposal for Change*. (Dublin: Department of Health and Children, 2005). Similarly, in the United States, the Intercountry Adoption Act 2000, 42 U.S.C.14901–14954 (2000).

[10] B. Yngvesson, *Belonging in an Adopted World: Race, Identity and Transnational Adoption*. (Chicago: Chicago University Press, 2010), p. 175.

[11] UNICEF, 'Intercountry Adoption', Press Release, 26 June 2015: www.unicef.org/media/media_41918.html.

[12] UNCRC, Art. 3 (1).

Guidance on the interpretation and application of 'the best interest of the child' is set out in General Comment No. 14.[13] In the area of intercountry adoption, the meaning and interpretation of 'best interests' underlies an intense debate between proponents of intercountry adoption, notably Bartholet, who argues that over-regulation impedes intercountry adoption to the detriment of children.[14] By contrast, Smolin argues that the current system of intercountry adoption violates the human rights of children due to the ineffective regulation of the placement process.[15] Seeking to provide a balance, Dillon recommends that there is a need for an international network for intercountry adoption as a human rights imperative because of its potential to provide homeless and children in state institutions an opportunity to 'exercise their right to a family'.[16]

In 2000 the Parliamentary Assembly of the Council of Europe expressed concerns about intercountry adoption. In Recommendation 1443, the Council stated that it wanted to 'alert the European public opinion to the fact that, sadly, international adoption may prove to be a practice that disregards children's rights and that does not necessarily serve their best interests'.[17] More recently, in 2012, the Council again noted in Resolution 1909, para. 4, that:

> ... persisting reports of cases of intercountry adoption where the best interest of children has evidently not been the paramount consideration or where their human rights have been severely violated. Certain children fall victim to 'child laundering' practices, involving the abduction and sale of children, the coercion or manipulation of birth parents and their family environment, falsification of documents and bribery. Both sending and

---

[13] Committee on the Rights of the Children, *General Comment No. 14 (2013) on the right of the child to have his or her best interests taken as a primary consideration (art. 3, para. 1)*, CRC/C/GC/14.

[14] See E. Bartholet, 'International adoption: Thoughts on the human rights issues' (2007) 13 *Buffalo Human Rights Law Review* 151, at 153–158. Bartholet is challenged on her approach in J. Oreskovic and T. Maskew 'Red thread or slender reed: Deconstructing Professor Bartholet's mythology of international adoption' (2008) 14 *Buffalo Human Rights Law Review* 7.

[15] D.M. Smolin 'Intercountry adoption as child trafficking' (2004) 39 *Valladolid University Law Review* 281, at 321–325.

[16] S. Dillon, 'Making legal regimes for intercountry adoption reflect human rights principles: transforming the United Nations Convention on the Rights of the Child with the Hague Convention on Intercountry Adoption' (2003) 21 *Boston University International Law Journal* 179, at 186.

[17] Council of Europe, 'Intercountry adoption: Respecting children's rights', Recommendation 1443. 1 March 2002.

receiving countries involved in intercountry adoptions must...live up to their responsibilities to prevent and fight such criminal activities at a global level.[18]

Therefore, the responsibility for ensuring the best interests of the child is placed squarely on both the sending and receiving countries. In the UK and the USA, the regulatory process for approval of intercountry adoptions is well documented and supplemented by UK and US official guidance on intercountry adoption from specific sending countries, including in the UK a block on all intercountry adoptions from Nepal. Describing the process for ensuring that the best interests of the child are paramount, Cantwell argues that 'determining the best interests needs to be a thorough and well prescribed process directed, in particular, towards identifying which of two or more rights-based solutions is most likely to enable children to realize their rights'.[19] Mr Justice Brennan perceptively commented that 'the best interest approach depends on the values systems of the decision maker. Absent any rule or guideline, that approach simply creates an unexaminable discretion in the repository of power'.[20] As we will see this presents challenges for the effective implementation of Article 3 in weak states, such as Nepal, which lack the ability to enforce rules or guidelines and in which values systems run counter to the UNCRC

Whilst the 'best interests of the child' is a general principle of the UNCRC, its meaning continues to be ambiguous. It is widely accepted that this presents a significant challenge for implementation, in particular, when the best interests of a child are to be the 'paramount consideration' in decisions about intercountry adoption. In these situations, the best interests of the child and the decisions about whether or not to allow intercountry adoption have to be balanced with a range of human rights.[21] Yet as highlighted by the Council of Europe, amongst others, disregard for the best interests of the child is a major concern in relation

---

[18] Council of Europe (2012) 'Intercountry adoption: ensuring that the best interests of the child are upheld', Resolution 1909, para. 4. Text adopted by the Standing Committee, acting on behalf of the Assembly, 30 November 2012.
[19] N. Cantwell, J. Davidson, S. Elsley, I. Milligan and N. Quinn, *Moving Forward: Implementing the 'Guidelines for the Alternative Care of Children'*. (Glasgow: Centre for Excellence for Looked After Children in Scotland, 2012), at p. 10.
[20] *Secretary of the Department of Health and Community Services v J.W.B and S.M.B (Marion's Case)*[1992] HCA 15; [199] 175 CLR 218, para. 14.
[21] Recognising the human rights of birth parents and the wider rights of children to their own identity, implicit within which is a right to their 'culture'.

to intercountry adoptions. In the following section, we turn to consider domestic and intercountry adoption in Nepal and India.

C Adoption in and from South Asia

Nepal: Civil Strife, the Internet and Adoption Tourism

The recent history of Nepal serves to illustrate a major challenge for the effective implementation of the UNCRC. Nepal emerged as a kingdom in the eighteenth century under the Shah dynasty. By the mid-nineteenth century political power was held by members of the Rana family. Following a coup in 1951 the Rana regime was ended and a move towards a parliamentary democracy began to emerge. This early move towards democracy was brought to a sudden end when, in 1960, King Mahendra imposed direct royal rule. Direct royal rule continued until a series of strikes and protests in 1989 forced King Birendra to agree to a new constitution promulgated in 1990. The 1990s witnessed a political impasse between the monarchy, the new political parties and the rise of a powerful Maoist party that declared a 'People's War' in 1996.

The civil war claimed, at least, 10,000 lives between 1996 and 2006. It destabilised Nepal's government and institutions. Since the end of the civil war and the abolition of the monarchy, Nepal has lurched from political crisis to political crisis as political parties fail to agree to the terms of a new constitution. The political turmoil of Nepal sets the context in which the UNCRC was introduced into Nepal after its ratification in 1990. Nepal was as with many other states an early 'adopter' of the UNCRC. In 1993 Nepal introduced the *Children's Act* that incorporated aspects of the UNCRC into national legislation

Adoption and Intercountry Adoption

Adoption in Nepal is covered by Chapter 15 of the *Muluki Ain* (General Code). Chapter 15 was amended by the Gender Equality Maintaining Some Nepal Acts Amendment Act 2006[22] to enable women, as well as men to adopt. Chapter 15 states that no adult may adopt a child if he or

---

[22] For ease of reference the Gregorian calendar year is given. The Nepali calendar year is 2063.

she already has a child of the same sex.[23] Following amendments to Chapter 15 in 1976, the Nepal Children's Organisation (NCO), established in 1964 by the royal family, became the only organisation authorised to conduct adoptions in Nepal. It is unclear how many domestic adoptions were overseen by the NCO between 1976 and 1996. Figures from the Central Child Welfare Board suggest that between 1996 and 2000, 327 children were adopted through the NCO.

In 1976 Chapter 15 of the *Muluki Ain* was amended to allow foreign nationals to adopt. Clause 12 A states that:

> if any foreign national wishes to adopt any citizen of Nepal, who may be adopted as a son or daughter in accordance with the law, the Government of Nepal may, after considering the character and economic condition of such a foreign national and on recommendation of the concerned foreign government or embassy, permit adoption of son or daughter on such terms and conditions as the Government of Nepal may consider appropriate.[24]

In 2000, the *Terms and Conditions* were issued by the Government of Nepal and opened up intercountry adoption to other child centres. Almost immediately there was a marked increase in the numbers of children adopted after 2000. By 2007 there were 47 child centres, mainly in Kathmandu, permitted to conduct adoptions. As a result, figures for adopted children rose sharply with 2,161 children adopted between 2000 and 2007. A report on *The State of the Rights of the Child* published in 2004 noted that there was an official intention to authorise the adoption of 510 children annually.[25] A recent study found that only four out of every hundred adoptions were domestic.[26] There are a number of factors why domestic adoption in Nepal is low, reflecting social/cultural norms and economic considerations. However, the official figures may not capture the local level, unregulated, adoptions that we know take place.[27] People create and recreate their families through a

---

[23] Chapter 15, Clause 1, *The Muluki Ain* (General Code), at 256. Available at: www.lawcommission.gov.np.
[24] Clause 12A *The Muluki Ain*, at 258–259.
[25] Child Workers in Nepal (CWIN), *State of the Rights of the Child in Nepal*. (Kathmandu: CWIN, 2004).
[26] Terres des hommes Foundation and UNICEF, *Adopting the Rights of the Child: A Study of Intercountry Adoption and Its Influence on Child Protection in Nepal*. (Kathmandu: Terres des hommes and UNICEF, 2008, pp. 27–29.
[27] During fieldwork in Nepal, the author encountered several children who had been adopted for a range of reasons in to local families without any formal process. Whilst

range of techniques that are meaningful to them whilst lacking the formality of state approval. We will return to consider these factors in the discussion at the end of the chapter.

The sharp rise in intercountry adoption occurred at the height of Nepal's civil war. This may reflect families in the most affected areas sending their children to the capital for safety. This was also the period that saw the expansion of the Internet in Nepal and the rise of adoption tourism. In 2007, shortly after the civil war ended, a report on intercountry adoption practices in Nepal drew attention to a range of serious concerns.[28] In his review of intercountry adoption practice in Nepal, S.P. Paudel concluded that as the number of intercountry adoptions rose sharply there was a significant increase in irregularities. Three key issues were identified. The first was that child centres were falsely declaring children to be abandoned. The second key concern identified was the purchasing of children from their biological parents for adoption. Finally, the child centres were charging excessive amounts of money from prospective adoptive parents.

The latest investigation by UNICEF found that 85 per cent of children in the orphanages they visited had at least one living parent.[29]. These orphanages often lack proper regulations, and regulations on who can operate a residential care institution for children are nonexistent. They have become a lucrative business in Nepal with profit to be made from both the families – who are deceived as to what will happen to their children – and from well-intentioned foreign tourists who donate funds in the belief they are supporting genuine orphans. Children are being trafficked into these orphanages internally from other parts of Nepal to meet the demands of volunteers and other donors who are prepared to pay to supposedly 'help' Nepal's orphans.

Article 3, Clause 5 of the Optional Protocol states that, 'State parties shall take all appropriate legal and administrative measure to ensure that all persons involved in the adoption of the child act in conformity with applicable international legal instruments.' Nepal ratified the Optional Protocol in 2006. It signed the Hague Intercountry Adoption Convention

---

this reflected the marginalised state of the families, the lack of official recognition of the child as a member of their new family potentially could affect their rights to state support and recognition of their rights to state citizenship.

[28] S.P. Paudel, *Inter-Country Adoption process in Nepal*, Paper presented at the International Conference on Intercountry Adoption, 11–13 March 2007, Kathmandu, Nepal.

[29] Terres des hommes Foundation and UNICEF, *Adopting the Rights of the Child*, p. 19.

on 28 April 2009. After signing the Hague Intercountry Adoption Convention, the Ministry of Women, Children and Social Welfare formed an Intercountry Adoption Management Committee on 14 May 2010 to regulate adoption effectively.

In May 2010 the UK Borders Agency issued a notice restricting adoptions from Nepal. Four specific concerns were set out in the notice: failure to adhere to the key principles of the UNCRC and in particular, 'the complete absence of the principle of the best interests of the child'; the absence of an adequate legal framework despite recent legislation; poor procedures; and finally the ongoing falsification of documents and lack of transparency and accountability for money brought in to Nepal for intercountry adoptions.[30] The restriction remains in force in the UK. In August 2010, the US Department of State and the US Immigration and Customs Enforcement agency suspended the processing of new adoption cases from Nepal that involved children who are claimed to have been found abandoned. Evidence showed that the likelihood that the children had actually been abandoned was very slim. As with the UK, the restriction remains in force.[31]

In 2011, the Nepali government announced that it received no applications for intercountry adoptions. The Ministry of Women, Children and Social Welfare (MWCSW) invited applications through concerned embassies, diplomatic missions and international adoption agencies ending the suspension introduced in 2009. Officials advised that prospective adoptive parents should apply online for the permission of the Nepali government. They should also submit permission from their respective governments for adoption and apply through registered adoption agencies. In 2011, twenty-nine child centres had their licenses renewed for intercountry adoption and seven new child centres were being licensed.[32] The US Department of State continues to

---

[30] International Adoption Guide, www.internationaladoptionguide.co.uk/from-which-countries-is-it-possible-to-adopt-from/nepal-adoption-criteria.html. Accessed 25 February 2015.

[31] US Department of State – Bureau of Consular Affairs, *Notice: U.S. Department of State Continues to Recommend Against Adopting from Nepal.* 31 December 2013. http://travel.state.gov/content/adoptionsabroad/en/country-information/alerts-and-notifications/nepal-5-html. See a critical online report on the US State Department's actions by American families affected by the restriction submitted to the US Congress, K.T. Dempsey, *Both Ends Burning Paper Chains*, no date, no place of publication. Available at https://bothendsburning.org/wp-content/Paper-Chains-Ful-Report.pdf.

[32] A. Poudel, 'Government opens applications for intercountry adoptions', 29 November 2014. Online news article accessible at www.myrepublica.com/portal/index.php?action=news_details&news_id=38929. Last accessed 6 October 2015.

strongly recommend that prospective adoptive parents refrain from adopting children from Nepal due to grave concerns about the reliability of Nepal's adoption system and credible reports that children have been stolen from birth parents, who did not intend to irrevocably relinquish parental rights.

India: National Assets and Scandals

Since gaining independence in 1947, India has emerged as the most populous country in South Asia. India is the federal union of twenty-nine states and seven territories. In recent years, after a failed policy of sterilisation introduced in the early 1970s, India's population exceeds one billion. According to a recent report, nearly one in five children in the world live in India.[33] At approximately 472 million, children make up almost 40 per cent of the Indian population. Whilst recent economic developments have boosted India's economy, the benefits are limited. Indian children continue to face significant deprivation, malnutrition and vulnerability (for example, the ongoing high rate of female infanticide).

India acceded to the UNCRC on 11 December 1992. In 2003, India ratified the Hague Intercountry Adoption Convention. This was followed in 2005 with the ratification of the Optional Protocol to the UNCRC on the sale of children, etc. These international treaties are set against an existing legislative framework based on colonial and post-colonial laws, notably the Guardian and Wards Act 1890, and the 1956 Adoption and Maintenance Act. More recently, there have been a series of child-focused Acts passed, notably the Juvenile Justice (Care and Protection of Children) Act 2000 and its 2006 amendment, the Commission for the Protection of Child Rights Act 2005 and the Protection of Children from Sexual Offences Act 2012. This brief summary of federal legislation demonstrates a significant difference in effective legal regulation between India and its neighbour, Nepal. However, whilst Nepal lacks a strong legal and regulatory framework, as we shall see there remain practical challenges to implementation in a federal state as large as India.

---

[33] Committee on the Rights of the Child, *Concluding observations on the consolidated third and fourth periodic report of India*, 13 June 2014, CRC/C/IND/CO/3-4.

Adoption and Intercountry Adoption

Adoption rights were until 2014 restricted in India. Prior to a Supreme Court decision in February 2014, adoption was restricted to Hindus, Buddhists and Jains.[34] The decision by the Supreme Court was a landmark judgment. The judgment held that any person, irrespective of religion, could adopt a child under the Juvenile Justice (Care and Protection) Act 2000. Indeed, recognising the separate personal laws for Muslims the Supreme Court held that this right to adopt prevailed even if 'the personal laws of the particular religion do not permit it'.[35] The petitioner, Shabnam Hashmi, had been advised in 2005 that she would only have 'guardianship rights' for the one-year-old girl that she adopted. In an interview after the Supreme Court issued its decision, Mrs Hashmi noted that 'We wanted to treat her like a naturally born child and wanted her to feel that way. But law and government officials stood in the way. The Supreme Court has passed a landmark verdict and now people of all religions can adopt'.[36]

Following the death of an Indian child travelling to the USA to be adopted, in 1981, a petition was submitted by an advocate to the Supreme Court complaining of the 'malpractices indulged in by the social organisation and voluntary agencies engaged in the work of offering Indian children in adoption to foreign parents'.[37] The petitioner accused the organisations and agencies of exposing such children to 'want of proper care'.[38] The *Laxmi Kant Pandey* case is a landmark. Justice Bhagwati noted that the Supreme Court directed child welfare organisations to develop domestic adoption programmes in India, whilst placing a quota on foreign adoptions (only 50 per cent of adoptions could be by foreigners). In addition, the decision expanded the mandate of child placement organisations to include a range of services for children. Drawing on the preamble to the National Policy for the Welfare of Children, which states that 'children are a "supremely

---

[34] *Shabnam Hashmi v Union of India & Others*, 19 February 2014. Available at: supremecourtofindia.nic.in/outtoday/wp4702005. Last accessed 15 July 2015.
[35] *Shabnam Hashmi v Union of India and Ors* at 34.
[36] H.V. Nair, 'Supreme Courts Gives Adoption Rights to Muslims,' *India Today*, 20 February 2014. Accessible at: Indiatoday.intoday.in/story/supreme-court-gives-adoption-rights-to-muslis/1/344463.
[37] *Laxmi Kant Pandey v Union of India & Anr* on 27 September, 1985, at 1. Accessible at http://indiankanoon.org/doc/1402035. Last accessed 6 October 2015.
[38] *Laxmi Kant Pandey v The Union of India*, at 1.

important national asset'",[39] Justice Bhagwati expressed concern for the impact of the loss to the nation arising from intercountry adoptions and the potential problems of assimilation by the children. For Justice Bhagwati, intercountry adoption should not be an 'independent activity in itself' because it could 'degenerate into trading' and promote abandonment.

As discussed previously, in relation to Nepal, children who are adopted transnationally generate immediate resources in the form of donations to the children's home.[40] Yngvesson suggests that as a result staff may therefore privilege or prefer intercountry adoptions and accept apparently abandoned children or those whose mothers wants to relinquish them, rather than seeking to trace birth kin.[41] However, Justice Bhagwati recognised barriers to domestic adoption. He states, 'it has been the experience ... of social welfare agencies working in the area of adoption that, by and large, Indian parents are not enthusiastic about taking a stranger child in adoption'.[42] Expanding on this observation, Justice Bhagwati noted that 'even if [Indian parents] decide to take such a [stranger] child in adoption they prefer to adopt a boy rather than a girl and they are wholly averse to adopting a handicapped child, with the result that the majority of abandoned, destitute or orphan girls and handicapped children have very little possibility of finding adoptive parents within the country and their future lies only in adoption by foreign parents'.[43]

The case did prompt a more aggressive policy of domestic adoption with an active campaign in 1990s. The campaign challenged existing ideas about 'the family' that inhibited adoption and fostering by presenting adopted and foster children as family forms like any other. By the late 1990s, directors of Indian child welfare societies reported waiting lists of Indian adoptive parents and a gradual shift in the bias against girls. Despite the apparent success of the campaign, there remain social and cultural barriers, for example, a preference for light-skinned children and for healthy, non-disabled children. Finally, there remains a reluctance to acknowledge adoptive status outside of the immediate family.

---

[39] *Laxmi Kant Pandey v The Union of India*, at 16.
 No date is given for the National Policy for the Welfare of Children.
[40] Yngvesson, *Belonging in an Adopted World*, chapter 3.   [41] Id.
[42] *Laxmi Kant Pandey v The Union of India*, at 30.   [43] Id.

As required by in the Hague Intercountry Adoption Convention the Indian authorities established the Central Adoption Resource Agency. In 2003, 39 per cent of children adopted were for intercountry adoptions (1,398). The main receiving country was the United States. In the same year, 60 per cent of adopted children were aged under five years (the percentage for intercountry adoptions is unclear).[44] On the face of it, it appears that India has implemented important legislation to improve and strengthen the administrative and regulatory framework to promote the 'best interests' of children. However, deep concerns remain about the efficacy and the political commitment to independent functioning of these statutory entities.[45]

One of the reasons for more federal level regulation arose from a series of adoption scandals. On three separate occasions in 1995, 1999 and 2000 in the state of Andhra Pradesh, allegations were made about the systematic buying of babies, in particular from the nomadic Lambadas.[46] Investigations of the orphanages at the centre of the allegations revealed other illicit practices.[47]

More recently, the Committee on the Rights of the Child made a number of recommendations in respect of the 'best interests of the child'. The Committee expressed concern at the lack of detailed information on measures taken to ensure that, in practice, the right of children to have their best interests taken as a primary consideration is consistently applied by professionals working for and with children in all areas affecting them. With reference to General Comment No. 14, the Committee recommended India to:

(a) Develop procedures and criteria to provide guidance to all relevant persons in authority for determining the best interests of the child in every area and for giving those interests due weight as a primary consideration; as well as ensure that such procedures and criteria are disseminated to courts of law, administrative authorities and

---

[44] A.S. Shenoy, *Child Adoption Policy in India – Review*. Paper presented at 1st International Conference on Intercountry Adoption, Kathmandu, Nepal, March 2007. Available at http://unstats.un.org/unsd/vitalstatkb/Attachment482.aspx

[45] S. Raha and A. Mehendale, 'Children's Commission: A Case of State Apathy', *Economic and Political Weekly*, 18 January 2014, 17.

[46] D. M. Smolin, 'The two faces of intercountry adoptions: The significance of the Indian adoption scandals' (2005) 35 *Seton Hall Law Review* 403, at 450.

[47] Smolin, 'The two faces of intercountry adoptions', at 493.

legislative bodies, public and private social welfare institutions, as well as traditional and religious leaders and the public at large;
(b) Establish effective monitoring and evaluation procedures in that regard.[48]

Although, as outlined India has enacted a range of child-focussed legislation, and the importance of the judicial decision in *Laxmi Kant Pandey* makes it clear that in a federal union the size of India that challenges remain at the local level to the effective implementation of Art. 3.

D Conclusion: States, Rights and Implementation

Bartholet argues that 'adoption abuses exist...But there is no persuasive evidence that adoption abuses are extensive'.[49] A vocal advocate for intercountry adoption, Bartholet is explicit in her opposition to increased restrictions of intercountry adoption. However, as discussed in the preceding section there is abuse and it is not taking place on 'an occasional basis'.[50] She criticises the UNCRC and the Hague Intercountry Adoption Convention subsidiarity provisions and strongly argues against the importance for a child of her or his 'heritage rights'. Whilst it is clear that Bartholet's stance is based on strong convictions in the right of all children to be raised in 'a nurturing family', the lack of detail in her article overlooks the evidence not only of abuse of the adoption system but the longer term issues experienced by children who are adopted through intercountry adoption. She does comment on the impact of long-term institutionalisation on children but in relation to babies and children under one years old. The evidence from Nepal and India demonstrates that it is often older children who have been put forward for intercoutry adoption. Bartholet in focussing on certain rights and playing down others illustrates the complexity of rights.

This chapter has focussed on the state parties and their obligations under Art. 3 of the UNCRC. From focussing on two South Asian states

---

[48] *Concluding observations on the combined third and fourth periodic reports of India*, 13 June 2014, para. 36. Accessible at: www.refworld.org/publisher,CRC,CONCOBSERVA TIONS,IND,541bee3e4,0.html. Last accessed 6 October 2015.

[49] E. Bartholet, 'International Adoption: The Human Rights Position', http://nrs.harvard.edu/urn-3:HUL.Inst.Repos:3228398, at 24. This is a pre-peer review version of the article 'International Adoption: The Human Rights Position' at Elizabeth Bartholet, International Adoption: The Human Rights Position, 1 *Global Policy* (2010).

[50] Bartholet, 'International Adoption', at 32.

we can gain important insights into the barriers to effective implementation. In recent years, anthropological and socio-legal research on human rights has highlighted the complexity of the rights claims and rights implementation. For example, research on the hybrid construction of women's rights in Iran through a blend of Shari'a law and international human rights illustrates that despite the global proliferation of rights talk, often anchored by reference to international conventions (e.g., CEDAW or UNCRC), it has not produced normative uniformity.[51] Others argue that there is a multiplication of rights constructions as international, national and local norms collide, merge and produce new hybrid meanings in different contexts. The production of new, hybrid, meanings has given rise to 'normative pluralism'.[52] However, whilst we can trace a flow of rights there are challenges between international rights and national or local norms. A range of scholars have illustrated how the 'very lightness of rights reconstructions' can lead to the limitation or denial of 'rights transformative powers'.[53] Specifically for this chapter are concerns over the failure of rights to deliver – notably the challenges at the national and local level – the effective and meaningful implementation of Art. 3. As Massoud demonstrates in his ethnographic research in Sudan, rights claims have little effect where the state lacks the institutional capacity.[54] Massoud notes that 'in a state embroiled in civil war', like Nepal, 'the law in not an unqualified human good'.[55] There remains in Nepal a lack of institutional capacity ranging from inadequate monitoring of child centres and an ineffective legal system to regulate and oversee intercountry adoptions from the perspective of the 'best interests' of the child.

Of course, it is important to recognise that states differ significantly in their acceptance of human rights depending on their political system

---

[51] A. Osanloo, *The Politics of Women's Rights in Iran* (Princeton: Princeton University Press, 2009), p. 207.
[52] M. Goodale, 'The Power of Rights: Tracking Empires of Law and New Forms of Social Resistance' in M. Goodale and S.E. Merry (eds.), *The Practice of Human Rights* (New York, NY: Cambridge University Press, 2007), 130, p. 135.
[53] M. McCann, 'The unbearable lightness of rights: On sociolegal inquiry in the global era', (2014) 48 *Law and Society Review* 245, at 263.
[54] M.F. Massoud, *Law's Fragile State: Colonial, Authoritarian and Humanitarian Legacies in Sudan* (New York, NY: Cambridge University Press, 2013), in particular Chapter 7, pp. 211–230
[55] M.F. Massoud, *Law's Fragile State*, p. 228.

and the actions of civil society.[56] Ratifying a convention, such as the UNCRC, can increase the resonance of human rights for its population. However, as Merry notes 'this raises a dilemma'.[57] Rights are more likely to be effective where they are resonant, where there are institutions that will respond to rights claims and where complainants can mobilize resources and allies to promote their claims. This is reflected to an extent in India, notably in the petition that initiated the case of Lakshmi Kant Pandey. Yet, rights frameworks are less successful in situations where, as in the case of child centres in Nepal, there is no single perpetrator but where certain groups are vulnerable, often children from remote mountainous communities, due to an unequal economic and political system.

By examining Art. 3 in the context of domestic and intercountry adoption in South Asia this chapter highlights the challenges to implementation of the UNCRC. The chapter's contribution is to remind us that the majority of children live in states that have weak state institutions, regimes that may be undemocratic and in which the 'voice of the child' remains unheard, if not, actually silent. From an anthropological perspective paying attention at the local level reveals a great deal. At the international level the state is the vehicle for the implementation of the UNCRC. This assumes that a state will be viewed as benevolent and on the side of its citizens. Yet as illustrated by a range of anthropological studies, we know that the state is not viewed as the neutral or the benevolent source of protection. Many ordinary people view the state with mistrust and do not comply with state norms. This raises significant concerns for children and young people separated from or abandoned by their parents or birth family, or without kin. As illustrated by the irregularities surrounding intercountry adoption these children are separated, without their consent or the ability to consent from their cultural and social roots. The sense of 'belonging' in two different worlds, the world of the birth parents and that of the adopted parents and yet not belonging fully in either is captured by Yngvesson. In her nuanced ethnographic study of intercountry adopted children in the USA and Sweden, Yngvesson's informants, adult adoptees, reflect on

---

[56] See B.A. Simmons, 'Reflections on mobilzing for human rights' (2012) 44 *International Law and Politics* 729.

[57] S.E. Merry, 'Inequality and rights: Commentary on Michael McCann's "The Unbearable Lightness of Rights"' (2014) 48(2) *Law and Society Review* 285, at 292.

their 'two different identities'.[58] The importance of identity and the impact on growing children should not be underestimated. Underlying the concerns over intercountry adoption, indeed why UNICEF and the Hague Intercountry Adoption Convention favour domestic adoption over intercountry adoption is a recognition of the potential psychological impact on the adoptee. For states to fully effect Art. 3 and in particular to ensure that state authorities do take the 'best interests' of the child into account the underlying, often complex, cultural and social values of the state and its representatives have to be addressed.

[58] Yngvesson, *Belonging in an Adopted World*, at 154–164.

PART IV

Parenting Disputes and the Best Interests of the Child

13

Canada's Controversy over Best Interests and Post-Separation Parenting

NICHOLAS BALA

A Introduction: Canada's Outdated Divorce Act

Over the past quarter century, many jurisdictions have reformed legislation that governs post-separation parenting and that articulates an approach to the 'best interests' of the child for this context. However, in Canada, the primary statute that governs post-separation parenting, the Divorce Act,[1] was enacted in 1985 and continues to use the traditional concepts of 'custody' and 'access,' with their 'winner and loser' connotations. Despite the constancy of the statute, there have been very significant changes in practice; some form of co-parenting is now the most common arrangement, though there is equal parenting time only in a minority of cases.

The present law is controversial and there have been efforts to reform the Divorce Act, including a bill that would have created a presumption of 'equal parenting time'. The proponents argued that this presumption would both promote the best interests of children and protect the rights of parents. While this proposal was opposed by many family justice professionals and not enacted, there is a need for reform. The present statute does not reflect social science research, and contains no reference to the effects of domestic violence on children or the views of children. The concepts of custody and access have unfortunate proprietary connotations, fail to reflect parenting realities, and tend to promote adversarial attitudes.

This chapter begins with a discussion of the evolution of Canada's laws on post-separation parenting,[2] and the adoption of the 'best interests of

---

[1] Divorce Act, RSC 1985, c. 3 (2nd Supp.), hereinafter referred to as 'the Divorce Act'.
[2] This chapter focuses on cases where a child has two opposite sex parents; similar issues arise with same-sex parents, though there is much less research on issues related to same-sex parents and their post-separation parenting.

the child' approach, as well as considering the evolution of practice. It then explores the controversy in Canada over the best interests of children, and various efforts at law reform.[3] The chapter concludes by sketching a proposal for reform, based on support of co-parenting after separation but not 'equal parenting', and by briefly considering the challenging question of the relationship between statutory articulations of the best interests of children and better outcomes for children.

B The Evolution of Parenting Law in Canada

During the latter part of the nineteenth century, legislation was enacted in Canada that began to recognize the rights of married women, and by the first part of the twentieth century courts applied the 'tender years doctrine' when parents separated. Reflecting the parenting arrangements within marriage during that period, mothers almost always were granted custody of the children.[4]

In 1968, Canada's first national divorce law was enacted. The Divorce Act 1968 gave judges little direction about how to deal with the issues of custody and access, leaving this to a judicial assessment of what was considered 'fit and just having regard to the conduct of the parties, and the condition, means and other circumstances of each of them'.[5] As recently as 1976, the Supreme Court of Canada considered it a matter of 'common sense' that children should normally be in the custody of

---

[3] There is a complex division of responsibility for family law in Canada between the federal Parliament and the provinces. Under the Constitution Act, 1867, RSC 1985, App. II, No. 11, ss. 91 & 92, the federal government has jurisdiction over divorce, including issues of support and parenting upon termination of marriage, while the provinces have jurisdiction over property issues for those getting divorced, and for all issues for those who cohabited outside of marriage or never lived together. The provinces also have jurisdiction over the 'administration of justice', including responsibility for the provision of support services such as mediation. While complex jurisdictional issues can arise, and there is some variation between provinces in some aspects of family law, there has been a strong tendency for legislators and judges to promote uniformity between provinces. The federal government, with its jurisdiction over divorce and its spending powers, has taken the lead on family justice reform in Canada over the past quarter century. Thus, while each province has its own post-separation parenting legislation that applies when parents are not getting a divorce, in practical terms, the Divorce Act provides the principal guidance for resolution of parenting disputes, and its reform has been a major focus of national controversy. See D. A. R. Thompson, 'Rules and Rulelessness in Family Law: Recent Developments, Judicial and Legislative', (2000)18 *Can Fam L Q* 25.
[4] See, e.g., *Bell v. Bell* [1955] OWN 341 at 344 (C.A.).
[5] Divorce Act, SC 1967–68, c. 24, s. 11.

their mothers in the event of separation,[6] though in deciding about child custody courts at that time continued to take account of a mother's conduct in 'breaking up a happy home' or committing adultery.[7] The parent with 'custody,' usually the mother, was 'exclusively' responsible for the 'care, upbringing and education of the child'.[8] The access parent, almost always the father, had a limited role, characterized by some judges as a 'passive bystander' or 'visitor' in the child's life.[9]

In 1985, a new Divorce Act was enacted, with adultery and cruelty retained as fault-based grounds for granting a divorce, and one year separation was added; this no-fault ground is now by far the most commonly used ground for divorce. This Act also adopted 'the best interests of the child' test for resolution of disputes over custody and access. However, it gives limited direction about this determination. One provision states that 'past conduct' of a parent (like adultery) is not to be taken into consideration 'unless the conduct is relevant to the ability... to act as a parent'.[10] At the time of its enactment in 1985, a number of American states had a statutory presumption of joint custody. While there was advocacy in Canada at that time for the enactment of similar legislation, the government was not prepared to enact this presumption, though the Act recognizes joint custody as an option. Subsection 16(10), the so-called 'maximum contact' provision, requires that courts should give effect to the 'principle that a child... should have as much contact with each spouse as is consistent with the best interests of the child'. In 1993, the Supreme Court observed:

> Parliament has expressed its opinion that contact with each parent is valuable, and that the judge should ensure that this contact is maximized. The modifying phrase 'as is consistent with the best interests of the child' means that the goal of maximum contact of each parent with the child is not absolute. To the extent that contact conflicts with the best interests of the child, it may be restricted. But only to that extent. *Parliament's decision to maintain maximum contact between the child and both parents is amply supported by the literature.*[11]

---

[6] *Talsky v. Talsky* [1976] 2 SCR 292.
[7] See, e.g., *Fishback v. Fishback* [1985] OJ1590 (Ont Dist Ct.).
[8] *Kruger v. Kruger* (1979) 11 RFL (2d) 52 (Ont. C.A.).
[9] See the comments of L'Heureux-Dubé J. in *Gordon v. Goertz* (1996) 19 RFL (4th) 117; although she was dissenting, her approach reflects the dominant views in the 1960s and 1970s about the limited role of 'access parents' after separation.
[10] RSC 1985 (2nd Supp.) c 3 s. 16(9).
[11] *Young v. Young* 1993 SCJ 112, at para. 204. Emphasis added.

Despite the Court's endorsement of subs. 16(10), there are concerns that this provision may increase the risk of harm in situations of domestic violence, by promoting contact between children and abusive parents, and exposing primary care parents to continued risk.[12] The silence of the Divorce Act about domestic violence heightens these concerns.

While there is only limited Canadian data tracking changes over the years in post-separation parenting, it is clear that a typical order now provides for significantly more involvement with a non-primary residential parent (usually the father) than was the case thirty years ago. It is now accepted that it is generally desirable for non-primary residential parents to not just be 'visitors', but to be involved in the education and extra-curricular activities of their children on a regular basis.

By the late 1970s, the concept of joint legal custody was starting to be used in Canada. Initially, the courts were very cautious about this approach, as reflected in a 1979 Ontario Court of Appeal decision, which held that 'joint custody [is] an exceptional disposition, reserved for a limited category of separated parents'.[13] Gradually, however, there has been a growing recognition that it is often valuable for children to have a strong relationship with both parents. While most joint custody arrangements are the result of negotiation or mediation, courts are now more willing to order joint custody, despite the objections of one or both parents.

In 2005, the Ontario Court of Appeal decided two cases involving joint legal custody. In *Kaplanis*,[14] the Court overturned an order for joint custody imposed by the lower court, but in *Ladisa*[15] the Court upheld the decision of the trial judge imposing joint legal custody. In both cases, the mother opposed joint legal custody and sought sole custody. The distinguishing feature of the cases was that in *Ladisa*, the Court was satisfied that the parents were able to put aside their differences and were able to cooperate effectively in the interests of the child.[16] In *Kaplanis*, the Court declined to order joint custody, stating:

> The fact that one parent professes an inability to communicate with the other parent does not, in and of itself, mean that a joint custody order

---

[12] See, e.g., J. Cohen & N. Gershbain, 'For the Sake of the Child Reforms and the Perils of Maximum Contact' (2001) 19 *Can J Fam L* 121.
[13] *Baker v. Baker* (1979) 23 OR (2d) 391 (CA).
[14] *Kaplanis v. Kaplanis* (2005) 10 RFL (6th) 373 (ONCA.).
[15] *Ladisa v. Ladisa* (2005) 11 RFL (6th) 50 (ONCA).
[16] See discussion in M. Shaffer, 'Joint Custody Since Kaplanis and Ladisa: A Review of Recent Ontario Case Law', (2007) 26 *Can Fam L Q* 315.

cannot be considered. On the other hand, hoping that communication between the parties will improve once the litigation is over does not provide a sufficient basis for the making of an order of joint custody. There must be some evidence ... that, despite their differences, the parties are able to communicate effectively with one another.[17]

These appellate decisions establish that judges should focus on the actual history of the parenting and relationships, not just on statements of parents about their feelings towards each other, which may be very negative, especially during litigation.

Canadian judges have also generally accepted that, in the absence of evidence that a parent poses a risk to a child, overnights with a father should begin in the first two years of a child's life, even if the mother objects.[18] In a 2015 decision, the Ontario Court of Appeal endorsed the use of concepts other than the Divorce Act's custody and access terminology as the basis for a 'parenting order', observing:

> For over twenty years, multi-disciplinary professionals have been urging the courts to move away from the highly charged terminology of 'custody' and 'access'. These words denote that there are winners and losers when it comes to children. They promote an adversarial approach to parenting and do little to benefit the child...
>
> It was therefore open to the trial judge to adopt the 'parenting plan' proposed by the assessor without awarding 'custody'.[19]

There is a tension in these litigated high-conflict cases over parenting. Judges do not want to give one parent (usually the mother) an effective veto over joint custody and substantial involvement of the other parent in the child's life, simply by asserting that co-operation is not possible or in the child's interests. However, the courts are also concerned about placing children in a situation where the parents are expected to co-operate closely in making decisions and caring for children but they display on-going anger for each other and cannot communicate effectively.

---

[17] *Kaplanis v. Kaplanis* (2005) 10 RFL (6th) 373, at para. 11 (ONCA).

[18] See, e.g., *Adams v. Nobili* [2011] OJ 3598 (SCJ), father to have overnights three nights a week for eighteen-month-old child; and *Lygouriatis v. Gohm* 2006 SKQB 448 overnights with father starting at three months.

[19] *M. v. F.* 2015 ONCA 277, at para. 39 and 40 per Benotto JA. The term 'custody assessor' is commonly used in Canada, while other jurisdictions use terms like 'evaluator' or 'investigator'. The evaluator in this case was an experienced psychologist, appointed by the court with the consent to both parties, to investigate the case and make recommendations to the parents and court. A 'parenting plan' is a detailed document that establishes a plan for the child; the concept is more fully discussed later in this chapter.

As a result, judges are willing to impose a regime of joint legal or physical custody even without parental consent, but generally are reluctant to do so if the parties get as far as a trial over parenting issues.[20] However, the judicial receptivity to consider some form of joint custody even for a relatively small portion of the litigated parenting cases has clearly had a major influence on the much larger number that are settled. The evolution of judicial approaches to joint custody reveal strong legal support for various forms of co-parenting, though they do not support a presumption of equal parenting time.[21]

Reflecting the evolution of the case law and the increased role of fathers in providing care for children in intact families,[22] there have been substantial changes in patterns of parenting after separation. Among separated parents, in about one in ten cases in Canada, the father now has primary care and in six out of ten the mother has primary residence.[23] However, in more than a fifth of cases, each parent has the child at least 40 per cent of the time, though less than one in ten involve equal residential care.[24]

The portion of cases in which there is shared decision-making or joint legal custody has gradually increased over the past three decades. Research suggests that about two-thirds of Canadian cases now involve some form of joint legal custody or shared parental responsibility for decision-making.

Relatively few parenting disputes in Canada are resolved by a judge after a court hearing.[25] Most cases result in a parenting arrangement based on negotiation, judicially led case conferencing or mediation, often resulting in some form of co-parenting arrangement.

---

[20] See M. Shaffer, 'Contested Joint Custody in the Ontario Courts: A Case Law Review', *AFCC*, Toronto, 29 May 2014.

[21] Alberta and British Columbia have enacted legislation to adopt concepts that replace 'custody' and 'access', and to support some form of shared parenting, though this legislation is generally only directly applicable if the parents cohabited outside of marriage: Family Law Act SA 2003,c F-4.5; and Family Law Act SBC 2011, c 25.

[22] Statistics Canada, *General Social Survey – 2010 Overview of Time Use of Canadians* (2011); and Statistics Canada, 'Converging Gender Roles', (July 2006), Vol. 7, no. 7, *Perspectives on Labour and Income*.

[23] Statistics Canada, *Fifty Years of Families in Canada: 1961 to 2011* (2013); and Statistics Canada, *Parenting and Child Support After Separation or Divorce* (February 2014).

[24] *Survey of Family Courts and Court File Review, Internal Analysis* (Department of Justice Canada, April 2013).

[25] Statistics Canada, *Divorce Cases in Civil Court, 2010/2011* (2012).

C Controversy over Best Interests Reforms

In the three decades since the enactment of the Divorce Act there has been significant controversy in Canada about its concepts and articulation of best interests of the child. Debates about these issues have engaged politicians, government officials, professionals and academics, and resulted in 'gender wars' of polemical rhetoric: fathers' groups[26] argue that the present law 'disenfranchises fathers', while feminists castigate some proponents of reform for 'demonizing mothers'.[27]

The Special Committee and Bill C-22 (1998–2002)

When federal *Child Support Guidelines* were introduced in 1996, there was vociferous criticism that Parliament was increasing the amounts of child support that would be paid, usually to mothers, while failing to address the concerns of fathers about a legal regime that failed to protect their relationships with their children. In response, the Liberal government established a Special Parliamentary Committee to consider changes to better protect the interests of children and the rights of parents in the context of divorce. At Committee hearings, fathers' groups and women's advocates often bitterly attacked one another.[28] In 1998, the Committee issued its report, *For the Sake of the Children*, with forty-eight recommendations for legislative reform and a broad range of changes to the family justice system, intended to increase the role of non-custodial parents in the lives of their children and encourage consensual resolution of family disputes.[29] The report

---

[26] While many refer to the supporters of Bill C-560 as 'fathers' rights advocates', and that terminology is used here, there are also women who support the 'equal parenting movement', just as there are many men who support the feminists' opposition to a presumption of equal parenting. For the views of one prominent female supporter of equal parenting and Bill C-560, see B. Kay, 'After a divorce, equal parenting rights should be the norm', *National Post*, March 19, 2014. For recent polemics supporting of a presumption of 'equal parenting' and respect for 'fathers' rights', see, e.g., E. Kruk, *The Equal Parent Presumption* (Montreal: McGill Queen's Press, 2013); and G. Brown, *Ideology and Dysfunction in Family Law: How Courts Disenfranchise Fathers* (Calgary, AB: Canadian Constitutional Foundation and Frontier Centre for Public Policy, 2014).

[27] See, e.g., S. Boyd, 'Demonizing Mothers: Fathers' Rights Discourses in Child Custody Law Reform Processes' (2004) 6 *J Assoc Res Mothering* 52.

[28] See N. Bala, 'A Report from Canada's Gender War Zone: Reforming the Child Related Provisions of the Divorce Act' (1999) 16 *Can J Fam L* 163.

[29] Canada, Parliament, Special Joint Committee of the Senate and Commons on Child Custody and Access Report, *For the Sake of the Children* (1998).

gave inadequate attention to issues like domestic violence, so further consultations were undertaken by the Department of Justice after its release. In 2002, the government proposed amendments to the Divorce Act in Bill C-22.[30] That Bill would have replaced the concepts of custody and access with 'parental responsibility' and 'contact', and supported use of shared parenting. It was criticized both by fathers' groups for not sufficiently advancing their rights and by feminists for still dealing inadequately with domestic violence.[31] It also failed to adequately recognize the rights of children. There was, however, significant support for this reform project, but the Bill died on the Order Paper due to the end of the parliamentary session. While the Liberal Minister of Justice at the time pledged to bring back a revised version of the Bill,[32] before this occurred the issue of same-sex marriage took over the family justice reform agenda in Canada, and then in 2006 the Liberals were voted out of office and replaced by the Conservatives.

Bill C-560 (2013–14)

Bill C-560 was proposed by backbench Conservative M.P. Maurice Vellacott in 2013,[33] proposing the adoption of a presumption of 'equal parenting time.' The Bill was a cause of considerable public controversy.[34] It was strongly supported by fathers' rights advocates, and had significant support from members of the caucus of the governing Conservative party. However, it was clearly at odds with the more balanced approaches to law reform of the Department of Justice, and many family justice professionals were opposed to the proposed legislation.[35]

---

[30] Bill C-22, 37th Parliament, 2nd Session, 1st Reading 10 December 2002.

[31] L. Neilson, 'Putting Revisions to the Divorce Act Through a Family Violence Research Filter: The Good, the Bad and the Ugly', (2003) 20 *Can J Fam L* 11.

[32] 'Cotler likes custody reform package', *Lawyers Weekly*, Feb. 20, 2004.

[33] Bill C-560, 2nd Session, 41st Parliament, 1st Reading Dec. 16, 2013; defeated May 27, 2014.

[34] The Bill resulted in considerable media coverage and public debate; see, e.g., B. Ludmer, 'Speaker's Corner: Time for Canada to embrace equal shared parenting,– *Law Times*, 5 May 2014; E. Kruk, 'Equal shared parenting – best for parents, best for children', *National Post*, 25 March 2014; T. Kheiriddin, '"Equal shared parenting" law doesn't put kids first', *National Post*, 20 March 2014; and N. Bala, 'Equal time for custody of children is a simplistic solution', *Toronto Star*, 10 March 2014.

[35] Canadian Bar Association, National Family Law Section, *In the Interests of Children Response to Bill C-560* (May 2014) www.cba.org/CBA/submissions/pdf/14-24-eng.pdf.

Unable to garner the support of opposition parties or even Cabinet, the Bill did not pass the first reading stage. The Conservative government, when faced with the alternatives of risking sustained opposition from family justice professionals and women's groups as a result of support for Bill C-560, or risking the wrath of its caucus by introducing a less radical set of reforms, opted to take no action.

Most Canadian families are not characterized by 'equal parenting time' when parents are living together, and it therefore unwise to have a presumption that this should be the best arrangement for children if they separate. Experience in Canada and elsewhere reveals that parental work schedules, relative location of residences and new relationships make equal parenting time practical in only a minority of situations of parental separation and social science research does *not* support enactment of such a presumption.

While a *presumption* of equal time is not appropriate, there are cases where this is an arrangement that is practicable and in a child's best interests. Indeed, as intact Canadian families slowly move towards greater equality in child care, one would expect that there will continue to be a gradual trend towards a increase in the number of equal parenting time arrangements for separated parents in the future.

Domestic Violence and Children's Best Interests

Social science research has clearly established that intimate partner violence (IPV) poses significant risks to children, whether or not it occurs in their presence.[36] Those who are victims of IPV may be less effective as parents as a result of the abuse; those who are perpetrators of violence are not good role models for their children, and are more likely to have poor parenting practices and to be physically or emotionally abusive towards their children. Further, children who are exposed to violence between their parents often find this experience traumatic. The safety of children and their caregivers must always be a priority.

Most jurisdictions have specific legislative provisions that recognize IPV as a factor to be taken into account when making best interests decisions, and many Canadian cases and the provincial statutes governing parenting for those who are not married recognize that domestic violence

---

[36] See, e.g., P. Jaffe, J. R. Johnston, L. Crooks & N. Bala, 'Custody Disputes Involving Allegations of Domestic Violence: The Need for Differentiated Approaches to Parenting Plans', (2008) 46 *FCR* 500.

is a serious concern when parenting decisions are being made.[37] The 1985 Divorce Act, however, makes no mention of domestic violence.

Bill C-560 minimized the issue of 'family violence', characterizing it is as an 'additional consideration' rather than a 'primary consideration', and indicating that partner violence is only to be taken into account in making parenting orders if 'committed in the presence of the child'. This approach is inconsistent with both the social science research and public policy. While a parental history that may include acts of IPV should not always be determinative of a child's best interests, there is no justification for treating it as a secondary consideration; IPV may be highly relevant to the child's best interests. It is also wrong to limit consideration to cases where violence has occurred 'in the presence of a child', as children often suffer from residing in a home where there is spousal violence, even if it is not proved that they actually witnessed the physical assaults. Further, an on-going threat to the safety of a child's primary caregiver is highly significant to a child's welfare.

While many Canadian judges, lawyers and mediators already take account of partner violence in making settlements and decisions, the failure of the Divorce Act to even mention this factor clearly gives IPV less salience than it merits. Inclusion of domestic violence as a statutory 'best interests' factor would help ensure professionals properly identify and respond to it, and may be especially important for alerting those parents who lack proper legal advice of its significance.[38]

Role of Children's Perspectives

Article 12 of the UN Convention on the Rights of the Child[39] establishes that children have the *right* to have their views considered when decisions are made about them, but notably the Divorce Act makes no mention of the perspectives or preferences of children. While children in litigated cases are often very wary of 'taking sides' and rarely want to be asked to 'decide' about their living arrangements, they often want to

---

[37] See, e.g., N. Bala, P. Jaffe & L. Crooks, 'Spousal Violence and Child-Related Cases: Challenging Cases Requiring Differentiated Responses', (2008) 27 *Can Fam L Q* 1.

[38] See, e.g., M. Brinig, L. Frederick & L. Drozd, 'Perspectives on Joint Custody Presumptions as Applied to Domestic Violence Cases', (2014) 52 *Fam Ct Rev* 271.

[39] United Nations Convention on the Rights of the Child, 20 November 1989, in force 2 September 1990, 1577 UNTS 3.

be consulted in some way.[40] Further, a child-focused decision should take account of *information from children* about their perceptions of their interests, needs, experiences and relationships with parents and other relatives.[41]

Although the views and perspectives of children are only one factor, and there are cases involving alienation or manipulation by one parent when children's wishes should be discounted, too often the views of children are not even solicited. Children whose parents are involved in litigation or a high-conflict separation[42] typically want a reduction in parental hostility and an arrangement that will have both parents significantly involved in their lives, and, especially as they become older, that will be flexible enough to evolve to take account of their views, for example about schooling, visiting friends and extracurricular activities. While the manner in which children's perspectives are ascertained will vary with the nature of the case, the resources available and the child's ideas about participation, it is important for parenting legislation like the Divorce Act to acknowledge the importance of children's views.[43]

D Reforming the Divorce Act and Changing Culture

Opinion polls in Canada reveal high levels of public concern about the family justice system, and support for reforms that will encourage involvement of both parents in the lives of their children,[44] and there will undoubtedly renewed demands for the reform of the parenting provisions of the Divorce Act. It is to be hoped that the new majority Liberal government led by Justin Trudeau, elected in October 2015, will undertake reform of the Divorce Act to better reflect interests of children and parents and children, completing a project begun by Justin

---

[40] R. Birnbaum & M. Saini, 'A Qualitative Synthesis of Children's Participation in Custody Disputes', (2012) 22 *Research on Social Work Practice* 400; and R. Bessner, *The Voice of the Child in Divorce, Custody and Access Proceedings: Background Paper* (Justice Canada, 2002).

[41] See, e.g., N. Semple, 'The Silent Child: A Quantitative Analysis of Children's Evidence in Canadian Custody and Access Cases', (2011) 29 *Can Fam L Q* 1.

[42] See, e.g., C. Smart, 'Children's Narratives of Post-divorce Family Life: From Individual Experience to an Ethical Disposition', (2006) 54 *Soc Rev* 155.

[43] See e.g., N. Bala, R. Birnbaum, F. Cyr & D. McColley, 'Children's Voices in Family Court: Guidelines for Judges Meeting Children', (2013) 47 *Fam L Q* 381.

[44] See B. Ludmer, 'Time for Canada to Embrace Equal Shared Parenting', *Law Times*, 5 May 2014.

Trudeau's father, Pierre, in 1968 when as Minister of Justice and introduced Canada's first national Divorce Act.

While limitations of space prevent setting out a detailed proposal here,[45] it is possible to sketch out the major elements of a reform package. The concepts of custody and access in the Divorce Act are archaic; many jurisdictions have adopted more child-focused concepts that reflect the issues that parents need to address, and that can help them to structure their plans. These include concepts such as a division or sharing of *parental responsibility* for making decisions and a schedule of *parenting time*, through the making of a voluntary *parenting plan*, or, if parents cannot agree, through, a court-imposed *parenting order*.

Parenting plans and orders establish a schedule for a child's time in the care of each parent, and will have provisions dealing with such issues as: decision-making about education, extracurricular activities, religious upbringing and health care; parental involvement with schools and health care providers; communication between parents and contact with children while in the care of the other parent. These plans normally provide for consultation between parents before significant decisions are made. In cases with higher conflict there should be provision for a method of resolving future disagreements, whether by reference to a third party or dividing final decision-making for different issues. In most cases, the parent with responsibility for the child at the relevant time should be making day-to-day decisions about such matters as daily routine, diet, discipline and religious observance.

Consistent with Article 3 of the UN Convention on the Rights of the Child,[46] in the context of parental separation the application of the 'best interests of the child test' appropriately recognizes that the decisions must be made based on an assessment of the needs of the individual child, and is focused on the child's interests rather than the rights or interests of the parents. While the best interests test is central to decision-making, its limitations must be recognized: it is very vague, and without further articulation of principles or factors that should be taken into account, the decisions of judges applying this test may be unpredictable or reflect their personal biases and experiences, while the negotiations of

---

[45] For a more detailed proposal for law reform, see N. Bala, 'Bringing Canada's Divorce Act into the New Millennium: Enacting a Child-Focused Parenting Law', (2015) 40 *Queen's L J* 425.

[46] United Nations Convention on the Rights of the Child, 20 November 1989, in force 2 September 1990, 1577 UNTS 3.

parents will be less structured and settlements more difficult to achieve due to the lack of legislative guidance.[47]

The present version of the 'best interests' test in Canada's Divorce Act was enacted in 1986, before the adoption of the *UN Convention on the Rights of the Child*,[48] and needs to be more fully developed. Better articulation of best interests principles in legislation can help structure decision-making of courts and negotiation of parenting arrangements, recognizing that there must always be discretion to make individualized parenting arrangements

Subsection 16(10) of the Divorce Act presently establishes the 'maximum contact' principle to guide decision-making, but this provision is vague and circular. It also uses the unfortunate term 'contact', which suggests a limited role rather than explicitly focusing on the interests of children in having two parents actively involved in their care and upbringing. This provision should be rearticulated to recognize that:

> It is usually in the best interests of children whose parents are divorcing to have a co-parenting arrangement, that allows for both parents to have a significant role in exercising parental responsibilities, and for each parent to have regular and significant involvement in the care of their children.

There should *not* be a legislative specification of an expected amount of parenting time, as these arrangements need to take account of individual circumstances of each child, and should be altered as children get older and their circumstances change. However, it would be appropriate to adopt a version of the Australian 'meaningful involvement' provision to indicate that 'where it is reasonably practicable' and consistent with the child's best interests, parenting time should include care not only on weekends and during holiday periods, but also some parenting time during the week. These statements of principle about co-parenting are *not* intended to establish a presumption of equal parenting time as found in Bill C-560, but rather is a presumption of significant involvement of both parents in the lives of their children.

The 'co-parenting principle' always needs to be balanced with consideration of other factors that also should be identified in legislation, such as the level of conflict between the parents, a history of family violence,

---

[47] See, e.g., E. Scott & R. Emery, 'Gender Politics and Child Custody: The Puzzling Persistence of the Best Interests Standard', (2014) 77 *Law Cont Prob* 69.

[48] United Nations Convention on the Rights of the Child, 20 November 1989, in force 2 September 1990, 1577 UNTS 3.

the ability of the parents to communicate and cooperate, the age and developmental needs of the child, the distance between the parents' homes and the closeness of the child's relationship with each parent. Enacting a provision that it is normally in the interests of children to have a co-parenting arrangement is consistent with widely shared Canadian values about the importance of both parents in the lives of their children, and with current Canadian post-separation parenting practices.

Other statements of principle about the promotion of the best interests of children that should be included in legislation include recognition that:

- Parents have a responsibility to support a child's relationship with the other parent and family members, unless such relationships are detrimental to their wellbeing;
- Children benefit from stability and continuity in their relationships; if a parent has not lived with and cared for a child, the parent's time with the child should be increased gradually, having regard to the child's age and adjustment;
- Parents should be discouraged from taking unilateral actions or steps without notice to the other parent, unless this is necessary to protect a child from significant harm;
- Parenting arrangements should take account of parenting capacity, including issues of impairment of parenting capacity by drugs, alcohol or mental illness;
- Parenting arrangements must not expose a child or parent to a risk of abuse or family violence;
- Parenting arrangements should be reviewed and revised as children grow older and the needs of children and circumstances of parents change.

All of these principles are recognized in some measure in Canadian case law and are reflective of social science research, but their articulation in legislation would benefit parents and their advisors, as well as the courts.

As with the omission of domestic violence, the absence of mention of the views of children as a factor in the Divorce Act has not prevented judges from taking the child's views into account in proceedings under the Act. However, its omission clearly illustrates that the parenting provisions of the Act are out-dated and need to be reformed. Further, its omission may result in some professionals and parents themselves failing to take appropriate account of the views and perspectives of children. While there must be real sensitivity in how children are involved in the making of parenting plans so that they do not feel 'caught in the middle' or manipulated by their parents, too often their views are not solicited at all. In particular when parents are making their own plans without court involvement, children are often ignored.[49]

One of the primary objectives for the reforms proposed here is to support efforts to increase the use of consensual dispute resolution for family cases, including mediation, collaborative law and negotiated resolution.[50] The reforms proposed here would both reflect and reinforce changes that have been occurring in Canadian social and legal culture towards increased use of consensual dispute resolution and co-parenting. While there must be recognition that in most cases some form of sharing of parental responsibilities is in the best interests of children and parents, an important premise of these proposals is that it essential to recognize that there are cases where co-parenting, or even contact, poses grave risks and should not occur. In appropriate cases, lawyers and judges need to be able to resist sharing of parental responsibilities and time by adducing evidence of on-going concerns of domestic violence, parental mental health or substance abuse issues, or serious alienating behaviour. Even in cases where there are not physical violence, abuse or mental health concerns, there may be a high level of parental conflict that is not responsive to available interventions and it may be necessary to resist co-parenting. It is important to recognize that exposure to prolonged high conflict is harmful to children and that ultimately neither courts nor mental health professionals can get all parents to effectively co-parent.[51]

Another important objective of these proposals is to recognize that children should have a voice in the resolution of proceedings, and to ensure that judges, lawyers, mediators and other professionals consider how children should be involved. While children should never be pressured to be involved, and often require professional intermediaries to ensure that they can be engaged in a sensitive fashion, they often have significant perspectives and insights, and can be important advocates for

---

[49] J. B. Kelly & M. K. Kisthardt, 'Helping Parents Tell Their Children about Separation and Divorce: Social Science Frameworks and the Lawyer's Counseling Responsibility', (2009) 22 *J Am Acad Mat L* 1401.

[50] For a recent Canadian report advocating more use of consensual dispute resolution, see Action Committee on Access to Justice in Civil and Family Matters, *Meaningful Change for Family Justice: Beyond Wise Words: Final Report of the Family Justice Working Group of the Action Committee on Access to Justice in Civil and Family Matters* (2013).

[51] J. McIntosh, 'Legislating for Shared Parenting: Exploring Some Underlying Assumptions', (2009) 47 *Fam Ct Rev* 389.

consensual resolution. Children have the right under the Convention to have their voices heard, and understanding their perspectives can also promote better outcomes for them.

Some commentators argue that changing 'the law cannot change [parenting] behavior',[52] and are resistant to legislative reforms that are intended to promote co-operative post-separation parenting. It is true that changing concepts and articulation of more child-focused principles will not cause bitterly conflicted parents to develop a harmonious post-separation relationship, but statutory reforms can send important messages that many professionals and parents will be affected by, and can help to encourage procedural, systemic and attitudinal changes that will affect how many cases are resolved.

Although the interrelationships between legislative reform, the provision of more support services for families and cultural change are complex and multidirectional, the legislative changes and increased access to dispute resolution services in Australia contributed to a gradual change in culture among the family bar and other professionals in that country.[53] While there will clearly be a need for research on the effects of legislative change on the family justice process and outcomes for children in Canada, experience elsewhere suggests that changing legislation can help to reduce the use of courts to resolve family disputes.

---

[52] F. Kaganas & C. Piper, 'Sharing Parenting – a 70% Solution', (2002) *Child & Fam L Q* 365, at 379.

[53] See B. Smyth, R. Chisholm, B. Rogers & V. Son, 'Legislating for Shared-Time Parenting After Parental Separation: Insights from Australia', (2014) 77 *Law Cont Prob* 109.

14

In Harm's Way: The Evolving Role of Domestic Violence in the Best Interests Analysis

D. KELLY WEISBERG

A Introduction

The best interests of the child is the prevailing standard in child custody disputes in all fifty American states as well as many countries. Article 3 of the UN Convention on the Rights of the Child (CRC) reflects this principle in its opening words by affirming that the best interests of children shall be the 'primary consideration' in all actions concerning children whether undertaken by courts of law, legislative bodies or social welfare institutions.[1] Yet, a *primary* consideration does not mean the *sole* consideration. Legal determinations invariably involve the weighing of competing considerations, as the next paragraph of CRC Article 3 recognizes when it refers to the need to respect parental rights.[2] Implicit in the language of Article 3 is the recognition that the child's best interests may sometimes conflict with parental rights. This conflict is particularly evident in the context of custody determinations in families experiencing domestic violence.

This chapter will explore the evolution of the prevailing best-interests standard for custody determinations in the context of domestic violence. In the process, it will highlight landmark legal developments in the state of Colorado and compare them with those in the country of Australia. Both jurisdictions recently adopted a 'safety-first' approach that prioritizes child protection over parental rights in custody determinations in the context of domestic violence.

B Setting the Stage for the Law Reform Movement

Domestic violence plays a role in many aspects of family law. However, nowhere is its role more poignant than in child custody proceedings.

---

[1] United Nations Convention on the Rights of the Child, 20 November 1989, in force 2 September 1990, 1577 UNTS 3, Article 3.
[2] Ibid., Art. 3(2).

A significant percentage of contested child custody cases (perhaps as many as two-thirds to three-fourths) involve allegations of domestic violence.[3] National recognition of domestic violence as a social problem prompted many American states to reform the prevailing best-interests standard in custody law.

Currently, laws in all American states require courts to consider domestic violence – to varying degrees – in custody and visitation disputes.[4] This approach is a far cry from the traditional view that *ignored* evidence of domestic violence in custody proceedings. According to the traditional approach, judges in divorce proceedings regarded a husband's acts of intimate partner violence as *irrelevant* to the abuser's parent-child relationship. The emergence of no-fault divorce further cemented this approach by permitting courts to exclude marital fault – such as acts of domestic violence – from consideration in divorce.[5]

In the 1980s, lawmakers began taking domestic violence into account in law reform. Legislators enacted reforms of the criminal law (i.e., warrantless arrest laws, mandatory arrest laws, marital rape laws) and passed civil restraining order laws.[6] Soon, policy makers turned their attention to reform of child custody law.

---

[3] *See* Peter G. Jaffe, Samantha E. Poisson and Alison Cunningham, 'Domestic Violence in High-Conflict Divorce: Developing a New Generation of Research for Children', in Sandra A. Graham-Bermann and Jeffrey L. Edleson (eds.), *Domestic Violence in the Lives of Children: The Future of Research, Intervention, and Social Policy* (American Psychological Ass'n, 2001), p. 192 (citing a Canadian study finding that domestic violence was an issue in 75 per cent of custody-related disputes at a children's mental health center); Janet Johnston, Vivienne Roseby and Kathryn Kuehnle, *In the Name of the Child: A Developmental Approach to Understanding and Helping Children of Conflicted and Violent Divorce* (Springer Pub. Co., 2d ed., 2009), p. 308 (finding that domestic violence was alleged in two-thirds to three-fourths of custody-litigating families).

[4] Leslie J. Harris, 'Failure to Protect from Exposure to Domestic Violence in Private Custody Disputes' (2010) 44 *Fam L. Q.* 169–195 at 170.

[5] Nancy K.D. Lemon, 'Statutes Creating Rebuttable Presumptions Against Custody To Batterers: How Effective Are They?' (2001) 28 *Wm. Mitchell L. Rev.* 601–676 at 603.

[6] Law suits against the police for failure to protect victims spearheaded law reform. On the traditional response of law enforcement to domestic violence, *see* Joan Zorza, 'The Criminal Law of Misdemeanor Domestic Violence, 1970–1990' (1992–1993) 83 *J. Crim. L. and Criminology* 46–72 at 46, 47–48 For early suits against police departments, *see Scott v. Hart*, No. C-76-2395 (N.D. Cal. filed Oct. 28, 1976); *Bruno v. Codd*, 396 N.Y.S.2d 974 (Sup. Ct. 1977), *rev'd*, 407 N.Y.S.2d 165 (App. Div. 1978), *aff'd* 393 N.E.2d 976 (N.Y. 1979).

C Stages in the Evolving Role of Domestic Violence in Custody Law

Consideration of the role of domestic violence in child custody law evolved in three stages. The first stage of custody law reform occurred in the 1980s and early 1990s. It may be called the 'one-factor approach'. The second stage, or the 'rebuttable-presumption' approach, occurred in the 1990s. The third stage, or the 'safety-first' approach, is occurring at present.

The first stage of law reform occurred as a backlash against the joint custody movement. Beginning in the 1970s, no-fault divorce led to an escalation in the numbers of spouses seeking divorce. The no-fault revolution had the unexpected consequence of enhancing the role of fathers in post-divorce parenting. Several social forces coalesced in this result: (1) women's rights groups called for greater paternal involvement in child care in order to distribute the work load more evenly at a time when increasing numbers of women were entering the work force; (2) research findings highlighted the adverse consequences of divorce for children and pointed out that children fared best post-divorce when they experienced continuity of care by both parents; and (3) social scientists revealed the important role that fathers play in child development.[7]

In response to these social forces, fathers' rights groups lobbied for laws that authorized parents to share physical and legal custody. From 1979, when California enacted the first joint custody statute, until 1991, virtually all states adopted some form of joint custody laws.[8] However, critics soon realized that joint custody was not appropriate in all circumstances and especially not for families experiencing domestic violence.[9] This recognition reached the national level when, in 1990, Congress adopted a resolution that children should not be placed in the custody of parents who perpetrated domestic violence.[10]

---

[7] Joan B. Kelly, 'The Determination of Child Custody' (1994) 4 *The Future of Children* 121–140 at 123.

[8] Ibid., at 123.

[9] See, e.g., Judith G. Greenberg, 'Domestic Violence and the Danger of Joint Custody Presumptions' (2005) 25 *N. Ill. U. L. Rev.* 403–431 at 404.

[10] House Concurrent Resolution 172, Domestic Violence and Custody, 101th Cong. 2d Sess. (October 25, 1990).

First Stage: Domestic Violence as One Factor among Many

The congressional resolution in 1990 had a significant impact on state law reform.[11] Before the 1990s, domestic violence played no role in the best-interests analysis in custody disputes. Influenced by the congressional resolution, however, state legislatures began enacting laws providing that domestic violence should be taken into account in child custody determinations.[12] By 1997, thirty-nine states and the District of Columbia required courts to consider domestic violence as one factor in the best-interests analysis.[13] The best-interests standard enumerates relevant factors in custody determinations, such as the physical and mental health of the parties, the age and wishes of the child, the child's interaction with parents and siblings, and the child's adjustment at home, school, and the community.[14] All these factors are equally weighted. In this first stage of law reform, domestic violence became an additional factor for courts to weigh in the best-interests determination.

In the late 1990s, however, many states began abandoning the 'one-factor' approach in response to concerns that the approach did not adequately protect children in families experiencing domestic violence. Dissatisfaction with the approach stemmed from several factors. First, evidence was accumulating on the detrimental effects on children from exposure to domestic violence.[15] Research revealed that the act of witnessing domestic violence had significant adverse impact (short-term and long-term) on children's well-being.[16]

Second, critics contended that the one-factor approach gave too much discretion to judges and custody evaluators. Critics lambasted the

---

[11] Ibid.
[12] For illustrative case law in the first stage, *see* Custody of Vaughn, 664 N.E.2d 434 (Mass. 1996).
[13] Philip C. Crosby, 'Custody of Vaughn: Emphasizing the Importance of Domestic Violence in Child Custody Cases' (1997) 77 *B.U. L. Rev.* 483–513 at 509.
[14] See Unif. Marriage and Divorce Act (UMDA) § 402.
[15] See, e.g., Jeffrey L. Edleson, 'Children's Witnessing of Adult Domestic Violence' (1999) 14 *J. Interpersonal Violence* 839–870 (reviewing thirty-one studies); Marjory D. Fields, 'Impact of Spouse Abuse on Children and its Relevance in Custody and Visitation Decisions in New York State' (1994) 3 *Cornell J. L. and Pub. Pol'y* 221–252 at 230; Alan J. Tomkins, Somaia Mohamed, Michael Steinman, Ruthann M. Macolini, Mary K. Kenning, and Jan Afrank, 'The Plight of Children Who Witness Woman Battering: Psychological Knowledge and Policy Implications' (1994) 18 *Law Psychol. Rev.* 137–187 at 137, 145–149.
[16] John W. Fantuzzo and Wanda K. Mohr, 'Prevalence and Effects of Childhood Exposure to Domestic Violence' (1999) 9 *The Future of Children: Domestic Violence and Children* 21–32.

overreliance of these decision makers on the 'parental alienation syndrome' (PAS), a term coined by child psychiatrist Richard Gardner to signify one parent's conscious or subconscious attempts to alienate a child from the other parent.[17] Despite vehement criticism of the doctrine by commentators,[18] many courts relied on PAS evidence to award custody to abusers.[19] The result, critics charged, was that the legal system favored custody awards to abusers at the expense of children's physical and emotional well-being.

Second Stage: Rebuttable Presumption Approach

State legislatures adopted a new approach to custody determinations in the late 1990s and early 2000s.[20] According to this approach, proof of domestic violence raised a rebuttable presumption that an award of custody to an abuser was not in the child's best interests. The law reform reflected the understanding that harm to children might be presumed whenever domestic violence occurred between the adult intimate partners.

Various interest groups lobbied during this period to enact laws precluding custody awards to abusers. The American Bar Association (ABA) passed a resolution in 1989 providing that joint custody was not appropriate in cases of spouse abuse, child abuse or parental kidnapping.[21] In 1996, the American Psychological Association (APA) passed a resolution recommending that states adopt laws that accorded a custodial preference to nonviolent parents.[22]

The most influential factor in the creation of rebuttable-presumption statutes was the Model Code on Domestic and Family Violence of the

---

[17] Richard A. Gardner, *The Parental Alienation Syndrome: A Guide for Mental Health and Legal Professionals* (Creative Therapeutics, 2d ed., 1998).

[18] For a summary of these criticisms, *see* Carol S. Bruch, 'Parental Alienation Syndrome and Alienated Children – Getting It Wrong in Child Custody Cases' (2002) 35 *Fam. L.Q.* 527–552.

[19] Rita Berg, 'Parental Alienation Analysis, Domestic Violence and Gender Bias in Minnesota Courts' (2011) 29 *Law and Ineq.* 5–26; Jennifer Hoult, 'The Evidentiary Admissibility of Parental Alienation Syndrome: Science, Law, and Policy' (2006) 26 *Child. Legal Rts. J.* 1–61.

[20] Massachusetts provides an illustrative example of this stage of law reform by its replacement of the one-factor approach with a rebuttable-presumption approach. *See* Mass. Gen. Laws Ann. Ch. 208 § 31A (enacted in 1998).

[21] ABA Resolution, Joint Custody (1)(Aug. 1989), available at www.americanbar.org/groups/child_law/tools_to_use/attorneys/joint_custody.html.

[22] Ibid.

National Council of Juvenile and Family Court Judges in 1994.[23] Drafted by experts in several fields (physicians, lawyers and domestic violence advocates), the Model Code recommended that states adopt rebuttable-presumption laws. By 2001, the rebuttable-presumption approach was so widely accepted that sixteen states plus the District of Columbia adopted it.[24] Today, twenty-two states have rebuttable presumptions against awards of custody to abusers.[25]

Stage Three: Prioritizing Safety

The law reform movement is currently witnessing the third stage of reform in the role of domestic violence in custody law. This stage prioritizes safety in the best-interests determination. Recent law reforms in the state of Colorado and country of Australia adopt this new approach.

D Roots of the Colorado Law Reform Movement

Wingspread Conference

The origins of the 'safety-first' approach in Colorado may be traced to 2007, when legal professionals and mental health experts in two national law-related organizations (the National Council of Juvenile and Family Court Judges and also the Association of Family and Conciliation Courts) convened a conference at the Wingspread Center in Racine, Wisconsin (called the 'Wingspread Conference'). The Wingspread Conference explored ways to improve the law's treatment of families in cases of domestic violence.[26] There, experts explored the tensions that hampered work with families experiencing domestic violence and suggested proposals for reform.

The experts' recommendations addressed ways that the legal and social service systems could better meet these families' needs. One recommendation was the prioritization of safety in the determination of custody

---

[23] Nat'l Council of Juvenile and Family Court Judges, Family Violence: A Model State Code §401 (1994), available at www.ncjfcj.org/resource-library/publications/model-code-domestic-and-family-violence.

[24] Lemon, *supra* note 5, at 611.

[25] Rebecca E. Hatch, 'Domestic Violence as Factor in Child Custody Cases' (2015) 129 *Am. Jur. Proof of Facts* 3d 217–304 (surveying law).

[26] For background on the conference, *see* Nancy Ver Steegh and Clare Dalton, 'Report from the Wingspread Conference on Domestic Violence and Family Courts' (2008) 46 *Fam. Ct. Rev.* 454–470.

arrangements.[27] Psychologist Janet Johnston, a conference participant, proposed a method for analyzing conflicts between child protection and parental rights in the context of domestic violence. She urged that if the safety of both the child and victim-parent could not be achieved at the same time as ensuring the child's access to both parents, then safety should take precedence.[28] This view that the child's safety should trump custodial rights of abusive parents, according to a legal commentator, constituted a 'paradigm shift' in child custody law.[29]

Protective Parents Movement

The recommendations of the Wingspread Conference fell on fertile ground because of the ongoing efforts of an interest group of 'protective parents' that was simultaneously pursuing the goal of safeguarding children's well-being in custody disputes. Influential research added fuel to their fire by shedding light on the many ways in which family courts failed battered mothers and their children.[30] Their findings were supported by increasing evidence documenting the co-occurrence of domestic violence and child abuse.[31]

The protective parents' movement launched an aggressive campaign to bring attention to the risks to children posed by family court decisions favoring abusers. Protective parents' coalitions were established in a dozen states, a national conference was held in Washington, D.C. (the first Battered Mothers Custody Conference), and an international association was formed (the Protective Mothers Alliance International). A documentary focused national attention on the problem.[32] Protective parents held court watches, conferences, public awareness campaigns and

---

[27] Ibid., at 463. [28] Ibid., at 464.
[29] Allen M. Bailey, 'Prioritizing Child Safety as the Prime Best-Interest Factor' (2013) 47 *Fam. L.Q.* 35–64 at 54.
[30] Ibid., at 37 (citing Jennifer L. Hardesty and Grace H. Chung, 'Intimate Partner Violence, Parental Divorce, and Child Custody: Directions for Intervention and Future Research' (2006) 55 *Fam. Relations* 200–210; Peter G. Jaffe, Janet R. Johnston, Claire V. Crooks and Nicholas Bala, 'Custody Disputes Involving Allegations of Domestic Violence: Toward a Differentiated Approach to Parenting Plans' (2008) 46 *Fam. Ct. Rev.* 500–522; Daniel G. Saunders and Angela Browne, 'Intimate Partner Homicide' (2000) 2 *Case Studies in Family Violence* 415–449 (Robert T. Ammerman and Michel Hersen, eds., 2000)).
[31] See, e.g., Jeffrey L. Edleson, 'The Overlap Between Child Maltreatment and Woman Battering' (1999) 5 *Violence Against Women* 134–154.
[32] See Garland Waller Productions, Small Justice: Little Justice in America's Family Courts (2001), *available at* https://www.youtube.com/watch?v=CNXqDgSAOt4.

marches in a concerted effort to reform the family court system to better protect mothers and children.[33]

The protective parents' movement lobbied for legislation to prevent the placement of children in the custody of abusers. Tennessee became the first state to enact a Protective Parent Reform Act (PPRA) in 2004.[34] New Hampshire and New York soon followed suit.[35] PPRA laws precluded courts from restricting a protective parent's custody or visitation rights based solely on the fact that the protective parent had accused the other parent of the commission of domestic violence or child abuse and then had taken reasonable actions (such as flight) based on that belief. The laws also safeguarded children by requiring courts to consider all admissible evidence of abuse in determining custodial arrangements that were in the best interest of the child.[36] The latter provision was intended to counter some judges' tendency to minimize or disregard evidence of abuse.

Meanwhile, concern about the exposure of children to violence reached the national level when U.S. Attorney General Eric Holder launched the Defending Childhood Initiative in 2010. A National Task Force made policy recommendations to address the problem.[37] One recommendation urged that, when domestic violence and child abuse co-occurred, the courts should collaborate with child protection services and domestic violence programs 'to create protocols and policies that protect children and adult victims'.[38] That recommendation suggested that the child's well-being was best served by continued custody in the victim-parent.[39] Both the gains of the protective parents' movement and the recommendations of the Wingspread Report reverberated in the state of Colorado.

E Law Reform in Colorado

In the midst of national attention on domestic violence, policy makers in Colorado enacted the strongest approach yet to child custody in the

---

[33] Battered Women's Testimony Project, Projects Description 2000–2004, Wellesley Centers for Women website, *available at* www.wcwonline.org/Archived-Projects/battered-mothers-testimony-project.
[34] Tenn. Code Ann. § 36-6-112(c).
[35] N.H. Rev. Stat. § 461-A: 6(IV)(a); N.Y. Dom. Rel. Law § 240(1).
[36] See, e.g., Tenn. Code Ann. § 36-6-112(c).
[37] Report of the Attorney General's Nat'l Task Force on Children Exposed to Violence (2012), available at www.justice.gov/defendingchildhood/task-force-children-exposed-violence.
[38] Ibid., at 16.   [39] Ibid.

context of domestic violence. Colorado's 'safety-first' approach prioritizes the protection of the child in the best-interests determination. The immediate catalyst for the pioneering legislation was several state cases in which battered mothers lost custody and, subsequently, their children were harmed by the abusive parent.[40] In response, the Colorado Coalition Against Domestic Violence (CCADV) voiced the need for stronger legislation and successfully lobbied for law reform.[41]

The aim of the ensuing Colorado law was to provide better protection for the child in custody decisions involving domestic violence and child abuse. It accomplished this goal in several ways. First, the statute adopts a rights-based perspective. The law's point of departure is the declaration that 'children have certain rights in the determination of matters relating to parental responsibilities'.[42] It confirms the child's right to have such determinations based on the best-interests principle.[43] Then, the statute sets forth two *new* rights of children in matters of parental rights and responsibilities: (1) the right 'to be emotionally, mentally, and physically safe when in the care of either parent'; and (2) the right to 'reside in and visit in homes that are free of domestic violence and child abuse or neglect'.[44]

Second, after setting forth the child's right to safety, the law provides that the court shall prioritize the factor of the child's safety in the determination of the best interests of the child. As the statute explains, the court must determine the allocation of parental responsibilities in accordance with the best interests of the child while '*giving paramount consideration to the child's safety*'.[45] This prioritization shall encompass both the child's physical care and legal decision making.[46] The concept of safety, according to the statute, shall extend to all dimensions (emotional, mental and physical) when the child is in either parent's physical care.[47] In addition, the law suggests that, after the court makes a finding of domestic violence or child abuse, all evidence must be evaluated through this lens of safety.[48] Further, the statute provides that a parent's protective actions to ensure her safety (such as her flight in response to domestic violence) shall not be held against that parent in the custody determination.[49]

---

[40] See Amy Miller, 'Colorado Passes Milestone Child Custody Law Reform' (2013) 19 *Domestic Violence Rep.* 1–11 at 10.
[41] Colo. Rev. Stat. § 14-10-123.4 (eff. July 1, 2013).   [42] Ibid., § 14-10-123.4(1).
[43] Ibid., § 14-10-123.4(a).   [44] Ibid., § 14-10-123.4(b)-(c).   [45] Ibid., § 14-10-124(1.5).
[46] Ibid.   [47] Ibid.   [48] Ibid., § 14-10-124(4)(a),(b).   [49] Ibid., § 14-10-124(4)(c).

Third, the Colorado law broadens the concept of the child's safety by provisions that address the safety of the abused *parent*. The new law requires a court to consider the issue of safety of *both* the child and parent before the court determines physical care or legal decision making.[50] Specifically, the law provides that, if the court finds that a party has committed domestic violence or child abuse, the court shall consider 'as the primary concern, the safety and well-being of the child *and* the abused party'.[51] Colorado law thereby recognizes that the child's safety is intimately connected with the safety of the abused parent. The law reflects the understanding that if the abused parent continues to be endangered by the abuser, then the child is also at risk of abuse (physical, sexual or psychological) or by exposure to the domestic violence.

Finally, the Colorado law mandates consideration of safety by authorizing the court to impose conditions on parenting time that promote safety. Once again, the focus is not limited to the child's safety but also encompasses the abused parent's safety.[52] The statute provides explicit examples of such conditions in the form of stay-away orders; restrictions on visitation exchanges; supervised visitation; restrictions on overnight visitation; restrictions against substance use during visitation; an order directing address confidentiality; an order limiting contact for purposes of payment of child support; and 'any other condition' necessary for the safety of the child or survivor.[53] Similar legislation has been introduced in Alaska and Vermont.[54]

F   Law Reform in Australia

The 'safety-first' paradigm also took root in Australia. The Australian Parliament adopted this approach in 2012 by the Family Violence Act, amending the Family Law Act (FLA) of 1975 (the country's major law regulating divorce, spousal support, property division, and parenting).[55]

---

[50] Ibid., § 14-10-124(4)(d)–(e).   [51] Ibid., § 14-10-124(4)(d) (emphasis added).
[52] Ibid., § 14-10-124(4)(e).   [53] Ibid., § 14-10-124(4)(e)(i–viii).
[54] Email communication from Amy Miller, Executive Director, Colorado Coalition Against Domestic Violence, to author (April 27, 2015) (on file with author). Recent decisions of the Alaska Supreme Court also prioritize domestic violence among the best-interest criteria. Bailey, *supra* note 29 at 56 (citing *Wee v. Eggener*, 225 P.3d 1120, 1125 (Alaska 2010); *Williams v. Barbee*, 243 P.3d 995, 1004 (Alaska 2010)).
[55] *See* Family Law Legislation Amendment (Family Violence and Other Measures) Act 2011 (Cth) (Austl.), [hereinafter cited as FLA 2011].

The recent amendments are the third stage of reform of custody law in that country to address domestic violence. In the first stage, the Australian Parliament in 1995 made domestic violence a factor in custody determinations.[56] In the second stage, Parliament adopted a presumption in 2006 against joint legal custody to an abuser.[57] The 2006 amendments also introduced two 'primary' considerations (i.e., overarching factors) that should apply to determinations of the best interests of the child. These primary considerations included:

- the benefit to the child of having a meaningful relationship with both parents[58] and
- the need to protect the child from physical or psychological harm from being subjected to, or exposed to, abuse, neglect or family violence.[59]

The 2006 law provided that these two primary considerations should be weighted equally.

The recent stage of reform in 2012 was prompted by considerable evaluation of the former law, consisting of three major reports including surveys of empirical research and criticisms by experts.[60] The most significant change in the recent Family Violence Act is the prioritization of the child's safety.

The new law accomplishes this goal in several ways. First, the law re-visits the weight given to the two primary considerations of prior law (i.e., the benefit to the child of a continuing relationship with both parents, and the need to protect the child from harm). Whereas prior law weighed these two factors equally, the recent amendments prioritize safety. That is, the new law provides that the consideration of the benefit to the child of a continuing relationship with both parents prevails *only*

---

[56] Family Law Reform Act 1995 (Cth), s 43(1)(ca) (Austl.).
[57] Family Law Amendment (Shared Parental Responsibility) Act 2006 (Cth) (Austl.) ss 61DA(1)–(4) [hereinafter cited as FLA 2006].
[58] Ibid., s 60CC(2)(a).   [59] Ibid., s 60CC(2)(b).
[60] Three reports were particularly influential: (1) the evaluation of the 2006 law by the Australian Institute of Family Studies that surveyed considerable empirical research before concluding that courts were ordering joint custody even in circumstances where the parents disclosed safety concerns; (2) a report by the Family Law Council criticizing the friendly-parent doctrine and urging broader definitions of family violence; and (3) a report by a professor/family court judge that also criticized the friendly-parent doctrine as well as the imposition of mandatory court costs for persons making allegedly false allegations of domestic violence and child abuse. For background on these reports, *see* Adiva Sifris and Anna Parker, 'Family Violence and Family Law: Where to Now?' (2014) 4 *Fam. L. Rev.* 3–24 (Austl.).

when concerns about the child's safety are absent. If such concerns exist, then the court is required to give *greater weight* to the need to protect the child from harm.[61] Thus, the new law explicitly ensures that the child's safety comes first, even in the face of the goal of shared parenting.

Second, the Australian law adds substantive and procedural protections that strengthen the law's response in the context of domestic violence. Among these substantive protections, the law provides for certain 'principles' to operate in conducting custody proceedings. One principle is that the proceedings should be conducted in a way that safeguards both the child and the abused parent from being exposed to violence.[62] To give effect to this principle, the law requires a court to ask each party whether the child has been exposed to either domestic violence or child abuse.[63] Another substantive protection is that the law provides for an absolute prohibition on joint legal custody. In 2006, as explained previously, the Australian Parliament enacted a presumption favoring joint custody. However, the recent amendments preclude joint legal custody ('equal shared parental responsibilities') in cases of domestic violence or child abuse.[64] In contrast to the American rebuttable-presumption approach, Australian law makes the presumption against joint legal custody absolute in such cases.

Procedural innovations also strengthen the law's response. For example, the law ensures the safety of the child and abused parent by improving the operation of protection orders. Sometimes, courts issue protection orders that conflict with custody orders. That is, a battered mother may obtain a protection order prohibiting the father from contacting her or the children. At the same time, however, the parents may have a custody order that grants him custody or visitation rights. The new law attempts to eliminate such inconsistencies by providing that courts must ensure that custody orders are consistent with protection orders and do not expose a person to 'an unacceptable risk of family violence'.[65] To further that goal, the law also permits the court to impose conditions ('safeguards') in parenting orders to ensure the safety of the child and abused parent.[66]

Third, the new law protects the child's safety by expanding definitions of harm. It revises the definitions of both 'family violence'[67] and

---

[61] FLA 2011, ss 4AB; 4(1).   [62] Ibid., s 69ZN.   [63] Ibid., s 69ZQ.
[64] Ibid., s 61DA(2) (if there are 'reasonable grounds' to believe that a parent has committed domestic violence or child abuse).
[65] Ibid., ss 60CG, 68N.   [66] Ibid., s 60CG(2).   [67] Ibid., s 4AB.

'exposure to abuse'[68] to reflect modern understanding of the terms. For example, the traditional definition of family violence includes such common acts as physical assault, sexual assault and stalking. But, the recent Australian law enlarges the definition of family violence by incorporating other acts of coercive control such as 'repeated derogatory taunts', pet abuse, isolating behavior, destruction of property and withholding financial support.[69]

Similarly, the statute broadens the definition of 'exposure to domestic violence'. The term generally includes the acts of seeing, hearing or experiencing the effects of domestic violence. However, the Australian law enlarges the focus to include such acts as overhearing threats to a family member, comforting the victim-parent, cleaning up the site of property destruction and seeing police arrive on the scene in response to the incident of abuse.[70] The law thereby encompasses a wider range of conduct in a better effort to safeguard the child from harm.

Fourth, the law enhances the likelihood of discovery of evidence of domestic violence. Often, evidence of intimate partner violence consists of protection orders. The new law requires the parents to disclose the existence of protective orders.[71] In addition, the statute permits the court to make inferences about the risk of harm from these protective orders.[72] Specifically, it provides that the court can take into account the nature of the order; the circumstances in which the protective order was made; any evidence admitted in proceedings for the order; any findings made by the court in, or in proceedings for, the order; and 'any other relevant matter' about the protective order.[73] The law thereby recognizes that protective orders constitute important evidence of past abuse as well as evidence regarding the risk of future harm both to the intimate partner and the child.

Evidence of domestic violence derives not only from the parties but also from child welfare agencies. The recent Australian law increases the likelihood of the discovery of such evidence in another way – by facilitating the reporting of evidence by child welfare agencies. Specifically, it provides that a court may order a child welfare agency to provide the court with 'documents or information' about suspected family violence or child abuse.[74] Documents may take the form of complaints to the agency, evidence gathered during the course of an investigation, or findings of the agency.[75] This reform addresses the problem that social

---

[68] Ibid., s 4(1). [69] Ibid., s 4AB(2). [70] Ibid., s 4AB(4). [71] Ibid., s 60CI.
[72] Ibid., s 60CC(3)(k). [73] Ibid., s 60CC(k). [74] Ibid., s 69ZW. [75] Ibid.

welfare agencies may have information that is not readily available to family courts and that such evidence may be highly relevant in the custody determination.

The new law increases the likelihood of discovery of evidence in still another way – by removing disincentives to disclosure of abuse. Prior law penalized a parent for taking actions that might undercut the presumption favoring shared parenting. That is, a 'friendly parent' provision required courts to take into account the willingness of each parent to facilitate a close relationship between the child and the other parent.[76] Former law also penalized a parent who knowingly made false allegations of abuse by mandating that the reporting parent pay court costs.[77] Both of these statutory provisions made battered mothers reluctant to disclose allegations of abuse for fear that the judge would deem them an 'unfriendly' parent or alternatively, would disbelieve their allegations and impose court costs on them in response. To improve access to evidence of abuse, the Family Violence Act repealed the friendly parent doctrine[78] as well as the provision imposing mandatory costs on a parent who made false allegations of abuse.[79]

G Statutory Comparison

The Colorado and Australian laws reflect two fundamental similarities. First, the goal of both laws is to prioritize the child's safety in the determination of the child's best interests in custody decision making in the context of domestic violence. Second, both laws take into account not only the child's safety but also that of the abused parent, thereby recognizing that the child's safety is intimately connected with that of the abused parent. By prioritizing safety, both laws revolutionize the traditional approach to custody that weighed all factors in the best-interests analysis equally.

Yet, the Colorado and Australian laws also manifest important variations. First, different forces influenced the passage of each law. In Colorado, anecdotal evidence stemming from several high-profile cases of battered mothers prompted the law reform movement. In contrast, the Australian law reform movement followed several years of evaluation and criticism of prior law by policy makers.

---

[76] FLA 2006, ss 60CC(3)(c); 60CC(4)(b).   [77] Ibid., s 117AB.
[78] FLA 2006, ss 60CC(3)(c), 60CC(4)(b), *repealed by* FLA 2011.
[79] FLA 2006, s 117AB, *repealed by* FLA 2011.

Second, the Australian law is stronger than the Colorado law. The Australian law introduces substantive and procedural protections that require the court to take evidence of domestic violence or child abuse especially seriously. For example, the law requires the court to ask each party to disclose the occurrence of domestic violence or child abuse, and then mandates the court to take 'prompt action' in response to such allegations to protect the child and the abused parent.[80] The law provides for an absolute prohibition of joint legal custody if a parent has committed domestic violence or child abuse.[81] The law also strives to eliminate any inconsistencies between custody orders and protective orders in an effort to keep the parties safe from harm.[82]

Third, the Australian law is more comprehensive than the Colorado law. The Australian law undertakes greater efforts to safeguard the child from harm. To accomplish this objective, the Australian law expands the definition of key terms ('family violence' and 'exposure to domestic violence'). The Australian law also safeguards the child better by improving access to evidence of domestic violence or child abuse. That is, the Australian Family Violence Act requires the parties to disclose evidence of protection orders, facilitates reporting of abuse to the courts by child welfare agencies and removes disincentives to disclosure of abuse.

Finally, these laws differ in their consideration of the UN Convention on the Rights of the Child. In Australia, the CRC plays an important role in the judicial consideration of family violence in custody law. Australia's recent custody amendments reflect and confirm the importance of the CRC. The amendments provide that an object of the legislation is to give effect to the CRC and also affirm the obligations of judicial actors under international law.[83]

In contrast, because the United States has not ratified the CRC, it is not surprising that the Colorado law contains no similar affirmation of CRC principles. Nonetheless, by its adoption of a rights-based perspective (i.e., the assertion that the child has an undeniable rights to safety and to live in a home free from abuse), the Colorado law is evocative of the CRC. Thus, it might be said that the Colorado law reflects the *spirit* of the CRC, although not its substance.

---

[80] FLA 2011, s 67ZBB.   [81] Ibid., s 61DA(2).   [82] Ibid., s 68N.
[83] Ibid., s 60B(4) ('An additional object of this Part is to give effect to the UN Convention on the Rights of the Child done at New York on 20 November 1989').

H Conclusion

From the time of the birth of the UN Convention on the Rights of the Child, the best-interests-of-the-child principle has developed 'far beyond its original conception as a principle of Anglo-American family law' to a doctrine which has 'global impact, creating a new area of law, that of children's rights'.[84] If we value children's rights, then it is time for legal professionals who are charged with children's welfare to ensure that custody law truly does serve children's best interests by prioritizing the child's safety in custody determinations. Hopefully, additional states and countries will adopt the 'safety-first' paradigm of Colorado and Australia. Only then will we be able to say that children's best interests are truly being served by child custody law.

---

[84] Lynne Marie Kohm, 'Tracing the Foundations of the Best Interests of the Child Standard in American Jurisprudence' (2008) 10 *J. L. Fam. Stud.* 337–376 at 351.

15

The Best Interests of the Child When There Is Conflict About Contact

LINDA D. ELROD

... when the custody of children is the question, ... the best interest of the children is the paramount fact. Rights of father and mother sink into insignificance before that.[1]

A Introduction

A child who refuses contact with a parent presents challenging issues for the lawyers, judges and mental health professionals who are involved in custody litigation. These cases raise questions of parent-child alienation, which require judges to determine what is in the best interests of this child. The UN Convention on the Rights of the Child uses the best interests of the child standard[2] as do judges hearing custody cases in all fifty states.[3] When parents fight over custody of their child, the trial judge has the responsibility to assess what placement would benefit the child physically, psychologically, and emotionally. For decades, judges had broad discretion and used a vague 'best interests' standard. Today's judges must review a growing list of statutory factors that include the child's preference, presumptions of shared parenting, evidence of spousal abuse, and 'friendly parent' provisions.[4]

---

[1] *Chapsky v. Wood*, 26 Kan. 650, 40 Am. Rep. 321 (1881).
[2] 'In all actions concerning children, whether undertaken by public or private social welfare institutions, courts of law ... the best interests of the child shall be a primary consideration.', Art 3(12) of the United Nations Convention on the Rights of the Child, 20 November 1989, in force 2 September 1990, 1577 UNTS 3.
[3] Linda D. Elrod and Robert G. Spector, 'A Review of the Year in Family Law 2013–2014: Same-Sex Couples Attain Rights to Marry and Parent' (2015) 48(4) *Family Law Quarterly* 609–674, at 656–659 (Chart 2: Custody Criteria, listing all fifty state statutes).
[4] Linda D. Elrod *Child Custody Practice and Procedure* (Minnesota: Thomson Reuters 2015), pp. 544–549.

Although the definition of 'best interest' has changed over the years,[5] generally, it benefits a child to maintain a loving, healthy relationship with both parents. Indeed, the majority of children are eager for contact with both parents.[6] When a child refuses to spend time with a parent, a judge must determine if there is a legitimate reason. Is the child going through a normal developmental stage or having a predictable reaction to the divorce? Or is there something deeper, such as violence in the family or one parent interfering with the other's relationship? Should parenting time be forced or residential custody changed? These are difficult questions that require the judge to focus on the best interests of the particular child and not punish the child.[7]

This chapter provides a brief history of child alienation, discusses the interrelationship of abuse, alienation and estrangement issues, and explores some recommendations of how the court system should respond when there are allegations of alienation. The chapter concludes that the best interest of an alienated child requires experienced judges and mental health professionals discovering and addressing the problems in the family.

B   Child Alienation and High Conflict

Divorce causes anxiety and life disruptions for parents and children alike. The majority of separating parents, however, work through their changing emotions and return to some semblance of 'normal' within two to three years.[8] The same is true for children. A small, but significant,

---

[5] Linda D. Elrod and Milfred D. Dale 'Paradigm Shifts and Pendulum Swings in Child Custody: The Interests of the Children in the Balance' (2008) 42(3) *Family Law Quarterly* 381–418.

[6] See *Mary E. v. Usher E.*, 967 N.Y.S.2d 868, 880 (Sup. Ct. 2013) (evaluator testified that hatred of a parent is not a natural emotion for a child). Janet R. Johnston 'Children of Divorce Who Reject a Parent and Refuse Visitation: Recent Research and Social Policy Implications for the Alienated Child' (2005) 38(4) *Family Law Quarterly* 757–775.

[7] Michigan judge ordered three children, the youngest of whom was nine years old, to juvenile detention until age eighteen for refusing to have lunch with their father allegedly because of the mother's alienating conduct. See www.foxnews.com/us/2015/07/10/Michigan-judge-detains-children. Perhaps in reaction to the outcry, the judge relented and sent the children to their scheduled summer camps.

[8] William G. Austin, Linda Fieldstone and Marsha Kline Pruett, 'Bench Book for Assessing Parental Gatekeeping in Parenting Disputes: Understanding the Dynamics of Gate Closing and Opening for the Best Interests of Children' (2013) 10(1)) *Journal of Child Custody* 1–16 at 9 (after two years 80 per cent of parents cooperate). See also Mavis Hetherington and John Kelly *For Better or For Worse: Divorce Reconsidered* (New York: Norton, 2002);

number of parents do not 'get over it'. They engage in a type of guerilla warfare, litigating repeatedly and harming their children.[9] These parents, one or both of whom are often demanding and manipulative, are the 'frequent flyers' of the court system.

> High-conflict custody cases are marked by a lack of trust between the parents, a high level of anger and a willingness to engage in repetitive litigation ... High-conflict custody cases can arise when parents, attorneys or mental health professionals become invested in the conflict or when parents are in a dysfunctional relationship, have mental disorders, are engaged in criminal or quasi-criminal conduct, substance abuse or there are allegations of domestic violence, or child abuse or neglect.[10]

Too often children are caught in the middle of the parental conflict. It is the high conflict, rather than the divorce, that harms the children.[11] Bitter, contentious divorcing parents provide the most common context for allegations of alienation. These are high conflict cases that may have devastating long-term effects on a child's well-being and self-esteem.[12]

Child Alienation or Parental Alienation

Many children of divorce go through stages of anxiety, mild depression, and may have loyalty conflicts in the aftermath of divorce. Most children, however, want to maintain contact with both parents. Even when a parent expresses negative opinions about the other, most children continue to want to see both parents. In approximately 20 per cent of cases, however children exhibit an alignment with one parent and

---

Judith S. Wallerstein and Joan Kelly, *Surviving the Break Up: How Children and Parents Cope with Divorce* (New York: Basic Books, 1980).

[9] Elrod and Dale, 'Paradigm Shifts and Pendulum Swings in Child Custody' 388, n. 32 (citing reports and studies).

[10] Wingspread Conferees, 'High-Conflict Custody Cases: Reforming the System for Children' (2001) 34(4) *Family Law Quarterly* 589–606 at 590; Linda D. Elrod, 'Reforming the System to Protect Children in High Conflict Custody Cases' (2001) 28 *William Mitchell Law Review* 495–551 at 500.

[11] Janet R. Johnston, Vivienne Roseby, and Kathryn Kuehnle, *In the Name of the Child: A Developmental Approach to Understanding and Helping Children of Conflicted and Violent Divorce* (New York: Springer Pub. 2009). See also Carla B. Garrity and Mitchell A. Baris, *Caught in the Middle: Protecting the Children of High-Conflict Divorce* 19 (New York: Lexington Books, 1994).

[12] Barbara Jo Fidler and Nicholas Bala, 'Children Resisting Postseparation Contact with a Parent: Concepts, Controversies and Conundrums' (2010) 48 *Family Court Review* 10, 20–21; Amy J.L. Baker, *Adult Children of Parental Alienation Syndrome: Breaking the Ties that Bind* (New York: W.W. Norton & Co., 2007).

may resist contact with the other parent.[13] In some cases a child appears to irrationally reject one parent as a result primarily of the negative influence of the other parent.[14] Dr. Richard Gardner in 1985 coined the term 'parental alienation syndrome', which depicted a vindictive, hostile parent (in his view, the mother), systematically programming the child to view the nonabusive father as evil, dangerous, or unnecessary to the child.[15] The immediate reactions to parental alienation syndrome were highly polarizing. Some called it 'junk science'.[16] Others agreed there was something going on whether it was called parental alienation,[17] indoctrination, or brainwashing.[18] Gardner's approach was to remove the child from the alienating parent who intentionally interfered through actions or words with the child's relationship with the other parent.[19]

In 2001, researchers argued that what was happening in family courts was more complex than Gardner portrayed. His theory ignored the context of divorce, the developmental stages of a child, the protective reactions of a parent who fears harm to the child, and the interpersonal

---

[13] Barbara Jo Fidler, Nicholas Bala, Rachel Birnbaum, and Katherine Kavassalis, *Challenging Issues in Child Custody Disputes: A Guide for Legal and Mental Health Professionals* (Canada: Carswell 2008), p. 205 (citing sources).

[14] See Judith S. Wallerstein and Joan B. Kelly, 'The Effects of Parental Divorce: Experience of the Child in Later Latency' (1976) 46(2) *American Journal of Orthopsychiatry* 256–269.

[15] Richard A. Gardner, *The Parental Alienation Syndrome: A Guide for Mental Health Professionals* (Cresskill, N.J.: Creative Therapeutics 1992) (describing eight symptoms, which included programming or brainwashing by one parent and a child's contributions to vilification of the target parent).

[16] Robert E. Emery, Randy Otto and W.T. O'Donohue, 'A Critical Assessment of Child Custody Evaluations: Limited Science and a Flawed System' (2005) 6(1) *Psychological Science in the Public Interest* 1–29 (scientific status of PAS is, to be blunt, nil); Carol S. Bruch, 'Parental Alienation Syndrome and Parental Alienation: Getting It Wrong in Child Custody Cases' (2001) 35(4) *Family Law Quarterly* 527–552, at 530.

[17] Douglas Darnall, 'Parental Alienation: Not in the Best Interest of the Children' (1999) 75 *North Dakota Law Review* 323, 325 (discussing differences between parental alienation syndrome and parental alienation). See also Fidler, Bala, Birnbaum, et al., *Challenging Issues in Custody Disputes*, note 13, 209–211.

[18] Stanley S. Clawar and Brynne V. Rivlin, *Children Held Hostage: Identifying Brainwashed Children, Presenting a Case, Crafting Solutions* 2nd edn. (Chicago: American Bar Association, 2013).

[19] Fidler, Bala, Birnbaum, et al., *Challenging Issues in Custody Disputes*, 214–217. See also Leslie M. Drozd, 'Rejection in Cases of Abuse or Alienation in Divorcing Families' in Robert M. Galatzer-Levy, Louis Kraus and Jeanne Galatzer-Levt (eds.), *The Scientific Basis of Child Custody Decisions* 2nd edn (Hoboken, NJ: Wiley & Sons, 2009) (noting the criticisms of parental alienation syndrome), pp. 403, 406

conflict between a parent and child.[20] Opining that there was too much focus on parental actions and not enough focus on the child, Johnston and Kelly recast the issue using a family systems framework:

> An alienated child expresses, freely and persistently, unreasonable negative feelings and beliefs (such as anger, hatred, rejection and or fear) towards a parent that are disproportionate to the child's actual experience with that parent.[21]

The child's rejection of a parent may be the result of multiple causes including possible alienating behavior by the favored or aligned parent, realistic estrangement due to child abuse or domestic violence, or poor parenting and family conflict.[22] The child's rejection of a parent is not always warranted by the rejected parent's behavior and is not always caused by actions of the other parent.[23]

Courts differ as to whether to admit evidence of alienation and what weight to give it.[24] Even recognizing the multiple factors that contribute to an 'alienated child', getting rid of the term 'parental alienation syndrome' has proven difficult. Despite a push by some mental health professionals, the American Psychiatric Association decided that parental alienation did not belong in the DSM-5 as a 'syndrome'.[25] While there is a growing body of literature, the debate remains as to whether there is enough data to make 'assertions about the etiology, prevalence and consequences of alienation'.[26]

---

[20] Joan B. Kelly and Janet R. Johnston, 'The Alienated Child: A Reformulation of Parental Alienation Syndrome' (2001) 39(3) *Family Court Review* 249–266.

[21] Kelly and Johnston, 'The Alienated Child', 251.

[22] Id. at 255–256 (stating that divorces characterized by bitter and protracted legal proceedings, continued verbal and/or physical aggression after separation, unsubstantiated allegations and counter allegations of child abuse, neglect or parental lack of interest are more likely to potentiate alienation in the child).

[23] Id. See Joan B. Kelly, 'Parents with Enduring Child Disputes: Multiple Pathways to Enduring Disputes' (2003) 9 *Journal of Family Studies* 37–50 (in one third of entrenched disputes, one parent was clearly responsible for the continuing conflict).

[24] *Pearson v. Pearson*, 5 P.3d 239, 243 (Alaska 2000); *Grove v. Grove*, 386 S.W.3d 603, 606 (Ark. App. 2011); *In re Marriage of Bates*, 819 N.E.2d 714, 731 (Ill. 2004).

[25] American Psychiatric Association, *Diagnostic and Statistical Manual of Mental Disorders, Fifth Edition* (Washington, DC: American Psychiatric Association, 2013) p. 715 (listing unwarranted feelings of estrangement as an example of Parent Child Relational Problems).

[26] See Michael Saini, Janet R. Johnston, Barbara Jo Fidler, and Nicholas Bala. 'Empirical Studies of Alienation' in Kathryn Kuehnle and Leslie Drozd (eds.), *Parenting Plan Evaluations: Applied Research for the Family Court* pp. 399, 434 (New York: Oxford, 2012) (parental alienation is not a diagnostic syndrome but rather a cluster of commonly recognized symptoms).

The Alienated Child or Abuse

A child needs to be safe. All states list spousal abuse as a negative factor in an award of child custody.[27] It is troubling that parental alienation is used as a counter allegation to an allegation of abuse. Children can be endangered if legal and mental health professionals ignore warning signs of domestic violence.[28] Some judges award shared parenting or unsupervised visitation even when there is evidence of spousal abuse on the theory that the child was not physically harmed. Research, however, confirms that a child can be harmed as much by witnessing violence as by being the object of it.[29]

Some believe that parental alienation theory has encouraged skepticism toward abuse allegations by directing attention to the purported misconduct of one parent, possibly deflecting attention from the existence of true abuse.[30] An abusive parent should be not able to use an allegation of alienation to gain rights to a child who has good reason to refuse contact.[31] If a child has witnessed intimate partner violence or has suffered physical or emotional abuse, the child may rationally resist contact with the abusive parent. The child may exhibit symptoms of 'post traumatic stress disorder'.[32]

---

[27] Elrod, *Child Custody Practice*, 522–539. See *Gjertsen v. Haar*, 347 P.3d 1117 (Wyo. 2015) (household abuse is always improper and contrary to the best interests of the children). See also Allen Bailey, 'Prioritizing Child Safety as the Prime Best-Interest Factor' (2013) 47(1) *Family Law Quarterly* 35–64, at 48–53.

[28] Peter G. Jaffe, Claire V. Crooks, and Nicholas Bala, 'Custody Disputes Involving Allegations of Domestic Violence: Toward a Differentiated Approach to Parenting Plans,' (2008) 46(3) *Family Court Review* 500–522; Johnston, Roseby and Kuehnle, *In the Name of the Child*, note 11, 307–334.

[29] Joan B. Kelly and Janet R. Johnston, 'Differentiation Among Types of Intimate Partner Violence: Research Update and Implications for Interventions' (2008) 46 (3) *Family Court Review* 476–499, at 489–490; Gregory K. Moffatt and Savannah L. Smith, 'Childhood Exposure to Conjugal Violence: Consequences for Behavioral and Neural Development' (2007) 56 *De Paul Law Review* 879–894 (exposure to domestic violence during childhood may have lifelong impact on children's developing brains).

[30] Joan S. Meier, 'Getting Real About Abuse and Alienation: A Critique of Drozd and Olesen's Decision Tree' (2010) 7(4) *Journal of Child Custody* 219–250 at 237 (alienation behaviors are commonly committed by abusive fathers); Fidler, Bala, Birnbaum, et al., *Challenging Issues in Custody Disputes*, 224 (a father's violent and abusive behavior toward the mother predicts his own tendency to exhibit alienating behaviors).

[31] Meier, 'Getting Real', 241.

[32] Fidler, Bala, Birnbaum, et al., *Challenging Issues in Custody Disputes*, at 221. See also Lynn Hecht Schafran, 'Domestic Violence, Developing Brains and the Lifespan: New Knowledge from Neuroscience' (2014) 3 *Judge's Journal* 32.

To keep the focus on the 'alienated child', courts should evaluate abuse claims carefully at the earliest stage possible. Abuse allegations should not be treated as if fabricated or exaggerated in the absence of a thorough and sophisticated investigation.[33] If the evaluation finds abuse of the child or of the other parent, safety becomes the priority. A risk assessment must be done to determine if the abuse is conflict-instigated abuse or the coercive, controlling type that is particularly harmful.[34]

If no abuse is found, there must be an inquiry into why the child refuses contact. The existence of an unproved allegation does not always mean that the parent is alienating the child.[35] There may be numerous reasons, including estrangement, restrictive parental gatekeeping, or the child's age and views. In a relatively small number of cases, it appears a parent has fabricated allegations of physical and sexual abuse and manipulated the children into making false allegations. Some courts have changed custody to the rejected parent.[36]

Friendly Parent Provisions and Child Alienation

About thirty states have cooperative or 'friendly parent' provisions, which encourage a judge to place a child with the parent who will do the most to facilitate a continuing positive relationship with the other parent.[37] This factor has increasingly become the tie-breaker factor when all others are equal. When a parent, however, is a victim of intimate partner violence or trying to protect a child from violence or abuse or other safety reasons, the friendly parent provisions should not be used.[38] A protective, abused

---

[33] Lundy Bancroft, Jay G. Silverman, and Daniel Ritchie, *The Batterer as Parent: Addressing the Impact of Domestic Violence on Family Dynamics* 2nd edn. (Thousand Oaks, Ca.: Sage, 2012). See also Bailey, 'Prioritizing Child Safety', 59–63 (noting it is better for a child to be placed in the custody of a parent who exaggerates a violence allegation than in the custody of an abusive parent).

[34] Kelly and Johnston, 'Differentiation Among Types of Violence'; Leslie M. Drozd and Nancy W. Olesen, 'Abuse and Alienation are Each Real: A Response to a Critique by Joan Meier' (2010) 7(4) *Journal of Child Custody* 253–265 at 259.

[35] Meier, 'Getting Real', 241. Drozd and Olesen, 'Abuse and Alienation are Each Real', 254.

[36] *Kirsch v. Kirsch*, 2015 WL 4597591 (La. Ct. App. 1st Cir. July 29, 2015); *C.M.J. v. L.M.C.*, 156 So. 3d 26 (La. 2014); *Noland-Vance v. Vance*, 321 S.W.3d 398 (Mo. App. 2010).

[37] Elrod, *Child Custody Practice*, 544; Elrod and Spector, 'A Review of the Year in Family Law', 656–659.

[38] Mary Ann Mason, *The Custody Wars: Why Children Are Losing the Legal Battle and What We Can Do About It* (N.Y. Basic Books, 2000), p. 169 (noting 'The transfer of custody to the "friendly parent" more often is done to punish the other parent than to meet the needs of the child'); Margaret Dore, 'The "Friendly Parent" Concept: A Flawed

parent may not present well and may be trying to protect the child by restrictive gatekeeping or by resisting shared parenting.[39]

When a parent is interfering with the other parent's access, there needs to be a thorough evaluation of whether there is a justifiable reason (child abuse, intimate partner violence, substance abuse, or safety issues) or if there are unresolved issues between the parents. Even if one parent has been noncooperative, the judge must look to the child's best interests in awarding custody and not use a residential custody award as a sanction. On the other hand, the court should not award custody to the alienating parent on the basis that the child lacks a healthy relationship with the rejected parent.[40] The friendly parent provision may be an appropriate tiebreaker if there is no abuse, intimate partner violence or other legitimate reasons for an alienated child to reject one parent.

Estrangement or Child Alienation

Sometimes a child who refuses contact is justifiably estranged from a parent. An estranged child is one who has a reasonable cause to have negative attitudes and beliefs about a parent based on the child's experience of that parent's parenting. A child may have an affinity or preference for one parent and an estrangement from the other that might be due to the parent's behavior and the child's reaction to it.[41] For example, estrangement is a reaction to neglect, poor, or marginal parenting by the estranged parent.[42] A maturing child may be angry at the parent perceived as causing the break up of the family.

C Dealing with Alienation in Custody Cases

Just as it takes a village to raise a child, it may take a village to save an alienated child. Cases in which a child refuses to visit or one parent

---

Factor for Child Custody' (2004) 6 *Loyola Journal Public International Law* 41–56 at 42 (criticizing factor as increasing litigation and conflict)

[39] See Bailey, 'Prioritizing Child Safety', 44–45, 58–59.
[40] *Nikolic v. Ingrassia*, 850 N.Y.S.2d 539 (App. Div. 2008).
[41] Leslie M. Drozd and Nancy W. Oleson, 'Is It Abuse, Alienation, and/or Estrangement? A Decision Tree' (2004) 1(3) *Journal of Child Custody* 65.
[42] Johnston, 'Children Who Reject', 763–765 (listing numerous legitimate reasons for a child's rejection of a parent); William G. Austin, Linda Fieldstone and Marsha Kline Pruett, 'Bench Book for Assessing Parental Gatekeeping in Parenting Disputes: Understanding the Dynamics of Gate Closing and Opening for the Best Interests of Children' (2013) 10(1)) *Journal of Child Custody* 1–16.

makes allegations of alienation or abuse need a quick assessment and active interventions. Such cases require early identification, strong judicial control, and a wide array of resources, including case management.[43]

Family law judges have the primary role in protecting the child from the harmful effects of the parental conflict.[44] The judge should act swiftly and authoritatively if the child is actually alienated and there is no evidence to support actual physical, mental or emotional abuse but there is affirmative evidence of significant conduct by one parent aimed at undermining the child's bond with the other parent. Doing nothing is not a good option. The judge should ensure continuity of contact with the rejected parent if it can be done safely because long delays with no contact can harm the child's long-term relationship with the parent. This may require a team to help the child reestablish a relationship with the parent that will include the family court judge, the lawyers for the parties (and maybe the child), one or more mental health professionals (custody evaluator, therapist for the child, therapist for each parent, coach for one or both parents), court service officers, and possibly neutral site coordinators or visitation supervisors.

Early Identification and Intervention

High conflict parents benefit from early identification and quick interventions. Potential alienation cases may be identified by the lawyers,[45] a mediator, court services personnel, or the judge when parties file repetitive motions to enforce temporary orders or present arguments at the first hearing. At the outset, the judge can compel parents to attend education and evaluation programs and issue protective orders to prevent them from inflicting violence on each other or abducting their children. If parent education does not modify behaviors, the court may require the parties to seek individual counseling, get counseling for the child, or appoint a mental health professional as a custody evaluator who

---

[43] Fidler, Bala, Birnbaum, et al., *Challenging Issues in Custody Disputes*, 231; 'Wingspread Conference Report', 597–599.

[44] Milfred D. Dale, 'Don't Forget the Children: Court Protection from Parental Conflict is in the Best Interests of Children' (2014) 52(4) *Family Court Review* 648–654 at 652 (court must match family needs to existing resources).

[45] 'Wingspread Conference Report', 595 (lawyers should help clients set realistic expectations and counsel clients to avoid inappropriate conduct and needless conflict because of the negative consequences on their child).

recommends interventions and protocols for selecting other professionals, such as treating professionals.

The judge can fast track the dates for submission of discovery and dates of hearing. The judge can refuse to tolerate violations of temporary orders. Ultimately, the judge determines the admission of evidence, weight to be given to the child's preference, and makes the best interest decision. Ideally one judge would handle the case from start to finish, including all motions, to eliminate repetitive litigation, assure continuity in decisions about early assessments and later interventions for the child and the parents, and keep a tight rein on the parties.

Early Neutral Evaluation

The judge needs to order an expedited evaluation to reveal if the child's refusal to visit or the parent's unwillingness to allow contact is an indication of abuse, alienation, or realistic estrangement.[46] Ideally, there would be a forensically sound, child-centered, abuse-sensitive, comprehensive, neutral evaluation with a mental health professional familiar with the current alienation literature and the dynamics of high conflict parents.[47] A child should not be taken to a therapist at the request of only one parent.[48] If there is evidence that the child is alienated, the evaluator can assess if it is mild, moderate or severe. The evaluator can recommended appropriate treatment or other measures that will protect the child and facilitate a rehabilitation of the parent-child relationship.

Hearing the Voice of the Child

The child's voice should be a part of the total picture that the judge should consider.[49] Alienation is not present just because a child has a strong preference for one parent over the other. The judge should listen to the child's reasons for not wanting to be with the other parent to see if there is genuine fear, if there have been threats or emotional blackmail, or

---

[46] Fidler, Bala, Birnbaum, et al., *Challenging Issues in Custody Disputes*, 239–253.

[47] Elrod, 'Reforming the System', 540–544; Richard A. Warshak, 'Ten Parental Alienation Fallacies That Compromise Decisions in Court and in Therapy' (2015) 46(4) *Professional Psychology: Research and Practice* 235–249 (professionals who are not current in alienation research and do not understand the family system may harm the child).

[48] Matthew J. Sullivan and Joan B. Kelly, 'Legal and Psychological Management of Cases with an Alienated Child' (2001) 39(2) *Family Court Review* 299–315 at 303. 'Wingspread Conference Report', 543–544.

[49] Linda D. Elrod, 'Client-Directed Lawyers for Children: It is the "Right" Thing to Do' (2007) 27(4) *Pace Law Review* 27 869, 899–903; Elrod, 'Reforming the System', 525–526.

if something else entirely is going on. Although an alienated child may 'vociferously voice their hatred and opposition to visitation',[50] the child should not get to decide whether to live with or visit a parent.[51] The UN Convention on the Rights of the Child provides a framework for hearing the child's voice, but not giving the child decision-making power. A judge can order a child to have parenting time over the child's objection but should proceed carefully and order interventions to help the child adjust to court orders requiring contact with a parent or placing the child with the other parent.[52] The court should consider appointing a lawyer for the child in high conflict cases to give the child a voice, and be an advocate for the child and help expedite the process.[53]

Minimize and Manage Conflict

If alienation is found, the judge should intervene to reduce the conflict level. A judge may require parents to attend an education class to learn about the impact of divorce on children, normal developmental stages, and the importance of both parents to a child.[54] Any parenting plans must be explicit and very detailed. The judge should avoid ordering joint decision making or plans requiring much contact between the parents. If the parents have difficulty complying, the judge can order therapy for one or more of the parties and appoint a parenting coordinator.

Specific, Highly Structured Parenting Plans

Vague parenting plans can lead to misinterpretation and ambiguities. To help the alienated child reestablish a relationship with the rejected parent, the court needs to order contact even if the parenting time is supervised, limited or during a therapy session. Ideally, the parents can

---

[50] Sullivan and Kelly, 'Legal and Psychological Management', 300.
[51] *Milligan v. Milligan*, 149 So. 3d 623 (Ala. Civ. App. 2014); *In re Marriage of Kimbrell*, 119 P.3d 684 (Kan. Ct. App. 2005); *Zubizaretta v. Hemminger*, 967 N.Y.S.2d 423 (App. Div. 2013); *Underwood v. Underwood*, 326 P.3d 793 (Wash. App. 2014).
[52] Warshak, 'Ten Fallacies', 241 (indicating that most children's protests evaporate when reunited with a parent).
[53] Elrod, 'Client-Directed Lawyers', 899–903; 'Wingspread Conference Report', 596.
[54] Susan L. Pollet and Melissa Lombreglia. 'A Nationwide Survey, of Mandatory Parent Education' (2008) 46 (3) *Family Court Review* 375–394; Peter Salem, Irwin Sandler & Sharlene Wolchik 'Taking Stock of Parent Education in the Family Courts: Envisioning a Public Health Approach' (2013) 51(1) *Family Court Review* 131–148, 133–134 (most effective programs include skills training, writing in workbooks, making reports, not just listening to speakers).

provide input into creation of the plan to deal with trust and safety issues. In any event, the details of parenting time must be set out clearly with definite and understandable terms that cannot be misinterpreted.

If the child has resisted physical contact or one parent has interfered with the other parent's time, the orders should affirm parental rights and restore child-appropriate contact. The order must specify the times and places for transitions and require a record of communication between parents. The how, when, and where of all visits must be listed. The plan should provide for dispute resolution and appropriate penalties for noncompliance with the agreement.

Avoid Shared Parenting and Joint Decision-Making

The court should protect the child from the conflict, not put the child in the middle of it. Even though many states prefer joint or shared parenting arrangements, successful shared parenting requires parents to isolate their personal conflicts from their role as parents. When parents are uncooperative and unable to communicate, ordering joint custody will not make them communicate better. The parents' animosity and inability to communicate may make shared parenting an impossibility.[55] Alienating behaviors should rebut the presumption of awarding shared parenting at the outset.[56] It may be better to award primary residential custody or parallel parenting with one parent having decision making for some items (education) and the other having decision making for other items (medical).[57]

Appoint Parent Coordinator

When parents cannot communicate, will not follow court orders or their parenting plan, the court may appoint an independent professional, called a parent coordinator, case manager, special master, or referee.

---

[55] See *Yetter v. Jones*, 706 N.Y.S.2d 782, 785 (App. Div. 2000) (not awarding joint custody where there was hostility and parental interference by both parents); *Reichert v. Hornbeck*, 63 A.3d 76 (Md. Spec. Ct. App. 2013); *Wright v. Kaura*. 964 N.Y.S.2d 573 (App. Div. 2013).

[56] Marsha Kline Pruett and Herbie DiFonzo, 'Closing the Gap: Research Policy Practice and Shared Parenting' (2014) 52(2) *Family Court Review* 152–174 at 162 (courts should not award shared parenting for parents who do not attempt to remove themselves or their child from the conflict and do not support the other parent's presence in the child's life). See also Elrod and Dale, 'Paradigm Shifts and Pendulum Swings in Child Custody',, 398-399; 'Wingspread Conference Report', 508–509.

[57] Elrod, 'Reforming the System', 507–509.

A parent coordinator can help the parents draft and implement their parenting plan. By monitoring compliance and helping parties with day-to-day decisions, the parenting coordinator can help reduce child-related conflicts and protect the child from the impact of their conflict.[58]

Require Therapeutic Intervention

In addition to seeking an evaluation of the child and the parents, the court can require expedited contact in therapeutic sessions to initiate access between the alienated child and rejected parent. In case of severe alienation, it may be that only intensive, family-focused therapy can resolve the case.[59] Therapeutic interventions can be individual or involve a team. The goals are to build the alienated child's relationship with the estranged parent, help the estranged parent understand the child's needs, and help the aligned parent be attuned to the child's short- and long-term needs. Both parents must be involved in resolution of the alienation. In addition, siblings may also be involved whether they are 'alienated' or not. There are some educational programs available when alienation is present. They range from skills-based communication programs at the courthouse to full-blown 'boot camps' for parents and children.[60]

Enforce Court Orders

When an order is made, judges must be willing to hold both parents accountable and allow quick and effective enforcement of orders. Deferring decisions, delays in hearings, and enforcing orders can harm the child's relationship with the rejected parent and reinforce the alienating parent's behaviors. Judges must be willing to impose penalties, but the penalty should be commensurate with the infraction. For example, if a parent denies the other parenting time, the judge can order compensatory or make up parenting time. If transportation is an issue for one parent, the court can order compensatory driving to facilitate contact. The court can require paying the financial expenses incurred by a parent

---

[58] AFCC Task Force on Parenting Coordination, *Guidelines for Parenting Coordination* 2 (2005). See *Hausladen v. Knoche*, 235 P.3d 399 (Idaho 2010).

[59] Sullivan and Kelly, 'Legal and Psychological Management', 302–303; Johnston et al., *In the Name of the Child*, 316.

[60] See Elrod, 'Reforming the System', 531–532 (discussing basic parent education programs); Matthew J. Sullivan, Peggie A. Ward and Robin M. Deutsch, 'Overcoming Barriers Family Camp: A Program for High-Conflict Divorced Families Where a Child Is Resisting Contact With a Parent' (2010) 48(1) *Family Court Review* 116-135.

because of the violation of the court order. A judge may hold a parent in contempt of court, require a parent to post a bond, order a fine, or any number of other remedies to ensure enforcement of the order.

While all agree that the best interests of the child should guide the response, there remains debate over the nature and extent of appropriate sanctions.[61] A frustrated judge may find that the alienation constitutes a material change of circumstances that makes it in the best interests of the child to modify the initial decree. A New York court indicated that alienation is an 'act so inconsistent with the best interest of the child as to, per se, raise a strong probability that the offending parent is unfit'.[62] While some courts do change residential custody to the rejected parent,[63] most mental health professionals do not advocate this result. Removing the child from the primary caregiver may cause the child acute distress and not resolve the child's feelings of anger or hostility to the alienated parent.[64] Therefore, in some instances, it may still be in a child's best interest to remain with the alienating parent.[65] The judge can order therapeutic interventions for parents and children.

D Conclusion

Conflict about contact is complicated. A child may reject parents for many reasons. The bottom line is that both parents' behaviors and the child's reactions affect the parent-child relationship. When judges, lawyers, or therapists fail to adequately identify, understand and deal with the variety of reasons why a child refuses to have contact with a

---

[61] Fidler, Bala, Birnbaum, et al., *Challenging Issues in Custody Disputes*, 281–283.

[62] *Bennett v. Schultz*, 110 A.D.3d 792, 973 N.Y.S.2d 244, 245 (2d Dep't. 2013). See also *Hibbard v. Hibbard*, 55 A.3d 301, 308 (Conn App. 2012); *Wade v. Hirschman*, 903 So. 2d 928 (Fla. 2005).

[63] See *Bowman v. Englehart*, 977 N.Y.S.2d 457 (App. Div. 2013); *In re Marriage of Rosenfeld*, 524 N.W.2d 212 (Iowa Ct. App. 1994) (transferring custody of children to the mother where father and stepmother had alienated the children).

[64] Sullivan and Kelly, 'Legal and Psychological Management', 313 (noting that the child may act out by running away or being self-destructive or further reject the parent in retaliation for obtaining a change of custody); Johnston, Roseby and Kuehnle, *In the Name of the Child*, note 11, 774 (custody should be changed if the alienating parent is psychotic, has serious parenting deficits or is emotionally abusive.). See also Fidler, Bala, Birnbaum, et al., *Challenging Issues in Custody Disputes*, 30.

[65] *Palazzolo v. Mire*, 10 So. 3d 748 (La. App. 2009); *Lew v. Sobel*, 46 A.D.3d 893, 849 N.Y.S.2d 586 (2007) (finding that a change of custody would be harmful to the children without extraordinary efforts by both parents and extensive therapeutic, psychological intervention).

parent, the child suffers either from continually being embroiled in conflict or from loss of a relationship with a parent.

The emphasis on the alienated child rather than on parental alienation is a positive movement if only courts and evaluators would start using it. Alienated children are undeniably caught in the middle of parental conflict. At stake is the child's independent sense of self in the eyes of one or both parents. Either the programming parent is using the child as a pawn, or the other parent is ignoring the child's self by interpreting the child as the other parent's pawn. For the child, loyalty binds to both parents may actually fuel alignments to one parent as a solution for the anxiety. The stakes for parents in alienation cases are high because sometimes there may be little possibility of salvaging the parent-child relationship.[66] Therefore, it is crucial that judges charged with looking out for the best interests of the child understand the family dynamics and focus on what the individual child needs to have as positive a relationship with each parent as possible.

---

[66] Elrod and Dale, 'Paradigm Shifts and Pendulum Swings in Child Custody', 397.

16

Relocation Disputes Following Parental Separation: Determining the Best Interests of the Child

NICOLA TAYLOR

A Introduction

Relocation disputes occur concurrently with, or more usually, following parental separation when the resident (or a shared care) parent seeks to relocate with the children and the impact of that geographical distance will significantly affect future contact between the children and their left-behind parent. In these cases, the parent wanting to move with the children is frequently the mother, while the parent opposing the move is most often the father. The gendered nature of relocation disputes thus places mothers' and fathers' interests in opposition to each other, such that any concessions gained from the courts are seemingly won at the other's expense.[1] Yet at the heart of these legal proceedings are the children of the ex-couple whose welfare and best interests are in danger of being overwhelmed by the dominance of their parents' respective interests. This chapter, focused on Article 3(1) of the United Nations Convention on the Rights of the Child (UNCRC),[2] examines why it is so challenging for children's best interests to be prioritised even though most Western jurisdictions 'place the welfare principle at the heart of their decision-making about relocation disputes'.[3]

B The Best Interests of the Child and Relocation Law

The UNCRC states very clearly in Article 3(1) that 'the best interests of the child shall be a primary consideration' when the courts of law are

---

[1] N.J. Taylor and M. Freeman, 'The gender agenda and relocation disputes' (2012) *International Family Law*, June, 184–191.

[2] UN Convention on the Rights of the Child (adopted 20 November 1989, entered into force 2 September 1990) 1577 UNTS 3.

[3] Quote from R. George, 'The international relocation debate' (2012) 34 *Journal of Social Welfare and Family Law*, 1, 141–152 at 143.

undertaking 'actions concerning children'. This principle attains an even higher threshold in those jurisdictions where it has been elevated from the 'primary' to the 'paramount' consideration. In New Zealand, for example, relocation law applies to proposed moves within and between provinces, as well as to proposed international moves. Guardians must agree on a change of the child's residence that may affect the child's relationship with their parents or guardians.[4] If they cannot agree, permission for the proposed relocation must be obtained from the Family Court.[5] The child's welfare and best interests then become 'the first and paramount consideration'[6] and there is no presumption for or against relocation in statute or in the case law.

While the welfare and/or best interests of the child is the well-established, and often overriding, principle in the law governing parenting disputes (including those concerning relocation) in Western countries, diverse approaches are nevertheless evident internationally. Some jurisdictions adopt a neutral, all-factor approach to relocation where decisions are made on a case-by-case basis (like Canada, Germany, New Zealand), while others are either in favor of relocation (for example, Indiana, Oklahoma, England/Wales, France, Spain) or against relocation (for example, Alabama, Louisiana, Sweden).[7] Presumptions or burdens of proof, definitions of what constitutes a relocation, and notice periods are incorporated within the law in various countries and states or are completely absent in others. Sometimes both guardians must agree on the child's place of residence (as in New Zealand and Australia), while in other jurisdictions (particularly civil law ones) the custodial parent has the right to solely determine where they and their child shall live.

The approach taken to determining the child's best interests also varies depending on whether the courts consider that children are more likely to attain their potential when they are in the care of a happy, well-functioning primary parent or instead benefit from security and stability

---

[4] Section 16(2)(b) Care of Children Act 2004.
[5] By an application under section 47(1)(a) of the Care of Children Act 2004 for a parenting order with a condition that the child may move, or by an application under section 44 of the Act for the Court to resolve a dispute between guardians.
[6] Section 4(1) Care of Children Act 2004.
[7] Family Law Council, *Relocation: A Report to the Attorney-General* (Canberra: Family Law Council, 2006) para. 5.3, p. 52; M. Messitte, 'Relocation of children: Law and practice in the United States' (2010) 16 *The Judges' Newsletter on International Child Protection*, Special Edition No. 1 on the International Judicial Conference on Cross-Border Family Relocation, 26–33 at 28–29.

in their existing environment where they can easily maintain relationships with both of their parents.[8] This latter approach is consistent with Article 9(3) of the UNCRC – one of the few other Articles in the Convention to mention the child's best interests:

> States Parties shall respect the right of the child who is separated from one or both parents to maintain personal relations and direct contact with both parents on a regular basis, except if it is contrary to the child's best interests.[9]

This diversity in the legal policies governing relocation disputes can be illustrated by contrasting the approach of England/Wales, where permission is required only for international relocations or where a court has made a prohibited steps order, with that of New Zealand.[10] Moves domestically within the United Kingdom are usually regarded as the prerogative of the parent who is primarily caring for the child. Applicants seeking to relocate internationally must, however, apply to the courts of England/Wales where the welfare principle in section 1(1) of the Children Act 1989 applies. Similar to the law in New Zealand, this states that 'the child's welfare shall be the court's paramount consideration' and, in certain circumstances, is supplemented by the welfare checklist in section 1(3). For many years the English courts have routinely granted applications to relocate internationally based on the likely effect of a 'refusal of the application on the mother's future psychological and emotional stability',[11] although more recently a different approach has applied in the context of shared care cases.[12] Conversely, in New Zealand the courts have tended to refuse more applications for both domestic or

---

[8] N.J. Taylor, M. Gollop and R.M. Henaghan, *Relocation Following Parental Separation: The Welfare and Best Interests of Children* (Dunedin: University of Otago Centre for Research on Children and Families and Faculty of Law, 2010) at 19.

[9] Article 9(3), UNCRC, 1989.

[10] R. George, *Reassessing Relocation: A Comparative Analysis of Legal Approaches to Disputes Over Family Migration After Parental Separation in England and New Zealand*, (2010) DPhil Thesis, University of Oxford; R. George, 'Practitioners' views on children's welfare in relocation disputes: Comparing approaches in England and New Zealand' (2011) 23 *Child and Family Law Quarterly*, 2, 178–201; R. George, *Relocation Disputes: Law and practice in England and New Zealand* (Oxford, UK: Hart Publishing, 2014) at 29.

[11] 'In most relocation cases the most crucial assessment and finding for the judge is likely to be the effect of the refusal of the application on the mother's future psychological and emotional stability'; *Payne v Payne* [2001] 1 WLR 1826; [2001] EWCA 166, para. 32 per Lord Justice Thorpe.

[12] M. Freeman and N.J. Taylor, 'The reign of Payne II' (2013) 4 *Journal of Family Law and Practice*, 2, 31–43.

international moves[13] as they work through a broader range of six statutory principles relating to a child's welfare and best interests that take account of the child's safety; the child's care, development and upbringing; the child's identity; the child's relationship with both parents; continuity of care; and the parents' role in consulting and co-operating with each other.[14] Worwood summarises the contrasting approaches between these two jurisdictions as follows:

> ... in England, considerable more weight appears to be given to the impact on the mother of a refusal of a relocation request than in some other countries where this factor is weighed alongside other factors, including the inevitable reduction in contact with the father ... In countries [like New Zealand] which apply a more all-factor approach, greater importance seems to be attached to the father's role in the child's life.[15]

Over recent years, debate about whether courts should be allowing or restricting international relocations has been fuelled by the increase in cross-border disputes within the courts as a result of the higher rates of relationship breakdown and increased levels of population mobility. Efforts have therefore been directed to achieving greater international consistency by reaching agreement on the common principles to be applied in the judicial determination of relocation disputes.[16] Resolutions to this effect have been passed at several international conferences since 2009.[17] In 2010, delegates at the International Judicial Conference on

---

[13] Taylor, Gollop and Henaghan, *Relocation Following Parental Separation*; R.M. Henaghan, 'Relocation cases – The rhetoric and reality of a child's best interests: A view from the bottom of the world' (2011) *Child and Family Law Quarterly*, 226–250 at 239.

[14] Section 5 Care of Children Act 2004. The importance of the six principles set out in s5 as relevant to a child's welfare and best interests have also been affirmed by the NZ Supreme Court in *Kacem v. Bashir* [2010] NZSC 112.

[15] A. Worwood, 'International relocation – The debate' (2005) *Family Law*, 35, 621–627 at 627.

[16] Lord Justice Thorpe, 'Relocation – The search for common principles' (2010) 1 *Journal of Family Law and Practice*, 1, 35–39.

[17] For example, the International Family Justice Judicial Conferences for Common Law and Commonwealth Jurisdictions held at Cumberland Lodge, Windsor, England, in 2009, and in Hong Kong in 2014; the 2010 and 2013 conferences hosted by the Centre for Family Law and Practice, London Metropolitan University, England; the International Judicial Conference on Cross-Border Family Relocation hosted by the Hague Conference on Private International Law and the International Center for Missing and Exploited Children, with the support of the US Department of State, held in Washington D.C., USA, in 2010; the 2012 Sixth Special Commission at the Hague on the Practical Operation of the 1980 Convention on the Civil Aspects of International Child Abduction

Cross-Border Family Relocation produced the Washington Declaration on International Family Relocation[18] aimed at closer international judicial co-operation in such cases. Lord Justice Thorpe, then Head of International Family Justice for England and Wales, convened a Relocation Working Group in 2012 with legal practitioners and academics from England/Wales and New Zealand to develop guidance on the most effective means of adopting a consistent international approach.[19] As well, legal scholars have contributed various initiatives including a 'discipline' incorporating primary caregiver and shared care decision-making pathways,[20] Relocation Advisory Guidelines (Canada),[21] and two sets of questions (George: five questions[22]; Parkinson and Cashmore: three questions[23]) to provide some landmarks for judges seeking to ascertain the child's best interests in relocation disputes.

However, the search for a more unified approach across Western jurisdictions has not yet been successful despite most of these countries placing the welfare and/or best interests of the child at the core of their approach to relocation disputes.[24] The neutral/all-factor, pro-relocation, or anti-relocation stances have instead led to differing interpretations of the 'best interests' or 'welfare' principle across the world. And even within a single jurisdiction, applying exactly the same statutory paramountcy provision, research has shown that adjudication trends in relocation cases can vary considerably over time in response to legislative reforms, the decisions of higher courts, and shifts in social science thinking about what is best for children. In New Zealand, for example, Professor Mark Henaghan has tracked the success rate of applications to relocate since 1988 and found that these have varied significantly over the past quarter century: 62% (1988–98), 48% (1999–2000), 21%

---

and the 1996 Child Protection Convention; and the 6th World Congress on Family Law and Children's Rights, held in Sydney, Australia, in 2013.
[18] www.hcch.net/upload/decl_washington2010e.pdf.
[19] R.M. Henaghan and N.J. Taylor, *Response to Robert George's paper on reforming relocation law* (2013) Paper prepared for the England/Wales and New Zealand Relocation Working Group convened by Lord Justice Thorpe, Head of International Family Justice for England and Wales.
[20] Henaghan, 'Relocation cases', 250.
[21] N. Bala and A. Wheeler, 'Canadian relocation cases: Heading towards guidelines' (2012) *Canadian Family Law Quarterly*, 271, 316.
[22] George, *Relocation disputes*, 157.
[23] P. Parkinson and J. Cashmore, 'Reforming relocation law: A reply to Prof. Thompson' (2015) 53 *Family Court Review*, 1, 56–65.
[24] George, 'The international relocation debate', 150.

(2005, immediately following the new Care of Children Act 2004 taking effect), 35% (2005–7), 50% (2008–9), 32% (2010), and 63% (2011, following the Court of Appeal and Supreme Court decisions in the current leading relocation case of *Kacem v. Bashir* [2010]).[25] It is thus hard to avoid the conclusion that the quest for uniformity may well prove futile given the continual wavering, both domestically and internationally, about what the best interests of the child really means when applications to relocate are being judicially determined.

C   The Best Interests of the Child and Research Evidence

Children whose parents seek to relocate experience the 'double whammy' of both parental separation and relocation, so it is important to consider both contexts when legal disputes arise between their parents over their care and/or location. Research evidence has been helpful, but not conclusive, in assisting with the application of the best interests principle in these cases.

The Impact of Parental Separation on Children

There is now a substantial body of research examining the impact of parental separation on children. Several early reviews of the research evidence have concluded that parental separation does pose a risk to children's well-being.[26] However, while short-term distress at the time of the separation is common, long-term negative outcomes are only experienced by a minority of children whose parents separate. These children, however, have approximately twice the risk of having adverse outcomes than those children from intact families.[27] Essentially, the majority of children from separated families do not experience long-term negative outcomes, but as a group, children whose parents have separated or divorced are more likely than those from intact families to have poorer outcomes.

---

[25] Henaghan, 'Relocation cases', 238.
[26] B. Rodgers and J. Pryor, *Divorce and Separation: The Outcomes for Children* (York: Joseph Rowntree Foundation, 1998); P.R. Amato and B. Keith, (1991). 'Consequences of parental divorce for children's well-being: A meta-analysis. *Psychological Bulletin*, 110, 26.
[27] Rodgers and Pryor, *Divorce and Separation*.

The contemporary approach is more concerned with evaluating which factors contribute to poorer outcomes for children and which ones act as buffers or protective mechanisms – a risk and resilience perspective[28] that views parental separation as a stressor for children. It is now also widely recognised that separation and divorce is not a discrete event but rather an ongoing process of family transition and adjustment that children and young people negotiate.[29] As such, the impact of separation on children and their adjustment to it is also an ongoing process with 'multiple changes and potential challenges for children'.[30] It is the presence of unalleviated or multiple stressors that can increase the risk of adverse outcomes for children[31] with the number of stressors that children experience predicting their post-separation well-being and adjustment.[32]

Many such stressors have been identified including: inter-parental conflict, loss of important relationships, economic hardship, poor parental adjustment and parenting competence, remarriage or repartnering, and stressful or negative life experiences, such as the initial separation, moving, or changing schools. Protective factors that can moderate these risk factors include: support from family and friends, the child's coping skills and resilience, therapeutic support, competent parenting, contact with non-resident parents, diminished inter-parental conflict, the quality of the parent-child relationship, and parents' ability to co-parent authoritatively.[33] It is therefore the particular combination of risk and protective factors in each child's individual situation that will determine how their parents' separation will initially impact on them and will then affect their adjustment and well-being over time.

The Impact of Relocation on Children

One particularly significant risk factor for children following their parents' separation is relocation. Residential mobility is often an

---

[28] J.B. Kelly and R.E. Emery, 'Children's adjustment following divorce: Risk and resilience perspective' (2003) *Family Relations*, 52, 352–362 at 352.

[29] Rodgers and Pryor, *Divorce and Separation*.

[30] Kelly and Emery, 'Children's adjustment following divorce', 352.

[31] Kelly and Emery, 'Children's adjustment following divorce', 352.

[32] P.R. Amato, 'The consequences of divorce for adults and children' (2000) *Journal of Marriage and Family*, 62, 1269–1287 at 1280.

[33] P.R. Amato, 'Parenting through family transitions' (2004) 23 *Social Policy Journal of New Zealand* 31–44 at 33.

inevitable consequence of relationship breakdown, with divorced parents being far more likely to shift and to change residences more often than those who remain married.[34] However, children tend to act as anchors in their separated parents' movement decisions. So while moving is common, the distance is usually restricted to enable each parent to continue playing a role in their child's life.[35] Legal disputes over relocation therefore arise when the distance is much greater and will affect the child's ability to easily retain contact with their non-moving parent.

While there is a substantial research literature on the effects of residential mobility on children in intact families and following parental separation, the findings are somewhat mixed.[36] Some studies reveal beneficial effects of relocating while others report negative outcomes for children.[37] The research in this field is highly diverse and negative outcomes associated with relocation may be explained by other factors that lead to frequent residential mobility.[38]

Overall, research findings indicate 'heightened risk' for a child who relocates, particularly when there have been multiple moves and changes to family structure,[39] which can increase or exacerbate the instability and disruption created by parental separation.[40] The risk of negative outcomes can be mediated by such factors as moving due to family disruption, a negative parental attitude towards the move, the number of moves and their frequency, the distance moved and the existence

---

[34] W.G. Austin, 'Relocation, research, and forensic evaluation, Part 1: Effects of residential mobility on children of divorce' (2008) *Family Court Review*, 46, 137.

[35] B. Smyth, J. Temple, J. Behrens, R. Kaspiew and N. Richardson, 'Post-separation mobility in Australia: Some preliminary data on behaviour, disputes and attitudes' in J. Behrens, B. Smyth and R. Kaspiew, (eds.), *Symposium Proceedings: Relocation Disputes in Australia: What Do We Know, What Are the Implications for Family Law and Policy?* (Canberra: The Australian National University, 2008), p. 13.

[36] For a review see B. Horsfall and R. Kaspiew, 'Relocation in separated and non-separated families: Equivocal research evidence from social science literature' (2010) *Australian Journal of Family Law* 24, 34–56.

[37] N.J. Taylor and M. Freeman, 'International research evidence on relocation: Past, present and future' (2010) 44 *Family Law Quarterly*, 3, 317–339.

[38] Taylor and Freeman, 'International research evidence on relocation'.

[39] J. Kelly, 'Relocation of children following separation and divorce: Challenges for children and considerations for judicial decision-making', Paper presented at the 5th World Congress on Family Law and Children's Rights, 23–26 August 2009, Halifax, Canada.

[40] K. Waldron, 'A review of social science research on post divorce relocation' (2005) *Journal of the American Academy of Matrimonial Lawyers*, 19, 337; Austin, 'Relocation, research, and forensic evaluation', 142.

of multiple stressors.[41] Whether relocation will have a positive or negative impact on a child depends on many variables,[42] and will be determined by the combination of risk and protective factors present in each individual case.[43] The principles and factors to be taken into account are generally identified in various statutes, caselaw, professional commentaries, and custody evaluation protocols.[44] However, no large-scale longitudinal research has yet been conducted to specifically identify the key risk and protective factors that can account for individual differences in outcomes for children who relocate after their parents' separation or who are the subject of a relocation dispute.[45] This void means that:

> ... value choices are being made based on the various ways families are seen after break-up, and how the issues in relocation cases are framed. The reality is not one of neutral fact finding ... Decision-making requires prioritising and giving more weight to some factors over others.[46]

Family Members' Perspectives on Relocation Disputes

A new line of qualitative socio-legal research on family members' perspectives on post-separation relocation disputes within the courts has been undertaken in Australia,[47] New Zealand,[48] and England/Wales[49]

---

[41] C. Humke and C. Schaefer, 'Relocation: A review of the effects of residential mobility on children and adolescents' (1995) *Psychology, A Journal of Human Behaviour*, 32, 16.

[42] M. Gindes, 'The psychological effects of relocation for children of divorce' (1998) *Journal of the American Academy of Matrimonial Lawyers*, 15, 119.

[43] Austin, 'Relocation, research, and forensic evaluation'; P. Parkinson, N.J. Taylor, J. Cashmore and W. Austin, 'Relocation, research, and child custody disputes' in L. Drozd, M. Saini and N. Olesen (eds.), *Parenting Plan Evaluations: Applied Research for the Family Court* (2nd ed.). (USA: Oxford University Press, in press).

[44] See, for example, W.D. Duggan, 'Rock-paper-scissors: Playing the odds with the law of child relocation' (2007) *Family Court Review*, 45, 193, who identifies thirty-six factors distilled from American Court decisions on relocation.

[45] Freeman and Taylor, 'The reign of Payne II', 41; Parkinson, Taylor, Cashmore and Austin, 'Relocation, research, and child custody disputes'.

[46] Henaghan, 'Relocation cases', 227.

[47] J. Behrens, B. Smyth and R. Kaspiew, 'Australian family law court decisions on relocation: Dynamics in parents' relationships across time' (2009) 23 *Australian Journal of Family Law*, 3, 222–46; P. Parkinson, J. Cashmore and J. Single, 'The need for reality testing in relocation cases' (2010) *Family Law Quarterly*, 44, 1.

[48] Taylor, Gollop and Henaghan, *Relocation Following Parental Separation*; N.J. Taylor, M. Gollop and R.M. Henaghan, 'Relocation following parental separation in New Zealand: Complexity and diversity' (2010) *International Family Law*, March, 97–105.

[49] M. Freeman, *Relocation: The reunite Research. Research Report* (London: Research Unit of the Reunite International Child Abduction Centre, 2009); R. George, *Relocation*

in recent times. All these studies explore the experiences of those most affected by the impact of a relocation or its refusal by a court. Parents applying to relocate, or those opposing their ex-partner's proposed move, were thus interviewed about the decision-making processes governing relocation, as well as the living arrangements and patterns of contact subsequently developing. The New Zealand[50] and Australian[51] studies also incorporated children's perspectives with forty-four children and thirty-three children aged seven to eighteen years being interviewed respectively. Directly placing children's own views at the heart of research enquiry honours Article 12 of the UNCRC and has shed new light on issues relevant to welfare and best interests determinations in parental disputes over relocation. It is also consistent with contemporary theoretical and methodological approaches (like Childhood Studies) that value the need to better undertand children's daily, lived experiences when their family is in transition.

Taken together, the children's and parents' findings have revealed that the interests of children are not necessarily the same as either of their parents. Children do not regard the relocation issue in quite the same 'black and white' way as their parents whose respective sole focus is being allowed to move (mother) or stopping the proposed move (father). Rather, children grapple with the complexity and poignancy of what is being asked of them including leaving their non-resident parent behind, the loss of their school, friends, wider family members, and familiar surroundings, while simultaneously starting afresh in a new location with many aspects of their lives and coping with the travel between their parents' homes on a regular, or more infrequent, basis. Some have to manage a custody reversal when the court refuses the relocation application and their mother decides to go without them anyway. Others regard the relocation as giving them an opportunity to experience the best of both worlds. Most of the New Zealand and Australian children adapted well to the relocation, although many missed their fathers very much and, unsurprisingly, reported a more distant relationship with him.

Disputes in England and Wales: First Findings from the 2012 Study (University of Oxford Legal Research Papers, 2012).

[50] M. Gollop and N.J. Taylor, 'New Zealand children and young people's perspectives on relocation following parental separation' in M. Freeman (ed.), *Law and Childhood Studies*, Current Legal Issues, vol. 14, (London: Oxford University Press, 2012, 219–42).

[51] J. Cashmore and P. Parkinson, *Children's 'Wishes and Feelings' in Relocation Disputes* (Australia: Sydney Law School Research Paper No. 14/100, 2014).

This research has thus been invaluable in reminding us that it is the children who live with the reality of the courts' decisions in relocation cases and whose adjustment to the outcome is often far more complex and nuanced than adults (both parents and family justice professionals) may perhaps initially think. Yet Professors Parkinson and Cashmore argue that:

> ... the debates in the literature still seem to us to be quite adult-centric, with arguments focusing on such issues as freedom of movement, fathers' rights as non-resident parents, and gendered impacts. ... There is a need to reaffirm a strong view of the paramountcy of children's interests in relocation cases, and to avoid an a priori assumption that their interests align with their primary caregiver.[52]

D Professor Eekelaar, the Best Interests Principle and Relocation

The welfare of the child principle has been firmly established in English law for 120 years, with nearly ninety years having passed since its elevation to paramountcy. Similar timeframes also apply in the law of New Zealand. It is therefore somewhat intriguing that courts still grapple with the principle's application, but perhaps this is less surprising when account is taken of the open-endedness of the welfare/best interests assessment and the nature of judicial discretion as hallmarks of modern family law.

To assist in providing a better structure for family law decision-making, Professor John Eekelaar has recently examined 'a distinction made, but not developed, between decisions about children and decisions about other matters which affect children indirectly'.[53] When decisions are directly *about* a child he argues that the decision-maker's focus 'should be on discovering a solution that has the best outcome for the child ... by *examining as wide a range of possible outcomes as is reasonably practicable*'.[54] In contrast, 'in cases indirectly affecting children, the focus of the decision-maker should be on reaching the "best" solution *to the issue to be decided*'.[55] Relocation cases are then cited as serving as a link between these two approaches to the best interests principle because

---

[52] Parkinson and Cashmore, 'Reforming relocation law', 60.
[53] J. Eekelaar, 'The role of the best interests principle in decisions affecting children and decisions about children' (2015) *International Journal of Children's Rights*, 23, 3–26 at 3. See also, Chapter 5 by John Eekelaar, 'Two Dimensions of the Best Interests Principle: Decisions About Children and Decisions Affecting Children', in this volume.
[54] Eekelaar, 'The role of the best interests principle', 5.
[55] Eekelaar, 'The role of the best interests principle', 5.

'while these are essentially directly about children, they have sometimes mistakenly been approached as if they were about the adults, affecting children only indirectly'.[56] Eekelaar argues that 'the decision is in fact about where the child should live and how the child is to maintain contact with both parents'.[57] It is not desirable or practical for the best interests principle to point to determinate outcomes; rather it needs 'to have regard to the child's perspective' and open the way 'for creative solutions that go beyond [social] rules. ... The law therefore needs to adopt a defensible basis upon which to relate the children's interests to those other interests'.[58] Jurisdictions that 'resist slippage from the proper approach of a decision about a child to a decision substantially about a parent'[59] are heading in the right direction.

E Conclusion

While the mobility research evidence is somewhat limited and equivocal[60] and research findings have had to be extrapolated from the parental separation field to the relocation context,[61] it is unarguable that children are adversely affected by conflict between parents that is frequent, intense and poorly resolved[62] and that this is especially detrimental when the conflict in question is *about* the child – as it is in a relocation dispute. Often the status quo is the only 'known' position in a relocation case and decision-makers are required to make 'predictions into the future concerning a child's adjustment, welfare and potential for negative outcomes under different sets of conditional living arrangements'.[63] Bala and Wheeler argue that judicial decision making in such circumstances is an 'inherently speculative exercise' since 'it will not be truly possible to know what would have happened to the child on the "road not taken".'[64]

---

[56] Eekelaar, 'The role of the best interests principle', 6.
[57] Eekelaar, 'The role of the best interests principle', 9.
[58] Eekelaar, 'The role of the best interests principle', 26.
[59] Eekelaar, 'The role of the best interests principle', 10.
[60] Horsfall and Kaspiew, 'Relocation in separated and non-separated families', 34; Taylor and Freeman, 'International research evidence on relocation', 318.
[61] J. Herring and R. Taylor, 'Relocating relocation' (2006) 18 *Child and Family Law Quarterly*, 4, 517–37.
[62] G. Harold and M. Murch, 'Interparental conflict and children's adaptation to separation and divorce: theory, research and implications for family law, policy and practice' (2005) 17 *Child and Family Law Quarterly* 2, 185–205.
[63] Austin, 'Relocation, research, and forensic evaluation', 194.
[64] Bala and Wheeler, 'Canadian relocation cases', 272.

This, of course, is not unique to the relocation field and is evident in much family law decision-making, including the removal and return of children to birth families from out-of-home care placements; adoption; neonatal baby swap cases; and so forth. It also serves as a timely reminder for just why Article 3(1) has such significance in the family justice sector and why our socio-legal research, policy, and practice efforts should be directed to refocusing on the child-centeredness of the best interests principle. This is consistent with i) Eekelaar's distinction regarding decisions *about* children and decisions about other matters that affect children indirectly; and ii) the qualitative research findings on family members' perspectives on relocation disputes that are aptly summarized by Parkinson and Cashmore as highlighting 'a need to focus resolutely on children's interests and not on adults rights' to 'improve the best interests analysis'.[65]

Prioritizing the child's welfare and/or best interests, as most Western jurisdictions do, is not enough unless this is realistically informed by what it is like (and *might* be like if the relocation goes ahead) to stand – and walk – in the shoes of the particular child(ren) living the reality of their family transition, their mother's relocation aspirations, and their father's opposition to this. The suggested reframing of the paramountcy principle is therefore vital in relocation disputes to help counter adult-centric perspectives, positions and interests, and to better respect the developmental safety and rights of children. It could also enhance dispute resolution processes and the weighing and balancing of statutory principles and risk and protective factors so central to determinations about the best interests of the child.

---

[65] Parkinson and Cashmore, 'Reforming relocation law', 60.

PART V

Best Interests and State Intervention

17

Making Best Interests Significant for Children Who Offend: A Scottish Perspective

CLAIRE MCDIARMID

A   Introduction

Overall, one of the outstanding qualities of the United Nations Convention on the Rights of the Child ('CRC')[1] is its universality. It is the most ratified[2] treaty in the world.[3] Through rights, then, it offers uniform protection and priority to almost all of the world's population aged under 18 years.[4] As part of this, the Article 3 'best interests' rubric holds out the promise of 'really good' decisions for children being taken by public bodies, courts and tribunals. Universalism, however, does not elide all concerns about access to, ability to exercise, and exclusion from, the rights apparently conferred. While all children have CRC rights, practical issues like poverty[5] or the scarcity, as a fact, of national resources may prevent their exercise and the status of the CRC as not directly incorporated into domestic law in many jurisdictions militates against the provision of mechanisms for addressing violations.[6] Alongside these practical issues, other *perceived* barriers also arise such as the risk of essentialism – that, whilst there is no 'universal' child, the CRC may be construed as applying an image of the western or northern or developed world's children for this purpose.[7] Similarly, the

---

[1] UN, General Assembly, 20 November 1989, in force 2 September 1990, 1577 UNTS 3.
[2] Radhika Coomaraswamy, 'Women and children: The cutting edge of international law' (2015) 30 *American University International Law Review* 1- 40 at 7.
[3] Only the USA has not ratified it. Somalia did so on 1 October 2015.   [4] CRC, Art. 1.
[5] See Wouter Vandenhole, 'Child poverty and children's rights: An uneasy fit?' (2014) 22 *Michigan State International Law Review* 609–636.
[6] The Third Optional Protocol to the CRC on a Communications Procedure, New York, 19 December 2011, in force 14 April 2014 creates a mechanism for reporting violations to the UN Committee on the Rights of the Child however this has not been ratified by the UK.
[7] See, for example, Jane Fortin, *Children's Rights and the Developing Law* (3rd ed) (Cambridge: Cambridge University Press, 2009), p. 45; Nicola Ansell, 'The Convention

perception of the child-offender sometimes engenders a view of lesser entitlement to the protection offered by rights. In the context of the Scottish legal system, this chapter adopts a literal, 'back-to basics' approach to the terms of Article 3, in order to highlight both its potential, and, indeed, its requirement, to achieve 'really good' outcomes for all children coming within its reach. The chapter takes the position of children who offend as its focal point considering particularly how the Article should apply in their cases. Its key argument is that Article 3 mandates 'really good' outcomes for all children including, equally, for those who do wrong, a position which is fully supported by the Committee on the Rights of the Child.[8]

The chapter will firstly consider the negative perception of children who offend in relation to their rights. It will then turn to the terms of Article 3 itself and examine the ways in which it is incorporated into Scots law as it applies to offenders, and its application. Finally, it will look at recent research reports compiled by the Centre for Youth and Criminal Justice and by the Scottish Children's Reporter Administration, which shed some light on young peoples' own views of decision-making allegedly in their best interests. Overall, it concludes that the terms of Article 3 provide the framework to offer and achieve much more in terms of outcome than is currently the case.

B The Rights of Children Who Offend

Children who commit crime are still children and, as such, are bearers of the rights conferred by the CRC.[9] In fact, the CRC specifically recognises them as in need of greater protection in certain respects by its inclusion of Article 37, which tempers the application of criminal sanctions to the young, and in Article 40, which makes provision for their right to a fair trial. Nonetheless, there is a particular rhetoric, stronger at historical

---

on the Rights of the Child: Advancing Social Justice for African Children?' in Afua Twum-Danso Imoh and Nicola Ansell (eds.) *Children's Lives in an Era of Children's Rights: The Progress of the Convention on the Rights of the Child in Africa* (London: Routledge, 2014), p. 235.

[8] United Nations Committee on the Rights of the Child, *General Comment No. 14 on the Right of the Child to Have His or Her Best Interests Taken as a Primary Consideration (Art. 3, para. 1)* (2013) (CRC/C/GC/14). Available at: www2.ohchr.org/English/bodies/crc/docs/GC/CRC_C_GC_14_ENG.pdf.

[9] Ibid., para. 28.

moments when youth crime is a highly politicised issue,[10] that child-offenders, through their (deemed) choice to commit wrongful acts, render themselves less entitled to other, so-called, protection rights.[11] Indeed, at the extreme, some might argue that these are forfeited.[12] Raymond Arthur has explained the issue in this way, in relation to English criminal procedure:

> The English youth justice system ... developed in a way which weakens and negates the protection rights stemming from the UN Convention by perpetuating the idea that if children are competent they are automatically assumed capable of negotiating their way through a liberal universe of choices, and the offender is no longer a child and no longer worthy of special protection of their rights.[13]

The issue arises partly because children who offend present a paradox[14] that law is not always equipped to resolve effectively. On the one hand, children, as a group, are regarded as vulnerable and in need of protection. On the other, 'offenders' are regarded as worthy of punishment because they have exercised an autonomous choice to do wrong. 'Child-offenders' belong to both of these groups at once, but the law is more used to dealing with each as a separate category. Child and family law is applied to the vulnerable; criminal law applies to the offender. Children's rights, conceived as a discrete area of law, has been relatively more successful in adopting the holistic approach, which is needed, in that Articles 37 and 40 specifically give cognisance to some of the unique vulnerabilities of the child-offender and Article 12 is widely recognised as at least a basic mechanism for giving credence to the child's autonomy (in the right to express views) but with some protection in that weight is to be given to these views 'in accordance with the age and maturity of the child'.[15] Nonetheless, in the context of the law as a whole, the rights of children

---

[10] For example, in England and Wales between 1997 and 2010 under New Labour, as exemplified by the White Paper, *No More Excuses* (London: TSO, 1997).

[11] Protection rights include, for example, rights to health (Art. 24), to benefit from social security (Art. 26) and to an adequate standard of living (Art. 27).

[12] See Fortin, *Children's Rights and the Developing Law*, (note 7,) p. 683.

[13] Raymond Arthur, 'Recognising children's citizenship in the youth justice system' (2015) 37 *Journal of Social Welfare and Family Law* 21–37 at 27 (reference omitted).

[14] See Claire McDiarmid, *Childhood and Crime* (Dundee: Dundee University Press, 2007), pp. 165–167.

[15] See, for example, Aoife Nolan, 'The child as "democratic citizen": challenging the "participation gap"' (2010) *Public Law* 767–782, particularly 780, though the author criticises the tendency to subjugate autonomy to protection.

who do wrong are not prominent and, in Scotland, there has been only very limited recourse to Articles 37 and 40.[16]

Another key issue is that 'the public interest' may sometimes be, or be perceived to be, in direct opposition to the interests of a child who commits a crime. For example, the CRC accords to a child 'in trouble' with the law at any stage of proceedings, a right 'to have his or her privacy fully respected'.[17] In a recent English case, a fifteen-year-old who murdered his teacher in a pre-meditated knife attack was named by the media following a specific order by the judge, who justified this by stating that he had come down 'firmly on the side of the public interest'.[18] It cannot therefore be said that children's rights are not affected by offending behaviour. The argument is the normative one that they *should not* be. Even where there must be some form of balancing of competing rights – for example, the child's right not to be separated from his/her parents[19] cannot be upheld where he or she has been sentenced to a period of detention by a criminal court[20] – there is no justification for the Article 3 protection ceasing to apply. Its content, and its application in the Scottish context, will now be considered.

C The Promise of the Best Interests Standard in Article 3

Article 3 sets the bar high in terms of expectation of outcome arising from its application. Art 3(1) states:

> In all actions concerning children, whether undertaken by public or private social welfare institutions, courts of law, administrative authorities or legislative bodies, the best interests of the child shall be a primary consideration.

This is not qualified. It includes '*all* actions concerning children' and *inter alia*, those undertaken by public social welfare institutions, courts of law and administrative authorities. The principle clearly extends, then, to institutions which take 'actions' concerning children who offend. In terms of what it means, if an element is a 'primary' consideration in reaching any decision both common sense and basic legal interpretative skills would

---

[16] See footnotes 45–49 and accompanying text.   [17] Art. 40(2)(vii).
[18] C. Brooke, 'Judge: why I was right to name the teacher's teen killer', Daily Mail, 6 Nov 2014. See also Ursula Smartt, "Why I was right to name the teacher's teen killer': naming teenagers in criminal trials and law reform in the internet age' (2015) 20 *Communications Law* 5–14 at 6.
[19] Art. 9(1).   [20] Criminal Procedure (Scotland) Act 1995, ss. 44 and 208.

indicate that it must be an *important* one in that decision-making process. Even if Article 3 stated only that it had to be <u>a</u> consideration (unqualified), 'best interests' would have to be part of the mix. 'Primary', if it is not just a weasel word, inserted without meaning, makes best interests *significant*. Indeed '*best*' means more than just the child's interests. If 'best interests' are 'a primary consideration' – and Article 3 says that they *shall* be, not that they may be[21] – a child about to enter a decision-making process armed with this information could reasonably expect that something really good *for him/her* is likely to come out of it. In other words:

> The expression "primary consideration" means that the child's best interests may *not* be considered on the same level as all other considerations. ... Viewing the best interests of the child as "primary" requires a consciousness about the place that children's interests must occupy in all actions and a willingness to give priority to those interests in all circumstances, but especially when an action has an undeniable impact on the children concerned.[22]

How, then, is this translated into Scots law, particularly in relation to child-offenders?

D Scots Law and Children Who Offend

It is first of all necessary to explain the mechanisms by which Scots law deals with children who offend. The primary route is through the children's hearings system, one of the grounds for referral to which is that 'the child has committed an offence'.[23] Children aged eight years and over may be so referred.[24] It is also possible for those aged twelve years and over to be prosecuted but only 'on the instructions of ..., or at the instance of[,] the Lord Advocate'[25] and usually for grave offences.[26] The vast majority of child-offenders are referred to the children's

---

[21] See UN Committee on the Rights of the Child *General Comment No. 14 (Art. 3(1))*, (2013) (note 8), para. 36.
[22] Ibid., at paras. 37 and 40 (emphasis added).
[23] Children's Hearings (Scotland) Act 2011, s. 67(2)(j).
[24] Criminal Procedure (Scotland) Act 1995, s. 41.
[25] Criminal Procedure (Scotland) Act 1995, s. 42(1).
[26] See the *Lord Advocate's Guidelines to the Chief Constable on the Reporting to Procurators Fiscal of offences alleged to have been committed by children* (2014) available at: www.crownoffice.gov.uk/images/Documents/Prosecution_Policy_Guidance/Lord_Advocates_Guidelines/Lord%20Advocates%20Guidelines%20offences%20committed%20by%20children.pdf.

hearings system,[27] which deals with such cases in the same way as those of children referred on each of its other fifteen (care and protection) grounds.[28] Decisions are taken by a panel of three lay members, trained for the function and, importantly, the determinative principle is the child's welfare. It is here, then, that Article 3 finds its first direct expression in Scots law.

E Article 3 in Scots Law

Best Interests and Welfare

Unlike the European Convention on Human Rights, the CRC as a whole is not incorporated into Scots law and, therefore, does not have direct effect. Despite this, the provisions of Article 3 *are* directly legislated but (like English law)[29] using the term 'welfare' instead of 'best interests'.

'Welfare' has a number of uses including the pejorative, if primarily tabloid, notion of the 'welfare scrounger'.[30] In Scottish child law, however, it has a long and well-respected history and denotes the principle that identifying and meeting hitherto unmet needs on the part of children will have a generally beneficial effect on their lives and will, specifically, operate to reduce to a vanishing point their offending behaviour. This argument is given passionate expression – quite specifically in relation to 'juvenile delinquency' – in the Kilbrandon Report of 1964 on the basis of which the children's hearings system was set up. It states:

---

[27] Statistics for prosecution and for referral to children's hearings on the offence ground are compiled separately and do not readily dovetail. In 2013/14, the official government statistics record that the number of children aged under sixteen years with a charge proved against them in court *per 1000 population* was zero. Eight per thousand sixteen-year-olds and twenty-five per thousand seventeen-year-olds were counted. The *Report* notes that 'In the past 10 years, the number of convictions for younger people has fallen at much faster rates than for older people.' (Scottish Government, *Statistical Bulletin Crime and Justice Series: Criminal Proceedings in Scotland 2013/14*, para. 3.5.1 and Table 5 (available at: www.gov.scot/Resource/0046/00469252.pdf). By contrast, 2764 children were referred to the children's hearings system for offending behaviour – a decrease of 20.4 per cent on the previous year: Scottish Children's Reporter Administration, *Annual Report 2013/14*, p. 22 (available at www.scra.gov.uk/wp-control/uploads/2016/04/SCRA-Annual-Report-2013-14-web-version.pdf). The Scottish Law Commission estimated that 99 per cent of children *aged under sixteen years* alleged to have committed an offence were dealt with in the children's hearings system: *Report on Age of Criminal Responsibility* (Scot Law Com No 185) (Edinburgh: TSO, 2002) at para. 3.10.

[28] Children's Hearings (Scotland) Act 2011, s. 67.   [29] Children Act 1989, s. 1(1).

[30] See, e.g., 'The welfies: recognising the country's scroungers and dossers', *The Sun*, 15 January 2015, p. 12.

> The object must be to effect, so far as this can be achieved by public action, the reduction, and ideally the elimination, of delinquency. If public concern must always be for the effective treatment of delinquency, the appropriate treatment measures in any individual case can be decided only on an informed assessment of the individual child's actual needs.[31]

There may be (though, in fact, this is rare) some debate as to the relationship between the Scottish legislation's preference for 'welfare' and the CRC's use of 'best interests',[32] but here they are used interchangeably.[33]

Scottish 'Article 3' Legislative Provisions
The Paramountcy Principle

For most decisions concerning children, the domestic Scottish legislation augments the Article 3 primacy requirement. The relevant provision (which does *not* cover the small number of children who are prosecuted) states:

> [W]here ... a children's hearing, pre-hearing panel or court is coming to a decision about a matter relating to a child [, ...it] is to regard the need to safeguard and promote the welfare of the child throughout the child's childhood as the paramount consideration.[34]

It would be hard to give a stronger statement of the importance of the child's welfare and this is applied to those who offend in the same way as to those referred on any other ground.[35]

Welfare as a Primary Consideration

In the immediately following section of the relevant Act, however, the paramountcy requirement *is* qualified so that the listed decision-making bodies (children's hearings, pre-hearing panels, courts) may depart from it where they deem this necessary 'for the purpose of protecting members of the public from serious harm (whether physical or not)', but in those

---

[31] Scottish Home and Health Department, Scottish Education Department *Report on Children and Young Persons, Scotland* (Edinburgh: HMSO, 1964) Cmnd. 2306, p. 8, para. 12.
[32] For an in-depth comparison, see Jonathan Herring and Charles Foster, 'Welfare means relationality, virtue and altruism' (2012) 32 *Legal Studies* 480 – 498, pp. 482-483.
[33] In fact, there is little clear distinction drawn in the case law. See, for example, *M* v. *K* 2015 CSIH 54.
[34] Children's Hearings (Scotland) Act 2011, s. 25(1) and (2).
[35] See *Merrin* v. *S* 1987 SLT 193.

circumstances the child's welfare must still be 'a primary consideration rather than the paramount consideration'.[36] This provision makes no specific reference to child-offenders, yet it is hard to think of circumstances where a child is likely to cause such 'serious harm' without breaking the criminal law. In fact, this power to depart from paramountcy first appeared, in a different form, in the Children (Scotland) Act of 1995[37] and an examination of the Parliamentary debate relating to it illustrates the point. Lord Macaulay of Bragar said:

> With this amendment we are seeking to deal with "a little monster" in society, a person who slashes car tyres, who breaks car windows and who is out of control. What is the paramount consideration? I do not know where the word "paramount" comes from. I think it is an Americanism, but it is a horrible word. It does not mean anything, but anyway it is in the Bill. Where does paramountcy go in achieving the balance between society and the individual?[38]

The shift away from paramountcy, then, seems to have been conceived as an intentional, government-sanctioned, dilution of the rights of children who offend with no clear statement of the way in which their welfare was to be considered instead.[39] In the current (2011) version of the provision, this public (safety) interest is only to be balanced in alongside best interests, which remain primary. It does not trump them. This can be taken as a welcome recognition that children's rights matter though, clearly, there is still some diminution between best interests as paramount and as a primary consideration.

But are these apparently different standards of best interests meaningful? What is the difference in practice between paramountcy and primacy in this context? There appears to be no reported case in which this power to depart from the paramountcy principle has been considered. This

---

[36] Children's Hearings (Scotland) Act 2011, s. 26(1) and (2).   [37] S. 16(5).
[38] Official Report of the Committee on the Children (Scotland) Bill, *Hansard*, HL Deb 06 June 1995 vol 564 cc1-66GC, at § 37GC (available at: http://hansard.millbanksystems.com/grand_committee_report/1995/jun/06/official-report-of-the-committee-on-the#S5LV0564P0_19950606_GCR_243).
[39] The original, 1995 version of s. 16(5)(a) stated:
'If, for the purpose of protecting members of the public from serious harm (whether or not physical harm)—

(a) a children's hearing consider it necessary to make a decision under or by virtue of this Part of this Act which (but for this paragraph) would not be consistent with their affording paramountcy to the consideration mentioned in subsection (1) above, they may make that decision'.

makes it difficult to know how to determine the difference *in law* between 'paramount' and 'primary' for these purposes. Indeed, the official training manual for children's panel members states of the public safety rule: '[t]his is an exception that panel members will very rarely use.'[40] While, clearly, the existence of the provision demonstrates that it is permissible to give less prominence to the welfare of children who are deemed a risk to public safety than to that of others, there is little to indicate that this is actually being done in the practice of the children's hearings system.

Welfare of Prosecuted Children

The final Scottish provision meriting consideration in the Article 3 context relates specifically to children who are prosecuted. It also considerably pre-dates both the CRC and the children's hearings system,[41] yet it still occupies the territory of welfare-based approaches. It states:

> Every court in dealing with a child who is brought before it as an offender shall have regard to the welfare of the child and shall in a proper case take steps for removing him from undesirable surroundings.[42]

This is not ambitious. It does not use 'significance' terminology like 'paramount' or 'primary' but it is unambiguous in its attachment to children who offend. It imposes a duty on all courts to consider their welfare. It is a provision for the tiny number of Scottish children who are prosecuted in the adult courts and it cannot be balanced against, or diluted by virtue of, offending behaviour because its *only* application is where such acts are alleged. As such, it seems valuable. It does, however, have some limitations.

First, it is unclear what would happen if a court failed to apply it. Second, the meaning to be attached to 'welfare' is not spelt out. Does it mean 'best interests' or 'ensuring the child's unmet needs are identified and met' or does it relate only to the child's comfort and understanding during the criminal proceedings in question – a more 'well-being' sense of the term? The fact that the section goes on to consider the child's residence – something beyond the scope of the instant proceedings – suggests the former. Again, a dearth of case law makes it difficult to put the matter beyond doubt.

---

[40] Children's Hearings Scotland, *Practice and Procedure Manual* (Edinburgh: Children's Hearings Scotland, 2013) p. 16, para. 3.4.

[41] It appeared in the Children and Young Persons (Scotland) Act 1937 (s. 49) and was repeated in the Criminal Procedure (Scotland) Act 1975 as s. 172.

[42] Criminal Procedure (Scotland) Act 1995, s. 50(6).

F The Temporal Dimension and Paternalism

This inquiry also brings into focus the temporal dimension of Article 3 and its domestic Scottish derivatives. In other words, for how long must the child's welfare weigh in the making of the decision? The Scottish paramountcy provision is unequivocal that decision-makers must take it into account 'throughout the child's childhood'. Article 3 and the Scottish public safety exception both make best interests primary, thereby giving it at least some longevity beyond the moment of making the decision, since it will continue to operate as the decision is implemented.

On the face of it, this seems to enhance its overarching 'real goodness' for the child. Not only must a decision-maker have that child's *best* interests in mind at the moment of making the decision but also for (possibly) years to come. In fact, however, as far as the child is concerned, this need to look to the future may operate to allow a particularly adultist or paternalist approach to come to the fore. The child's wishes and his/her welfare are not the same even if these wishes (or 'views')[43] should be taken into account in determining best interests. Child-friendly statements of the principle of Article 3 make clear just how little weight needs to be conferred on these wishes however. UNICEF states:

> All adults should do what is best for you. When adults make decisions, they should think about how their decisions will affect children.

The Scottish Government states:

> If a decision is being made by any organisation about your well-being, then your interests must be considered when making the final decision. What is best for YOU is what matters. For example, if a local authority is planning a new road they have to think about how their plans affect your safety.[44]

The child who has read the original Article and is expecting a decision in which his/her best interests are, at least, a primary consideration will realise that it is an adult view of his/her good that is definitive. Adults have also, by definition, proceeded to the end of the period of the lifespan called childhood. There may be an argument that this equips them to know better how a decision will bear 'throughout' that period than the child who is in the midst of it. If this revelation is disappointing for a

---

[43] Art. 12; Children's Hearings (Scotland) Act 2011, s. 27.
[44] *The UN Convention on the Rights of the Child: A Guide for Children and Young People* (Edinburgh: The Scottish Government, 2008) (emphasis in original).

child expecting his/her own version of the 'really good' to emerge from a process, it does not detract from the overarching principle that the outcome should still *be* 'really good'. To what extent is this the case? This chapter will look firstly at prosecuted children and then at those who are processed through the children's hearings system.

G   The Best Interests of Children Who Are Prosecuted

Only a very small number of children (for this purpose, those aged seventeen years and under) are prosecuted in the adult courts. At the outset of this process, a decision will have been taken jointly to refer such a child to the reporter to the children's panel and to the procurator fiscal to decide whether his/her case should be processed through the children's hearings system or by prosecution. It is noteworthy that the Lord Advocate's Guidelines,[45] which govern this process, make no reference to the child-accused's best interests, though the existence of Article 3 is at least noted in the Crown Office's *Book of Regulations*.[46] Nonetheless, the Scottish High Court has noted with approval resort being made to the CRC where the accused is a child. In *HM Advocate* v. *P*,[47] Lord Reed made reference to Article 40 (right to a fair trial) and to the Beijing Rules,[48] noting that the European Court of Human Rights had used each 'as a source of guidance as to the requirements imposed by the European Convention in relation to proceedings involving juvenile offenders'.[49] Little seems to have been said beyond this in any subsequent

---

[45] *Lord Advocate's guidelines on reporting of offences alleged to have been committed by children* (2014) (above note 26).
[46] Crown Office and Procurator Fiscal Service, *Prosecution Policy and Guidance – Book of Regulations*, Chapter 16 – Children (1998), p. 1 available at: www.crownoffice.gov.uk/images/Documents/Prosecution_Policy_Guidance/Book_of_Regulations/Book%20of%20Regulations%20-%20Chapter%2016%20-%20Children.PDF. Similar guidance provided by the Crown Prosecution Service in England and Wales on *Youth Offenders* (available at: www.cps.gov.uk/legal/v_to_z/youth_offenders/#a01) is more nuanced and, in places, makes reference to the types of information that should be obtained in deciding whether to prosecute (e.g., 'views of local authority Children's and Young People's Service' in relation to rape and other offences against children under 13 (where the defendant is also a child under 13)). See Laura Hoyano, 'Decision to prosecute: Whether decision of defendant to prosecute a child for alleged sexual abuse by her of her two younger sisters amenable to judicial review' (2012) *Criminal Law Review* 39–46.
[47] 2001 SLT 924.
[48] The UN Standard Minimum Rules for the Administration of Juvenile Justice, Beijing, 29 November 1985.
[49] *HM Advocate* v. *P* 2001 SLT 924, at p. 927 para. 11.

case – and, in fact, the accused's status as a child is not necessarily noted in case reports suggesting that, once the decision to prosecute has been taken, it is not seen as particularly significant.

In relation to the sentencing of juveniles though, it has been stated, in Hibbard v. HM Advocate,[50] that

> the court has no difficulty with the proposition that, when sentencing a child for any offence, the sentence selected ought to take into account, as a primary consideration, the welfare of the child and the desirability of his reintegration into society. It is not the only primary consideration, since the legislation requires that the seriousness of the offence be taken into account and that the period selected satisfies the requirements for retribution and deterrence. But it is one. In this way, the sentencing of a child will differ in the degree of emphasis or weight placed on the welfare of the person sentenced. With an adult, it is also a consideration, but it may not always be categorised as a primary one, at least where murder is concerned.[51]

Subsequent cases have also articulated the principle but the emphasis on welfare as only one among a number of important considerations means that the outcome is not always necessarily *in* the child's best interests. In HM Advocate v. KH,[52] for example, while the judgment states that court 'had specific regard to the welfare of the respondent as a primary consideration'[53] the accused's sentence (absolute discharge) was quashed as unduly lenient and a community payback order was imposed instead. He was fifteen years old at the time of the offence and had pled guilty to a sexual assault against a classmate. A competing interest – the need for a punitive element – was considered definitive. It might be questioned *how* 'primary' the child-offender's welfare was deemed to be in a decision, taken by the state, to appeal a sentence in order to have it made more severe where the young person has already been through a court process, accepted his guilt and, to some extent, moved on.

On the other hand, in HM Advocate v. Smith,[54] another Crown appeal against an unduly lenient sentence, the original sentence remained in place. It had been reached after careful assessment of a range of factors including the accused's troubled home background. While there is no overt reference to welfare or best interests, it appears that considerations relevant to these issues were applied.

---

[50] 2011 JC 149. [51] Ibid., at pp. 153–154 per Lord Carloway. [52] 2014 SCCR 485.
[53] Ibid., at p. 487, para. 11 per Lord Justice-Clerk Carloway. [54] 2014 SCCR 39.

The extent to which best interests looks to collapse into leniency is of some relevance. The Committee on the Rights of the Child is unequivocal in its view that 'protecting the child's best interests means that the traditional objectives of criminal justice, such as repression or retribution, must give way to rehabilitation and restorative justice objectives, when dealing with child offenders'.[55]

H Children's Hearings System: Young People's Views of 'Best Interests' in Practice

Finally, then, views on the extent to which actual decisions taken within the children's hearings system are perceived as 'really good' by the young people in respect of whom they are taken will be considered, through examination of two, recent, small-scale research projects. The first, entitled *Youth In Justice: Young People Explore What Their Role in Improving Youth Justice should be*[56] was produced jointly by the Centre for Youth and Criminal Justice ('CYCJ')[57] and by Space Unlimited,[58] and the young people who participated were all either 'involved in, or at risk of becoming involved in, youth justice services'.[59] Accordingly, they are well qualified to comment. Overall, they were between the ages of thirteen and twenty-five and participated as three separate groups.[60] The other study was conducted by the Scottish Children's Reporter Administration ('SCRA') and was entitled *The Children's Hearings System: Understood and Making a Difference: Young People's Views*.[61] SCRA's members – children's reporters – are the gatekeepers and administrators of the children's hearings system. The twenty-one young participants in the study were between the ages of eleven and seventeen and had experience of the hearings system, some in relation to offending behaviour.[62]

---

[55] UN Committee on the Rights of the Child *General Comment No. 14 (Art. 3(1))*, (2013) (note 8), para. 28.
[56] (Glasgow: Space Unlimited, 2015).
[57] Which exists to support improvements in youth justice through practice development, research and knowledge exchange. See its own website at: www.cycj.org.uk/about-us/background/.
[58] A social enterprise and charity that helps 'young people, organisations, and communities to design and take action together'. See Space Unlimited's website at: www.spaceunlimited.org/.
[59] Space Unlimited, *Youth in Justice* (2015) (note 56), at p. 2.   [60] Ibid., at pp. 5–6.
[61] (Stirling: SCRA, 2011) (available at: www.scra.gov.uk/wp-content/uploads/2016/07/Young-peoples-views-on-decisions-services-and-outcomes.pdf).
[62] Ibid., at pp. 6–7 and p. 21.

The two studies are partly concerned with the participants' experience of the children's hearings *process*. In principle, Article 3 relates to decisions and their consequences. Article 12, which affords to the child who wishes to do so the right to express views and have these taken into account, seems more directly relevant to process. There is, however, a close link between views and decisions such that the Committee on the Rights of the Child has specifically stated that 'there can be no correct application of article 3 if the components of article 12 are not respected'.[63] There is also an argument that the fairness of any such process has a direct impact on perceptions of the justice or acceptability of the final decision[64] and will, therefore, have an impact on the individual young person's view of its relationship to his/her best interests. Process and outcome or views and best interests are, thus, closely linked. With this in mind, what do the reports say about children's hearings? The view of CYCJ participants was 'mostly negative' and they described 'feeling judged, ignored, not listened to, sometimes barely even addressed when in the room, and talked about being excluded from the process and not understanding it'.[65] While this may tell us little about outcomes, the participants' perception of the decision was that it had not been good.

The SCRA study asked a question that was more directly relevant to Article 3, but that still took the processes into account: '[d]oes the Children's Hearings System make a difference to the lives of children and young people?'[66] Some young people felt, specifically, that their views had *not* been heard in the process and '*[a]ll* the young people had experienced a Hearing that made a decision that was against their wishes. However, there still appeared to be widespread acceptance that it was a fair process'.[67] The study's overall conclusion relates to outcomes. It found that:

> [m]ost of the young people in this research felt their lives had got better since being involved in the Hearings System. ... Hearings could provide

---

[63] United Nation Committee on the Rights of the Child, *General Comment* No. 12: *The Right of the Child to be Heard* (2009), CRC/C/GC/12, (available at: www2.ohchr.org/english/bodies/crc/docs/AdvanceVersions/CRC-C-GC-12.pdf) at para. 74.
[64] Victoria Weisz, Twila Wingrove and April Faith-Slaker, 'Children and Procedural Justice' (2007) 44 *Court Review* 36–43.
[65] Space Unlimited, *Youth in Justice* (2015) (note 56), p. 8.
[66] *The Children's Hearings System: Understood and Making a Difference: Young People's Views* (2011)(note 61) at p. 6.
[67] Ibid., p. 12 (emphasis added).

the impetus for change – for young people and their parents. . . . Overall, young people said that it was their own commitment to change that had improved their lives.[68]

On the one hand then, these young people do *not* report that the decision of the children's hearing was 'really good' for them – that as a direct consequence of it, their lives improved. On the other, there is a sense that they themselves converted a, probably paternalistic, decision about what would be best for them, into a catalyst for positive change. They reclaimed their agency to achieve the good outcome. Thus, if the hearing's decision was not 'really good', it was, equally, not wholly bad. 'Welfare as being paramount throughout childhood' became 'an improved life'.

I   Conclusion

Overall then, in its clear terms, Article 3 holds out considerable promise of 'really good' outcomes for all children in respect of whom official decisions are taken including, on the same terms, those who offend. Within the children's hearings setting, the commitment to welfare is paramount. In other words, it could not have greater significance yet the young people about whom its decisions are taken do not always experience its decisions as 'really good'. For children who are prosecuted, the status of best interests as a primary consideration may allow other primary considerations to be balanced in alongside, rather than the overarching concentration on welfare, rehabilitation and reintegration into society, which the UN children's rights regime, taken as a whole, envisages. Article 3 states that *best* interests *shall* be *primary*. Decision-makers, and particularly those deciding about children who offend who may have fewer advocates, must welcome the opportunity this provides to ensure those really good outcomes.

---

[68] Ibid., p. 27.

18

The Child's Best Interests and Religion: A Case Study of the Holy See's Best Interests Obligations and Clerical Child Sexual Abuse

IOANA CISMAS

A Introduction

Does religion and belief carry any relevance for the child's best interests? The United Nations Committee on the Rights of the Child provides indicia in General Comment 14. Therein, the treaty body stipulates that in assessing a child's best interests, the right to preserve her identity as guaranteed by the Convention on the Rights of the Child (CRC) in article 8 must be taken into consideration; whereby religion and beliefs, form part of a child's identity.[1] Thus, in considerations related to foster home and placement for a child, adoption, separation of parents and divorce, for instance, the assessment of the child's best interests should pay due regard to the 'desirability of continuity in a child's upbringing and to the child's ... religious... background'.[2]

Yet, the relation between religious interpretations and the child's best interests proves to be much more complex. Reflecting this complexity, the UN Committee emphasizes:

> Although preservation of religious and cultural values and traditions as part of the identity of the child must be taken into consideration, practices that are inconsistent or incompatible with the rights established in the Convention are not in the child's best interests.[3]

Consistent with these cautionary words, the Committee holds that authorities may not invoke the preservation of a child's identity in their attempt to propagate 'traditions and cultural values that deny

---

[1] Committee on the Rights of the Child, General comment No. 14, The right of the child to have his or her best interests taken as a primary consideration (art. 3, para. 1), U.N. Doc. CRC/C/GC/14 (2013), para. 55.
[2] Ibid., para. 56.   [3] Ibid., para. 57.

the child ... the rights guaranteed by the Convention'.[4] Against this background, a question that adds another layer of complexity to our considerations regarding religion and the child's best interest emerges: are religious state actors[5] bound by a similar obligation to that of (assumingly secular) authorities? In other words, should they consider a child's best interests in their interpretations of religion, i.e., their rules and actions? And do they consider the child's best interests? This chapter addresses these two questions in relation to a very specific religious actor, the Holy See, while employing the context of clerical child sexual abuse as a case study.

The chapter is structured in three parts. The first analytical part will establish whether the Holy See, as a party to the CRC, has international legal obligations related to the child's best interests and whether these are different in nature compared to those of other (secular) state parties. In answering these questions, the analysis challenges the dual personality scenario proposed by the Holy See and supported by parts of doctrine. The second part of the study draws on doctrinal and judicial developments in the area of extraterritoriality and argues that the Holy See's child rights obligations do not stop at the tiny borders of the Vatican. In reaching this conclusion it discusses critically the UN Committee's 2014 Concluding Observations on the Holy See's report. Third, normative and institutional changes undertaken by the Holy See in recent years with the aim to address child sexual abuse will be examined in order to ascertain whether and to what extent such changes take into account the child's best interests at the Vatican and extraterritorially.

B When Status Matters

Much of the work on the Holy See in general international law manuals and specialised literature starts (and often ends) with a discussion of the international legal status of the actor. The fascination of scholars with the Holy See's status can be seen as an intellectual exercise aimed at

---

[4] Ibid., para. 57.
[5] This chapter defines religious actors as those entities that assume the authority to interpret religion, i.e., by using religion as an important or primary source of law, whose executive and judiciary enforce religious laws, or who grant religious authorities a principal role in the executive. See I. Cismas, *Religious Actors and International Law* (Oxford: Oxford University Press, 2014), pp. 51–58 and especially p. 53.

clarifying the odd contours of an actor that defies traditional criteria of statehood. Or, it reflects an understanding that status in international law matters; and that the exact form that such status takes – statehood or not – is of great significance, for therefrom flows a specific set of rights and obligations.

With the loss of the Papal States to Italy in 1870, it is generally accepted that the Holy See ceased its existence as a state.[6] Thus, some early writers argued that, alongside statehood, the Holy See lost its international legal status;[7] others concede 'a degree of international personality'[8] to the Holy See due to custom and acquiescence of other states rooted not in statehood but in the important religious role of the actor.[9] Instead of putting to rest such debates, the conclusion of the Lateran Treaty between the Holy See and Italy in 1929 – whereby the latter granted the Vatican territory to the Holy See – amplified confusion. Legal scholars appear to have resorted to mathematics, exploring permutations between two elements: international legal personality and statehood (or absence thereof). The result is a multitude of variants: the Holy See as a state or as a non-state actor; the Holy See having one international legal personality, that of the state, or alternatively that of the Roman Catholic Church; and, the Holy See's self-portrayal of a dual personality.[10] This latter variant portrays the Holy See as enjoying two international legal personalities, as the government of the Vatican and, *separately*, as the government of the Catholic Church.

Over the years and in various circumstances the legal implications of this latter arrangement have become apparent. One such consequence of the dual personality scenario is that it facilitates the 'shifting of the two personae', thereby allowing the Holy See to avail itself of the

---

[6] See J. L. Kunz, 'The Status of the Holy See in International Law' (1952) 46 *American Journal of International Law* 308, at 311.

[7] For an overview of early writings on the Holy See and the various positions of scholars see C. G. Fenwick, 'The New City of the Vatican' (1929) 23 *American Journal of International Law* 371, at 371.

[8] See J. Crawford, *The Creation of States in International Law*, 2nd ed., (Oxford: Oxford University Press, 2006), p. 226; see also P. Fauchille, *Traité de droit international public*, 8ème ed., Entièrement refondue, complétée et mise au courant, du Manuel de droit international public de M. Henry Bonfils ed., vol. I, (Paris: Rousseau & Co., 1922), pp. 732–755.

[9] Expressed elsewhere as 'religious legitimacy'. See discussion in Cismas, *Religious Actors and International Law*, pp. 163–164.

[10] On the self-perception of the Holy See and the logic of the dual personality scenario see, Cismas, *Religious Actors and International Law*, pp. 185–188.

privileges of statehood, while at times denying the corresponding statal obligations.[11] It is relevant to note, as an illustration, that the Holy See has become party to a number of human rights treaties open for membership exclusively to states, among which is the CRC.[12] When the validity of the Holy See's general reservations entered to the CRC were challenged by a member of the Committee,[13] the Holy See specifically invoked its right qua state to join treaties and make reservations.[14] In turn, an analysis of the review processes of the Holy See by various treaty bodies, including the UN Committee on the Rights of the Child, demonstrates that the party understands its obligations arising from human rights instruments as 'moral obligations', drawing on its personality qua Catholic Church.[15]

Another example illustrates a second use of the dual personality scenario, whereby the Holy See invokes at the same time rights qua state *and* non-state entity. In *O'Bryan v. the Holy See*, the plaintiffs brought a putative class action on behalf of all victims of sexual abuse by Catholic clerics in the United States; they alleged that the Holy See was liable under the doctrine of *respondeat superior*, and *inter alia*, for violations of customary international human rights law.[16] In this case, the Holy See argued that it should enjoy state immunity under the Foreign Sovereign Immunities Act – it did so successfully. In the same breath, however, the Holy See also argued that the freedom of religion clause entailed by the First Amendment to the US Constitution should bar the plaintiffs' claim. In denying this path of defense, the judge appeared mystified:

---

[11] Described in Cismas, *Religious Actors and International Law*, pp. 10, 13, 158–159.

[12] Among the ratified human rights treaties of significance for the analysis here are: Convention on the Rights of the Child, New York, 20 November 1989, into force 2 September 1990, 1577 UNTS 3 (ratified 20 April 1990) (Hereafter, CRC); Optional Protocol on the Sale of Children, Child Prostitution and Child Pornography, New York, 25 May 2000, in force18 January 2002, A/54/49, Vol. III (2000), (ratified 24 October 2001).

[13] For an analysis the reservations entered by the Holy See upon ratification of the CRC see Cismas, *Religious Actors and International Law*, pp. 219–223.

[14] UN Committee on the Rights of the Child, Compte rendu analytique de la 255ème seance, Examen des rapports présentés par les Etats parties: Rapport initial du Saint-Siège, UN Doc. CRC/C/SR.255, 24 novembre 1995, para. 47.

[15] See for instance UN Committee on the Rights of the Child, UN Doc. CRC/C/SR.255, para. 19.

[16] *O'Bryan v. Holy See*, 490 F. Supp. 2d 826 (W.D. Ky. 2005) and *O'Bryan v. Holy See*, 471 F.Supp.2d 784 (W.D. Ky. 2007). See also L. C. Martinez Jr, 'Sovereign Impunity: Does the Foreign Sovereign Immunities Act Bar Lawsuits Against Holy See in Clerical Sexual Abuse Cases?' (2008) 44 *Texas International Law Journal* 123.

'Defendant Holy See cannot simultaneously seek the protections of the Foreign Sovereign Immunities Act and the United States Constitution.'[17]

Perhaps unsurprisingly, challenges to the legal status of the Vatican have flared up in contexts in which the Holy See has exercised in a visible manner rights restricted to states in international conferences, and in instances where it arguably eluded some of the concurrent state obligations.[18] Clerical child sexual abuse is the most prominent of such contexts.

In a systematic study of the question of the personality of the Holy See, this author has shown that the dual personality scenario is legally untenable and fails to garner consequential support from state practice.[19] While the international personality of the Holy See (but not as a state) continued to exist after the extinction of the Papal States by virtue of its religious legitimacy, it was only as a result of the Lateran Treaty that the construct (not the Holy See, nor the Vatican on its own) could 'clothe'[20] itself with the semblance of statehood. On the one hand, by reading the Lateran Treaty in the light of the effectiveness criteria for statehood (territory, population, government, and independence), the Holy See's claim to an external, separate international personality invalidates its other invoked personality qua state, mainly because the requirement of independence would not be realized. On the other hand, when divorced from the construct, the Vatican is essentially a territory and has *on its own* no legal basis to support the claim for a distinct international legal personality. Instead, the study posited that the Holy See and the Vatican form a construct with one single international personality, which, however, derives from two sources: international custom recognizing the religious legitimacy of the Holy See and the state-like resemblance conferred upon the construct by the Lateran Treaty in 1929. It demonstrated that the construct personality reflects history, is supported by the Lateran Treaty and general international law, domestic case law and the monitoring of human rights bodies, and 'makes sense of what otherwise would be erratic state practice'.

---

[17] *O'Bryan v. Holy See*, 471 F.Supp.2d 784 (W.D. Ky. 2007), at 794.
[18] See for example Y. Abdullah, 'The Holy See at United Nations Conferences: State or Church?' (1996) 96 *Columbia Law Review* 1835–1875.
[19] Cismas, *Religious Actors and International Law*, chapter 4.
[20] The notion 'clothing itself with the formal attributes of statehood' was used by H. Lauterpacht, 'General Rules of the Law of Peace', in E. Lauterpacht (ed.), *International Law Being the Collected Papers of Hersch Lauterpacht, vol. I, The General Works*, (Cambridge: Cambridge University Press, 1970), p. 306.

Crucially, it has shown that the Holy See-Vatican construct enjoys the rights *and* incurs the obligations of a state.[21]

For the purpose of this chapter, a brief review of the UN Committee on the Rights of the Child's monitoring activity of the Holy See's obligations under the CRC is in order. The treaty body's early practice accommodated the dual personality claimed by the Holy See and thereby, to a certain extent, also the shifting of personalities and the invocation of rights qua both state and church.[22] Yet, even in the 1995 Concluding Observations the Committee underscored that the best interests of the child, alongside the principles of non-discrimination and respect for the views of the child, should be 'fully taken into account in the conduct of all the activities of the Holy See and of the various Church institutions and organizations dealing with the rights of the child'.[23]

Recent practice accepts *formally* the dual personality variant, but proceeds *substantively* as if the Holy See has only one international legal personality. In the 2014 review of the Holy See's obligations under the Convention and its Optional Protocol on the sale of children, child prostitution and child pornography (OPSC), the UN Committee was uncompromising: it regarded the Holy See as a party with obligations no different than those of any of other state party to these instruments – regardless of its invoked special, religious nature.[24]

Best interests obligations appeared prominently in the 2014 Concluding Observations. As such, the treaty body noted with concern that the Holy See's legislative, administrative and judicial proceedings and other programmes impacting children have failed to sufficiently incorporate children's best interests as a primary consideration.[25] The Committee showed itself particularly concerned with the Holy See's handling of clerical child sexual abuse allegations as 'the Holy See has consistently placed the preservation of the reputation of the Church and the

---

[21] Cismas, *Religious Actors and International Law*, chapter 4, pp. 308–309, and citations at 156.

[22] For an examination of the review processes of the UN Committee on the Rights of the Child, see discussion in Cismas, *Religious Actors and International Law*, pp. 218–237.

[23] Concluding Observations of the Committee on the Rights of the Child: Holy See, UN Doc. CRC/C/15/Add.46, 27 November 1995, para. 14.

[24] Concluding Observations on the Second Periodic Report of the Holy See, U.N. Doc. CRC/C/VAT/CO/2, 25 February 2014 (Hereafter, CRC/C/VAT/CO/2); See also I. Cismas, 'Introductory Note to Committee on the Rights of the Child Concluding Observations on the Second Periodic Report of the Holy See', *International Legal Materials*, Vol. 53, No. 3 (2014), 580–596.

[25] CRC/C/VAT/CO/2, para. 29.

protection of the perpetrators above the child's best interests'.[26] Finally, it drew the attention of the Holy See to General Comment 14 and recommended that it 'strengthen its efforts to ensure that this right is appropriately integrated and consistently applied in all legislative, administrative and judicial proceedings as well as in all policies, programmes and projects that are relevant to and have an impact on children'.[27]

It is beyond doubt that the Holy See has *legal* obligations in relation to the child best interests, in particular in the context of child sexual abuse. Unlike in previous monitoring cycles the actor appears to assume the legality of these obligations, however, it recognizes their applicability only within the territory of the Vatican.[28] Given that there are a handful of children at the Vatican, and the vast majority of cases of clerical sexual abuse have occurred outside the Vatican's borders, what do these best interests obligations signify? If the Holy See's obligations under the CRC, including those related to the child's best interests, are to have any meaning, their extraterritorial application is crucial.

C Beyond the Borders

International courts,[29] treaty bodies,[30] UN Special Procedures,[31] and an increasingly solid body of scholarly work[32] have tackled extraterritoriality.

---

[26] Ibid.   [27] Ibid., para. 30.
[28] Mission permanente du Saint-Siège auprès de l'Office des Nations Unies et des Organisations internationales à Genève, Comments of the Holy See on the Concluding observations of the Committee on the Rights of the Child, 23 September 2014, para. 3. [Hereafter Comments, 2014].
[29] See, for example, *Case Concerning Armed Activities on the Territory of the Congo (Democratic Republic of the Congo v. Uganda)*, Judgment, ICJ Report 2005, p. 168. See also *infra* note 35.
[30] See Human Rights Committee, General Comment 31, Nature of the General Legal Obligation on States Parties to the Covenant, CCPR/C/21/Rev.1/Add.13 (2004), para. 10; Committee on the Rights of the Child, General comment 16, State Obligations Regarding the Impact of the Business Sector on Children's Rights, CRC/C/GC/16 (2013), paras. 40.
[31] Special Rapporteurs with socioeconomic rights and with civil and political rights mandates have examined extraterritorial obligations in their thematic reports and communications to states.
[32] Notable works are: M. Milanovic, *Extraterritorial Application of Human Rights Treaties: Law, Principles, and Policy* (Oxford: Oxford University Press, 2011); R. Wilde, 'The Extraterritorial Application of International Human Rights Law on Civil and Political Rights' in S. Sheeran and N. Rodley (eds.), *Routledge Handbook of International Human Rights Law* (Abingdon: Routledge, 2013), 435–461; Olivier De Schutter, et al, 'Commentary to the Maastricht Principles on the Extraterritorial Obligations of States in the Area of Economic, Social and Cultural Rights' (2012) 34 *Human Rights Quarterly* 1084.

Writing in 2011, Françoise Hampson summarized the state of the debate as follows: 'the principal argument is not between those who think there is some extra-territorial applicability of human right law and those who think there is none... the dispute is over the precise scope of such applicability'.[33] Her conclusion, that the extra-territorial applicability of 'human rights law would depend on the control exercised by the state over the harm inflicted' on an individual, whereas the 'scope of the state's responsibility would depend on the degree of control exercised by the state over the conduct alleged to constitute a violation of human rights law'[34] appears to have been also validated by recent case law of the European Court of Human Rights.[35]

These judicial and doctrinal developments have taken place over the past decade or so – roughly the same period that elapsed since the last review of the Holy See by the Committee on the Rights of the Child and the most recent monitoring exercise. It is against this dynamic, that the 2014 Concluding Observations, which place a paramount emphasis on the Holy See's extraterritorial obligations, should be understood. Therein, paragraph 8 states:

> The Committee is aware of the dual nature of the Holy See's ratification of the Convention as the Government of the Vatican City State, and also as a sovereign subject of international law having an original, non-derived legal personality independent of any territorial authority or jurisdiction. While being fully conscious that bishops and major superiors of religious institutes do not act as representatives or delegates of the Roman Pontiff, the Committee nevertheless notes that subordinates in Catholic religious orders are bound by obedience to the Pope in accordance with Canons 331 and 590. The Committee therefore reminds the Holy See that by ratifying the Convention, it has committed itself to implementing the Convention not only on the territory of the Vatican City State but also as the supreme power of the Catholic Church through individuals and institutions placed under its authority.[36]

---

[33] F. Hampson, 'The Scope of the Extra-territorial Applicability of International Human Rights Law', in G. Gilbert, F. Hampson and C. Sandoval (eds.), *The Delivery of Human Rights: Essays in Honour of Professor Sir Nigel Rodley* (Abingdon: Routledge, 2011), 157–182, p. 158.
[34] Ibid., p. 182.
[35] For the evolution of extraterritoriality in the case law of the European Court of Human Rights see M. Milanovic, 'Al-Skeini and Al-Jedda in Strasbourg' (2012) 23(1) *European Journal of International Law* 121–139.
[36] CRC/C/VAT/CO/2, para. 8.

A similar statement, which places the onus on the Holy See to respect its obligations *extraterritorially*, can be found in the Concluding Observations on the Holy See's report on the implementation of the OPSC.[37]

While acknowledging that concluding observations are not the most convenient instruments for the theoretization of complex concepts such as extraterritoriality, both more and less (or rather different) conceptualization may have strengthened the Committee's argument.

First, paragraph 8 could have listed those provisions of the Convention with an explicit extraterritorial reach, thereby clarifying the intention of the drafters of the CRC in what regards extraterritoriality.[38] In a review of the *travaux préparatoires*, Sigrun Skogly shows that 'for large parts of the drafting process, international cooperation was linked to all rights in the Convention' and it was only in the technical phase that this was placed in the area of socio-economic rights, in an attempt to ensure textual conformity with other instruments.[39] By no means, the scholar suggests, is the extraterritorial effect of the Convention limited to articles 4 and 24, given the centrality of extraterritoriality in the conceptual architecture of the CRC.[40]

Article 34 – whereby 'States Parties undertake to protect the child from all forms of sexual exploitation and sexual abuse' through 'national, bilateral and multilateral measures'[41] – would have been worth recalling in an enumeration of extraterritorial provisions of the CRC. This stipulation showcases the strong grounding of such obligations in the text of the Convention, and specifically in the area of protection against child sexual abuse. Article 34 thus provides a solid extraterritorial anchor for the Committee to 'encourage' the Holy See to provide 'guidance to all relevant persons in authority with a view to ensuring that the best interests of the child is a primary consideration' and for it to 'urge' that

---

[37] UN Committee on the Rights of the Child, Concluding Observations on the report submitted by the Holy See under article 12, paragraph 1, of the Optional Protocol to the Convention on the Rights of the Child on the sale of children, child prostitution and child pornography, CRC/C/OPSC/VAT/CO/1, 25 February 2014.

[38] Notably, in its Comments on the Concluding observations, the Holy See argues that it should be '[o]f general concern, for all States Parties, ... the fact that para. 8 ... offers a controversial new approach to "jurisdiction", which clearly contradicts the general understanding of this concept in international law.'

[39] S. Skogly, *Beyond National Borders: States' Human Rights Obligations in International Cooperation* (Antwerpen: Intersentia, 2006), pp. 103–104.

[40] Ibid., p. 104. Other clauses with explicit extraterritorial effect are CRC, arts. 7.2, 11.2, 17.b, 21.e, 22.2, 23.4, 24.4, 27.4, 28.3, 34 and 35.

[41] CRC, article 34.

the state party 'disseminate such guidance to all Catholic churches, organizations and institutions worldwide'.[42]

Second, the main conceptual vulnerability of the Concluding Observations lies in the UN Committee's acceptance of the Holy See's dual personality scenario, and thus of the actor's submission that these two personalities are separate (or distinct) one from the other. The treaty body's attempt to conceptualize extraterritoriality to fit with the dual personality scenario[43] exposes the Concluding Observations to an unusually ingenious critique.

In its striking Comment on the Observations, the Holy See denies the existence of obligations that may arise from the CRC, requiring it to respect and protect the rights stipulated in the Convention beyond its borders.[44] In doing so, it cites precisely the separateness of the two personalities as evidence. First, the Holy See argues that its personality qua government of the Vatican lacks the capacity to be in control over the acts of 'bishops and major superiors of religious institutes'; it thus claims to have such capacity solely over the citizens at the Vatican 'as well as, where appropriate, the diplomatic personnel of the Holy See or its Officials residing outside the territory of Vatican City State'.[45] Second, as to the Holy See's personality qua Church, it submits that it enjoys church autonomy defined as 'the exclusive power of faith communities to organize and govern their internal affairs'.[46] Overall, the Holy See's submission in response to the 2014 Concluding Observations provide the most vivid illustration of the legal consequences that the acceptance of the dual personality scenario entails: enabling the actor to shift its personalities to enjoy state privileges, yet denying its obligations, and permitting it to invoke at the same time rights qua state and non-state entity.

Had the treaty body chosen to regard the Holy See-Vatican as a construct, with one single international personality – the variant, which

---

[42] CRC/C/VAT/CO/2, para. 30.
[43] The Committee added another layer of confusion by calling on the Holy See to exercise its 'moral authority' and 'moral leadership'. CRC/C/VAT/CO/2, para. 26 and CRC/C/OPSC/VAT/CO/1, paras. 16 and 21. While certainly the Holy See may well possess such moral powers, the terms are unfortunate in the context of a review process of *legal* obligations, not least because in the past the Holy See had claimed to incur solely 'moral' obligations under the CRC. See *supra* note 15. Ironically, in its response to the Concluding observations, the Holy See did not hesitate to call the Committee out on this point. Comments, 2014, para. 6, footnote 9.
[44] Comments, 2014, paras. 3 and 10.   [45] Ibid., para. 3
[46] Ibid., para. 8. See also para. 18.

despite the Holy See's insistence to the contrary, is the only one consistent with international law and supported by state practice – the possibility for the actor to elude state obligations, while claiming state privileges *and* church autonomy would simply not exist.

What is certain is that extraterritoriality does not mean that the Holy See, in becoming party to the Convention, has ratified a treaty '*on behalf of every Catholic* in the world' and that it has 'obligations to "implement" the Convention within the territories of other States Parties *on behalf of Catholics*, no matter how they are organized'.[47] Such an understanding seems to implicate the absurd outcome that if a Catholic anywhere in the world should suffer any sort of harm, the Holy See would by a mysterious linkage incur responsibility for such harm. These propositions are misinterpretations of extraterritoriality – on this author's reading, the Concluding Observations do not advance such an understanding of extraterritoriality.

On the other hand, picture the following hypothetical. Through a letter of the Apostolic Nuncio in Ireland, the Holy See's Congregation for the Clergy informs the Irish Bishops that the procedures and dispositions, which they had established in response to clerical child sexual abuse, do not conform to canonical norms – as they should. The Congregation emphasizes that 'in particular, the situation of "mandatory reporting" [to civil authorities] gives rise to serious reservations of both a moral and a canonical nature'.[48] It proceeds by directing the nuncio 'to inform the individual Bishops of Ireland [. . .] that in the sad cases of accusations of sexual abuse by clerics, the procedures established by the Code of Canon Law must be meticulously followed under pain of invalidity of the acts involved if the priest so punished were to make hierarchical recourse against his Bishop'.[49] If as a result, the bishops feel compelled or even only encouraged not to cooperate with Irish authorities, then we would move away from the register of the absurd, towards that of extraterritoriality. Evidence demonstrates that the above is not within the realm of the hypothetical, but has in fact occurred.[50]

In this context, the Holy See acts are acts of authority with an extraterritorial effect, which resulted in the Irish bishops' non-reporting of cases

---

[47] Ibid., para. 10.c. [Emphasis added].
[48] See Apostolic Nunciature in Ireland, N. 808/97, Strictly Confidential, Dublin, 31 January 1997, accessed January 2012, http://graphics8.nytimes.com/packages/pdf/world/Ireland-Catholic-Abuse.pdf.
[49] Ibid.
[50] Ibid.; Commission of Investigation, Report into the Catholic Diocese of Cloyne, December 2010, accessed March 2012, www.dacoi.ie/; especially paras. 1.18 and 1.76.

of clerical child sexual abuse. This is in stark disaccord with the Holy See's obligation under the CRC, article 34, taken together with article 19 and article 3 on the child's best interests. These acts may have also interfered with Ireland's obligations to comply with the said provisions of the Convention. Ironically thus, whereas the Holy See considers extraterritorial human rights obligations to be in contradiction to the principle of non-interference in the internal affairs of third states,[51] the extraterritorial effect of its actions, in this context, apparently amounted to interference. As Marco Milanovic put it, '[t]he bottom line of the Committee's approach is that if, for instance, there are reports of sexual abuse of children by Catholic clergy in Ireland, both Ireland and the Holy See have a positive obligation to protect and ensure the human rights of these children'.[52] Such an approach is largely consistent with the European Court of Human Rights' (ECtHR) judgment in *O'Keeffe v. Ireland*.[53]

D On Norms and Institutions

It flows from the reading of the 2014 Concluding Observations, together with provisions of General Comment 14, that the child's best interests should be employed by the Holy See as a fundamental legal principle and a rule of procedure in decision-making related to clerical child sexual abuse even when, or particularly when, such abuse occurs extraterritorially. Such conclusion has important implications for prevention, identification, reporting, referral, investigation, treatment and follow-up of clerical child sexual abuse victims.

Passages in the Concluding Observations, as well as reports produced at domestic level by commissions of inquiries, portray a damning picture of the Holy See's handling of past clerical child sexual abuse and specifically the failure to accord primacy to the child's best interests. It remains to be seen whether and to what extent the Holy See-Vatican's normative

---

[51] Comments, 2014, para. 3.
[52] M. Milanovic, 'CRC Concluding Observations on the Holy See', *EJILTalk!*, 5 February 2014, www.ejiltalk.org/crc-concluding-observations-on-the-holy-see/; CRC/C/VAT/CO/2, paras. 37–38, 43–44.
[53] Ibid., *O'Keeffee v. Ireland*, Application no. 35810/09, Judgment of 28 January 2014. Ireland was found in violation of its obligation to prevent ill-treatment of children because it continued to entrust the management of the primary education to National Schools (privately run by Catholic clerics) without establishing an effective mechanism of state control over them.

and institutional changes incorporate article 3 requirements, and other relevant provisions of the CRC and OPSC.

The Holy See's norms and procedures aimed at addressing clerical child sexual abuse are contained in the *Normae de gravioribus delictis* approved by Pope Benedict XVI on 21 May 2010, and canons 1717–1719 of the Code of Canon Law of 1983.[54] Under the current *Normae*, bishops or major superiors are responsible for dealing with cases of sexual abuse of minors. If an accusation 'has the semblance of truth', they must carry out a preliminary investigation in accordance with canon 1717 and communicate the outcome to the Congregation for the Doctrine of the Faith (CDF). As the Supreme Apostolic Tribunal for 'delicts' of child sexual abuse by clerics, the CDF will then direct the bishops how to proceed. Alternatively, the case may be referred directly to the CDF, which will itself undertake the preliminary investigation.[55]

Two aspects deserve emphasis at this stage. First, the aim of these norms and procedures should not be confused with the purpose of criminal law proper; under the *Normae*, the maximum penalty that a cleric who was found guilty of abusing a minor can incur is dismissal from the clergy.[56] As the Holy See itself clarifies, these norms and procedures are not designed to replace criminal investigations of local authorities wherever such clerical abuse occurs.[57] However, the procedure in the *Normae* may prove to be a formidable obstacle to attempts of local authorities to investigate clerical sexual abuse – investigations that should be seen as a minimum threshold in ensuring a child's best interests in such contexts. Article 30 of the *Normae* suggests that as soon as a bishop starts his preliminary investigation into an allegation of sexual abuse he would be bound by pontifical secret and would therefore be prevented from informing civil authorities.[58] A CDF Circular Letter

---

[54] The Normae amend the 2001 issued Norms of the *Motu Proprio Sacramentorum sanctitatis tutela*. See *Normae de gravioribus delictis* (2010), www.vatican.va/resources/index_en.htm (Hereafter, *Normae*); J. P. Beal, 'The 1962 Instruction *Crimen sollicitationis*: Caught Red-handed or Handed a Red Herring?' 41 *Studia Canonica* (2007) 199–236, at 199–201.

[55] See *Normae*, arts. 1, 16 and 17; Congregation for the Doctrine of the Faith, *Circular Letter to Assist Episcopal Conference in Developing Guidelines for Dealing with Cases of Sexual Abuses of Minors Perpetrated* by Clerics, Rome, 3 May 2011, www.vatican.va/roman_curia/congregations/cfaith/documents/rc_con_cfaith_doc_20110503_abuso-minori_en.html. (Hereafter, Circular Letter).

[56] Circular Letter, para. II.   [57] Comments, 2014, para. 9.d.

[58] Normae, art. 30. See also G. Robertson, *The Case of the Pope: Vatican Accountability for Human Rights Abuse*, (London: Penguin Books, 2010), pp. 57–62, 116.

sought to assist bishops in developing guidelines for dealing with cases of child sexual abuse seems to relativise this provision; nonetheless, it explicitly maintains that information obtained during confession is not to be reported to local authorities.[59]

The absurdity of the situation is fully revealed when one considers that as a result of the current *Normae*, the Holy See's authorities seeking to implement new penal legislation in the Vatican territory may be hampered in doing so. In 2013, Pope Francis adopted supplementary norms on criminal matters and amendments to the criminal code and criminal procedure at the Vatican. Crimes against children (sale of children, child prostitution, child pornography, sexual violence against children, sexual acts with children) were entrusted to the competent judicial authorities of the Vatican City State whereby their penal jurisdiction was to be exercised when these crimes were committed by persons deemed 'public officials' – including those working within the Roman Curia and related institutions, and diplomatic personnel serving worldwide.[60] Would a priest at the Vatican hearing confession from a Vatican public official as to its role in child sexual be able to share this information with Vatican judicial authorities? The answer is at best unclear, at worse negative.

These previously mentioned legislative additions and amendments are of crucial importance.[61] Yet, a proper understanding of the Holy See's obligations under the CRC and OPSC, and an acknowledgment of the extraterritorial reach of the instruments' provisions, would require amendments to canon law whereby a procedure of mandatory reporting to local authorities is introduced to replace the current qualifications in article 30 of the *Normae* including in respect to confessional secret.

Second, and central to this chapter, is the absence of any express reference to the best interests of the child in canon law norms on addressing child sexual abuse. This is an area where article 3 of the CRC is not only applicable, but its extraterritorial application, as noted previously, is paramount. Interestingly, the Pontifical Commission for

---

[59] Circular Letter, para. I.e.
[60] Vatican City State Law No. VIII of 11 July 2013; Vatican City State Law No. IX of 11 July 2013; Apostolic Letter Issued *Motu Proprio* of the Supreme Pontiff Francis on the Jurisdiction of the Judicial Authorities of the Vatican City State in Criminal Matters, September 2013.
[61] They are indeed giving effect to provisions of the OPSC and OPAC.

the Protection of Minors established by Pope Francis in December 2013, appears to embrace extraterritoriality in as far as its mission is to 'study present programmes in place for the protection of children' and to 'formulate suggestions for new initiatives on the part of the Curia, in collaboration with bishops, Episcopal conferences, religious superiors and conferences of religious superiors'.[62] The mandate of the Commission does not explicitly adopt a child rights perspective, nor does it expressly stipulate the child's best interests as a primary consideration. It does include former child sexual abuse victims, but no children are part of the Commission. However, on this author's reading of the Commission's public declarations it is the child's best interests, rather than the Church's reputation, which appear to implicitly guide its work. To clarify matters and focus its work, the adoption of an explicit child rights and best interests approach would be invaluable in view of the Commission's role as guidance hub to bishops across the world on procedures for protecting children.

E Conclusion

This chapter has shown that the Holy See incurs legal obligations under the CRC and that the treaty body monitoring these obligations emphasizes the crucial importance of their extraterritorial reach. Having reviewed the Holy See's Comments on the 2014 Concluding Observations, on the one hand, and recent legislative additions at the Vatican and the work of the new Pontifical Commission, on the other, what appears most striking is their dissonance. The former are characterized by obstinacy in their rejection of extraterritorial obligations under the CRC, obstinacy that in turn can be explained by the enarmoration with the Holy See's dual personality scenario. Yet, Pope Francis' new legislative and institutional additions, present a promise to translate into practice child rights obligations extraterritorially. In Pope Francis' words: 'I believe that the Commission can be a new, important and effective means for helping me to encourage and advance the commitment of the Church at every level – Episcopal Conferences, Dioceses, Institutes of Consecrated Life and Societies of Apostolic Life, and others – to take whatever steps are necessary to ensure the protection

---

[62] Briefing on the Meeting of the Council of Cardinals, 5 December 2013, www.vatican.va/resources/resources_briefing-consiglio-cardinali_20131205_en.html.

of minors and vulnerable adults, and to respond to their needs with fairness and mercy.'[63]

In the end, complexity stemming from this dissonance characterizes the answer that we can provide to the two initial questions of this study: Should the Holy See consider a child's best interests in its rules and actions? They should and they say they should not. And do they consider the child's best interests? They did not but there is some (institutional and legislative) hope that they will, even if not necessarily as an expression of the acknowledgment of legal obligations with extraterritorial reach.

---

[63] Letter of His Holiness Pope Francis to the Presidents of the Episcopal Conferences and Superiors of Institutes of Consecrated Life and Societies of Apostolic Life concerning the Pontifical Commission for the Protection of Minors, 2 February 2015, https://w2.vatican.va/content/francesco/en/letters/2015/documents/papa-francesco_20150202_lettera-pontificia-commissione-tutela-minori.html

19

'Best Interests' in Care Proceedings: Law, Policy and Practice

JUDY CASHMORE

A 'Best interests' in Care Proceedings

Making decisions about children's care and protection, and particularly whether children need to be removed from their family home, is a very significant responsibility because of the seriousness of the intrusion and impact on children's lives and that of their family. It is one that is therefore strongly regulated and governed by specific legislation, and policy and practice guidelines. The 'best interests of the child' is the standard that is commonly invoked or explicitly articulated in legislation concerning the care and protection of children. The context in which this principle is used and the degree of specificity associated with it varies significantly across countries and jurisdictions. As Skivenes[1] points out, the legislation in different countries in relation to the adoption and welfare of children varies in the degree of leeway or prescription provided to decision-makers concerning the 'best interests' principle. This ranges, for example, from providing no instructions beyond the principle to providing specific factors to consider or even instructing decision-makers to strongly emphasise certain values or concerns.[2]

The New South Wales legislation falls into the fairly prescriptive camp, with 'best interests' specified in a number of sections of the Children and Young Persons (Care and Protection) Act 1998 (the 1998 Act). This includes references in sections relating to children's need for a 'safe, nurturing, stable and secure environment'[3] following their removal from the care of a parent or parents, and permanency, contact, and cultural

---

[1] M. Skivenes, 'Judging the child's best interests: Rational reasoning or subjective presumptions?' *Acta Sociologica* 53(4) (2010), 339–353 at 340.
[2] Skivenes, 'Judging the child's best interests', 340.
[3] Sections 8(a)(1), s. 9 (2) (e), and s.10(a)(1).

considerations.[4] Section 9(1) of the 1998 Act states that 'in any action or decision concerning a particular child or young person, the safety, welfare and well-being of the child or young person are paramount'. The other principles outlined in sections 9 and 10 are consistent with the basic elements specified in the United Nations Committee on the Rights of the Child's General Comment No. 14 (General Comment 14) as the major considerations in assessing the child's best interests.[5] These include the need to consider the child's views, identity issues associated with culture, language, religion, disability and sexuality, and the requirement to take the appropriate 'least intrusive intervention in the life of the child' and his or her family; and if the child is placed in out-of-home care, the importance of maintaining family and other relationships with significant people in that child's life as well as ensuring a 'safe, nurturing, stable and secure environment'.[6] Recent amendments to the 1998 Act[7] in relation to permanent placement principles now prioritise adoption over long-term placement in foster care, with restoration to the child's parents as the first preference 'if it is practicable and in the best interests of a child or young person' to do so. Where there is any conflict between these principles, the 'paramount concern [is] to protect the child from harm and promote his or her development'.[8]

It is significant, too, that from 2011 a number of court judgments, at first instance and on appeal, specifically refer to the United Nations Conventions on the Rights of the Child (UN CRC).[9] This follows an important appeal judgment in 2011 in the New South Wales Court of Appeal, a somewhat unusual escalation of appeal to this court in a child welfare matter. In this case, the Chief Justice and another senior judge

---

[4] The term 'best interests of the child' is specifically used in at least sixteen sections of the NSW Children and Young Persons (Care and Protection) Act 1998 in reference to permanency planning, the various types of orders including contact orders, the scope of parental responsibilities, dispute resolution processes, and the Aboriginal and Torres Strait Islander Placement Principles.
[5] United Nations Committee on the Rights of the Child, *General Comment No. 14 on the Right of the Child to have his or her Best Interests Taken as a Primary Consideration (Art. 3, para. 1)* (2013) (CRC/C/GC/14) at paras 52–84.
[6] United Nations Committee on the Rights of the Child, *General Comment No. 14*, paras 53–54 and 55–57 and 58–70 and 71–74.
[7] Amended section 10(a) of NSW Children and Young Persons (Care and Protection) Act 1998 amended by Children and Young Persons (Care and Protection) Amendment (Permanency Planning) Act 2001 (s. 10a).
[8] Children and Young Persons (Care and Protection) Act 1998 section 10a.
[9] *Re Kerry* (No 2) [2012] NSWCA 127, at paras 33–35; *Re Elizabeth* [2011] NSWDC 245, 7–74, 173–174.

determined that the judge had erred 'by rejecting the relevance of the various provisions of the CROC [sic]'.[10] In a first instance decision in the same year, the magistrate commented that the principles and objects of the New South Wales Children and Young Persons (Care and Protection) Act 1998 as stated in sections 8 and 9 'appear to go beyond the stated objects of the Convention, in that section 9 states that the safety, security and wellbeing of a child or young person are *paramount* whilst the Convention states that the best interest of the child should be a *primary* consideration'.[11]

Court processes and the New South Wales legislation are also largely consistent with the procedural safeguards outlined in *General Comment* 14 to guarantee the implementation of the child's best interests. These include, again, the child's right to express his or her own views and have those taken into consideration, to have appropriate legal representation when these interests are being formally assessed and determined by courts or similar bodies, trained professionals establishing the facts and assessing the child's best interests, and the requirement for appropriate legal reasoning and mechanisms to review or revise decisions.[12] Consideration of children's need for timely decision-making, particularly in relation to periods of rapid brain development and greatest vulnerability rather than explicitly the child's perceptions of time, as outlined in *General Comment 14*,[13] underpin the permanency planning principles and the need to protect children and promote their development.

One of the most contentious issues in determining what level of intervention is required is how to balance children's safety and their connections with parents and family. Such decisions generally involve a number of professionals: caseworkers in statutory child protection departments, clinicians and paediatricians providing assessments and expert reports, and at the end of the line when the courts are involved, lawyers representing children and parents, and specialist or non-specialist magistrates making the decision. Each plays a very different role and is likely to have different understandings of what constitutes the 'best interests of the child'.

---

[10] *Re Tracey* [2011] NSWCA 43, at para 45.
[11] *In the matter of D, R, J and W* [2011] NSWChC 3 para 14 [emphasis added].
[12] United Nations Committee on the Rights of the Child, *General Comment No. 14*, paras 97–98.
[13] United Nations Committee on the Rights of the Child, *General Comment No. 14*, para 93.

The focus of this chapter is on judicial decision-making, and in particular, on the types of evidence that Children's Court magistrates base their decisions upon, and how their decisions and orders align with the expert clinical reports and social science research available to them. The broader question is how lawyers, judges, and magistrates understand and use social science evidence in formulating their case and making their decisions.

In cases that reach the Children's Court for determination, specialist or generalist magistrates in Australia are required to determine whether children are 'in need of care and protection',[14] and whether they can remain at home safely (with or without conditions) or whether they need to be placed away from their parents, and if so, for how long. If children are removed from parents, a further set of issues arises – how to achieve some certainty and permanence in children's lives when the state assumes parental responsibility for them and what contact they will have with their parents.[15]

These decisions often require difficult judgments about both past events and the likelihood of achieving change.[16] Their decision-making is constrained by the inevitable uncertainty of future events and by the need to gather and make sense of information from others. That information may be incomplete or difficult to interpret. Allegations of emotional abuse and neglect, for example, which together comprise the majority of substantiated reports to child protection agencies, are particularly problematic in evidentiary terms because the real harm to children is cumulative and less easy to provide evidence for than more obvious physical injuries.[17] In many cases, the use of emotional and psychological abuse appears to act as a catch-all.[18]

---

[14] 1998 Act, ss. 71–72.
[15] P. Parkinson, 'Child protection, permanency planning and children's right to family life', *International Journal of Law, Policy and the Family* 17 (2003), 147–172.
[16] Mary Ballou, James Barry, Kerry Billingham, *et al.*, 'Psychological model for judicial decision making in emergency or temporary child placement', *American Journal of Orthopsychiatry* 71 (2001), 416–425; R. Mnookin, 'Child-custody adjudication: Judicial functions in the face of indeterminacy', *Law and Contemporary Problems* 39 (1975), 226–293 at 229–231.
[17] Australian Institute of Health and Welfare (AIHW) (2011). *Child Protection Australia 2010-11*. Child welfare series no. 53. Cat. no. CWS 41. Canberra: AIHW; R. Sheehan, 'Emotional harm and neglect: The legal response', *Child Abuse Review* 15 (2006), 38–54 at 41–42.
[18] Sheehan, 'Emotional harm and neglect', at 48–49.

B Establishing the Facts – The Forms of Evidence Available

The decisions Children's Court magistrates make in New South Wales, and in most states of Australia, are based on several different types of documentary evidence and in-court testimony. The most important of these are the care application and supporting documents provided by caseworkers in the statutory authority; reports from authorised Children's Court Clinicians and other professionals; and the in-court evidence provided by the case-worker, the parents (or their lawyer), and the children's lawyer. These sources of evidence are dealt with in a process that remains largely adversarial despite various reform attempts to allow a more inquiry-based approach.[19] There have, however, been increased moves in New South Wales, and in other Australian states and territories, to divert these matters to be dealt with as far as possible via alternative dispute resolution processes.

Children's Courts in Australia, like those in most common law jurisdictions, are not courts of record.[20] Since there are also closed courts, and most of the decisions go unreported, there is little external scrutiny of what these courts do and how decisions are made.[21] There has also been limited research in this area, perhaps partly for these reasons, but there is now increasing interest in research in this to date neglected field in the UK, United States, and Australia.[22]

The following discussion is based on a mixed-method research study of decision-making processes in the New South Wales (NSW)

---

[19] P. Parkinson, 'Child Protection Law in Australia' in M. Freeman (ed.), *Overcoming Child Abuse: A Window on a World Problem* (Aldershot, England: Ashgate, 2000), pp. 15–38; *Victoria's Vulnerable Children Inquiry*. Melbourne. www.childprotectioninquiry.vic.gov.au/report-pvvc-inquiry.html accessed 28 February 2012, at section 15.4.

[20] *Family Justice: The Work of Family Judges in Uncertain Times*. (Oxford: Hart Publishing, 2013 at 147): Public law children's cases have called for greater transparency in care and adoption proceedings with judgments 'an important and usually necessary feature of the judicial process' because they provide to the parties, and the public, 'the legal and rational basis for the outcome' and also provide a record for children 'to explain to them what happened at this crucial stage of their life'.

[21] J. Masson, "What are care proceedings really like?', *Adoption & Fostering* 36 (2012) 5–12 at 10–11 provides a useful and plausible account of why care proceedings have evolved as they have: 'the ethos and culture surrounding the process; legal principles about rights; beliefs about the value of different interventions; and practicalities associated with cost and diversionary tactics'.

[22] A. Borowski and R. Sheehan (eds.), *Australia's Children's Courts Today and Tomorrow* (New York: Springer, 2013); J. Eekelaar and M. Maclean, *Family Justice: The Work of Family Judges in Uncertain Times* (Oxford: Hart Publishing, 2013); J.M. Masson, J.F. Pearce and K.F. Bader, *Care Profiling Study* (London: Ministry of Justice, 2011).

Children's Courts in Australia.[23] It focuses on some preliminary analyses of forty-nine first instance judgments in the NSW Children's Court, forty-seven appeals dealt with in the NSW District Court, and thirteen adoption determinations in the NSW Supreme Court over the period from 2008 to 2015.[24] The judgments that are available through the NSW Caselaw site are predominantly those of the former Senior Children's Magistrate, former and current President of the Children's Court and matters that go to appeal. While these are not representative of the judgments that all magistrates dealing with these cases may make, appeal judgment and the Presidents' written judgments are intended to provide a model for the way such matters should be considered. The other written judgments in the Children's Court are generally reported when they address a significant point of law.

C Judicial Considerations Concerning the Best Interests of the Child

Not surprisingly, there was clear reference in the judgments to the principles in section 9 governing the administration of the NSW Children and Young Persons (Care and Protection) Act 1998, and in particular to the paramountcy of the 'safety, welfare and wellbeing' of the child or young person involved. 'Best interests' were frequently linked to this phrase, and there were several clear statements to the effect that the court is required to consider and prioritise the best interests of the child, not those of the parents or prospective adoptive parents, grandparents or other relatives, or foster carers. In an appeal judgment, for example, the judge stated:

> In my opinion his Honour did place undue emphasis on the needs and condition of the mother, and less on the interests of the children. His Honour appeared to see the issue before him as a contest between the mother and the carer.[25]

---

[23] This research is funded by an Australian Research Council Discovery Grant DP130104812. The coding and analysis of the judgments was conducted by Sarah Hoff, a lawyer with experience in relation to children's rights and in preparing Australia's non-government report to the United Nations Committee on the Rights of the Child.

[24] These cases were derived from the NSW Caselaw site and from cases involved in the Australian Research Council study.

[25] *Re Louise and Belinda* [2009] NSWSC 534 para 45.

And in another appeal:

> ... it does not sit well with the objects of the Care Act. The argument seems focused on the parents' interests rather than Campbell's. The principle that 'the safety, welfare and wellbeing of [Campbell] are paramount' (Care Act, s 9(1)) may mean that the parents may have to forego a last opportunity to restore Campbell to their care.[26]

One consideration articulated in a number of judgments was the importance of parental 'insight' and parents' acknowledging the impact of their behaviour, commonly substance abuse and family violence, on their children and recognising the need for intervention to ensure their children's safety, welfare and well-being.

Magistrates and judges articulated in their judgments their proper consideration of the key concepts associated with the 'best interests of the child'. The President of the Children's Court specifically listed the factors for consideration in one case concerning a paternal grandmother's application to vary the contact orders with her young grandchildren in long-term foster care when the foster carers relocated some distance away:

> The decision should be based on relevant, reliable and current information.
>
> Factors include the level of attachment to the relevant member of the birth family, the degree of animosity displayed by the birth family against the carers, the level of demonstrated co-operation and engagement with the carers, and the commitment to supporting the placement, the degree of any abusive experience while in the care of the birth family and any ongoing emotional sequelae, the competing demands of the children's educational, cultural, social and sporting activities, the proposed location of the contact, the travel and other disruption involved, the quality of the contact, the safety of the children during contact, and any other risk factors associated with contact, including the potential for denigration of the carers or other undermining of the placement, and the potential for other negative persons or influences to be present at the visit.[27]

In particular, the security and stability of children's relationships and 'attachments' were commonly endorsed important factors in judicial considerations of what constitute 'best interests' for children, in line with

---

[26] *In the matter of Campbell* [2011] NSWSC 761 referring to the Children and Young Persons (Care and Protection) Act 1998.
[27] *Community Services (NSW) and the Knoll Children* [2014] NSWChC 6 paras 59–60.

one of the main objects of the Children and Young Persons (Care and Protection) Act 1998. Section 8(a1) refers to 'recognition that the primary means of providing for the safety, welfare and well-being of children and young persons is by providing them with long-term, safe, nurturing, stable and secure environments through permanent placement'.

> There was also an emphasis on the need for timely decisions to provide a sense of certainty so 'children can get on with their lives'.

The Aboriginal child placement principle[28] is also an important principle in the NSW legislation, with preferential ordering of Aboriginal and Torres Strait Islander children being placed within their cultural and kinship groups, and in non-Aboriginal placement as the last preference. This principle was not applied, however, without regard to the paramount consideration of the 'safety, welfare and well-being of children', as required in section 9(1). As expressed in one judgment, this also includes avoiding the harm that can result from disrupting secure attachments:

> It would clearly not be in the best interests of these children to now remove them from their carers and place them with appropriate Aboriginal carers in accordance with the Aboriginal placement regime in section 13(1) of the Act. This is because of the real risk of significant psychological harm being caused to the children by severing the strong attachment, which has developed between them and the carers.[29]

D Children's Views

While certainty, stability and security as well as timeliness were very important considerations in judicial thinking as evident in their judgments, consideration of children's views about their placements in child welfare matters was less common. There were various references in the judgments to the age and maturity of the children involved, consistent with Article 3, and not surprising given the children involved in a number of cases were very young children. There were some clear statements about the importance of taking the views of older children and adolescents into account, particularly in relation to contact. For example: 'Hilary and Sarah are 14 years of age and Joseph is 13 years

---

[28] Section 13 of the NSW Children and Young Persons (Care and Protection) 1998 Act.
[29] In the Matter of Victoria and Marcus [2010] No. 49/08 and 50/08 para 53.

of age and their wishes are very important and I must and do take them into account'.[30] In several cases where the actual placement was made against the expressed wishes of the child, there was explicit consideration of those views in relation to contact arrangements.[31] There was also, however, concern about protecting children from the power and responsibility of making the decision, and concerns about children being subject to adult pressure and manipulation, especially where this may create loyalty conflicts for them.[32] For example, the judge determining an adoption matter said:

> Nor is it in the child's interests effectively to cede responsibility for making a decision about his best interests to him, and potentially to place him in an invidious position of having to choose.[33]

Discussion of this kind concerning the value of children's views, their authenticity, and how they should be balanced against the child's best interests are not unique to care proceedings; they are also common in private family law matters.[34] It is also consistent with recent findings by Magnussen and Skivenes[35] in their analysis of fifty-three county board rulings in Norway concerning the care and protection of children aged five to eleven years. While children's views were mentioned in 70 per cent of these cases, they were assessed and elaborated upon in only 13 per cent of these matters and given some consideration in 15 per cent.[36]

---

[30] *In the Matter of Hilary and Ors* [2008] para 11.

[31] For example: 'The children need a safe and secure environment and they need to know it is not going to change dependant on some circumstances. These children have proved themselves resilient and whilst I acknowledge Alison Claire may have strong views of wanting to live with her mother, it is not in her best interests to do so. It is important though to recognise the significant bond she has with her mother and I will deal with that in the context of contact.' (*Re Alison Claire, Lauren Donovan and Victoria Claire*, para 55.)

[32] These are views that are commonly expressed by parents, lawyers, counsellors, and judges in private law matters: P. Parkinson and J. Cashmore, *The Voice of a Child in Family Law Disputes* (Oxford: Oxford University Press, 2008), at pp. 93–96, 113–114.

[33] *Adoption of NG* (No 2) [2014] NSWSC 680 at para 98.

[34] J. Eekelaar, 'The interest of the child and the child's wishes: The role of dynamic self-determinism', *International Journal of Law, Policy and the Family* 8 (1994), 42–61; Parkinson and Cashmore, *The Voice of a Child in Family Law Disputes*, at p. 121.

[35] A-M. Magnussen and M. Skivenes, 'The child's opinion and position in care order proceedings: An analysis of judicial discretion in County Boards' decision-making', *International Journal of Children's Rights* 23 (2015), 1–19.

[36] Magnussen and Skivenes, 'The child's opinion and position in care order proceedings, at 14.

E Judicial Alignment with Expert Reports and Clinical Assessments

Clinical and other assessment reports on parents and children prepared by a social science-trained 'expert' are now a relatively common form of evidence in courts dealing with both private and public law children's matters. In Australia, courts may order expert reports in child welfare matters, and several states also have access to clinical assessments by Children's Court Clinicians. In England and Wales, reports in both public and private law matters are prepared by professionally qualified social work staff in the Children and Family Court Advisory and Support Service (Cafcass).[37] In the United States, parenting capacity assessments are common in public law matters and custody evaluation reports in private law matters. Assessment orders usually specify in some detail the particular questions that the judge or magistrate requires the assessment to address; this generally involves an assessment of parental capacity of those involved in the child's life and the likely options for a child who is to be removed from the parental home. Such assessments often draw upon the reports from other agencies, interviews with the parents and carers, teachers and medical professionals, and may include standardised assessments. They are commonly conducted by qualified professionals in social work, psychology, or related mental health disciplines.

Given the nature of the court's powers in care proceedings and the uncertainty of positive outcomes for children and families, it is not surprising that courts look for strong evidence on which to base these decisions. The main role of an assessment report is to provide information 'from a credible, neutral source' that might not otherwise be available to the court making decisions in the child's best interests.[38] Indeed, the President of the Children's Court in New South Wales commented on the value of such reports in very similar terms in a recent judgment:

> the Children's Court can derive considerable assistance from independent clinicians appointed by the Children's Court Clinic. In addition to providing independent expert opinion, the clinicians can provide a hybrid factual form of evidence not otherwise available.
>
> Because they observe the protagonists over a period of time, interview parents, children and others in detail and on different occasions, in neutral or non-threatening environments, away from courts and lawyers,

---

[37] For further information on CAFCASS, see: www.cafcass.gov.uk.
[38] A. Schepard, 'Editorial notes: Mental health evaluations in child custody disputes', *Family Court Review* 43 (2005), 187–190 at 187.

untrammelled by court formalities and processes, clinicians can provide the Court with insights and nuances that might not otherwise come to its attention.

Thus, clinicians can provide impartial, independent, objective information not contained in other documents, give context and detail to issues that others may not have picked up on, and which the Court, trammelled by the adversarial process and the 'snapshot' nature of a court hearing, would not otherwise have the benefit of.[39]

While there is some evidence and anecdotal reports that these assessment reports can be influential, there is limited empirical research in Australia and elsewhere that the courts make orders in accordance with the expert's or assessor's recommendations.[40] The propriety of experts, including mental health professionals, providing opinions on the 'ultimate legal issue' – properly the province of the judge or magistrate – is also a matter of some debate.[41] Some judges are also at pains to point out that the decisions they are making are their own, noting that they have taken into account the observations of the expert report writer. For example:

That decision is my own, reached for the reasons set out above, but I note that it accords with the recommendation of Ms L [clinical psychologist] and with that of Ms B in the s 91 report.[42]

Preliminary analysis of court files and judgments in the current research study does indicate a substantial degree of reliance and alignment between the report's recommendations and the judicial views as expressed in the judgment and evident in the final orders. Judicial comments about Children's Court Clinicians and psychologists were generally positive and in agreement with the expert's recommendations. A number of judges and magistrates referred in positive terms to the value of such expert reports, and the reliability and compelling nature of the evidence of various expert witnesses. For example:

---

[39] *DFaCS and Colt Children* [2013] NSWChC 5 paras 291–293.
[40] K.S. Budd and R.E. Springman, 'Empirical analysis of referral issues and "ultimate issue" recommendations for parents in child protection cases', *Family Court Review* 49 (2011), 34–45; N. Jamieson, T. Tranah and E.C. Sheldrick, 'The impact of expert evidence on care proceedings', *Child Abuse Review* 8 (1999), 183–192.
[41] Budd and Springman, 'Empirical analysis of referral issues', at 34; G. B. Melton, J. Petrila, N. G. Poythress and C. Slobogin, *Psychological Evaluations for the Courts: A Handbook for Mental Health Professionals and Lawyers* (3rd ed.) (New York: Guilford, 2007).
[42] *Adoption of SRB, CJB and RDB* [2014] NSWSC 138 para 72.

> The Clinician in this case was thorough and detailed, and to my mind convincing, and I am persuasively guided by her observations and opinions.[43]

And:

> Perhaps the most telling evidence of the level of abuse was that of Dr P in her report ... Dr P is a psychologist who was requested by the Children's Court Clinic to provide assessments in respect of the children and the potential impact of restoration to the care of the parents. She also gave evidence in these proceedings, and I found her a compelling witness. Her experience and qualifications are most impressive.[44]

Clear expressions of disagreement and lack of alignment with the clinical assessment and report were not common – indeed, evident in only a handful of cases. On the mild end of the critical continuum, one appeal judge noted:

> It seems to me that the opinions of Mr F..., whilst reasoned and legitimate, tended too much to the conservative side of the equation of balancing the benefits and detriments of altering the level of contact between 'AA' and his birth family.[45]

Another judge was robust in his criticism of a Children's Court Clinician, referring to the 'reasoning process' underlying the clinician's recommendations as 'demonstrably flawed' because it 'downplayed the nature and extent of the domestic violence and disharmony that was prevalent'.[46]

> Sadly in this case I am compelled to reject the opinion of the Children's Court clinician... She is a lone voice in the evidence supporting a restoration of these children to their parents, albeit on a staged basis....[47]

Other judges and magistrates have also been critical of some psychologists' reports and recommendations, again referring to flawed reasoning or lack of objectivity or balance, and the failure to have access to or properly test relevant materials.[48] These matters were concerned with the possibility of children being restored to their parents' care and the allocation of parental responsibility in first instance matters, as well as appeals in relation to the frequency of contact between children and their parents.

---

[43] *DFaCS and Colt Children* [2013] NSWChC 5 paras 291–293.
[44] *Re Saunders and Morgan v DoCS* [2009] NSW DC para 21.
[45] *DCS v AA* [2010] NSWDC 19 para 67.
[46] *DFaCS re Amanda and Tony* [2012] NSWChC 13 para 76. [47] Ibid.
[48] *Re Henry* [2015] NSWCA 89 para 75.

Typically, however, the orders made by judges and magistrates were consistent with the recommendations of the expert report writer and commentary in relation to children's safety, emotional and psychological welfare and wellbeing. The judgments commonly referred to the 'evidence' or advice' of the Children's Court Clinicians or other expert report writers in relation to the 'security' and 'stability' of the options for children, in considerations about their possible restoration to their parents or their placement in out of home care.

'Security' was referred to in two main ways – as 'secure' or 'insecure attachment' based on attachment theory, and as 'felt security' – which went beyond the reference to certainty in relation to 'secure environments'. The judge in an adoption matter, for example, commented on the importance of 'a very emotionally vulnerable' young child 'deprived of the opportunity to develop secure attachments' during his 'turbulent first three years' needing 'understanding, support and above all stability and security' to 'develop secure attachments while the opportunity remains to do so'.[49] The benefits of 'felt security' – 'the legal and psychological sense of belonging'[50] and a secure identity – were referred to in a range of cases, including adoption matters and applications for variations in relation to the frequency and supervision of contact for children in out-of-home care, and particularly contact with siblings.

F   Value of Social Science Evidence to Legal Decision-Makers

The reliance on expert reports and clinical assessments raises the broader issue of the role of social science research and social science evidence in legal processes where decisions are being made about children's care and protection. On the positive side, social science research is seen as providing the fact-finder with background knowledge for better understanding what children need for healthy physical and psycho-social development and the factors that might be important in the determination of the child's 'best interests'. Others take a more critical view, pointing to the differences in philosophy, language, methods, processes, and definition and use of evidence between law and social science, and between research and practice.[51]

---

[49] *Adoption of NG* (No. 2) [2014] NSWSC 680 para 23.
[50] *Adoption of BS* (No. 3) [2013] NSWSC 2033 para 59.
[51] A. Fineman and A. Opie, 'The uses of social science data in legal policymaking: Custody determinations at divorce', *Wisconsin Law Review* (1987), 107–158; M. King and

It is significant then that some senior judges are citing social science evidence and literature, particularly in relation to children's attachments and the comparative outcomes for children in adoption and long-term foster care. In a recent adoption case in the New South Wales Supreme Court, for example, the judge indicated his consideration of the evidence of the clinical psychologist and her references to the social science literature:

> With reference to literature, Ms L has expressed a number of opinions which, while she accepted ought not be applied invariably to every case, nonetheless provide some useful statements of general principle so far as the social science is concerned.[52]

This reference points to a critical issue in the application of social science research to legal decision-making – the tension between the probabilistic and general nature of such research findings and the need to make decisions for a particular child, taking account of all of the circumstances for that child. This is of course complicated by the uncertainty of the best interests principle, and the unpredictability of future events. The value-laden indeterminacy of the 'best interests' standard has been the subject of much discussion and criticism[53] but also defended for its capacity to reflect shifting social values and circumstances and importantly to focus on the individual child's developmental and socio-emotional needs.[54] Kelly, for example, commented positively that:

> The best interest standard represents a willingness on the part of the court and the law to consider children on a case-by-case basis rather than adjudicating children as a class or a homogeneous grouping with identical needs and situations.[55]

On the other hand, Kelly[56] and Lamb[57] and others are critical of the lack of consensus about the meaning and weighting of legal criteria in making

---

J. Trowell, *Children's Welfare and the Law - The Limits of Legal Intervention*, (London: Sage Publications Ltd, 1992); J. P. Shonkoff, 'Science, policy and practice: Three cultures in search of a shared mission', *Child Development* 71 (2000), 181–187.

[52] *Adoption of SRB, CJB and RDB* [2014] NSWSC 138 para 54.

[53] R. Mnookin, 'Child-custody adjudication'; S. Parker, 'The best interests of the child: Principles and problems', *International Journal of Law and the Family* 8 (1994), 26–41.

[54] J.B. Kelly, 'The best interests of the child: a concept in search of meaning', *Family and Conciliation Courts Review* 35 (1997), 377–387 at 385–386; M. Rutter, 'Nature, nurture, and development: from evangelism through science toward policy and practice', *Child Development* 73 (2002), 1–21 at 11–12.

[55] Kelly, 'The best interests of the child'.   [56] Ibid., at 379–381.

[57] M. Lamb, 'Dangers associated with the avoidance of evidence-based practice', *Family Court Review* 52 (2014) 194–198.

such decisions, and urge the use of evidence-based decision-making. As Eekalaar and Maclean state:

> Mechanisms for serious scrutiny that direct attention at the circumstances of the child in question, informed but not dictated by knowledge about the generality of cases, and respecting the value of procedural fairness to all parties, are essential to prevent ... convictions about children's welfare, leading to harmful actions.[58]

Understanding the value, but also the limits of social science research, and what it can offer legal and social work professionals in making these decisions in and out of court requires clear communication by researchers and processes by which lawyers and judges can become intelligent consumers of research.

---

[58] J. Eekelaar and M Maclean, *Family Justice: The Work of Family Judges in Uncertain Times* (Oxford: Hart Publishing, 2013) at p.146.

20

Judicial Discretion and the Child's Best Interests: The European Court of Human Rights on Adoptions in Child Protection Cases

MARIT SKIVENES AND KARL HARALD SØVIG

A Introduction

This chapter examines how the European Court of Human Rights (ECtHR) makes decisions about the termination of parental rights and adoptions in child protection cases. In these cases, two very strong but broad principles meet – the child's best interests, as outlined in the United Nations Convention of the Rights of the Child (CRC) Article 3, and the right to respect private and family life, as delineated in Article 8 of the European Convention of Human Rights (ECHR). How do judges exercise judicial discretion in these immensely difficult cases?

CRC provides clear guidelines that oblige states to protect children from harm and abuse and to primarily consider children's best interests.[1] One of the basic rights in the convention is the *best interest* principle:

> In all actions concerning children, whether undertaken by public or private social welfare institutions, courts of law, administrative authorities or legislative bodies, the best interests of the child shall be a primary consideration.[2]

Through the child protection system,[3] the State assumes parental responsibility or terminates parental rights when parents are unable or unwilling to perform parental responsibilities and obligations.

---

[1] D. Archard (ed.), *Children: Rights and Childhood* (Oxford: Routledge, 2004) at p. 58.
[2] United Nations Convention of the Rights of the Child, UN, General Assembly, 20 November 1989, in force 2 September 1990, 1577 UNTS 3. Article 3, para 1
[3] The term *child protection* characterises systems that are responsible for children who are at risk for harm or neglect from their caregivers or who may be at risk of harm to themselves or others. In some countries, these may be referred to as *child welfare* systems.

Children are removed from homes and placed in foster homes or residential units, or are adopted. These decisions are necessary because the child's welfare, childhood and future may be at stake. However, terminating or severely curtailing parental rights and responsibilities is an invasive and consequential decision that is made by the State. These interventions are decisions that represent the State's power, because family is at the core of humanity and because these decisions challenge individuals' freedoms and the privacy and autonomy of family life. Thus, the court or court-like decision-making bodies are often given the authority to make decisions about serious interventions into family life.[4] The courts must negotiate the tension between parental rights and children's rights that are often overlooked when we discuss the State's responsibility for children who may be at risk of harm and abuse. The increasing focus on children and their situation and position in modern society reflects child-centric policies and societies – in contrast to family-centric orientations – which are likely to increase this tension.[5]

Child protection adoption cases will fall within the ambit of ECHR Article 8 and the right to respect private and family life, which reads:

> 1. Everyone has the right to respect for his private and family life, his home and his correspondence.
> 2. There shall be no interference by a public authority with the exercise of this right except such as is in accordance with the law and is necessary in a democratic society in the interests of national security, public safety or the economic well-being of the country, for the prevention of disorder or crime, for the protection of health or morals, or for the protection of the rights and freedoms of others.

This chapter examines how an important legal institution — the supranational ECtHR — uses and interprets children's rights in their judgments for terminating parental rights and adoptions in child protection cases. The 'best interest of the child' is not laid down in Article 8 or other provisions, but the ECtHR has in its jurisprudence seen this interest as an integrated part of Article 8. We focus on how the child's best interest principle is understood when it is balanced against other important principles and considerations. The material

---

[4] K. Burns, T. Pösö and M. Skivenes (eds.) *When the State Takes Children from Their Home* (New York: Oxford University Press, in press), chapter 10.

[5] N. Gilbert, N. Parton, and M. Skivenes (eds.), *Child Protection Systems: International Trends and Orientations* (New York: Oxford University Press, 2011) p. 251ff.

for our analysis includes child protection judgments that involve the termination of parental rights and adoptions (n=15). Specifically, we analyse judgments that focus on considerations about the child's best interest (n = 6).

The next section outlines theoretical platform, which is followed by a methodological section. Then, we present background information about the ECtHR, as well as a result and discussion section, with concluding remarks in the final section.

B Theoretical Platform – Best Interests and Judicial Discretion

The principle of the 'best interests of the child' is ambiguous.[6] The legal scholars Mnookin and Szwed have extensively written about this topic, and state that: 'the flaw is that what is best for any child or even children in general is often indeterminate and speculative and requires a highly individualized choice between alternatives'.[7] Elster and others strongly support Mnookin's criticism that the principle is useless as a guideline in decision-making.[8] Nevertheless, this is the principle that decision makers apply in cases that concern children and thus should be a vital consideration for the ECtHR. Judges have authorisation to exercise discretion when they weigh differing arguments and considerations for deciding a child's best interest. Best interest decisions in child protection are discretionary, in which national legislation and international conventions authorise court decision-makers to solve conflicts and use discretion when parental rights and responsibilities are restricted or terminated. Discretion is necessary in child protection cases, but is also problematic because it challenges the principles of the rule of law, democratic control and influence, as well as the legitimacy

---

[6] J. Elster, *Solomonic Judgements: Studies in the Limitations of Rationality* (Cambridge: Cambridge University Press, 1989) p. 130; C. Breen, *The Standard of the Best Interest of the Child* (The Hague, London and New York, Martinus, 2002) p. 43; M. Freeman, *Article 3: The Best Interests of the Child* (Leiden and Boston, MA: Martinus Nijhoff, 2007) p. 13; M. Skivenes, *Legislation and Legitimacy – an Evaluation of the Law Making Process of the Child Welfare Act of 1992* ... ≪UiB, Dept. of Political Science, Rapport Nr. 79PhD Monograph, in Norwegian, 2002, p. 187≫.
[7] R. Mnookin and E. Szwed, 'The Best Interest Syndrome as the Allocation Of Power In Child Care', in H. Geach and E. Szwed (eds.), *Providing Civil Justice for the Child* (London: Edward Arnold, 1983), pp. 7–20.
[8] Elster, *Solomonic Judgements*, p. 130; Breen, *The Standard of the Best Interest of the Child*, p. 44.

and quality of decisions.[9] Discretionary decisions can also be non-authorised and can represent an intentional misuse of power.[10]

Discretion was a controversial topic in the United States and Europe several decades ago amongst prominent scholars, including Dworkin, Goodin, Handler, Hawkins and Mnookin, among others. Dworkin's 1967 piece, *The Models of Rules*, is a classic conceptual outline of legal decision-making and discretion that is still used today and constitutes a platform for renewed theoretical work on discretion.[11] In Dworkin's words, 'discretion is at home in only one sort of context: when someone is in general charged with making a decision subject to standards set by a particular authority'.[12] Thus, the concept is clearly relative, and we can expect that the standards that governments set will differ. For example, a study of child-protection systems found that the United States and England set stricter regulations (or 'standards' in Dworkin's words) for decision makers' use of discretion in care-order preparations than Norway and Finland.[13] From Dworkin's position, decision-makers can exercise either weak or strong discretion. Weak discretion may be expressed in two forms, one that relates to having some authority to use judgment; for example, when the English Children's Act instructs which aspects are relevant for best interest and the judge must decide how they are considered.[14] Another form of weak discretion occurs when

---

[9] R. M. Dworkin, *The Model of Rules* (Yale: Faculty Scholarship Series, Paper 3609, 1967) p. 33; Elster, *Solomonic Judgements*, p. 132; J. Handler, *The Conditions of Discretion: Autonomy, Community, Bureaucracy* (Russel Sage Foundation, 1986) at p. 161; J. Herring, 'The Welfare Principle and the Children: Presumably it's about Welfare?' (2014) 36 *Journal of Social Welfare and Family Law*, 1, 14–25; Hawkins, K., *The Uses of Discretion* (Oxford: Clarendon Press, 1992); A. Molander, H. Grimen, and E. O. Eriksen, 'Professional discretion and accountability in the welfare state' (2012) 29 *Journal of Applied Philosophy*, 214–230; C. Piper, 'Assumptions about Children's Best Interests' (2000) 22 *Journal of Social Welfare and Family Law*, 261–276; Archard, *Children: Rights and Childhood*.

[10] Dworkin, *The Model of Rules*; E. C., Schneider, 'Discretion and Rules', in K. Hawkins (ed.), *The Uses of Discretion* (Oxford: Clarendon press, 1992), pp. 47–88; J. E. Artis, 'Judging the Best Interests of the Child: Judges' Accounts of the Tender Years Doctrine' (2004) 38 *Law & Society Review*, 4, 769–806.

[11] Hawkins, *The Uses of Discretion*, p. 13; cf. Molander, Grimen, and Eriksen, 'Professional Discretion and Accountability', p. 229

[12] Dwordkin, *The Model of Rules*, p. 32.

[13] J. Berrick, S. Peckover, T. Pösö and M. Skivenes 'The formalized framework for decision-making in child protection: A cross-country comparison' (2015) *Journal of European Social Policy*, 25(4), 366–378 at p. 9–10.

[14] Cf. D. Archard and M. Skivenes, 'Deciding best interests: General principles and the cases of Norway and the UK' (2010) 5(4) *Journal of Children's Services*, 43–54, at p. 47.

decision-makers are given the final authority to decide particular questions, with no appeals against these decisions. The example Dworkin uses is from baseball: he discusses how instant observations of which player reached second base first are delegated and cannot be appealed.[15] Similar situations are less evident in child protection cases, but it is possible that individual case testimonies will have elements of this type of weak discretion. However, we believe that an important aspect of weak discretion is that it is related to fact-oriented situations in which clear 'game' rules exist. Strong discretion concerns decisions that are not 'bound by any standards set by an authority'.[16] An example of this occurs when judges are given the authority to decide the best interests of the child without any particular instruction on how to do so. Hence, discretion relates to how decision-makers are instructed by relevant authorities.

We believe that the judges in the ECtHR have the authority to exercise strong discretion, and following the outline of Dworkin, this implies that these decision makers can more or less act as they please because there are no limits to their authority on particular issues, except for institutional and professional standards. The ECtHR has rule-building discretion, as judges have the authority to develop norms and first-order rules with the aim to develop better regulations and practices.[17] However, judges can still be criticised for making good or bad decisions based on the strength of the reasoning of their decisions.

C Methodological Approach

Although only 4 per cent of the applications to the ECtHR are accepted for further review, there have been an enormous amount of cases that have been decided upon since the court began in 1960 – approximately 18,000 court rulings.[18] About 1,000 of these cases involve violations of ECHR Article 8, 'Respect for private and family life'. These cases are frequently written in English and provide substantive descriptions of the proceedings from each family's first contact with child-protection services to the final ECtHR decision. Although national courts are responsible for the procedural aspects, the cases provide an in-depth understanding of how the ECtHR makes decisions and allows us to

---

[15] Dworkin, *The Model of Rules*, p. 33.   [16] Ibid.
[17] Cf. Schneider, 'Discretion and Rules', p. 54.
[18] Cf. the court's publication *Overview 1959–2014*, available at www.echr.coe.int/Pages/home.aspx?p=reports&c= (last retrieved 10 November 2015).

identify similarities and trends in how this court, as well as nation-states, decides adoption cases using the principle of the child's best interest.

We used the HUDOC database, which contains all the judgments, decisions and resolutions that were made by the ECtHR[19] and focused on case law judgments that were decided in grand chamber and chamber, importance levels 1 and 2 and ECHR Article 8 that were available in English. We employed two search strategies. First, we searched text strings that included (all of these words): 'child*'; 'adopt*'; and 'welfare.*' Second, we searched for 'Johansen', which is a reference to an adoption case from 1996 that ECtHR frequently uses in child protection adoption cases. These searches resulted in a total of 174 cases. Then, we reviewed all the cases to examine if they were adoption cases, and then child protection adoption cases. The omitted cases included step-child adoptions (against the wishes of the other natural parent)[20] or cross-border adoptions (against the wishes of the child),[21] despite the cases having similarities to adoption in child protection, with ECtHR using similar approaches. Additionally, we omitted cases that were on selecting the adoptive parents[22] and annulling adoptions.[23] This resulted in fifteen cases that were about terminating parental rights or abandoning a child in which the child had been adopted or was going to be adopted. First, we examined all cases for themes of children's participation that included the CRC and whether the best interests of the child were present in the cases. Then, we carefully examined the courts' reasoning in these cases to identify whether the court emphasised procedural or the substantial elements in best interest considerations. Based on this criteria, we identified nine cases that focused on procedural aspects of the complaint of violations of the ECHR – leaving us with six core cases that we examined in depth.[24]

---

[19] We have not included cases from the former Commission, see as example *U. and G.F. v. Germany*, appl. no. 11588/85, decision 15 May 1986, DR 47 p. 259.

[20] See as an example *Eski v. Austria*, appl. no. 21949/03, judgment 25 January 2007.

[21] See as an example *Pini et al v. Romania*, appl. no. 78028/01, judgment 22 June 2004.

[22] See *Bronda v. Italy*, appl. no. 40/1997/824/1030, judgment 9 June 1998 (grandparents' request for being a foster home) and *Moretti and Benedetti v. Italy*, appl. no. 16318/07, judgment 27 April 2010 (foster parents' request for being adoptive parents).

[23] See *Kurochkin v. Ukarine*, appl. no. 42276/08, judgment 20 May 2010.

[24] The fifteen cases are (six core cases emboldened): *B. v. The United Kingdom*, appl. no. 9840/82, judgment 8 July 1987; *H. v. The United Kingdom*, appl. no. 9580/81, judgment 8 July 1987; *O. v. The United Kingdom*, appl. no. 9276/81, judgment 8 July 1987; *R. v. The United Kingdom*, appl. no. 1049/83, judgment 8 July 1987; *W. v. The United Kingdom*, appl. no. 9749/82, judgment 8 July 1987; *McMichael v. The United*

We are aware that this choice may be controversial because many appeal applications and their decisions on best interests are interwoven with the procedural aspects of a decision.

The remaining six cases are the core focus of our examination, and we analyse the parts of the written judgments in which the court presents their interpretation and reasoning for their conclusions. The six judgments are part of a larger material, thus, it is important to be careful drawing concrete conclusions. However, examining the judgments highlight material may be of interest for future discussion.

D Background

Involuntary adoptions are controversial. In some countries, such as Finland, there is no legal mechanism for involuntary adoptions, and in some countries, it is hardly used (e.g., Denmark and Norway), while in other countries it is an important measure of permanence for children (e.g., the United States).

The ECtHR was constructed to observe the engagements undertaken by the contracting parties in ECHR and the Protocols thereto, cf. Article 19. The number of judges is equal to the number of contracting parties. The ECtHR can receive applications from any person, non-governmental organisation or group of individuals that claim to be the victim of a violation by one of the contracting parties, cf. Article 34. There is also a potential for inter-state cases, but this option is rarely used. There are no age limits for being a victim of human rights violations, and in some cases children have acted as applicants, often represented by their parents.[25] An application can be declared inadmissible by a single judge. In practice, most applications are dismissed as 'manifestly ill-founded', cf. Article 35(3)(a). A judgment is normally delivered by a chamber that consists of seven judges, cf. Article 26, but other compositions are also possible. For many years, the ECtHR

Kingdom, appl. no. 16424/90, judgment 24 February 1995; *Johansen v. Norway*, appl. no. 17383/90, judgment 7 July 1996; *Bronda v. Italy*, appl. no. 22430/93, judgment 9 June 1998; *E.P. v. Italy*, appl. no. 31127/96, judgment 16 November 1999; *X. v. Croatia*, appl. no. 11223/04, judgment 17 July 2008; *Aune v. Norway*, appl. no. 52502/07, judgment 28 October 2010; *R. and H. v. The United Kingdom*, appl. no. 35348/06, judgment 31 May 2011; *Y.C. v. The United Kingdom*, appl. no. 4547/10, judgment 13 March 2012; *A.K. and L. v. Croatia*, appl. no. 37956/11, judgment 8 January 2013; *R.M.S v. Spain*, appl. no. 28775/12, judgment 18 June 2013.

[25] As an example, see *A.K. and L. v. Croatia*, appl no. 37956/11, judgment 8 January 2013.

has been burdened with an increasing number of cases, and several reforms have been introduced to meet these challenges. In 2014, the ECtHR decided 86,063 cases, of which 2,388 were judgments and 83,675 were decisions (declared inadmissible or struck from the list).[26]

The task of the ECtHR is to supervise the implementation of the ECHR in the contracting states based on applications that are primarily coming from citizens. The ECtHR can only address the matter after all 'domestic remedies' have been exhausted, cf. Article 35(1). The ECtHR does not represent a 'fourth instance' (referring to the fact that most jurisdictions have three court levels), and its function is not to 'deal with errors of fact or law allegedly committed by a national court unless and insofar as they may have infringed rights and freedoms protected by the Convention'.[27]

In adoption cases, Article 8 is the crucial provision and the core of the case is the protection of 'family life'. An adoption amounts to an interference in the natural parents' family life,[28] and must conform to the conditions provided in Article 8(2). Normally, an adoption will be well-founded in national legislation and, therefore, in 'accordance with the law' and will pursue a legitimate aim, namely 'the protection of the rights and freedoms' of the concerned child. Accordingly, the crux of the case is whether an adoption is 'necessary in a democratic society'.

We can expect that discussions about the best interest principle in these cases will minimally include considerations of parental rights and whether removal is a necessary action in a modern democracy. Further, we expect that there will be considerations of the child's opinion and views on the case, as well as the child's right to a family and the child's interest in being with his/her parents/family; the short- and long-term consequences for the child, the child's needs, for example, for education, permanence, and attachment to significant others. According to the recommendations of the Committee on the Rights of the Child *General Comment No. 14*, there are seven elements to consider in a best interest assessment: 1) the child's views; 2) the child's identity; 3) preserving the

---

[26] For statistics, see www.echr.coe.int/Pages/home.aspx?p=reports&c=#n1347956867932_pointer (last retrieved 16 October 2015).
[27] See as an example, *García Ruiz v. Spain*, appl. no. 20544/96, judgment (GC) 21 January 1999, para. 28.
[28] See *Bronda v. Italy*, appl. no. 40/1997/824/1030, judgment 9 June 1998 concerning grandparents request for being a foster home.

family environment and maintaining relations; 4) care, protection and the safety of the child; 5) the situation of vulnerability; 6) the child's right to health and 7) the child's right to education. The committee underscores the general character of these elements and, thus, can make individual and context specific adjustments.[29]

E Findings and Discussion

The Starting Points of the ECtHR Assessments

To assess whether an adoption or restriction in access or parental responsibility with a potential for adoption is 'necessary in a democratic society', the ECtHR relies on case law from other child protection measures (such as taking into care),[30] as well as other related areas, including custody cases[31] and child abductions.[32] We omitted cases that concern procedural requirements, but it is important to acknowledge that substantial and procedural requirements are interrelated. The need for broad discretion in assessing whether adoption should occur leads to an even greater call for protection against arbitrary interferences in the form of procedural guarantees.[33]

In *Johansen*, the ECtHR stated that they would consider, 'whether, in the light of the case as a whole, the reasons adduced to justify them were relevant and sufficient',[34] while emphasizing the variability in laws and practices in the member states for public intervention in family life. The ECtHR also stressed in *Johansen* that the national authorities had the benefit of direct contact with all persons concerned. Therefore, 'the Court's task is not to substitute itself for the domestic authorities',

---

[29] United Nations Committee on the Rights of the Child, *General Comment No. 14 on the Right of the Child to have his or her Best Interests Taken as a Primary Consideration (Art. 3, para. 1)* (2013) (CRC/C/GC/14), paras. 52–79.

[30] See *inter alia* the reference to *Scozzari and Giunta v. Italy*, appl. nos. 39221/98 and 41963/98, judgment (GC) 13 July 2000 (and several other cases concerning removal and restrictions of access) in *R.M.S. v. Spain*, para. 71.

[31] See *inter alia* the reference to *Elsholz v. Germany*, appl. no. 25735/94, judgment (GC) 13 July 2000 in *R. and H. v. UK* (2011), para. 81.

[32] See *inter alia* the reference to *Neulinger and Shuruk v. Switzerland*, appl. no. 41615/07, judgment (GC) 6 July 2010 *in R. and H. v. UK* (2011), para. 73.

[33] See *X. v. Croatia*, appl. no. 11223/04, judgment 17 July 2008, para. 47–49 with references to previous case law.

[34] *Johansen v. Norway*, appl. no. 17383/90, para. 64.

but 'rather to review under the Convention the decisions that those authorities have taken'.[35]

This approach was used in *R. and H. v. UK*, in which the ECtHR emphasized that the national authorities have duties to protect children and 'cannot be held liable every time genuine and reasonably held concerns about the safety of children vis-à-vis members of their family are proved, retrospectively, to have been misguided'.[36] This self-restraint is closely related to the doctrine of 'margin of appreciation', which, in *Johansen*, is developed and formulated to target the different phases of child protection cases:

> The margin of appreciation so to be accorded to the competent national authorities will vary in the light of the nature of the issues and the seriousness of the interests at stake ... Thus, the Court recognises that the authorities enjoy a wide margin of appreciation in assessing the necessity of taking a child into care. However, a stricter scrutiny is called for both of any further limitations, such as restrictions placed by those authorities on parental rights and access, and of any legal safeguards designed to secure an effective protection of the right of parents and children to respect for their family life. Such further limitations entail the danger that the family relations between the parents and a young child are effectively curtailed.[37]

As the ECtHR noted in *Y.C. v. United Kingdom*, decisions that are made by the national courts are 'often irreversible', which necessitates 'an even greater call than usual for protection against arbitrary interferences'.[38]

According to established case law, 'taking a child into care should normally be regarded as a temporary measure' that should be 'discontinued as soon as circumstances permit'.[39] This temporariness also indicates a positive obligation for authorities: 'any measures of implementation of temporary care should be consistent with the ultimate aim of reuniting the natural parent and the child'.[40]

A key issue in *E.P. v. Italy* was that there was a total ban on contact between the applicant and her daughter immediately after she was taken into care.[41] The ECtHR continued to emphasize that no steps had been taken to re-unite the bond between mother and daughter. Additionally, there had been no expert. The latter also illustrates the interplay between

---

[35] Ibid., para. 64. [36] *R. and H. v. The United Kingdom*, appl. no. 35348/06, para. 81.
[37] *Johansen v. Norway*, para 64.
[38] *Y.C. v. The United Kingdom*, appl. no. 4547/10, para. 126.
[39] *Johansen v. Norway*, para. 78. [40] Ibid.
[41] *E.P. v. Italy*, appl. no. 31127/96, para. 65.

substantial and procedural requirements. However, the obligation for reunification is limited. In *R. and H. v. UK*, the ECtHR held that Article 8 does not require that domestic authorities 'make endless attempts at family reunification'; it only requires that they take 'all the necessary steps that can reasonably be demanded to facilitate the reunion of the child and his or her parents'.[42] The ECtHR continued to observe that when 'a considerable period of time has passed since a child was originally taken into public care', the interest of a child not to have his or her de facto family situation changed again 'may override the interests of the parents to have their family reunited'.[43] The best interest of the child also applies when the national authorities are obligated to reunify the family.

General Descriptions of the Cases in This Study

The fifteen cases are from the time period between 1987 and 2013, and include the United Kingdom (8), Italy (2), Croatia (2), Norway (2) and Spain (1). Seven cases had unanimous conclusions, two cases were registered as dissenting, and seven cases were registered as a partial consensus and/or partial dissenting. After examining the fifteen cases and excluding the five cases that were from before 1989 when the CRC was adopted, we find that six cases had no references to the CRC. In the four cases that had such references, there are citations from Articles 9 and 21 (*A.K. and L. v. Croatia*; *X v. Croatia*[44]); Articles 1, 3 and 21 (*Johansen v. Norway*[45]); and Article 12 (*Aune v. Norway*[46]). In all fifteen cases there are references to the 'best interests of the child'. However, there are distinct differences between the cases. Some cases only mention the child's interests once or a few times, as illustrated in *A.K. and L. v. Croatia* from 2013, in which the best interest of the child is mentioned once (para. 24). In other cases, the child´s best interest is quite often or very often discussed throughout the case. Only in three of the cases are children´s wishes or opinion a matter for the court (*R.M.S v. Spain*; *Y.C. v. United Kingdom*; *Aune v. Norway*[47]), showing us that children´s participation is not an important consideration in these judgments.

Directing our lenses towards the six cases that are the focus of the analysis shows that there are some discretionary considerations in the

---

[42] *R. and H. v. The United Kingdom*, appl. no. 35348/06, para. 88. [43] Ibid.
[44] For individual case citations, see note 24.   [45] Appl. no. 17383/90.
[46] Appl. no. 52502/07.   [47] For individual case citations, see note 24.

content of the best interest principle. Of these cases, one is from Spain (2013), two are from the United Kingdom (2012 and 2011), two are from Norway (2011 and 1996) and one is from Italy (1999). Two cases have consensus decisions (Spain and Norway 2011), and the remaining cases have dissenting decisions. In four cases there is no reference to the Convention on the Rights of the Child, while the CRC is mentioned in both Norwegian cases.

The first case in which the possibility of adoption was a key issue and there were material discussions of the child's best interests was *Johansen v. Norway* (1996). We previously reviewed the important assessment criteria that the ECtHR formulated in this and other judgments. The core issue in all the selected cases was whether the impugned measures were 'necessary in a democratic society'. In brief, this necessity test includes the states obligation to respect family life for both the child and the parents; protect children; the margin of appreciation; and the irreversible nature of the decisions.

We systematically examine the six judgments and their considerations for the child's best interest and use *Johansen v. Norway* as reference for our analysis. We include material from the five other judgments where the cases either develop or deviate from *Johansen*.

When reiterating the general principles of the convention, the ECtHR stated in *Johansen* that the 'consideration of what is in the best interest of the child is in any event of crucial importance'.[48] When assessing the merits of this individual case, the ECtHR elaborated this point:

> In this regard, a fair balance has to be struck between the interests of the child in remaining in public care and those of the parent in being reunited with the child ... In carrying out this balancing exercise, the Court will attach particular importance to the best interests of the child, which, depending on their nature and seriousness, may override those of the parent. In particular, as suggested by the Government, the parent cannot be entitled under Article 8 of the Convention to have such measures taken as would harm the child's health and development.[49]

In *R. and H. v. UK* (2011), the ECtHR underlined that, in all decisions concerning children, their best interests must be 'paramount'.[50] This is

---

[48] *Johansen v. Norway*, appl. no. 17383/90, para. 64.

[49] Para. 78. It should be noted that the government made a reference to UN Convention on the rights of the Child (CRC) Article 3, and it is not unlikely that the latter impacted the words used by the ECtHR.

[50] *R. and H. v. The United Kingdom*, appl. no. 35348/06, para. 73.

more strongly formulated in *R.M.S v. Spania* (2013): 'In the pursuit of a balance between these different interests, the child's best interests must always be a paramount consideration.'[51] In *Aune v. Norway*[52] (2011), the ECtHR did not specifically state assessment criteria besides what had already been expressed in *Johansen*, and followed a concrete, case-specific approach that considered the limited contact between the child and the mother; the expert opinion that the child had a significant need for security and belonging; and the child's wishes.

For the specific issues of depriving the mother's parental rights and her access to a permanent placement for her daughter in a foster home with the potential for adoption by the foster parents, the ECtHR held in *Johansen*:

> These measures were particularly far-reaching in that they totally deprived the applicant of her family life with the child and were inconsistent with the aim of reuniting them. Such measures should only be applied in exceptional circumstances and could only be justified if they were motivated by an overriding requirement pertaining to the child's best interests.[53]

Based on this standard and an assessment of the facts of the case, the ECtHR held that depriving access and parental rights did not 'correspond to any overriding requirement in the child's best interests'.[54] The ECtHR emphasized that whether an interference is justified must be assessed in light of the circumstances that were obtained during the time in which the decisions were taken, 'and not with the benefit of hindsight'.[55] The ECtHR noted that less than a year after the applicant's daughter was taken into care, a national court found that the applicant's material conditions had improved to the point where she would have been able to provide her daughter with a satisfactory upbringing. However, the court refused to terminate care due to the lack of contact between the applicant and her daughter. The child's situation was far more permanent in *Aune*, as he had been in foster care since the age of six months. The mother saw him on six of the fifteen opportunities that were offered, and for approximately a year she did not see him because of her drug abuse. The ECtHR held that this 'must have implications for the degree of protection that ought to be afforded' to the mother's right to respect

---

[51] *R.M.S v. Spain*, appl. no. 28775/12, para. 74. With reference to *Moretti and Benedetti v. Italy*, appl. no. 16318/07, judgment 27 April 2010, para. 67.
[52] Appl. no. 52502/07.   [53] Appl. no. 17383/90, para. 78.   [54] Ibid., para. 84.
[55] Ibid., para. 80.

for family life when assessing the necessity of the interference.[56] In *R.M.S. v. Spain* (2013), the child was taken into care in early childhood, but the main reason was the mother's financial hardship. The ECtHR observed that in cases concerning family life, the 'breaking-off of contact with a very young child may result in the progressive deterioration of the child's relationship with his or her parent'.[57] A core element was that the child's care situation could have been solved with less intrusive measures. Clearly, according to the ECtHR, a lack of economic resources cannot be the sole reason for removal.

In 2012, there was a slight shift in how the ECtHR outlines the important elements in cases that consider the child's best interest. In *Y.C. v. United Kingdom* (2012), they clearly prescribe the totality of the factors and elements that need to be accounted for in child's best interest decisions.

> The identification of the child's best interests and the assessment of the overall proportionality of any given measure will require courts to weigh a number of factors in the balance. The Court has not previously set out an exhaustive list of such factors, which may vary depending on the circumstances of the case in question. However, it observes that the considerations listed in section 1 of the 2002 Act (see paragraph 103 above) broadly reflect the various elements inherent in assessing the necessity under Article 8 of a measure placing a child for adoption. In particular, it considers that in seeking to identify the best interests of a child and in assessing the necessity of any proposed measure in the context of placement proceedings, the domestic court must demonstrate that it has had regard to, inter alia, the age, maturity and ascertained wishes of the child, the likely effect on the child of ceasing to be a member of his original family and the relationship the child has with relatives.[58]

We noticed that the ECtHR is formulating elements for the best interest of the child assessment. In the first part of the statement, the ECtHR is careful in its wording, while in the last part the language is firm and operational. Particular elements are emphasized that are both more specific and child-oriented than in previous cases. In earlier case law, the child was predominantly an interest worthy of protection, whereas it is now considered an individual with independent interests. Another aspect that indicates a shift in approach is the attention that is given to

---

[56] Appl. no. 52502/07, para. 69.   [57] Appl. no. 28775/12, para. 79.
[58] Appl. no. 4547/10, para. 135.

the assessments that were developed by the national courts. Although the ECtHR emphasized the need for thorough scrutiny of the intrusive measure of adoption in earlier case law, it is now examining whether the national courts have taken the relevant factors into consideration. We see a resemblance to the Committee of the CRC's General Comment No. 14[59] (2013) on best interests, which outlines and distinguishes between the seven elements to be considered, cf. our outline of this earlier in the chapter.

A core element when assessing the best interest of the child is to involve ('hear') the child (CRC Article 12), although it may be difficult to weigh the view of the child in these cases. Several of these judgments concern young children. In *Aune v. Norway* (2011) the child was twelve years old when the ECtHR made their judgment. Relying on findings from the national courts, the ECtHR saw 'no reason to doubt that the impugned measures' corresponded to the child's wishes.[60] In the quotation from the case of *Y.C. v. United Kingdom*, the wishes and the feelings of the child are emphasized as important components of best interest considerations,.[61] In *R.M.S v. Spain* (2013), there is no mention of the child's participation, view, or opinion, which is similar to *E.P. v. Italy*.[62] In the latter case, the child's view is presented in the government's case presentation with a reference to psychological reports that expressed the child's reluctance and fear of being in contact with her mother. We cannot say whether this influenced the ECtHR, but the lack of attention to the child's view and wishes is in contrast to the *Y.C. v. UK* judgment.

The findings show that children's wishes and views are, to varying degrees, included in the judgments. Overall, children's perspectives are not given a prominent place in the case proceedings. It remains to be seen whether we now are standing at a crossroads based on the promising stepping stone that was provided in *Aune v. Norway* and in particular in *Y.C. v. United Kingdom*. Here, the ECtHR was consistent with the UN Committee on the Rights of the Child, General Comment No. 12, which states that in adoption cases it: '...is vitally important that the child is heard'.[63]

---

[59] CRC/C/GC/14, paras. 52–79.   [60] Appl. no. 52502/07, para. 72.
[61] See text accompanying footnote 58.   [62] Appl. no. 31127/96.
[63] Appl. no. 4547/10, para. 55. General Comment No. 12 (2009). The right of the child to be heard (CRC/C/GC/12).

F Concluding Remarks

How should we cautiously draw conclusions on the ECtHR's interpretations of children´s rights and best interest assessments? We clearly show that the CRC is not a prominent source for the ECtHR and that the child, to a varying degree, is represented in the case material. The best interest principle is absolutely evident in the cases, although with great variability. We also notice that the best interest principle is, with one exception, presented with a reference to previous judgments in the ECtHR and not the CRC.

At the outset, the ECtHR appears to reiterate the points that were established in the *Johansen* case from 1996, with developments occurring over time. All cases stemmed from applications by the natural parents, which may have resulted in a focus on intervening in the parents' family life. The child´s need of protection was not absent in the first cases, and in *Johansen* the ECtHR stated that, 'the parent cannot be entitled under Article 8 of the Convention to have such measures taken as would harm the child's health and development'.[64] However, a more child-centric approach appears to be in the forefront in recent judgments. This is exemplified by the use of the term 'paramount' in weighing the child´s interests against the parent´s right for reunification and is in accord with developments that have been found in several high-income countries.[65]

The ECtHR has strong discretionary power, and we see how the court can decide to be critical and detailed in their judgment, as evident in the *R.M.S. v. Spain* (2013) case. This is within the discretionary power that is held by the court and is found within the sovereign authority of the ECtHR in interpreting the ECHR – a convention that has not changed in content since it was made, besides adding new provisions. The discretionary power and practice of the ECtHR is somewhat bound by the national states legislation, but the court decides how much they wish to exercise their powers. Surely, developments that may influence how the court exercises power are the alarming increases in the amount of submitted court cases.

The literature on best interest decisions claims that these decisions are not only highly complex but also impossible to resolve. Nevertheless, these decisions are made on a daily basis. One explanation for the

---

[64] Appl. no. 17383/90, para. 78.
[65] Gilbert, Parton and Skivenes (eds.), *Child Protection Systems Orientations* pp. 253–254.

trend in listing elements that should be considered in a best interest assessment may be that these guidelines can help overcome the challenge of making these impossible decisions. Obviously, there may be other explanations, but this process may result in more streamlined decision-making in the ECtHR. Consequentially, the variations that we find in children's participation may disappear in the coming years.

Appendix I

The United Nations Convention on the Rights of the Child (1989) 1577 U.N.T.S. 3

Preamble

The States Parties to the present Convention,

Considering that, in accordance with the principles proclaimed in the Charter of the United Nations, recognition of the inherent dignity and of the equal and inalienable rights of all members of the human family is the foundation of freedom, justice and peace in the world,

Bearing in mind that the peoples of the United Nations have, in the Charter, reaffirmed their faith in fundamental human rights and in the dignity and worth of the human person, and have determined to promote social progress and better standards of life in larger freedom,

Recognizing that the United Nations has, in the Universal Declaration of Human Rights and in the International Covenants on Human Rights, proclaimed and agreed that everyone is entitled to all the rights and freedoms set forth therein, without distinction of any kind, such as race, colour, sex, language, religion, political or other opinion, national or social origin, property, birth or other status,

Recalling that, in the Universal Declaration of Human Rights, the United Nations has proclaimed that childhood is entitled to special care and assistance,

Convinced that the family, as the fundamental group of society and the natural environment for the growth and wellbeing of all its members and particularly children, should be afforded the necessary protection and assistance so that it can fully assume its responsibilities within the community,

Recognizing that the child, for the full and harmonious development of his or her personality, should grow up in a family environment, in an atmosphere of happiness, love and understanding,

Considering that the child should be fully prepared to live an individual life in society, and brought up in the spirit of the ideals proclaimed in the Charter of the United Nations, and in particular in the spirit of peace, dignity, tolerance, freedom, equality and solidarity,

Bearing in mind that the need to extend particular care to the child has been stated in the Geneva Declaration of the Rights of the Child of 1924 and in the Declaration of the Rights of the Child adopted by the General Assembly on 20 November 1959 and recognized in the Universal Declaration of Human Rights, in the International Covenant on Civil and Political Rights (in particular in articles 23 and 24), in the International Covenant on Economic, Social and Cultural Rights (in particular in article 10) and in the statutes and relevant instruments of specialized agencies and international organizations concerned with the welfare of children,

Bearing in mind that, as indicated in the Declaration of the Rights of the Child, "the child, by reason of his physical and mental immaturity, needs special safeguards and care, including appropriate legal protection, before as well as after birth",

Recalling the provisions of the Declaration on Social and Legal Principles relating to the Protection and Welfare of Children, with Special Reference to Foster Placement and Adoption Nationally and Internationally; the United Nations Standard Minimum Rules for the Administration of Juvenile Justice (The Beijing Rules); and the Declaration on the Protection of Women and Children in Emergency and Armed Conflict,

Recognizing that, in all countries in the world, there are children living in exceptionally difficult conditions, and that such children need special consideration,

Taking due account of the importance of the traditions and cultural values of each people for the protection and harmonious development of the child,

Recognizing the importance of international co-operation for improving the living conditions of children in every country, in particular in the developing countries,

Have agreed as follows:

Part I

Article 1

For the purposes of the present Convention, a child means every human being below the age of eighteen years unless under the law applicable to the child, majority is attained earlier.

Article 2

1. States Parties shall respect and ensure the rights set forth in the present Convention to each child within their jurisdiction without discrimination of any kind, irrespective of the child's or his or her parent's or legal guardian's race, colour, sex, language, religion, political or other opinion, national, ethnic or social origin, property, disability, birth or other status.
2. States Parties shall take all appropriate measures to ensure that the child is protected against all forms of discrimination or punishment on the basis of the status, activities, expressed opinions, or beliefs of the child's parents, legal guardians, or family members.

Article 3

1. In all actions concerning children, whether undertaken by public or private social welfare institutions, courts of law, administrative authorities or legislative bodies, the best interests of the child shall be a primary consideration.
2. States Parties undertake to ensure the child such protection and care as is necessary for his or her well-being, taking into account the rights and duties of his or her parents, legal guardians, or other individuals legally responsible for him or her, and, to this end, shall take all appropriate legislative and administrative measures.
3. States Parties shall ensure that the institutions, services and facilities responsible for the care or protection of children shall conform with the standards established by competent authorities, particularly in the areas of safety, health, in the number and suitability of their staff, as well as competent supervision.

Article 4

States Parties shall undertake all appropriate legislative, administrative, and other measures for the implementation of the rights recognized in the present Convention. With regard to economic, social and cultural rights, States Parties shall undertake such measures to the maximum extent of their available resources and, where needed, within the framework of international co-operation.

Article 5

States Parties shall respect the responsibilities, rights and duties of parents or, where applicable, the members of the extended family or community as provided for by local custom, legal guardians or other persons legally responsible for the child, to provide, in a manner consistent with the evolving capacities of the child, appropriate direction and guidance in the exercise by the child of the rights recognized in the present Convention.

Article 6

1. States Parties recognize that every child has the inherent right to life.
2. States Parties shall ensure to the maximum extent possible the survival and development of the child.

Article 7

1. The child shall be registered immediately after birth and shall have the right from birth to a name, the right to acquire a nationality and, as far as possible, the right to know and be cared for by his or her parents.
2. States Parties shall ensure the implementation of these rights in accordance with their national law and their obligations under the relevant international instruments in this field, in particular where the child would otherwise be stateless.

Article 8

1. States Parties undertake to respect the right of the child to preserve his or her identity, including nationality, name and family relations as recognized by law without unlawful interference.
2. Where a child is illegally deprived of some or all of the elements of his or her identity, States Parties shall provide appropriate assistance and protection, with a view to re-establishing speedily his or her identity.

Article 9

1. States Parties shall ensure that a child shall not be separated from his or her parents against their will, except when competent authorities subject to judicial review determine, in accordance with applicable law and procedures, that such separation is necessary for the best interests of the child. Such determination may be necessary in a particular case such as one involving abuse or neglect of the child by the parents, or one where the parents are living separately and a decision must be made as to the child's place of residence.

2. In any proceedings pursuant to paragraph 1 of the present article, all interested parties shall be given an opportunity to participate in the proceedings and make their views known.
3. States Parties shall respect the right of the child who is separated from one or both parents to maintain personal relations and direct contact with both parents on a regular basis, except if it is contrary to the child's best interests.
4. Where such separation results from any action initiated by a State Party, such as the detention, imprisonment, exile, deportation or death (including death arising from any cause while the person is in the custody of the State) of one or both parents or of the child, that State Party shall, upon request, provide the parents, the child or, if appropriate, another member of the family with the essential information concerning the whereabouts of the absent member(s) of the family unless the provision of the information would be detrimental to the well-being of the child. States Parties shall further ensure that the submission of such a request shall of itself entail no adverse consequences for the person(s) concerned.

Article 10

1. In accordance with the obligation of States Parties under article 9, paragraph 1, applications by a child or his or her parents to enter or leave a State Party for the purpose of family reunification shall be dealt with by States Parties in a positive, humane and expeditious manner. States Parties shall further ensure that the submission of such a request shall entail no adverse consequences for the applicants and for the members of their family.
2. A child whose parents reside in different States shall have the right to maintain on a regular basis, save in exceptional circumstances, personal relations and direct contact with both parents. Towards that end and in accordance with the obligation of States Parties under Article 9, paragraph 1, States Parties shall respect the right of the child and his or her parents to leave any country, including their own, and to enter their own country. The right to leave any country shall be subject only to such restrictions as are prescribed by law and which are necessary to protect the national security, public (*ordre public*), public health or morals or the rights and freedoms of others and are consistent with the other rights recognized in the present Convention.

Article 11

1. States Parties shall take measures to combat the illicit transfer and non-return of children abroad.
2. To this end, States Parties shall promote the conclusion of bilateral or multilateral agreements or accession to existing agreements.

Article 12

1. States Parties shall assure to the child who is capable of forming his or her own views the right to express those views freely in all matters affecting the child, the views of the child being given due weight in accordance with the age and maturity of the child.
2. For this purpose, the child shall in particular be provided the opportunity to be heard in any judicial and administrative proceedings affecting the child, either directly, or through a representative or an appropriate body, in a manner consistent with the procedural rules of national law.

Article 13

1. The child shall have the right to freedom of expression; this right shall include freedom to seek, receive and impart information and ideas of all kinds, regardless of frontiers, either orally, in writing or in print, in the form of art, or through any other media of the child's choice.
2. The exercise of this right may be subject to certain restrictions, but these shall only be such as are provided by law and are necessary:
   (a) For respect of the rights or reputations of others or
   (b) For the protection of national security or of public order (*ordre public*), or of public health or morals.

Article 14

1. States Parties shall respect the right of the child to freedom of thought, conscience and religion.
2. States Parties shall respect the rights and duties of the parents and, when applicable, legal guardians, to provide direction to the child in the exercise of his or her right in a manner consistent with the evolving capacities of the child.
3. Freedom to manifest one's religion or beliefs may be subject only to such limitations as are prescribed by law and are necessary to protect public safety, order, health or morals, or the fundamental rights and freedoms of others.

Article 15

1. States Parties recognize the rights of the child to freedom of association and to freedom of peaceful assembly.
2. No restrictions may be placed on the exercise of these rights other than those imposed in conformity with the law and which are necessary in a democratic society in the interests of national security or public safety, public order (*ordre public*), the protection of public health or morals or the protection of the rights and freedoms of others.

Article 16

1. No child shall be subjected to arbitrary or unlawful interference with his or her privacy, family, home or correspondence, nor to unlawful attacks on his or her honour and reputation.
2. The child has the right to the protection of the law against such interference or attacks.

Article 17

States Parties recognize the important function performed by the mass media and shall ensure that the child has access to information and material from a diversity of national and international sources, especially those aimed at the promotion of his or her social, spiritual and moral well-being and physical and mental health.

To this end, States Parties shall:

(a) Encourage the mass media to disseminate information and material of social and cultural benefit to the child and in accordance with the spirit of Article 29;
(b) Encourage international co-operation in the production, exchange and dissemination of such information and material from a diversity of cultural, national and international sources;
(c) Encourage the production and dissemination of children's books;
(d) Encourage the mass media to have particular regard to the linguistic needs of the child who belongs to a minority group or who is indigenous;
(e) Encourage the development of appropriate guidelines for the protection of the child from information and material injurious to his or her well-being, bearing in mind the provisions of articles 13 and 18.

Article 18

1. States Parties shall use their best efforts to ensure recognition of the principle that both parents have common responsibilities for the upbringing and development of the child. Parents or, as the case may be, legal guardians, have the primary responsibility for the upbringing and development of the child. The best interests of the child will be their basic concern.
2. For the purpose of guaranteeing and promoting the rights set forth in the present Convention, States Parties shall render appropriate assistance to parents and legal guardians in the performance of their child-rearing responsibilities and shall ensure the development of institutions, facilities and services for the care of children.
3. States Parties shall take all appropriate measures to ensure that children of working parents have the right to benefit from child-care services and facilities for which they are eligible.

Article 19

1. States Parties shall take all appropriate legislative, administrative, social and educational measures to protect the child from all forms of physical or mental violence, injury or abuse, neglect or negligent treatment, maltreatment or exploitation, including sexual abuse, while in the care of parent(s), legal guardian(s) or any other person who has the care of the child.
2. Such protective measures should, as appropriate, include effective procedures for the establishment of social programmes to provide necessary support for the child and for those who have the care of the child, as well as for other forms of prevention and for identification, reporting, referral, investigation, treatment and follow-up of instances of child maltreatment described heretofore, and, as appropriate, for judicial involvement.

Article 20

1. A child temporarily or permanently deprived of his or her family environment, or in whose own best interests cannot be allowed to remain in that environment, shall be entitled to special protection and assistance provided by the State.
2. States Parties shall in accordance with their national laws ensure alternative care for such a child.

3. Such care could include, *inter alia,* foster placement, *kafalah* of Islamic law, adoption or if necessary placement in suitable institutions for the care of children. When considering solutions, due regard shall be paid to the desirability of continuity in a child's upbringing and to the child's ethnic, religious, cultural and linguistic background.

Article 21

States Parties that recognize and/or permit the system of adoption shall ensure that the best interests of the child shall be the paramount consideration and they shall:

(a) Ensure that the adoption of a child is authorized only by competent authorities who determine, in accordance with applicable law and procedures and on the basis of all pertinent and reliable information, that the adoption is permissible in view of the child's status concerning parents, relatives and legal guardians and that, if required, the persons concerned have given their informed consent to the adoption on the basis of such counselling as may be necessary;
(b) Recognize that inter-country adoption may be considered as an alternative means of child's care, if the child cannot be placed in a foster or an adoptive family or cannot in any suitable manner be cared for in the child's country of origin;
(c) Ensure that the child concerned by inter-country adoption enjoys safeguards and standards equivalent to those existing in the case of national adoption;
(d) Take all appropriate measures to ensure that, in inter-country adoption, the placement does not result in improper financial gain for those involved in it;
(e) Promote, where appropriate, the objectives of the present article by concluding bilateral or multilateral arrangements or agreements, and endeavour, within this framework, to ensure that the placement of the child in another country is carried out by competent authorities or organs.

Article 22

1. States Parties shall take appropriate measures to ensure that a child who is seeking refugee status or who is considered a refugee in accordance with applicable international or domestic law and procedures shall, whether unaccompanied or accompanied by his or her

parents or by any other person, receive appropriate protection and humanitarian assistance in the enjoyment of applicable rights set forth in the present Convention and in other international human rights or humanitarian instruments to which the said States are Parties.
2. For this purpose, States Parties shall provide, as they consider appropriate, co-operation in any efforts by the United Nations and other competent intergovernmental organizations or non-governmental organizations co-operating with the United Nations to protect and assist such a child and to trace the parents or other members of the family of any refugee child in order to obtain information necessary for reunification with his or her family. In cases where no parents or other members of the family can be found, the child shall be accorded the same protection as any other child permanently or temporarily deprived of his or her family environment for any reason, as set forth in the present Convention.

Article 23

1. States Parties recognize that a mentally or physically disabled child should enjoy a full and decent life, in conditions which ensure dignity, promote self-reliance and facilitate the child's active participation in the community.
2. States Parties recognize the right of the disabled child to special care and shall encourage and ensure the extension, subject to available resources, to the eligible child and those responsible for his or her care, of assistance for which application is made and which is appropriate to the child's condition and to the circumstances of the parents or others caring for the child.
3. Recognizing the special needs of a disabled child, assistance extended in accordance with paragraph 2 of the present article shall be provided free of charge, whenever possible, taking into account the financial resources of the parents or others caring for the child, and shall be designed to ensure that the disabled child has effective access to and receives education, training, health care services, rehabilitation services, preparation for employment and recreation opportunities in a manner conducive to the child's achieving the fullest possible social integration and individual development, including his or her cultural and spiritual development.
4. States Parties shall promote, in the spirit of international cooperation, the exchange of appropriate information in the field of preventive health

care and of medical, psychological and functional treatment of disabled children, including dissemination of and access to information concerning methods of rehabilitation, education and vocational services, with the aim of enabling States Parties to improve their capabilities and skills and to widen their experience in these areas. In this regard, particular account shall be taken of the needs of developing countries.

Article 24

1. States Parties recognize the right of the child to the enjoyment of the highest attainable standard of health and to facilities for the treatment of illness and rehabilitation of health. States Parties shall strive to ensure that no child is deprived of his or her right of access to such health care services.
2. States Parties shall pursue full implementation of this right and, in particular, shall take appropriate measures:
   (a) To diminish infant and child mortality;
   (b) To ensure the provision of necessary medical assistance and health care to all children with emphasis on the development of primary health care;
   (c) To combat disease and malnutrition, including within the framework of primary health care, through, *inter alia*, the application of readily available technology and through the provision of adequate nutritious foods and clean drinking water, taking into consideration the dangers and risks of environmental pollution;
   (d) To ensure appropriate pre-natal and post-natal health care for mothers;
   (e) To ensure that all segments of society, in particular parents and children, are informed, have access to education and are supported in the use of basic knowledge of child health and nutrition, the advantages of breast-feeding, hygiene and environmental sanitation and the prevention of accidents;
   (f) To develop preventive health care, guidance for parents and family planning education and services.
3. States Parties shall take all effective and appropriate measures with a view to abolishing traditional practices prejudicial to the health of children.
4. States Parties undertake to promote and encourage international co-operation with a view to achieving progressively the full realization of the right recognized in the present article. In this regard, particular account shall be taken of the needs of developing countries.

Article 25

States Parties recognize the right of a child who has been placed by the competent authorities for the purposes of care, protection or treatment of his or her physical or mental health, to a periodic review of the treatment provided to the child and all other circumstances relevant to his or her placement.

Article 26

1. States Parties shall recognize for every child the right to benefit from social security, including social insurance, and shall take the necessary measures to achieve the full realization of this right in accordance with their national law.
2. The benefits should, where appropriate, be granted, taking into account the resources and the circumstances of the child and persons having responsibility for the maintenance of the child, as well as any other consideration relevant to an application for benefits made by or on behalf of the child.

Article 27

1. States Parties recognize the right of every child to a standard of living adequate for the child's physical, mental, spiritual, moral and social development.
2. The parent(s) or others responsible for the child have the responsibility to secure, within their abilities and capacities, the conditions of living necessary for the child's development.
3. States Parties, in accordance with national conditions and within their means, shall take appropriate measures to assist parents and others responsible for the child to implement this right and shall in case of need provide material assistance and support programmes, particularly with regard to nutrition, clothing and housing.
4. States Parties shall take all appropriate measures to secure the recovery of maintenance for the child from the parents or other persons having financial responsibility for the child, both within the State Party and from abroad. In particular, where the person having financial responsibility for the child lives in a State different from that of the child, States Parties shall promote the accession to international agreements or the conclusion of such agreements as well as the making of other appropriate arrangements.

Article 28

1. States Parties recognize the right of the child to education, and with a view to achieving this right progressively and on the basis of equal opportunity, they shall, in particular:
   (a) Make primary education compulsory and available free to all;
   (b) Encourage the development of different forms of secondary education, including general and vocational education, make them available and accessible to every child, and take appropriate measures such as the introduction of free education and offering financial assistance in case of need;
   (c) Make higher education accessible to all on the basis of capacity by every appropriate means;
   (d) Make educational and vocational information and guidance available and accessible to all children;
   (e) Take measures to encourage regular attendance at schools and the reduction of drop-out rates.
2. States Parties shall take all appropriate measures to ensure that school discipline is administered in a manner consistent with the child's human dignity and in conformity with the present Convention.
3. States Parties shall promote and encourage international cooperation in matters relating to education, in particular with a view to contributing to the elimination of ignorance and illiteracy throughout the world and facilitating access to scientific and technical knowledge and modern teaching methods. In this regard, particular account shall be taken of the needs of developing countries.

Article 29

1. States Parties agree that the education of the child shall be directed to:
   (a) The development of the child's personality, talents and mental and physical abilities to their fullest potential;
   (b) The development of respect for human rights and fundamental freedoms, and for the principles enshrined in the Charter of the United Nations;
   (c) The development of respect for the child's parents, his or her own cultural identity, language and values, for the national values of the country in which the child is living, the country from which he or she may originate, and for civilizations different from his or her own;
   (d) The preparation of the child for responsible life in a free society, in the spirit of understanding, peace, tolerance, equality of sexes,

and friendship among all peoples, ethnic, national and religious groups and persons of indigenous origin;
(e) The development of respect for the natural environment.
2. No part of the present article or article 28 shall be construed so as to interfere with the liberty of individuals and bodies to establish and direct educational institutions, subject always to the observance of the principles set forth in paragraph 1 of the present article and to the requirements that the education given in such institutions shall conform to such minimum standards as may be laid down by the State.

Article 30

In those States in which ethnic, religious or linguistic minorities or persons of indigenous origin exist, a child belonging to such a minority or who is indigenous shall not be denied the right, in community with other members of his or her group, to enjoy his or her own culture, to profess and practise his or her own religion, or to use his or her own language.

Article 31

1. States Parties recognize the right of the child to rest and leisure, to engage in play and recreational activities appropriate to the age of the child and to participate freely in cultural life and the arts.
2. States Parties shall respect and promote the right of the child to participate fully in cultural and artistic life and shall encourage the provision of appropriate and equal opportunities for cultural, artistic, recreational and leisure activity.

Article 32

1. States Parties recognize the right of the child to be protected from economic exploitation and from performing any work that is likely to be hazardous or to interfere with the child's education, or to be harmful to the child's health or physical, mental, spiritual, moral or social development.
2. States Parties shall take legislative, administrative, social and educational measures to ensure the implementation of the present article. To this end, and having regard to the relevant provisions of other international instruments, States Parties shall in particular:
   (a) Provide for a minimum age or minimum ages for admission to employment;

(b) Provide for appropriate regulation of the hours and conditions of employment;
(c) Provide for appropriate penalties or other sanctions to ensure the effective enforcement of the present article.

Article 33

States Parties shall take all appropriate measures, including legislative, administrative, social and educational measures, to protect children from the illicit use of narcotic drugs and psychotropic substances as defined in the relevant international treaties, and to prevent the use of children in the illicit production and trafficking of such substances.

Article 34

States Parties undertake to protect the child from all forms of sexual exploitation and sexual abuse. For these purposes, States Parties shall in particular take all appropriate national, bilateral and multilateral measures to prevent:

(a) The inducement or coercion of a child to engage in any unlawful sexual activity;
(b) The exploitative use of children in prostitution or other unlawful sexual practices;
(c) The exploitative use of children in pornographic performances and materials.

Article 35

States Parties shall take all appropriate national, bilateral and multilateral measures to prevent the abduction of, the sale of or traffic in children for any purpose or in any form.

Article 36

States Parties shall protect the child against all other forms of exploitation prejudicial to any aspects of the child's welfare.

Article 37

States Parties shall ensure that:

(a) No child shall be subjected to torture or other cruel, inhuman or degrading treatment or punishment. Neither capital punishment nor

life imprisonment without possibility of release shall be imposed for offences committed by persons below eighteen years of age;
(b) No child shall be deprived of his or her liberty unlawfully or arbitrarily. The arrest, detention or imprisonment of a child shall be in conformity with the law and shall be used only as a measure of last resort and for the shortest appropriate period of time;
(c) Every child deprived of liberty shall be treated with humanity and respect for the inherent dignity of the human person, and in a manner which takes into account the needs of persons of his or her age. In particular, every child deprived of liberty shall be separated from adults unless it is considered in the child's best interest not to do so and shall have the right to maintain contact with his or her family through correspondence and visits, save in exceptional circumstances;
(d) Every child deprived of his or her liberty shall have the right to prompt access to legal and other appropriate assistance, as well as the right to challenge the legality of the deprivation of his or her liberty before a court or other competent, independent and impartial authority, and to a prompt decision on any such action.

Article 38

1. States Parties undertake to respect and to ensure respect for rules of international humanitarian law applicable to them in armed conflicts which are relevant to the child.
2. States Parties shall take all feasible measures to ensure that persons who have not attained the age of fifteen years do not take a direct part in hostilities.
3. States Parties shall refrain from recruiting any person who has not attained the age of fifteen years into their armed forces. In recruiting among those persons who have attained the age of fifteen years but who have not attained the age of eighteen years, States Parties shall endeavour to give priority to those who are oldest.
4. In accordance with their obligations under international humanitarian law to protect the civilian population in armed conflicts, States Parties shall take all feasible measures to ensure protection and care of children who are affected by an armed conflict.

Article 39

States Parties shall take all appropriate measures to promote physical and psychological recovery and social reintegration of a child victim of:

any form of neglect, exploitation, or abuse; torture or any other form of cruel, inhuman or degrading treatment or punishment; or armed conflicts. Such recovery and reintegration shall take place in an environment which fosters the health, self-respect and dignity of the child.

Article 40

1. States Parties recognize the right of every child alleged as, accused of, or recognized as having infringed the penal law to be treated in a manner consistent with the promotion of the child's sense of dignity and worth, which reinforces the child's respect for the human rights and fundamental freedoms of others and which takes into account the child's age and the desirability of promoting the child's reintegration and the child's assuming a constructive role in society.
2. To this end, and having regard to the relevant provisions of international instruments, States Parties shall, in particular, ensure that:
   (a) No child shall be alleged as, be accused of, or recognized as having infringed the penal law by reason of acts or omissions that were not prohibited by national or international law at the time they were committed;
   (b) Every child alleged as or accused of having infringed the penal law has at least the following guarantees:
      (i) To be presumed innocent until proven guilty according to law;
      (ii) To be informed promptly and directly of the charges against him or her, and, if appropriate, through his or her parents or legal guardians, and to have legal or other appropriate assistance in the preparation and presentation of his or her defence;
      (iii) To have the matter determined without delay by a competent, independent and impartial authority or judicial body in a fair hearing according to law, in the presence of legal or other appropriate assistance and, unless it is considered not to be in the best interests of the child, in particular, taking into account his or her age or situation, his or her parents or legal guardians;
      (iv) Not to be compelled to give testimony or to confess guilt; to examine or have examined adverse witnesses and to obtain the participation and examination of witnesses on his or her behalf under conditions of equality;

(v) If considered to have infringed the penal law, to have this decision and any measures imposed in consequence thereof reviewed by a higher competent, independent and impartial authority or judicial body according to law;
(vi) To have the free assistance of an interpreter if the child cannot understand or speak the language used;
(vii) To have his or her privacy fully respected at all stages of the proceedings.
3. States Parties shall seek to promote the establishment of laws, procedures, authorities and institutions specifically applicable to children alleged as, accused of, or recognized as having infringed the penal law, and, in particular:
   (a) The establishment of a minimum age below which children shall be presumed not to have the capacity to infringe the penal law;
   (b) Whenever appropriate and desirable, measures for dealing with such children without resorting to judicial proceedings, providing that human rights and legal safeguards are fully respected.
4. A variety of dispositions, such as care, guidance and supervision orders; counselling; probation; foster care; education and vocational training programmes and other alternatives to institutional care shall be available to ensure that children are dealt with in a manner appropriate to their well-being and proportionate both to their circumstances and the offence.

Article 41

Nothing in the present Convention shall affect any provisions which are more conducive to the realization of the rights of the child and which may be contained in:

(a) The law of a State Party or
(b) International law in force for that State.

Part II

Article 42

States Parties undertake to make the principles and provisions of the Convention widely known, by appropriate and active means, to adults and children alike.

Article 43

1. For the purpose of examining the progress made by States Parties in achieving the realization of the obligations undertaken in the present Convention, there shall be established a Committee on the Rights of the Child, which shall carry out the functions hereinafter provided.
2. The Committee shall consist of [eighteen][1] experts of high moral standing and recognized competence in the field covered by this Convention. The members of the Committee shall be elected by States Parties from among their nationals and shall serve in their personal capacity, consideration being given to equitable geographical distribution, as well as to the principal legal systems.
3. The members of the Committee shall be elected by secret ballot from a list of persons nominated by States Parties. Each State Party may nominate one person from among its own nationals.
4. The initial election to the Committee shall be held no later than six months after the date of the entry into force of the present Convention and thereafter every second year. At least four months before the date of each election, the Secretary General of the United Nations shall address a letter to States Parties inviting them to submit their nominations within two months. The Secretary-General shall subsequently prepare a list in alphabetical order of all persons thus nominated, indicating States Parties which have nominated them, and shall submit it to the States Parties to the present Convention.
5. The elections shall be held at meetings of States Parties convened by the Secretary-General at United Nations Headquarters. At those meetings, for which two thirds of States Parties shall constitute a quorum, the persons elected to the Committee shall be those who obtain the largest number of votes and an absolute majority of the votes of the representatives of States Parties present and voting.
6. The members of the Committee shall be elected for a term of four years. They shall be eligible for re-election if renominated. The term of five of the members elected at the first election shall expire at the end of two years; immediately after the first election, the names of these five members shall be chosen by lot by the Chairman of the meeting.

---

[1] Amended by U.N. Doc. CRC/SP/1995/L.1/Rev.1 of 18 November 1995.

7. If a member of the Committee dies or resigns or declares that for any other cause he or she can no longer perform the duties of the Committee, the State Party which nominated the member shall appoint another expert from among its nationals to serve for the remainder of the term, subject to the approval of the Committee.
8. The Committee shall establish its own rules of procedure.
9. The Committee shall elect its officers for a period of two years.
10. The meetings of the Committee shall normally be held at United Nations Headquarters or at any other convenient place as determined by the Committee. The Committee shall normally meet annually. The duration of the meetings of the Committee shall be determined, and reviewed, if necessary, by a meeting of the States Parties to the present Convention, subject to the approval of the General Assembly.
11. The Secretary-General of the United Nations shall provide the necessary staff and facilities for the effective performance of the functions of the Committee under the present Convention.
12. With the approval of the General Assembly, the members of the Committee established under the present Convention shall receive emoluments from United Nations resources on such terms and conditions as the Assembly may decide.

Article 44

1. States Parties undertake to submit to the Committee, through the Secretary-General of the United Nations, reports on the measures they have adopted which give effect to the rights recognized herein and on the progress made on the enjoyment of those rights
   (a) Within two years of the entry into force of the Convention for the State Party concerned;
   (b) Thereafter every five years.
2. Reports made under the present Article shall indicate factors and difficulties, if any, affecting the degree of fulfilment of the obligations under the present Convention. Reports shall also contain sufficient information to provide the Committee with a comprehensive understanding of the implementation of the Convention in the country concerned.
3. A State Party which has submitted a comprehensive initial report to the Committee need not, in its subsequent reports submitted in accordance with paragraph 1(b) of the present article, repeat basic information previously provided.

4. The Committee may request from States Parties further information relevant to the implementation of the Convention.
5. The Committee shall submit to the General Assembly, through the Economic and Social Council, every two years, reports on its activities.
6. States Parties shall make their reports widely available to the public in their own countries.

Article 45

In order to foster the effective implementation of the Convention and to encourage international co-operation in the field covered by the Convention:

(a) The specialized agencies, the United Nations Children's Fund, and other United Nations organs shall be entitled to be represented at the consideration of the implementation of such provisions of the present Convention as fall within the scope of their mandate. The Committee may invite the specialized agencies, the United Nations Children's Fund and other competent bodies as it may consider appropriate to provide expert advice on the implementation of the Convention in areas falling within the scope of their respective mandates. The Committee may invite the specialized agencies, the United Nations Children's Fund, and other United Nations organs to submit reports on the implementation of the Convention in areas falling within the scope of their activities;

(b) The Committee shall transmit, as it may consider appropriate, to the specialized agencies, the United Nations Children's Fund and other competent bodies, any reports from States Parties that contain a request, or indicate a need, for technical advice or assistance, along with the Committee's observations and suggestions, if any, on these requests or indications;

(c) The Committee may recommend to the General Assembly to request the Secretary-General to undertake on its behalf studies on specific issues relating to the rights of the child;

(d) The Committee may make suggestions and general recommendations based on information received pursuant to articles 44 and 45 of the present Convention. Such suggestions and general recommendations shall be transmitted to any State Party concerned and reported to the General Assembly, together with comments, if any, from States Parties.

Part III

Article 46

The present Convention shall be open for signature by all States.

Article 47

The present Convention is subject to ratification. Instruments of ratification shall be deposited with the Secretary-General of the United Nations.

Article 48

The present Convention shall remain open for accession by any State. The instruments of accession shall be deposited with the Secretary-General of the United Nations.

Article 49

1. The present Convention shall enter into force on the thirtieth day following the date of deposit with the Secretary-General of the United Nations of the twentieth instrument of ratification or accession.
2. For each State ratifying or acceding to the Convention after the deposit of the twentieth instrument of ratification or accession, the Convention shall enter into force on the thirtieth day after the deposit by such State of its instrument of ratification or accession.

Article 50

1. Any State Party may propose an amendment and file it with the Secretary-General of the United Nations. The Secretary-General shall thereupon communicate the proposed amendment to States Parties, with a request that they indicate whether they favour a conference of States Parties for the purpose of considering and voting upon the proposals. In the event that, within four months from the date of such communication, at least one third of the States Parties favour such a conference, the Secretary-General shall convene the conference under the auspices of the United Nations. Any amendment adopted by a majority of States Parties present and voting at the conference shall be submitted to the General Assembly for approval.
2. An amendment adopted in accordance with paragraph 1 of the present article shall enter into force when it has been approved by

the General Assembly of the United Nations and accepted by a two-thirds majority of States Parties.
3. When an amendment enters into force, it shall be binding on those States Parties which have accepted it, other States Parties still being bound by the provisions of the present Convention and any earlier amendments which they have accepted.

Article 51

1. The Secretary-General of the United Nations shall receive and circulate to all States the text of reservations made by States at the time of ratification or accession.
2. A reservation incompatible with the object and purpose of the present Convention shall not be permitted.
3. Reservations may be withdrawn at any time by notification to that effect addressed to the Secretary General of the United Nations, who shall then inform all States. Such notification shall take effect on the date which it is received by the Secretary-General.

Article 52

A State Party may denounce the present Convention by written notification to the Secretary-General of the United Nations. Denunciation becomes effective one year after the date of receipt of the notification by the Secretary-General.

Article 53

The Secretary-General of the United Nations is designated as the depositary of the present Convention.

Article 54

The original of the present Convention, of which the Arabic, Chinese, English, French, Russian and Spanish texts are equally authentic, shall be deposited with the Secretary-General of the United Nations.

Appendix II

United Nations Committee on the Rights of the Child

General Comment No. 14 (2013) on the right of the child to have his or her best interests taken as a primary consideration (art. 3, para. 1), CRC/C/GC/14

Adopted by the Committee at its sixty-second session (14 January – 1 February 2013).

Contents
- I. Introduction
  - A. The best interests of the child: a right, a principle and a rule of procedure
  - B. Structure
- II. Objectives
- III. Nature and scope of the obligations of states parties
- IV. Legal analysis and links with the general principles of the Convention
  - A. Literal analysis of article 3, paragraph 1
    1. "In all actions concerning children"
    2. "By public or private social welfare institutions, courts of law, administrative authorities or legislative bodies"
    3. "The best interests of the child"
    4. "Shall be a primary consideration"
  - B. The best interests of the child and links with other general principles of the Convention
    1. The child's best interests and the right to non-discrimination (art. 2)
    2. The child's best interests and the right to life, survival and development (art. 6)
    3. The child's best interests and the right to be heard (art. 12)
- V. Implementation: assessing and determining the child's best interests
  - A. Best interests assessment and determination
    1. Elements to be taken into account when assessing the child's best interests
    2. Balancing the elements in the best-interests assessment

B. Procedural safeguards to guarantee implementation of the child's best interests
VI. Dissemination

> "In all actions concerning children, whether undertaken by public or private social welfare institutions, courts of law, administrative authorities or legislative bodies, the best interests of the child shall be a primary consideration."
>
> Convention on the Rights of the Child (art. 3, para. 1)

I. Introduction

A. The best interests of the child: a right, a principle and a rule of procedure

1. Article 3, paragraph 1, of the Convention on the Rights of the Child gives the child the right to have his or her best interests assessed and taken into account as a primary consideration in all actions or decisions that concern him or her, both in the public and private sphere. Moreover, it expresses one of the fundamental values of the Convention. The Committee on the Rights of the Child (the Committee) has identified article 3, paragraph 1, as one of the four general principles of the Convention for interpreting and implementing all the rights of the child,[1] and applies it is a dynamic concept that requires an assessment appropriate to the specific context.

2. The concept of the "child's best interests" is not new. Indeed, it predates the Convention and was already enshrined in the 1959 Declaration of the Rights of the Child (para. 2), the Convention on the Elimination of All Forms of Discrimination against Women (arts. 5 (b) and 16, para. 1 (d)), as well as in regional instruments and many national and international laws.

3. The Convention also explicitly refers to the child's best interests in other articles: article 9: separation from parents; article 10: family reunification; article 18: parental responsibilities; article 20: deprivation of family environment and alternative care; article 21: adoption; article 37 (c): separation from adults in detention; article 40, paragraph 2 (b) (iii): procedural guarantees, including presence of parents at court hearings for penal matters involving children in conflict with the law.

---

[1] The Committee's General Comment No. 5 (2003) on the general measures of implementation of the Convention on the Rights of the Child, para. 12; and No. 12 (2009) on the right of the child to be heard, para. 2.

Reference is also made to the child's best interests in the Optional Protocol to the Convention on the sale of children, child prostitution and child pornography (preamble and art. 8) and in the Optional Protocol to the Convention on a communications procedure (preamble and arts. 2 and 3).

4. The concept of the child's best interests is aimed at ensuring both the full and effective enjoyment of all the rights recognized in the Convention and the holistic development of the child.[2] The Committee has already pointed out[3] that "an adult's judgment of a child's best interests cannot override the obligation to respect all the child's rights under the Convention." It recalls that there is no hierarchy of rights in the Convention; all the rights provided for therein are in the "child's best interests" and no right could be compromised by a negative interpretation of the child's best interests.

5. The full application of the concept of the child's best interests requires the development of a rights-based approach, engaging all actors, to secure the holistic physical, psychological, moral and spiritual integrity of the child and promote his or her human dignity.

6. The Committee underlines that the child's best interests is a threefold concept:

(a) A substantive right: The right of the child to have his or her best interests assessed and taken as a primary consideration when different interests are being considered in order to reach a decision on the issue at stake, and the guarantee that this right will be implemented whenever a decision is to be made concerning a child, a group of identified or unidentified children or children in general. Article 3, paragraph 1, creates an intrinsic obligation for States, is directly applicable (self-executing) and can be invoked before a court.
(b) A fundamental, interpretative legal principle: If a legal provision is open to more than one interpretation, the interpretation which most effectively serves the child's best interests should be chosen. The rights enshrined in the Convention and its Optional Protocols provide the framework for interpretation.

---

[2] The Committee expects States to interpret development as a "holistic concept, embracing the child's physical, mental, spiritual, moral, psychological and social development" (General Comment No. 5, para. 12).
[3] General Comment No. 13 (2011) on the right to protection from all forms of violence, para. 61.

(c) A rule of procedure: Whenever a decision is to be made that will affect a specific child, an identified group of children or children in general, the decision-making process must include an evaluation of the possible impact (positive or negative) of the decision on the child or children concerned. Assessing and determining the best interests of the child require procedural guarantees. Furthermore, the justification of a decision must show that the right has been explicitly taken into account. In this regard, States parties shall explain how the right has been respected in the decision, that is, what has been considered to be in the child's best interests; what criteria it is based on; and how the child's interests have been weighed against other considerations, be they broad issues of policy or individual cases.

7. In the present general comment, the expression "the child's best interests" or "the best interests of the child" covers the three dimensions developed above.

B. Structure

8. The scope of the present general comment is limited to article 3, paragraph 1, of the Convention and does not cover article 3, paragraph 2, which pertains to the well-being of the child, nor article 3, paragraph 3, which concerns the obligation of States parties to ensure that institutions, services and facilities for children comply with the established standards, and that mechanisms are in place to ensure that the standards are respected.

9. The Committee states the objectives (chapter II) of the present general comment and presents the nature and scope of the obligation of States parties (chapter III). It also provides a legal analysis of article 3, paragraph 1 (chapter IV), showing the links to other general principles of the Convention. Chapter V is dedicated to the implementation, in practice, of the principle of best interests of the child, while chapter VI provides guidelines on disseminating the general comment.

II. Objectives

10. The present general comment seeks to ensure the application of and respect for the best interests of the child by the States parties to the Convention. It defines the requirements for due consideration, especially in judicial and administrative decisions as well as in other actions concerning the child as an individual, and at all stages of the adoption

of laws, policies, strategies, programmes, plans, budgets, legislative and budgetary initiatives and guidelines – that is, all implementation measures – concerning children in general or as a specific group. The Committee expects that this general comment will guide decisions by all those concerned with children, including parents and caregivers.

11. The best interests of the child is a dynamic concept that encompasses various issues which are continuously evolving. The present general comment provides a framework for assessing and determining the child's best interests; it does not attempt to prescribe what is best for the child in any given situation at any point in time.

12. The main objective of this general comment is to strengthen the understanding and application of the right of children to have their best interests assessed and taken as a primary consideration or, in some cases, the paramount consideration (see paragraph 38 below). Its overall objective is to promote a real change in attitudes leading to the full respect of children as rights holders. More specifically, this has implications for:

(a) The elaboration of all implementation measures taken by governments;
(b) Individual decisions made by judicial or administrative authorities or public entities through their agents that concern one or more identified children;
(c) Decisions made by civil society entities and the private sector, including profit and non-profit organizations, which provide services concerning or impacting on children;
(d) Guidelines for actions undertaken by persons working with and for children, including parents and caregivers.

III. Nature and scope of the obligations of States parties

13. Each State party must respect and implement the right of the child to have his or her best interests assessed and taken as a primary consideration, and is under the obligation to take all necessary, deliberate and concrete measures for the full implementation of this right.

14. Article 3, paragraph 1, establishes a framework with three different types of obligations for States parties:

(a) The obligation to ensure that the child's best interests are *appropriately integrated and consistently applied* in every action taken by a public institution, especially in all implementation measures, administrative and judicial proceedings which directly or indirectly impact on children;

(b) The obligation to ensure that all judicial and administrative decisions as well as policies and legislation concerning children demonstrate that the child's best interests have been a primary consideration. This includes describing how the best interests have been examined and assessed, and what weight has been ascribed to them in the decision.
(c) The obligation to ensure that the interests of the child have been assessed and taken as a primary consideration in decisions and actions taken by the private sector, including those providing services, or any other private entity or institution making decisions that concern or impact on a child.

15. To ensure compliance, States parties should undertake a number of implementation measures in accordance with articles 4, 42 and 44, paragraph 6, of the Convention, and ensure that the best interests of the child are a primary consideration in all actions, including:

(a) Reviewing and, where necessary, amending domestic legislation and other sources of law so as to incorporate article 3, paragraph 1, and ensure that the requirement to consider the child's best interests is reflected and implemented in all national laws and regulations, provincial or territorial legislation, rules governing the operation of private or public institutions providing services or impacting on children, and judicial and administrative proceedings at any level, both as a substantive right and as a rule of procedure;
(b) Upholding the child's best interests in the coordination and implementation of policies at the national, regional and local levels;
(c) Establishing mechanisms and procedures for complaints, remedy or redress in order to fully realize the right of the child to have his or her best interests appropriately integrated and consistently applied in all implementation measures, administrative and judicial proceedings relevant to and with an impact on him or her;
(d) Upholding the child's best interests in the allocation of national resources for programmes and measures aimed at implementing children's rights, and in activities receiving international assistance or development aid;
(e) When establishing, monitoring and evaluating data collection, ensure that the child's best interests are explicitly spelled out and, where required, support research on children's rights issues;
(f) Providing information and training on article 3, paragraph 1, and its application in practice to all those making decisions that directly or

indirectly impact on children, including professionals and other people working for and with children;

(g) Providing appropriate information to children in a language they can understand, and to their families and caregivers, so that they understand the scope of the right protected under article 3, paragraph 1, as well as creating the necessary conditions for children to express their point of view and ensuring that their opinions are given due weight;

(h) Combating all negative attitudes and perceptions which impede the full realization of the right of the child to have his or her best interests assessed and taken as a primary consideration, through communication programmes involving mass media and social networks as well as children, in order to have children recognized as rights holders.

16. In giving full effect to the child's best interests, the following parameters should be borne in mind:

(a) The universal, indivisible, interdependent and interrelated nature of children's rights;
(b) Recognition of children as right holders;
(c) The global nature and reach of the Convention;
(d) The obligation of States parties to respect, protect and fulfill all the rights in the Convention;
(e) Short-, medium- and long-term effects of actions related to the development of the child over time.

IV. Legal analysis and links with the general principles of the Convention

A. Legal Analysis of article 3, paragraph 1

1. "In all actions concerning children"

(a) "in all actions"

17. Article 3, paragraph 1 seeks to ensure that the right is guaranteed in all decisions and actions concerning children. This means that every action relating to a child or children has to take into account their best interests as a primary consideration. The word "action" does not only include decisions, but also all acts, conduct, proposals, services, procedures and other measures.

18. Inaction or failure to take action and omissions are also "actions", for example, when social welfare authorities fail to take action to protect children from neglect or abuse.

(b) "concerning"

19. The legal duty applies to all decisions and actions that directly or indirectly affect children. Thus, the term "concerning" refers first of all, to measures and decisions directly concerning a child, children as a group or children in general, and secondly, to other measures that have an effect on an individual child, children as a group or children in general, even if they are not the direct targets of the measure. As stated in the Committee's General Comment No. 7 (2005), such actions include those aimed at children (e.g. related to health, care or education), as well as actions which include children and other population groups (e.g. related to the environment, housing or transport) (para. 13 (b)). Therefore, "concerning" must be understood in a very broad sense.

20. Indeed, all actions taken by a State affect children in one way or another. This does not mean that every action taken by the State needs to incorporate a full and formal process of assessing and determining the best interests of the child. However, where a decision will have a major impact on a child or children, a greater level of protection and detailed procedures to consider their best interests is appropriate.

Thus, in relation to measures that are not directly aimed at the child or children, the term "concerning" would need to be clarified in the light of the circumstances of each case in order to be able to appreciate the impact of the action on the child or children.

(c) "children"

21. The term "children" refers to all persons under the age of 18 within the jurisdiction of a State party, without discrimination of any kind, in line with articles 1 and 2 of the Convention.

22. Article 3, paragraph 1, applies to children as individuals and places an obligation on States parties to assess and take the child's best interests as a primary consideration in individual decisions.

23. However, the term "children" implies that the right to have their best interests duly considered applies to children not only as individuals, but also in general or as a group. Accordingly, States have the obligation to assess and take as a primary consideration the best interests of children

as a group or in general in all actions concerning them. This is particularly evident for all implementation measures. The Committee[4] underlines that the child's best interests is conceived both as a collective and individual right, and that the application of this right to indigenous children as a group requires consideration of how the right relates to collective cultural rights.

24. That is not to say that in a decision concerning an individual child, his or her interests must be understood as being the same as those of children in general. Rather, article 3, paragraph 1, implies that the best interests of a child must be assessed individually. Procedures for establishing the best interests of children individually and as a group can be found in chapter V below.

2. "By public or private social welfare institutions, courts of law, administrative authorities or legislative bodies"

25. The obligation of the States to duly consider the child's best interests is a comprehensive obligation encompassing all public and private social welfare institutions, courts of law, administrative authorities and legislative bodies involving or concerning children. Although parents are not explicitly mentioned in article 3, paragraph 1, the best interests of the child "will be their basic concern" (art. 18, para. 1).

(a) "public or private social welfare institutions"

26. These terms should not be narrowly construed or limited to social institutions *stricto sensu*, but should be understood to mean all institutions whose work and decisions impact on children and the realization of their rights. Such institutions include not only those related to economic, social and cultural rights (care, health, environment, education, business, leisure and play, etc.), but also institutions dealing with civil rights and freedoms (birth registration, protection against violence in all settings, etc.). Private social welfare institutions include private sector organizations – either for-profit or non-profit – which play a role in the provision of services that are critical to children's enjoyment of their rights, and which act on behalf of or alongside Government services as an alternative.

---

[4] General Comment No.11 (2009) on indigenous children and their rights under the Convention, para. 30.

(b) "courts of law"

27. The Committee underlines that "courts" refer to all judicial proceedings, in all instances – whether staffed by professional judges or lay persons – and all relevant procedures concerning children, without restriction. This includes conciliation, mediation and arbitration processes.

28. In criminal cases, the best interests principle applies to children in conflict (i.e. alleged, accused or recognized as having infringed) or in contact (as victims or witnesses) with the law, as well as children affected by the situation of their parents in conflict with the law. The Committee[5] underlines that protecting the child's best interests means that the traditional objectives of criminal justice, such as repression or retribution, must give way to rehabilitation and restorative justice objectives, when dealing with child offenders.

29. In civil cases, the child may be defending his or her interests directly or through a representative, in the case of paternity, child abuse or neglect, family reunification, accommodation, etc. The child may be affected by the trial, for example in procedures concerning adoption or divorce, decisions regarding custody, residence, contact or other issues which have an important impact on the life and development of the child, as well as child abuse or neglect proceedings. The courts must provide for the best interests of the child to be considered in all such situations and decisions, whether of a procedural or substantive nature, and must demonstrate that they have effectively done so.

(c) "administrative authorities"

30. The Committee emphasizes that the scope of decisions made by administrative authorities at all levels is very broad, covering decisions concerning education, care, health, the environment, living conditions, protection, asylum, immigration, access to nationality, among others. Individual decisions taken by administrative authorities in these areas must be assessed and guided by the best interests of the child, as for all implementation measures.

(d) "legislative bodies"

31. The extension of States parties' obligation to their "legislative bodies" shows clearly that article 3, paragraph 1, relates to children in

---

[5] General comment No. 10 (2007) on children's rights in juvenile justice, para. 10.

general, not only to children as individuals. The adoption of any law or regulation as well as collective agreements – such as bilateral or multilateral trade or peace treaties which affect children – should be governed by the best interests of the child. The right of the child to have his or her best interests assessed and taken as a primary consideration should be explicitly included in all relevant legislation, not only in laws that specifically concern children. This obligation extends also to the approval of budgets, the preparation and development of which require the adoption of a best-interests-of-the-child perspective for it to be child-rights sensitive.

3. "The best interests of the child"

32. The concept of the child's best interests is complex and its content must be determined on a case-by-case basis. It is through the interpretation and implementation of article 3, paragraph 1, in line with the other provisions of the Convention, that the legislator, judge, administrative, social or educational authority will be able to clarify the concept and make concrete use thereof. Accordingly, the concept of the child's best interests is flexible and adaptable. It should be adjusted and defined on an individual basis, according to the specific situation of the child or children concerned, taking into consideration their personal context, situation and needs. For individual decisions, the child's best interests must be assessed and determined in light of the specific circumstances of the particular child. For collective decisions – such as by the legislator –, the best interests of children in general must be assessed and determined in light of the circumstances of the particular group and/or children in general. In both cases, assessment and determination should be carried out with full respect for the rights contained in the Convention and its Optional Protocols.

33. The child's best interests shall be applied to all matters concerning the child or children, and taken into account to resolve any possible conflicts among the rights enshrined in the Convention or other human rights treaties. Attention must be placed on identifying possible solutions which are in the child's best interests. This implies that States are under the obligation to clarify the best interests of all children, including those in vulnerable situations, when adopting implementation measures.

34. The flexibility of the concept of the child's best interests allows it to be responsive to the situation of individual children and to evolve knowledge about child development. However, it may also leave room for manipulation; the concept of the child's best interests has been abused

by Governments and other State authorities to justify racist policies, for example; by parents to defend their own interests in custody disputes; by professionals who could not be bothered, and who dismiss the assessment of the child's best interests as irrelevant or unimportant.

35. With regard to implementation measures, ensuring that the best interests of the child are a primary consideration in legislation and policy development and delivery at all levels of Government demands a continuous process of child rights impact assessment (CRIA) to predict the impact of any proposed law, policy or budgetary allocation on children and the enjoyment of their rights, and child rights impact evaluation to evaluate the actual impact of implementation.[6]

4. "Shall be a primary consideration"

36. The best interests of a child shall be a primary consideration in the adoption of all measures of implementation. The words "shall be" place a strong legal obligation on States and mean that States may not exercise discretion as to whether children's best interests are to be assessed and ascribed the proper weight as a primary consideration in any action undertaken.

37. The expression "primary consideration" means that the child's best interests may not be considered on the same level as all other considerations. This strong position is justified by the special situation of the child: dependency, maturity, legal status and, often, voicelessness. Children have less possibility than adults to make a strong case for their own interests and those involved in decisions affecting them must be explicitly aware of their interests. If the interests of children are not highlighted, they tend to be overlooked.

38. In respect of adoption (art. 21), the right of best interests is further strengthened; it is not simply to be "**a primary** consideration" but "**the paramount** consideration". Indeed, the best interests of the child are to be the determining factor when taking a decision on adoption, but also on other issues.

39. However, since article 3, paragraph 1, covers a wide range of situations, the Committee recognizes the need for a degree of flexibility in its application. The best interests of the child – once assessed and determined – might conflict with other interests or rights (of other

---

[6] General Comment No. 5 (2003) on general measures of implementation of the Convention on the Rights of the Child, para. 45.

children, the public, parents, etc.). Potential conflicts between the best interests of a child, considered individually, and those of a group of children or children in general have to be resolved on a case-by-case basis, carefully balancing the interests of all parties and finding a suitable compromise. The same must be done if the rights of other persons are in conflict with the child's best interests. If harmonization is not possible, authorities and decision-makers will have to analyse and weigh the rights of all those concerned, bearing in mind that the right of the child to have his or her best interests taken as a primary consideration means that the child's interests have high priority and not just one of several considerations. Therefore, a larger weight must be attached to what serves the child best.

40. Viewing the best interests of the child as "primary" requires a consciousness about the place that children's interests must occupy in all actions and a willingness to give priority to those interests in all circumstances, but especially when an action has an undeniable impact on the children concerned.

B. The best interests of the child and links with other general principles of the Convention

1. The child's best interests and the right to non-discrimination (art. 2)

41. The right to non-discrimination is not a passive obligation, prohibiting all forms of discrimination in the enjoyment of rights under the Convention, but also requires appropriate proactive measures taken by the State to ensure effective equal opportunities for all children to enjoy the rights under the Convention. This may require positive measures aimed at redressing a situation of real inequality.

2. The child's best interests and the right to life, survival and development (art. 6)

42. States must create an environment that respects human dignity and ensures the holistic development of every child. In the assessment and determination of the child's best interests, the State must ensure full respect for his or her inherent right to life, survival and development.

3. The child's best interests and the right to be heard (art. 12)

43. Assessment of a child's best interests must include respect for the child's right to express his or her views freely and due weight given to said views in all matters affecting the child. This is clearly set out in the Committee's General Comment No. 12 which also highlights the inextricable links between articles 3, paragraph 1, and 12. The two articles have complementary roles: the first aims to realize the child's best interests, and the second provides the methodology for hearing the views of the child or children and their inclusion in all matters affecting the child, including the assessment of his or her best interests. Article 3, paragraph 1, cannot be correctly applied if the requirements of article 12 are not met. Similarly, article 3, paragraph 1, reinforces the functionality of article 12, by facilitating the essential role of children in all decisions affecting their lives.[7]

44. The evolving capacities of the child (art. 5) must be taken into consideration when the child's best interests and right to be heard are at stake. The Committee has already established that the more the child knows, has experienced and understands, the more the parent, legal guardian or other persons legally responsible for him or her have to transform direction and guidance into reminders and advice, and later to an exchange on an equal footing.[8] Similarly, as the child matures, his or her views shall have increasing weight in the assessment of his or her best interests. Babies and very young children have the same rights as all children to have their best interests assessed, even if they cannot express their views or represent themselves in the same way as older children. States must ensure appropriate arrangements, including representation, when appropriate, for the assessment of their best interests; the same applies for children who are not able or willing to express a view.

45. The Committee recalls that article 12, paragraph 2, of the Convention provides for the right of the child to be heard, either directly or through a representative, in any judicial or administrative proceeding affecting him or her (see further chapter V.B below).

V. Implementation: assessing and determining the child's best interests

46. As stated earlier, the "best interests of the child" is a right, a principle and a rule of procedure based on an assessment of all elements

---

[7] General Comment No. 12, paras. 70–74. [8] Ibid., para. 84.

of a child's or children's interests in a specific situation. When assessing and determining the best interests of the child in order to make a decision on a specific measure, the following steps should be followed:

(a) First, within the specific factual context of the case, find out what are the relevant elements in a best-interests assessment, give them concrete content, and assign a weight to each in relation to one another;
(b) Secondly, to do so, follow a procedure that ensures legal guarantees and proper application of the right.

47. Assessment and determination of the child's best interests are two steps to be followed when required to make a decision. The "best-interests assessment" consists in evaluating and balancing all the elements necessary to make a decision in a specific situation for a specific individual child or group of children. It is carried out by the decision-maker and his or her staff – if possible a multidisciplinary team –, and requires the participation of the child. The "best-interests determination" describes the formal process with strict procedural safeguards designed to determine the child's best interests on the basis of the best-interests assessment.

A. Best interests assessment and determination

48. Assessing the child's best interests is a unique activity that should be undertaken in each individual case, in the light of the specific circumstances of each child or group of children or children in general. These circumstances relate to the individual characteristics of the child or children concerned, such as, *inter alia*, age, sex, level of maturity, experience, belonging to a minority group, having a physical, sensory or intellectual disability, as well as the social and cultural context in which the child or children find themselves, such as the presence or absence of parents, whether the child lives with them, quality of the relationships between the child and his or her family or caregivers, the environment in relation to safety, the existence of quality alternative means available to the family, extended family or caregivers, etc.

49. Determining what is in the best interests of the child should start with an assessment of the specific circumstances that make the child unique. This implies that some elements will be used and others will not, and also influences how they will be weighted against each other. For children in general, assessing best interests involves the same elements.

50. The Committee considers it useful to draw up a non-exhaustive and non-hierarchical list of elements that could be included in a best-interests assessment by any decision-maker having to determine a child's best interests. The non-exhaustive nature of the elements in the list implies that it is possible to go beyond those and consider other factors relevant in the specific circumstances of the individual child or group of children. All the elements of the list must be taken into consideration and balanced in light of each situation. The list should provide concrete guidance, yet flexibility.

51. Drawing up such a list of elements would provide guidance for the State or decision-maker in regulating specific areas affecting children, such as family, adoption and juvenile justice laws, and if necessary, other elements deemed appropriate in accordance with its legal tradition may be added. The Committee would like to point out that, when adding elements to the list, the ultimate purpose of the child's best interests should be to ensure the full and effective enjoyment of the rights recognized in the Convention and the holistic development of the child. Consequently, elements that are contrary to the rights enshrined in the Convention or that would have an effect contrary to the rights under the Convention cannot be considered as valid in assessing what is best for a child or children.

1. Elements to be taken into account when assessing the child's best interests

52. Based on these preliminary considerations, the Committee considers that the elements to be taken into account when assessing and determining the child's best interests, as relevant to the situation in question, are as follows:

(a) **The child's views**

53. Article 12 of the Convention provides for the right of children to express their views in every decision that affects them. Any decision that does not take into account the child's views or does not give their views due weight according to their age and maturity, does not respect the possibility for the child or children to influence the determination of their best interests.

54. The fact that the child is very young or in a vulnerable situation (has a disability, belongs to a minority group, is a migrant, etc.) does

not deprive him or her of the right to express his or her views, nor reduces the weight given to the child's views in determining his or her best interests. The adoption of specific measures to guarantee the exercise of equal rights for children in such situations must be subject to an individual assessment which assures a role to the children themselves in the decision-making process, and the provision of reasonable accommodation[9] and support, where necessary, to ensure their full participation in the assessment of their best interests.

(b) The child's identity

55. Children are not a homogeneous group and therefore diversity must be taken into account when assessing their best interests. The identity of the child includes characteristics such as sex, sexual orientation, national origin, religion and beliefs, cultural identity, personality. Although children and young people share basic universal needs, the expression of those needs depends on a wide range of personal, physical, social and cultural aspects, including their evolving capacities. The right of the child to preserve his or her identity is guaranteed by the Convention (art. 8) and must be respected and taken into consideration in the assessment of the child's best interests.

56. Regarding religious and cultural identity, for example, when considering a foster home or placement for a child, due regard shall be paid to the desirability of continuity in a child's upbringing and to the child's ethnic, religious, cultural and linguistic background (art. 20, para. 3), and the decision-maker must take into consideration this specific context when assessing and determining the child's best interests. The same applies in cases of adoption, separation from or divorce of parents. Due consideration of the child's best interests implies that children have access to the culture (and language, if possible) of their country and family of origin, and the opportunity to access information about their biological family, in accordance with the legal and professional regulations of the given country (see art. 9, para. 4).

57. Although preservation of religious and cultural values and traditions as part of the identity of the child must be taken into consideration,

---

[9] See Convention on the Rights of Persons with Disabilities, art. 2: "Reasonable accommodation" means necessary and appropriate modification and adjustments not imposing a disproportionate or undue burden, where needed in a particular case, to ensure [...] the enjoyment or exercise on an equal basis with others of all human rights and fundamental freedoms.

practices that are inconsistent or incompatible with the rights established in the Convention are not in the child's best interests. Cultural identity cannot excuse or justify the perpetuation by decision-makers and authorities of traditions and cultural values that deny the child or children the rights guaranteed by the Convention.

(c) **Preservation of the family environment and maintaining relations**

58. The Committee recalls that it is indispensable to carry out the assessment and determination of the child's best interests in the context of potential separation of a child from his or her parents (arts. 9, 18 and 20). It also underscores that the elements mentioned above are concrete rights and not only elements in the determination of the best interests of the child.

59. The family is the fundamental unit of society and the natural environment for the growth and well-being of its members, particularly children (preamble of the Convention). The right of the child to family life is protected under the Convention (art. 16). The term "family" must be interpreted in a broad sense to include biological, adoptive or foster parents or, where applicable, the members of the extended family or community as provided for by local custom (art. 5).

60. Preventing family separation and preserving family unity are important components of the child protection system, and are based on the right provided for in article 9, paragraph 1, which requires "that a child shall not be separated from his or her parents against their will, except when [...] such separation is necessary for the best interests of the child". Furthermore, the child who is separated from one or both parents is entitled "to maintain personal relations and direct contact with both parents on a regular basis, except if it is contrary to the child's best interests" (art. 9, para. 3). This also extends to any person holding custody rights, legal or customary primary caregivers, foster parents and persons with whom the child has a strong personal relationship.

61. Given the gravity of the impact on the child of separation from his or her parents, such separation should only occur as a last resort measure, as when the child is in danger of experiencing imminent harm or when otherwise necessary; separation should not take place if less intrusive measures could protect the child. Before resorting to separation, the State should provide support to the parents in assuming their parental responsibilities, and restore or enhance the family's capacity to take care of the child, unless separation is necessary

to protect the child. Economic reasons cannot be a justification for separating a child from his or her parents.

62. The Guidelines for the Alternative Care of Children[10] aims to ensure that children are not placed in alternative care unnecessarily; and that where alternative care is provided, it is delivered under appropriate conditions responding to the rights and best interests of the child. In particular, "financial and material poverty, or conditions directly and uniquely imputable to such poverty, should never be the only justification for the removal of a child from parental care [...] but should be seen as a signal for the need to provide appropriate support to the family" (para. 15).

63. Likewise, a child may not be separated from his or her parents on the grounds of a disability of either the child or his or her parents.[11] Separation may be considered only in cases where the necessary assistance to the family to preserve the family unit is not effective enough to avoid a risk of neglect or abandonment of the child or a risk to the child's safety.

64. In case of separation, the State must guarantee that the situation of the child and his or her family has been assessed, where possible, by a multidisciplinary team of well-trained professionals with appropriate judicial involvement, in conformity with article 9 of the Convention, ensuring that no other option can fulfil the child's best interests.

65. When separation becomes necessary, the decision-makers shall ensure that the child maintains the linkages and relations with his or her parents and family (siblings, relatives and persons with whom the child has had strong personal relationships) unless this is contrary to the child's best interests. The quality of the relationships and the need to retain them must be taken into consideration in decisions on the frequency and length of visits and other contact when a child is placed outside the family.

66. When the child's relations with his or her parents are interrupted by migration (of the parents without the child, or of the child without his or her parents), preservation of the family unit should be taken into account when assessing the best interests of the child in decisions on family reunification.

67. The Committee is of the view that shared parental responsibilities are generally in the child's best interests. However, in decisions regarding

[10] General Assembly resolution 64/142, annex.
[11] Convention on the Rights of Persons with Disabilities, art. 23, para. 4.

parental responsibilities, the only criterion shall be what is in the best interests of the particular child. It is contrary to those interests if the law automatically gives parental responsibilities to either or both parents. In assessing the child's best interests, the judge must take into consideration the right of the child to preserve his or her relationship with both parents, together with the other elements relevant to the case.

68. The Committee encourages the ratification and implementation of the conventions of the Hague Conference on Private International Law,[12] which facilitate the application of the child's best interests and provide guarantees for its implementation in the event that the parents live in different countries.

69. In cases where the parents or other primary caregivers commit an offence, alternatives to detention should be made available and applied on a case-by-case basis, with full consideration of the likely impacts of different sentences on the best interests of the affected child or children.[13]

70. Preservation of the family environment encompasses the preservation of the ties of the child in a wider sense. These ties apply to the extended family, such as grandparents, uncles/aunts as well friends, school and the wider environment and are particularly relevant in cases where parents are separated and live in different places.

(d) Care, protection and safety of the child

71. When assessing and determining the best interests of a child or children in general, the obligation of the State to ensure the child such protection and care as is necessary for his or her well-being (art. 3, para. 2) should be taken into consideration. The terms "protection and care" must also be read in a broad sense, since their objective is not stated in limited or negative terms (such as "to protect the child from harm"), but rather in relation to the comprehensive ideal of ensuring the child's "well-being" and development. Children's well-being, in a broad sense includes their basic material, physical, educational, and emotional needs, as well as needs for affection and safety.

---

[12] These include No. 28 on the Civil Aspects of International Child Abduction, 1980; No. 33 on Protection of Children and Co-operation in Respect of Intercountry Adoption, 1993; No. 23 on the Recognition and Enforcement of Decisions Relating to Maintenance Obligations, 1973; No. 24 on the Law Applicable to Maintenance Obligations, 1973.

[13] See recommendations of the Day of general discussion on children of incarcerated parents (2011).

72. Emotional care is a basic need of children; if parents or other primary caregivers do not fulfil the child's emotional needs, action must be taken so that the child develops a secure attachment. Children need to form an attachment to a caregiver at a very early age, and such attachment, if adequate, must be sustained over time in order to provide the child with a stable environment.

73. Assessment of the child's best interests must also include consideration of the child's safety, that is, the right of the child to protection against all forms of physical or mental violence, injury or abuse (art. 19), sexual harassment, peer pressure, bullying, degrading treatment, etc.,[14] as well as protection against sexual, economic and other exploitation, drugs, labour, armed conflict, etc.(arts. 32–39).

74. Applying a best-interests approach to decision-making means assessing the safety and integrity of the child at the current time; however, the precautionary principle also requires assessing the possibility of future risk and harm and other consequences of the decision for the child's safety.

(e) Situation of vulnerability

75. An important element to consider is the child's situation of vulnerability, such as disability, belonging to a minority group, being a refugee or asylum seeker, victim of abuse, living in a street situation, etc. The purpose of determining the best interests of a child or children in a vulnerable situation should not only be in relation to the full enjoyment of all the rights provided for in the Convention, but also with regard to other human rights norms related to these specific situations, such as those covered in the Convention on the Rights of Persons with Disabilities, the Convention relating to the Status of Refugees, among others.

76. The best interests of a child in a specific situation of vulnerability will not be the same as those of all the children in the same vulnerable situation. Authorities and decision-makers need to take into account the different kinds and degrees of vulnerability of each child, as each child is unique and each situation must be assessed according to the child's uniqueness. An individualized assessment of each child's history from birth should be carried out, with regular reviews by a

---

[14] General Comment No. 13 (2011) on the right of the child to freedom from all forms of violence.

multidisciplinary team and recommended reasonable accommodation throughout the child's development process.

(f) **The child's right to health**

77. The child's right to health (art. 24) and his or her health condition are central in assessing the child's best interest. However, if there is more than one possible treatment for a health condition or if the outcome of a treatment is uncertain, the advantages of all possible treatments must be weighed against all possible risks and side effects, and the views of the child must also be given due weight based on his or her age and maturity. In this respect, children should be provided with adequate and appropriate information in order to understand the situation and all the relevant aspects in relation to their interests, and be allowed, when possible, to give their consent in an informed manner.[15]

78. For example, as regards adolescent health, the Committee[16] has stated that States parties have the obligation to ensure that all adolescents, both in and out of school, have access to adequate information that is essential for their health and development in order to make appropriate health behaviour choices. This should include information on use and abuse of tobacco, alcohol and other substances, diet, appropriate sexual and reproductive information, dangers of early pregnancy, prevention of HIV/AIDS and of sexually transmitted diseases. Adolescents with a psycho-social disorder have the right to be treated and cared for in the community in which he or she lives, to the extent possible. Where hospitalization or placement in a residential institution is necessary, the best interests of the child must be assessed prior to taking a decision and with respect for the child's views; the same considerations are valid for younger children. The health of the child and possibilities for treatment may also be part of a best-interests assessment and determination with regard to other types of significant decisions (e.g. granting a residence permit on humanitarian grounds).

---

[15] General Comment No. 15 (2013) on the right of the child to the enjoyment of the highest attainable standard of health (art. 24), para. 31.

[16] General Comment No. 4 (2003) on adolescent health and development in the context of the Convention on the Rights of the Child.

(g) The child's right to education

79. It is in the best interests of the child to have access to quality education, including early childhood education, non-formal or informal education and related activities, free of charge. All decisions on measures and actions concerning a specific child or a group of children must respect the best interests of the child or children, with regard to education. In order to promote education, or better quality education, for more children, States parties need to have well-trained teachers and other professionals working in different education-related settings, as well as a child-friendly environment and appropriate teaching and learning methods, taking into consideration that education is not only an investment in the future, but also an opportunity for joyful activities, respect, participation and fulfilment of ambitions. Responding to this requirement and enhancing children's responsibilities to overcome the limitations of their vulnerability of any kind, will be in their best interests.

2. Balancing the elements in the best-interests assessment

80. It should be emphasized that the basic best-interests assessment is a general assessment of all relevant elements of the child's best interests, the weight of each element depending on the others. Not all the elements will be relevant to every case, and different elements can be used in different ways in different cases. The content of each element will necessarily vary from child to child and from case to case, depending on the type of decision and the concrete circumstances, as will the importance of each element in the overall assessment.

81. The elements in the best-interests assessment may be in conflict when considering a specific case and its circumstances. For example, preservation of the family environment may conflict with the need to protect the child from the risk of violence or abuse by parents. In such situations, the elements will have to be weighted against each other in order to find the solution that is in the best interests of the child or children.

82. In weighing the various elements, one needs to bear in mind that the purpose of assessing and determining the best interests of the child is to ensure the full and effective enjoyment of the rights recognized in the Convention and its Optional Protocols, and the holistic development of the child.

83. There might be situations where "protection" factors affecting a child (e.g. which may imply limitation or restriction of rights) need to be

assessed in relation to measures of "empowerment" (which implies full exercise of rights without restriction). In such situations, the age and maturity of the child should guide the balancing of the elements. The physical, emotional, cognitive and social development of the child should be taken into account to assess the level of maturity of the child.

84. In the best-interests assessment, one has to consider that the capacities of the child will evolve. Decision-makers should therefore consider measures that can be revised or adjusted accordingly, instead of making definitive and irreversible decisions. To do this, they should not only assess the physical, emotional, educational and other needs at the specific moment of the decision, but should also consider the possible scenarios of the child's development, and analyse them in the short and long term. In this context, decisions should assess continuity and stability of the child's present and future situation.

B. Procedural safeguards to guarantee the implementation of the child's best interests

85. To ensure the correct implementation of the child's right to have his or her best interests taken as a primary consideration, some child-friendly procedural safeguards must be put in place and followed. As such, the concept of the child's best interests is a rule of procedure (see para. 6 (b) above).

86. While public authorities and organizations making decisions that concern children must act in conformity with the obligation to assess and determine the child's best interests, people who make decisions concerning children on a daily basis (parents, guardians, teachers, etc.) are not expected to follow strictly this two-step procedure, even though decisions made in everyday life must also respect and reflect the child's best interests.

87. States must put in place formal processes, with strict procedural safeguards, designed to assess and determine the child's best interests for decisions affecting the child, including mechanisms for evaluating the results. States must develop transparent and objective processes for all decisions made by legislators, judges or administrative authorities, especially in areas which directly affect the child or children.

88. The Committee invites States and all persons who are in a position to assess and determine the child's best interests to pay special attention to the following safeguards and guarantees:

(a) Right of the child to express his or her own views

89. A vital element of the process is communicating with children to facilitate meaningful child participation and identify their best interests. Such communication should include informing children about the process and possible sustainable solutions and services, as well as collecting information from children and seeking their views.

90. Where the child wishes to express his or her views and where this right is fulfilled through a representative, the latter's obligation is to communicate accurately the views of the child. In situations where the child's views are in conflict with those of his or her representative, a procedure should be established to allow the child to approach an authority to establish a separate representation for the child (e.g. a guardian ad litem), if necessary.

91. The procedure for assessing and determining the best interests of children as a group is, to some extent, different from that regarding an individual child. When the interests of a large number of children are at stake, Government institutions must find ways to hear the views of a representative sample of children and give due consideration to their opinions when planning measures or making legislative decisions which directly or indirectly concern the group, in order to ensure that all categories of children are covered. There are many examples of how to do this, including children's hearings, children's parliaments, children-led organizations, children's unions or other representative bodies, discussions at school, social networking websites, etc.

(b) Establishment of facts

92. Facts and information relevant to a particular case must be obtained by well-trained professionals in order to draw up all the elements necessary for the best-interests assessment. This could involve interviewing persons close to the child, other people who are in contact with the child on a daily basis, witnesses to certain incidents, among others. Information and data gathered must be verified and analysed prior to being used in the child's or children's best-interests assessment.

(c) Time perception

93. The passing of time is not perceived in the same way by children and adults. Delays in or prolonged decision-making have particularly adverse effects on children as they evolve. It is therefore advisable

that procedures or processes regarding or impacting children be prioritized and completed in the shortest time possible. The timing of the decision should, as far as possible, correspond to the child's perception of how it can benefit him or her, and the decisions taken should be reviewed at reasonable intervals as the child develops and his or her capacity to express his or her views evolves. All decisions on care, treatment, placement and other measures concerning the child must be reviewed periodically in terms of his or her perception of time, and his or her evolving capacities and development (art. 25).

(d) Qualified professionals

94. Children are a diverse group, with each having his or her own characteristics and needs that can only be adequately assessed by professionals who have expertise in matters related to child and adolescent development. This is why the formal assessment process should be carried out in a friendly and safe atmosphere by professionals trained in, *inter alia*, child psychology, child development and other relevant human and social development fields, who have experience working with children and who will consider the information received in an objective manner. As far as possible, a multidisciplinary team of professionals should be involved in assessing the child's best interests.

95. The assessment of the consequences of alternative solutions must be based on general knowledge (i.e. in the areas of law, sociology, education, social work, psychology, health, etc.) of the likely consequences of each possible solution for the child, given his or her individual characteristics and past experience.

(e) Legal representation

96. The child will need appropriate legal representation when his or her best interests are to be formally assessed and determined by courts and equivalent bodies. In particular, in cases where a child is referred to an administrative or judicial procedure involving the determination of his or her best interests, he or she should be provided with a legal representative, in addition to a guardian or representative of his or her views, when there is a potential conflict between the parties in the decision.

(f) Legal reasoning

97. In order to demonstrate that the right of the child to have his or her best interests assessed and taken as a primary consideration has been respected, any decision concerning the child or children must be motivated, justified and explained. The motivation should state explicitly all the factual circumstances regarding the child, what elements have been found relevant in the best-interests assessment, the content of the elements in the individual case, and how they have been weighted to determine the child's best interests. If the decision differs from the views of the child, the reason for that should be clearly stated. If, exceptionally, the solution chosen is not in the best interests of the child, the grounds for this must be set out in order to show that the child's best interests were a primary consideration despite the result. It is not sufficient to state in general terms that other considerations override the best interests of the child; all considerations must be explicitly specified in relation to the case at hand, and the reason why they carry greater weight in the particular case must be explained. The reasoning must also demonstrate, in a credible way, why the best interests of the child were not strong enough to be outweigh the other considerations. Account must be taken of those circumstances in which the best interests of the child must be the paramount consideration (see paragraph 38 above).

(g) Mechanisms to review or revise decisions

98. States should establish mechanisms within their legal systems to appeal or revise decisions concerning children when a decision seems not to be in accordance with the appropriate procedure of assessing and determining the child's or children's best interests. There should always be the possibility to request a review or to appeal such a decision at the national level. Mechanisms should be made known to the child and be accessible by him or her directly or by his or her legal representative, if it is considered that the procedural safeguards had not been respected, the facts are wrong, the best-interests assessment had not been adequately carried out or that competing considerations had been given too much weight. The reviewing body must look into all these aspects.

(h) Child-rights impact assessment (CRIA)

99. As mentioned above, the adoption of all measures of implementation should also follow a procedure that ensures that the child's best

interests are a primary consideration. The child-rights impact assessment (CRIA) can predict the impact of any proposed policy, legislation, regulation, budget or other administrative decision which affect children and the enjoyment of their rights and should complement ongoing monitoring and evaluation of the impact of measures on children's rights.[17] CRIA needs to be built into Government processes at all levels and as early as possible in the development of policy and other general measures in order to ensure good governance for children's rights. Different methodologies and practices may be developed when undertaking CRIA. At a minimum, they must use the Convention and its Optional Protocols as a framework, in particular ensuring that the assessments are underpinned by the general principles and have special regard for the differentiated impact of the measure(s) under consideration on children. The impact assessment itself could be based on input from children, civil society and experts, as well as from relevant Government departments, academic research and experiences documented in the country or elsewhere. The analysis should result in recommendations for amendments, alternatives and improvements and be made publicly available.[18]

VI. Dissemination

100. The Committee recommends that States widely disseminate the present general comment to parliaments, governments and the judiciary, nationally and locally. It should also be made known to children – including those in situations of exclusion –, all professionals working for and with children (including judges, lawyers, teachers, guardians, social workers, staff of public or private welfare institutions, health staff, teachers, etc.) and civil society at large. To do this, the general comment should be translated into relevant languages, child-friendly/appropriate versions should be made available, conferences, seminars, workshops and other events should be held to share best practices on how best to implement it. It should also be incorporated into the formal pre- and in-service training of all concerned professionals and technical staff.

---

[17] General Comment No. 16 (2013) on State obligations regarding the impact of the business sector on children's rights, paras. 78–81.

[18] States may draw guidance from the Report of the Special Rapporteur on the right to food on Guiding principles on human rights impact assessments of trade and investment agreements (A/HRC/19/59/Add.5).

101. States should include information in their periodic reporting to the Committee on the challenges they face and the measures they have taken to apply and respect the child's best interests in all judicial and administrative decisions and other actions concerning the child as an individual, as well as at all stages of the adoption of implementation measures concerning children in general or as a specific group.

INDEX

Aboriginal child placement principle, 333
ACRWC. *See* African Charter on the Rights and Welfare of the Child
administrative authorities
  Article 3(1) and, 58
  defined, 390
adoptions. *See also* intercountry adoptions
  Article 3(1) and, 197
  Article 8 and, 348
  Article 21 and, 197–199
  under child protection laws, 342
  children's right to identity in, 176
  children's rights in, 72–76
    in England, 73–74
    in Italy, 76
    in Scotland, 74–75
  de facto, 190–191
  domestic, under Hague Inter-Country Adoption Convention, 229
  in ECHR, 72–76
  ECtHR and, 72–73, 76
  in England, 200–204
    children's rights as part of, 73–74
    children's rights in, 73–74
    judicial approaches to, 202–204
    legislation for, 200–202
    paramountcy principle and, 202–204
  equitable, 191
  within India, 223–226
    gender bias in, 224
    restrictions on, 223
  involuntary, 347–349
  in Nepal, 218–222
    informal, 219–220
    NCO oversight of, 219
  parental orders compared to, 176–177
  in Scotland, 74–75, 204–212
    absence of threshold criteria for, 211–212
    compulsory supervision orders for, 208–209
    judicial approaches to, 209–212
    legislation for, 204–209
    paramountcy principle and, 205
    permanence orders for, 207–208
    by step-parents, 212
  in South Africa, under customary law, 194
African Americans
  in child welfare system, 142
  in developmental equality model, 118–119
African Charter on the Rights and Welfare of the Child (ACRWC), 8, 12–13, 28
  best interests principle in, 186–188
  children's rights in, 186–188
American Bar Association (ABA), 253
American Psychiatric Association, 269
American Psychological Association (APA), 253
APA. *See* American Psychological Association
appeals. *See* final appeals/appellate court
appellate courts. *See* final appeals/appellate court
Arthur, Raymond, 297

artificial insemination. *See* assisted reproduction
assisted reproduction, 164. *See also* surrogacy
Australia. *See also* New South Wales, Australia
  best interests principle in, 65
  child custody law in, 258–259
  child protection agencies in, 140
  child protection law in, 132–134
    poor outcomes for children under, 143
    systemic racism in, 141–142
  domestic violence laws in, 258–262
    safety first paradigm in, 258–259
  relocation cases for particular child in, 85–86
  significant harm concept in, 132–134
  UNCRC delegations from, 28

baby switching
  historical precedents for, 180
  legislative measures for, 184
    international benchmarks for, 184–188
  in South Africa, 181–182
    best interests principle as factor in, 191–193
    cultural tradition as influence on, 194
    under customary law, 193–195
    de facto adoptions and, 190–191
    equitable adoptions and, 191
    paramountcy principle and, 192–193
    parental rights and responsibilities in, 189–190
    psychological parenthood and, 190–191
  under UNCRC standards, 184–186
Bala, Nicholas, 11–12
belief. *See* religious belief
best interests principle, 10–12, 33–35, 382–384. *See also* developmental equality model
  academic critique of, 52
  in African Charter on the Rights and Welfare of the Child, 186–188
  in Article 3(2), 40–41
  in Article 9(1), 54
  in Article 12, 34–35
  in Article 18, 26–27
  in Article 37(c), 54
  in Article 40(2)(b)(iii), 54
  assessment of, 395–404
    procedural safeguards in, 404–408
  in Australia, 65
  in Canada, 94
    in final appellate court cases, 94
  in care proceedings, 326–329
  child protection laws and, 343–345, 356
  child sexual abuse by clerics and, 315–316
  child-offenders and, 298–299
    in Article 3(1), 298
    for prosecuted children, 305–307
    youth perspectives on, 296–309
  children refusing contact with parents and, 265
    assessment of, 266
  children's views under, 14–15, 396–397
  Committee on the Rights of the Child and, 58–59
  content of, 11–12
  critique of, 22
  decisions about children and, 101–102
    defined, 99–100, 111
    in private law cases, 102
    in public law cases, 102
  decisions affecting children and
    in ambiguous and contestable instances, 109–110
    in custodial sentencing, 105
    defined, 99–100, 111
    in deportation cases, 106–107
    ECHR and, 108–109
    ECtHR and, 108–109
    in extradition cases, 106–107
    through indirect means, 103–107
    in international cases, 103–105

best interests principle (cont.)
  in relocation cases, 110
  defined, 48, 341, 391–392
  determination of, 395–404
  development of, as free-standing principle, 52–56
  dissemination of, 408–409
  drafting process for, 53–54
  ECtHR and, 101
  for Eekelaar, in relocation cases, 290–291
  in final appellate court, 91–96
    adult-focused prioritisation and, 92–93
    in Canada, 94
    in New Zealand, 95
    true prioritisation of, 93–95
    in U.K., 92–94
  flexibility of, 36
  foundation of, 21–22, 35–39
  gender biases and, 37
  in Germany, 64
  goals of, 51–52
  Holy See and, 315–316
  implementation of, 394–408
  indeterminacy of, 37–38
  in intercountry adoptions, 215–218
    from India, 225–226
  in international documents, 188
  international support for, 63–64
  as interpretive legal principle, 46–47
  in Ireland, 64
  known biological father disputes and, 149–152
    under Article 3(1), 150–152, 157–158
    genetic definitions in, 149
    role of parenthood in, 157–159
    in U.K., 149–152
  language use in, 55–56
  in New Zealand, 95
    in relocation disputes, 281–285, 288–290
  in Norway, 63
  in paragraph 1, 27–29
  preservation of family environment, 398–400
  prioritisation as factor in, 12–13
  prosecuted children under, 305–307
  religious belief and, 310–311
  relocation law and, 280–285
    alternative interpretations of, 284–285
    in Australia, 288–290
    family members' perspectives on, 288–290
    for international cross-border cases, 283–284
    jurisdictional approach to, 281–285
    long-term impact on children, 286–288
    in New Zealand, 281–285, 288–290
    parental emotional stability and, 282
    parental separation as influence in, 285–286
    prioritizing of, 292
    research evidence on, 285–290
    risk and resilience perspective on, 286
    in U.K., 282–285, 288–290
  as right, 56–59
  right to be heard in, 394
  right to education in, 403
  right to health in, 402
  right to life, survival and development in, 393
  right to non-discrimination in, 393
  as rule of procedure, 55
  Russian Federation and, 45–46
  the Seychelles and, 45–46
  situation of vulnerability in, 401–402
  status of parental relationships and, 36–37
  surrogacy under, 165–166, 178–179
  in Sweden, 63
  in U.K., 92–94
  vagueness of, 11–12
biological parentage
  competing concepts of, 152–155
    under international legislation, 153
    in U.K., 154–155
  defined, 149, 152–153

INDEX 413

in international legislation, 152
parental orders under, 166–169
judicial generalities for, 155–157
known biological father disputes and, 149–152
under Article 3(1), 150–152, 157–158
genetic definitions in, 149
role of parenthood in, 157–159
in U.K., 149–152
legal reform of, 163–164
assisted reproduction and, 164
non-heterosexual relationships and, 163–164
parental authority and, 153
legal claims for, 154
for step-parents, 164
parental responsibility and, 153
in South Africa, 181
statutory particulars of, 155–157
Boezaart, Trynie, 10
Bolivia, constitution of, 28
Bronfenbrenner, Uri, 116

Canada
best interests principle
in final appellate court cases, 94
biological parentage in, legislative definitions for, 151
child protection law in, 132–133
poor outcomes for children under, 143
systemic racism in, 141–142
family law in, 234
parenting law in, 234–238
custody assessors in, 237
for heterosexual parents, 233
joint legal custody under, 236–238
parenting plans, 237
shared parenting, 238
relocation cases for particular child in, 83–85
significant harm concept in, 132–133
UNCRC delegation from, 28
care proceedings, bests interests in, 326–329
Cashmore, Judy, 11–12

Catholic Church. *See* Holy See
CCADV. *See* Colorado Coalition Against Domestic Violence
CDF. *See* Congregation for the Doctrine of Faith
Centre for Youth and Criminal Justice (CYCJ) research project, 307–309
Charter of Fundamental Rights of the European Union, 28
child alienation, 266–278
as child-focused, 279
child's voice and, 274–275
custody transfers and, 271–272
domestic abuse and, 270–271
early neutral evaluation of, 274
estrangement and, 272
through family systems framework, 268–269
friendly parent provisions and, 271–272
IPV and, 270
multiple causes of, 269
parental causes of, 269
child custody law
in Australia, 258–259
children refusing contact with parents under, 266–267, 272–278
child alienation and, 271–272
conflict management and minimization, 275–277
enforcement of court orders, 277–278
high conflict identification and intervention in, 273–275
joint custody and, 276
parent coordinators, 276–277
parenting deficits as factor in, 278
parenting plans, 275–276
primary role of judges, 273
shared parenting in, 276
therapeutic interventions in, 277
in Colorado, 256–258
safety provisions in, 258
domestic violence as influence on, 252–253
fathers' rights movement and, 251

child custody law (cont.)
  joint custody movement and, 251
  in law reform movement, 251–262
  PAS and, 252–253
  rebuttable presumption approach, 253–254
  safety as priority under, 254, 258
child development, 26
child protection agencies, 132–133, 137–139
  in Australia, 140
  limitations to intervention by, 139–141
  in New Zealand, 140
  in U.S., 140
child protection laws. *See also* well-being
  adoption cases under, 342
  in Canada, 132–133
    intervention legalistic model of, 132–133
    poor outcomes for children under, 143
    systemic racism in, 141–142
  under ECHR, 342, 345–347
  ecological approach to, 144–146
  under ECtHR, 342
    assessment reports, 349–351
    best interests principle and, 343–345, 356
    international case studies, 351–355
    for involuntary adoptions, 347–349
    judicial discretion for, 343–345, 356
    methodological approach to, 345–347
  exosystems and, 145–146
  failure of, 132
  intervention legalistic model of, 131–141
    in Australia, 132–134
    in Canada, 132–133
    through child protection agencies, 132–133, 137–141
    as counter-productive, 136–139
    limitations of, 139–141
    in New Zealand, 132–133, 135–136
    resources for, 141
    in Scotland, 134
    significant harm concept in, 131, 133–139
    in U.K., 132–134
  macrosystems and, 145–146
  microsystems and, 145–146
  ontogenic development and, 145–146
  poor outcomes for children, 142–144
    in Australia, 143
    in Canada, 143
    colonialism as influence on, 143–144
    in New Zealand, 143
  state responsibilities for, 341–343
  systemic racism in, 141–142
  threshold criteria for, 131
child sexual abuse, by clerics, 320
  autonomy of church and, 319
  best interests principle and, 315–316
  CDF and, 322
  human rights treaties and, 313–314
  extraterritorial applicability of, 316–321
  institutional implications for, 321–324
  norms and procedures for, 321–324
  OPSC and, 315, 323–324
  penal jurisdiction for, 323
  UNCRC obligations, 323–324
child-offenders
  best interests principle and, 298–299
  in Article 3(1), 298
  for prosecuted children, 305–307
  youth perspectives on, 296–309
  as legal paradox, 297–298
  perceptions of, 295–296
  prosecuted children
    under best interests standard, 305–307
    under Scottish law, 303
  public interest and, 298
  rights of, 296–298

under Scottish law, 299–305
   under Article 3, 300–305
   legal mechanisms for, 299–300
   legislative provisions, 301–303
   paramountcy principle and, 301
   prosecuted children and, 303
   prosecution statistics for, 300
   temporal dimensions of, 304–305
   welfare principle in, 300–303
 in U.K., 297
children refusing contact with parents
 best interests principle and, 265
 assessment of, 266
 child alienation and, 266–278
   as child-focused, 279
   child's voice and, 274–275
   custody transfers and, 271–272
   domestic abuse and, 270–271
   early neutral evaluation of, 274
   estrangement and, 272
   through family systems
      framework, 268–269
   friendly parent provisions and,
      271–272
   IPV and, 270
   multiple causes of, 269
   parental causes of, 269
 in custody cases, 266–267, 272–278
   child alienation and, 271–272
   conflict management and
      minimization, 275–277
   enforcement of court orders,
      277–278
   high conflict identification and
      intervention in, 273–275
   joint custody and, 276
   parent coordinators, 276–277
   parenting deficits as factor in, 278
   parenting plans, 275–276
   primary role of judges, 273
   shared parenting in, 276
   therapeutic interventions in, 277
 during divorce, 266–267
 high conflict as factor in, 266–272
   identification of, 273–275
   interventions for, 273–275
 legal discretion for, 265
 legal judgments against, 266

 parental alienation syndrome and,
      267–269
   diagnostic criteria for, 269
   skepticism of, 270
 as unnatural, 266
Children's Courts, in New South Wales,
      Australia
 best interests principle in, judicial
      considerations for, 331–333
 children's views as factor in,
      333–334
 clinical assessment reports, 335–338
 decision-making in, 330–331
 forms of evidence for, 330–331
 judicial alignment in, 335–338
 mixed-method research in,
      330–331
 security assessments by, 338
 social science evidence in, value of,
      338–340
children's rights. *See also* child
      protection laws; children
      refusing contact with parents;
      well-being
 in ACRWC, 186–188
 in adoptions, 72–76
   in England, 73–74
   in Italy, 76
   in Scotland, 74–75
 Article 3(1) and, 62–66
   in domestic law, 62–64, 99
   language in, 65–66
 Article 3(2) and, 68
 for child-offenders, 296–298
 components of, 3
 to dignity, 26
 under ECHR, 68–70
   in adoptions, 72–76
   in Article 8, 71–72
   decision-making protections as
      part of, 78–80
   protection of family life as part of,
      70–72
   protection of future relationships
      as part of, 72–76
   U.K. violations of, 68–69, 73–74
   welfare protections as part of,
      76–78

children's rights. (cont.)
  in ECtHR, 72
    in adoptions, 72–73, 76
    best interests principle and, 101
    decision-making protections as part of, 78–79
    protection of family life as part of, 70–72
    welfare protections as part of, 76–77
  to freedom, 26
  to health, 26
  in Ireland, 69–70
  opponents of, 3
  opposition to, 65
  in South Africa, 184–186
  in U.K., 68–69
    in adoptions, 73–75
  under UNCRC, 184–186
  with working mothers, 24
child-rights impact assessment (CRIA), 407–408
Cismas, Ioana, 11–12
Claire, Alison, 334
Cleland, Alison, 15
Colorado, U.S., child custody law in, 256–258
  law reform movement and, 254–258
  statutory comparisons for, 262–263
  safety provisions in, 258
Colorado Coalition Against Domestic Violence (CCADV), 257
Committee on the Rights of the Child, 58–59
compulsory supervision orders, for adoptions, 208–209
Congregation for the Doctrine of Faith (CDF), 322
co-parenting principle, 245
Council of Europe, 61
  intercountry adoption and, 216–217
courts of law
  Article 3(1) and, 58
  defined, 390
CRIA. *See* child-rights impact assessment
custodial sentencing, 105

custody assessors, in Canada, 237
custody cases. *See* child custody law
CYCJ research project. *See* Centre for Youth and Criminal Justice research project

decision-making protections
  in Children's Courts, 330–331
  under ECHR, 78–80
  in ECtHR, 78–79
decisions about children, in best interests principle, 101–102
  defined, 99–100, 111
  in private law cases, 102
  in public law cases, 102
decisions affecting children, best interests principle and
  in ambiguous and contestable instances, 109–110
  in custodial sentencing, 105
  defined, 99–100, 111
  in deportation cases, 106–107
  ECHR and, 108–109
  ECtHR and, 108–109
  in extradition cases, 106–107
  through indirect means, 103–107
  in international cases, 103–105
  in relocation cases, 110
deportation cases
  in decisions affecting children, 106–107
  decisions affecting children in, 106–107
  of particular child, 91–95
developmental equality model
  African American males in, 118–119
  ecological perspective for, 115–129
  exosystems in, 116
  limitations of, 118–129
  macrosystems in, 116–118
  mesosystems in, 116
  microsystems in, 116–118
  risk and resilience model in, 121–122
  function of, 112
  as integrative model, 126–129
  adaptive cultures in, 128–129
  component parts of, 127–128

purpose of, 113–114
PVEST and, 122–126
　coping strategies in, 125–126
　risk contributors in, 123–125
　Roma children in, 118–119
　in U.S. law, 113
dignity, as right, 26
divorce, children refusing contact with parents during, 266–267
domestic adoptions. See adoptions
domestic violence, protections against. See also intimate partner violence
　child alienation and, 270–271
　child custody law influenced by, 252–253
　incidence rates for, 250
　law reform movement and, 249–250
　　in Australia, 258–262
　　for child custody law, 251–262
　　in Colorado, 254–258
　　law enforcement in, 250
　　Protective Parents Movement, 255–256
　　stages of, 251–262
　　statutory comparisons, 262–263
　　under UNCRC, 263
　　Wingspread Conference, 254–255
Donnelly, Jack, 3
Dowd, Nancy E., 11–12

ECHR. See European Convention on Human Rights
ECtHR. See European Court of Human Rights
Eekelaar, John, 13, 38
　on best interests principle, in relocation cases, 290–291
Elrod, Linda D., 16
England and Wales
　adoptions in, 200–204
　　children's rights as part of, 73–74
　　judicial approaches to, 202–204
　　legislation for, 200–202
　　paramountcy principle and, 202–204
　relocation cases in, 282–285

equal parenting time, 240–241. See also Bill C-560
equality. See developmental equality model
equitable adoptions, 191
essentialism, 295
estrangement, 272
Ethiopia, constitution of, 28
European Convention on Human Rights (ECHR)
　child protection laws under, 342, 345–347
　children's rights under, 68–70
　　in adoptions, 72–76
　　in Article 8, 71–72, 101
　　decision-making protections as part of, 78–80
　　protection of family life as part of, 70–72
　　protection of future relationships as part of, 72–76
　　U.K. violations of, 68–69, 73–74
　　welfare protections as part of, 76–78
　goals of, 68
　as living instrument, 68
　surrogacy time limit provisions under, 172–173
European Convention on the Exercise of Children's Rights 1995, 8, 28, 188
European Court of Human Rights (ECtHR), 8, 68, 321
　child protection laws under, 342
　　assessment reports for, 349–351
　　best interests principle and, 343–345, 356
　　international case studies, 351–355
　　for involuntary adoptions, 347–349
　　judicial discretion for, 343–345, 356
　　methodological approach to, 345–347
　children's rights in, 72
　　in adoptions, 72–73, 76
　　best interests principle and, 101

European Court of Human Rights (ECtHR) (cont.)
  decision-making protections as part of, 78–79
  protection of family life as part of, 70–72
  welfare protections as part of, 76–77
  Hague Convention on the Civil Aspects of International Child Abduction, 77
Every Child Matters: Change for Children initiative, 139–141
extradition cases
  in decisions affecting children, 106–107
  for particular child, 91–95

families, family life and. *See also* parents
  in Article 5, 3
  protections of, under ECHR, 70–72
  in Article 8, 71–72
family law. *See also* child custody law; child protection laws; domestic violence; joint legal custody
  in Canada, 234
family systems framework, 268–269
Farson, Richard, 3
fathers' rights movement, 251
Fiji, constitution of, 28
final appeals/appellate court
  best interests principle in, for particular child, 91–96
    adult-focused prioritisation and, 92–93
    in Canada, 94
    in New Zealand, 95
    true prioritisation of, 93–95
    in U.K., 92–94
  deportation cases, 91–95
  extradition cases, 91–95
  fundamental principles of justice in, 90–91
  Hague Convention cases, 91–95

parental rights cases for particular child, 87–90
paramountcy principle in, 87–88
  in U.K., 87–90
  in U.S., 88–89
purpose of, 81
relocation cases for particular child, 83–87
  in Australia, 85–86
  in Canada, 83–85
  in New Zealand, 86–87
Francis (Pope), 323–325
freedom, as right, 26
friendly parent provisions, 271–272

Garcia Coll, Cynthia, 126–129
Gardner, Richard, 252–253, 268
  parental alienation syndrome and, 267–269
  diagnostic criteria for, 269
  skepticism of, 270
gender biases, 37
  in India adoptions, 224
gender neutrality, 29–30
General Comments, on Article, 32, 48
George, Rob, 103, 110
Germany, best interests principle in, 64
guardians. *See* legal guardians
Guidelines on Child-friendly Justice, 61

Hague Convention cases, for particular child, 91–95
Hague Convention on Child Protection 1996, 103
Hague Convention on the Civil Aspects of International Child Abduction 1980, 77, 82, 103–104
Hague Intercountry Adoption Convention 1993, 214–215, 222, 225–226
  heritage rights and, 226
  preference for domestic adoptions, 229
Hammarberg, Thomas, 3–4

Hampson, Françoise, 317
Hashmi, Shabnam, 223
health, as right, 26
Henaghan, Mark, 14, 284–285
heritage rights, 226
Holder, Eric, 256
Holt, John, 3
Holy See
  autonomy of church and, 319
  best interests principle and, 315–316
  CDF and, 322
  human rights treaties and, 313–314
    extraterritorial applicability of, 316–321
    international legal status for, 311–316
  Lateran Treaty and, 312, 314–315
  loss of statehood for, 312
  moral authority of, 319
  norms and procedures for, 321–324
  OPSC and, 315, 323–324
  UNCRC obligations, 323–324
Howard, Rhoda, 3
human rights. *See also* children's rights; European Convention on Human Rights; rights
  Holy See and, 313–314
    extraterritorial applicability for, 316–321
  intercountry adoptions and, 217
    implementation of, challenges in, 227

identity. *See* right to identity
identity contact, 160
ILO. *See* International Labour Organisation
indeterminacy
  of best interests principle, 37–38
  welfare checklists and, 38
India, 222–226
  adoptions within, 223–226
    gender bias in, 224
    restrictions on, 223
  child population in, 222
  intercountry adoptions from, 223–226
    best interests principle in, 225–226
    under Hague Inter-Country Adoption Convention, 222, 225–226
    scandals as result of, 225
    as sender country, 213
integrative model, 126–129
  adaptive cultures in, 128–129
  component parts of, 127–128
intent, in parental orders, 175–176
intercountry adoptions
  acceleration of, 214–218
  under Article 3, 228–229
  under Article 21, 214–215
  under best interests principle, 215–218
  Council of Europe and, 216–217
  under Hague Inter-Country Adoption Convention, 214–215
  heritage rights and, 226
  human rights considerations in, 217
    implementation of, challenges in, 227
  implementation strategies for, 226–229
  from India, 223–226
    best interests principle in, 225–226
    under Hague Inter-Country Adoption Convention, 222, 225–226
    scandals as result of, 225
    as sender country, 213
  from Nepal, 213, 218–222
    during civil conflicts, 220
    historical increase in, 219–220
    international restrictions on, 221
    as sender country, 213
  receiving countries for, 217
  from sender countries, 213–214
  U.K. and, 217
  under UNCRC, 226–229
  U.S. and, 217
International Federation of Human Rights, 29

International Labour Organisation (ILO), 30
intervention legalistic model, of child protection law, 131–141
  in Australia, 132–134
  in Canada, 132–133
  through child protection agencies, 132–133, 137–141
  as counter-productive, 136–139
  limitations of, 139–141
  in New Zealand, 132–133, 135–136
  resources for, 141
  in Scotland, 134
  significant harm concept in, 131, 133–139
  in U.K., 132–134
intimate partner violence (IPV), 241–242
  child alienation and, 270
  defined, 241
involuntary adoptions, 347–349
IPV. *See* intimate partner violence
Ireland
  best interests principle in, 64
  children's rights in, 69–70
Italy, adoptions in, 76

Johnson, Janet, 255
joint legal custody
  in Canada, 236–238
    through parenting plans, 237
    through shared parenting, 238
  child custody law and, 251
  children refusing contact with parents and, 276
judges, in child custody cases, 273

Kenya, constitution of, 28
Kilkelly, Ursula, 2–10
known biological father disputes
  best interests principle and, 149–152
    under Article 3(1), 150–152, 157–158
  genetic definitions in, 149
  role of parenthood in, 157–159
  in U.K., 149–152
identity contact in, 160
judicial consensus on, 159–163
  broad consensus, 159–160
  expansion of terminology for, 161–163
  lack of, 160–163
  social research as influence on, 162–163
legal reform for, 163–164

language use, in best interests principle, 55–56, 65–66
Lateran Treaty, 312, 314–315
law reform movement, for domestic violence protections, 249–250
  in Australia, 258–262
  for child custody law, 251–262
  in Colorado, 254–258
  law enforcement in, 250
  Protective Parents Movement, 255–256
  stages of, 251–262
  statutory comparisons for, 262–263
  under UNCRC, 263
  Wingspread Conference, 254–255
LeBlanc, Lawrence J., 3
legal guardians, 29–30
  well-being of children influenced by, 42
legal parents, defined, 153
legislation, best interests principle and, 46–47
legislative bodies, defined, 390–391

Macfarlane, Lesley-Anne Barnes, 12
margin of appreciation doctrine, 350
maximum contact principle, 245
McDiarmid, Claire, 13–14
Milanovic, Marco, 321
Millennium Development Goals, 40–41, 48–49
Mnookin, Robert, 22
moral authority, of Holy See, 319
Munby, James, 74, 163, 170
Muntarbhorn, Vitit, 3

NCO. *See* Nepal Children's
    Organisation
Nepal, 218–222
  adoption in, 218–222
    informal, 219–220
    NCO oversight of, 219
  civil conflict in, 218
    intercountry adoptions during,
      220
  intercountry adoptions from, 213,
    218–222
    during civil conflicts, 220
    historical increase in, 219–220
    international restrictions on, 221
    as sender country, 213
Nepal Children's Organisation (NCO),
  219
New South Wales, Australia
  Children's Courts in
    best interests principle in, judicial
      considerations for, 331–333
    children's views as factor in,
      333–334
    clinical assessment reports,
      335–338
    decision-making in, 330–331
    forms of evidence for, 330–331
    judicial alignment in, 335–338
    mixed-method research in,
      330–331
    security assessments by, 338
    social science evidence in, value of,
      338–340
New Zealand
  bests interests principle, in final
    appellate court, 95
  child protection agencies in, 140
  child protection law in, 132–133,
    135–136
    poor outcomes for children under,
      143
    systemic racism in, 141–142
  relocation cases for particular child
    in, 86–87
  significant harm concept in,
    132–133, 135–136
Norrie, Kenneth McK., 11
Norway, best interests principle in, 63

obligations, of Convention
  under Article 3, 31–43
  under Article 3(1), 32–39
  under Article 3(2), 39–42
  under Article 3(3), 42–43
offenders. *See* child-offenders
Optional Protocol on the sale of
    children, child prostitution
    and child pornography
    (OPSC), 315, 323–324

paramountcy principle, 33–35, 45–46,
    49
  adoptions and
    in England, 202–204
    in Scotland, 205
  in Article 3(1), 197–199
  child-offenders and, 301
  in parental rights cases for particular
    child, 87–88
  relocation law and, 292
parent coordinators, 276–277
parental alienation syndrome,
    267–269
  diagnostic criteria for, 269
  skepticism of, 270
parental alienation syndrome (PAS),
    252–253
parental authority, 153
  legal claims for, 154
  for step-parents, 164
parental orders, 166–169
  adoption orders compared to,
    176–177
  children's right to identity in,
    176
  intent in, 175–176
  marital status as factor in, 167
parental responsibility, 153
parental rights cases for particular
    child, in final appellate
    courts, 87–90
  paramountcy principle in,
    87–88
  in U.K., 87–90
  in U.S., 88–89
parenting plans, 237, 244, 275–276
parenting time, 245

parents. *See also* biological parentage; children refusing contact with parents; step-parents
   best interests principle and, 36–37
   child alienation and, parental causes of, 269
   defined, 152–153
   in known biological father disputes, 157–159
   legal, 153
   shared parenting, 182
   well-being of children influenced by, 42
PAS. *See* parental alienation syndrome
permanence orders, for adoptions, 207–208
phenomenological variant of ecological systems theory (PVEST), 122–126
   coping strategies in, 125–126
   risk contributors in, 123–125
Polish draft, of Article 3, 25
Portugal, UNCRC delegation from, 28
primacy. *See also* paramountcy principle
   in Article 3, 45–46, 49
   in Article 3(1), 33–35, 197–199
private law, decisions about children, best interests principle and, 102
prosecuted children
   under best interests standard, 305–307
   under Scottish law, 303
Protective Parents Movement, 255–256
public law, decisions about children, best interests principle and, 102
PVEST. *See* phenomenological variant of ecological systems theory

racism, in child protection laws, 141–142
rebuttable presumption approach, 253–254
religious actors
   defined, 311
   international legal status for, 311–316

religious belief
   best interests principle and, 310–311
   children's identity influenced by, 310
   under UNCRC, 310–311
relocation law
   in appellate courts, for particular child, 83–87
   in Australia, 85–86
   in Canada, 83–85
   decisions affecting children in, 110
   in New Zealand, 86–87
   best interests of the child and, 280–285
   alternative interpretations of, 284–285
   in Australia, 288–290
   family members' perspectives on, 288–290
   for international cross-border cases, 283–284
   jurisdictional approach to, 281–285
   long-term impact on, 286–288
   in New Zealand, 281–285, 288–290
   parental emotional stability and, 282
   parental separation as influence on, 285–286
   prioritizing of, 292
   research evidence on, 285–290
   risk and resilience perspective on, 286
   in U.K., 282–285, 288–290
   occurrence rates for, 280
   paramountcy principle and, 292
reproduction. *See also* biological parentage
   assisted, 164
resilience. *See* risk, resilience and
right to be heard, for children, 394
right to education, for children, 403
right to health, for children, 402
right to identity, for children, 176, 397–398
right to life, survival and development, for children, 393

right to non-discrimination, for
children, 393
rights. *See also* children's rights
in Article 3, prioritisation of, 49
in Article 3(1), 60
best interests principle as, 56–59
dignity, 26
freedom, 26
health, 26
risk, resilience and
in developmental equality model,
121–122
in relocation law, 286
Roma children, in developmental
equality model, 118–119
rules of procedure
Article 3(1) as, 54–55, 59–61
best interests principle as, 55
Russian Federation, best interests
principle and, 45–46

safety provisions
under child custody law, 254, 258
Scotland
adoptions in, 74–75, 204–212
absence of threshold criteria for,
211–212
compulsory supervision orders
for, 208–209
judicial approaches to, 209–212
legislation for, 204–209
paramountcy principle and, 205
permanence orders for, 207–208
by step-parents, 212
child protection law in, 134
child-offenders in, 299–305
under Article 3, 300–305
legal mechanisms for, 299–300
legislative provisions, 301–303
paramountcy principle and, 301
prosecuted children and, 303
prosecution statistics for, 300
temporal dimensions of law for,
304–305
welfare principle and, 300–303
parental authority claims in, 154
significant harm concept in, 134
Scott, Janys M., 10

Scottish Children's Reporter
Administration (SCRA)
study, 307–309
self-reporting, 43–44
Senegal, UNCRC delegation from, 28
the Seychelles, 45–46
shared parenting, 182, 238, 276
significant harm, as legal concept, 131,
133–139
in Australia, 132–134
in Canada, 132–133
in New Zealand, 132–133, 135–136
in Scotland, 134
threshold criteria, 135, 137–138
in U.K., 132–134
situation of vulnerability, 401–402
Skivenes, Marit, 10
Skogly, Sigrun, 318
Sloan, Brian, 13
social welfare institutions, 58
African Americans in, 142
defined, 389
Somalia, constitution of, 28
South Africa
adoptions in, under customary law,
194
baby switching in, 181–182
parental rights and responsibilities
after, 189–190
children's rights in, 184–186
parental rights and responsibilities
in, 181
acquisition of, 188–190
for baby switching, 189–190
Søvig, Karl Harald, 10
Spencer, Margaret Beale, 122–126
step-parents
parental authority provisions for, 164
in Scottish adoptions, 212
surrogacy
under best interests principle,
165–166, 178–179
children's welfare and, subjectivity
of, 177–178
legal limitations of, 177–178
parental orders and, 166–169
adoption orders compared to,
176–177

surrogacy (cont.)
  children's right to identity in, 176
  intent in, 175–176
  marital status as factor in, 167
  time limit provisions, 169–177
  under ECHR, 172–173
Sutherland, Elaine E, 10–11
Sweden, best interests principle in, 63

Taylor, Nicola, 15
Trudeau, Justin, 243–244
Trudeau, Pierre, 243–244

U.K. *See* United Kingdom
United Nations Convention on the Elimination of all Forms of Discrimination against Women, 188
United Nations Convention on the Rights of the Child (UNCRC). *See also* best interests principle
  Article 1, 359
  Article 2, 360
  Article 3, 360. *See also specific paragraphs*
    content of obligations under, 31–43
    drafting of, 24–31
    implementation of, 15–17
    intercountry adoptions under, 228–229
    legislation and, 15–17
    Polish draft, 25
    primacy in, 45–46
    prioritisation of rights in, 49
    scope of, 4–5
  Article 3(1), 10–15. *See also* best interests principle
    administrative authorities and, 58
    adoptions and, 197
    child-offenders under, 298
    children's rights and, 62–66
      in domestic law, 62–64, 99
      language in, 65–66
    content of obligations in, 32–39
    courts of law and, 58
    drafting process for, 53–54
    General Comments in, 32, 48
    Guidelines on Child-friendly Justice and, 61
    holistic reading of, 60
    as interpretive tool, 61–62
    known biological father disputes under, 150–152
    legislative bodies and, 58
    paramountcy in, 197–199
    parental rights and duties in, 185
    primacy in, 33–35, 197–199
    as right of principle, 54–55, 57–58
    rights-based approach to, 60
    as rule of procedure, 54–55, 59–61
    social welfare institutions and, 58
  Article 3(2)
    bests interests in, 40–41
    children's rights and, 68
    content of obligations under, 39–42
    implementation issues in, 47–48
    parental rights and duties in, 185
    well-being under, 23, 40–41, 48–49
  Article 3(3), 31
    content of obligations in, 42–43
    implementation issues in, 47–48
    parental rights and duties in, 185–186
  Article 4, 60–61, 112, 360
  Article 5, 360–361
    expansion of family models under, 3
  Article 6, 361
  Article 7, 361
  Article 8, 71–72, 101, 361
    adoptions and, 348
  Article 9, 54, 361–362
  Article 10, 362
  Article 11, 363
  Article 12, 363
    best interests principle in, 34–35
    children's views under, 14–15
  Article 13, 363
  Article 14, 363
  Article 15, 364
  Article 16, 364
  Article 17, 364

Article 18, 26, 30–31, 365
  best interests principle in, 26–27
Article 19, 365
Article 20, 365–366
Article 21, 197–199, 366
Article 22, 366–367
Article 23, 367–368
Article 24, 318–319, 368
Article 25, 369
Article 26, 369
Article 27, 369
Article 28, 370
Article 29, 370–371
Article 30, 371
Article 31, 371
Article 32, 371–372
Article 33, 372
Article 34, 372
Article 35, 372
Article 36, 372
Article 37, 54, 372–373
Article 38, 373
Article 39, 373–374
Article 40, 54, 374–375
Article 41, 375
Article 42, 375
Article 43, 376–377
Article 44, 377–378
Article 45, 378
Article 46, 379
Article 47, 379
Article 48, 379
Article 49, 379
Article 50, 379–380
Article 51, 380
Article 52, 380
Article 53, 380
Article 54, 380
baby switching under, 184–186
child sexual abuse by clerics and, 323–324
children's rights under, 184–186
classification of, 3–4
content of, 1–4
domestic violence law reform movement under, 263
dynamism of, 5–9
evolution of, 5–9
global and holistic application of, 2
Holy See and, 323–324
intercountry adoptions and, 226–229
international incorporation of, 9
legal analysis of, 387–393
long-term impact of, 5–9, 43–48
objectives of, 384–385
Optional Protocols to, 7
Preamble to, 2, 358–359
ratification of, 5–6
religious belief under, 310–311
scope of, 1–4
self-reporting under, 43–44
state party obligations under, 385–387
structure of, 384
United Nations Convention on the Rights of People with Disabilities, 188
United Nations Declaration of the Rights of the Child 1959, 24, 27, 188
UNCRC. *See* UN Convention on the Rights of the Child
UNICEF UK, 63
United Kingdom (U.K.). *See also* England and Wales; Scotland
  best interests of the child and, in relocation cases, 282–285, 288–290
  best interests principle and, in final appellate court, 92–94
  biological parentage in, 154–155
    known biological father disputes and, 149–152
  child protection law in, 132–134
    systemic racism in, 142
  children's rights in, 68–69
    in adoptions, 73–75
  ECHR violations, 68–69
  intercountry adoptions and, 217
  legal parents in, defined, 153
  non-heterosexual relationships in, legal status of, 163–164
  parental authority claims in, 154
    for step-parents, 164

United Kingdom (U.K.). (cont.)
  parental rights cases for particular child in, 87–90
  significant harm concept in, 132–134
  surrogacy in, under best interests principle, 165–166
United States (U.S.). *See also* Colorado, U.S.
  biological parentage in, legislative definitions for, 151
  child protection agencies in, 140
  child protection law in, 142
  developmental equality model in, 113
  intercountry adoptions and, 217
  paragraph 1 text, 27–29
  parental rights cases for particular child in, 88–89

Vatican. *See* Holy See
Vellacott, Maurice, 240–241. *See also* Bill C-560
Vienna Convention on the Law of Treaties, Article 31, 57
Vienna Declaration and Programme of Action, 2

violence. *See* domestic violence; intimate partner violence

Wales. *See* England and Wales
Washington Declaration on International Family Location (2010), 28
Weisberg, D. Kelly, 17
welfare checklists, 38
welfare institutions. *See* social welfare institutions
welfare principle, 300–303
well-being, of children
  under Article 3(2), 23, 40–41, 48–49
  defined, 40–42, 48–49
  historical context for, 23
  Millennium Development Goals for, 40–41, 48–49
  role of parents and guardians in, 42
Whitecross, Richard, 11–12
Wingspread Conference, 254–255, 273
Woodhouse, Bennett, 59–60
working mothers, children's rights with, 24

Zimbabwe, constitution of, 28